THE CAMBRIDGE COMPANION TO

Sherlock Holmes is the most famous fictional detective in history, with a popularity that has never waned since catching the imagination of his late-Victorian readership. This *Companion* explores Holmes's popularity and his complex relationship to the late-Victorian and modernist periods; on the one hand bearing the imprint of a range of Victorian anxieties and preoccupations, while on the other shaping popular conceptions of criminality, deviance and the powers of the detective. This collection explores these questions in three parts. 'Contexts' explores late-Victorian culture, from the emergence of detective fiction to ideas of evolution, gender and Englishness. 'Case Studies' reads selected Holmes adventures in the context of empire, visual culture and the Gothic. Finally, 'Reinventions and Adaptations' investigates the relationship between Holmes and literary theory, film and theatre adaptations, new Holmesian novels and the fandom that now surrounds him.

Janice M. Allan is Associate Dean Academic, School of Arts and Media, University of Salford. She has published widely on nineteenth-century popular fiction as well as constructions of gender and literary value and is Executive Editor of *Clues: a Journal of Detection*.

Christopher Pittard is Senior Lecturer in English Literature at the University of Portsmouth. He is the author of *Purity and Contamination in Late Victorian Detective Fiction* (2011) and numerous articles and chapters on Victorian popular culture and detective fiction.

A complete list of books in the series is at the back of this book.

THE CAMBRIDGE
COMPANION TO
SHERLOCK HOLMES

EDITED BY

JANICE M. ALLAN

University of Salford

&

CHRISTOPHER PITTARD

University of Portsmouth

CAMBRIDGE
UNIVERSITY PRESS

CAMBRIDGE
UNIVERSITY PRESS

University Printing House, Cambridge CB2 8BS, United Kingdom

One Liberty Plaza, 20th Floor, New York, NY 10006, USA

477 Williamstown Road, Port Melbourne, VIC 3207, Australia

314–321, 3rd Floor, Plot 3, Splendor Forum, Jasola District Centre,
New Delhi – 110025, India

79 Anson Road, #06–04/06, Singapore 079906

Cambridge University Press is part of the University of Cambridge.

It furthers the University's mission by disseminating knowledge in the pursuit of
education, learning, and research at the highest international levels of excellence.

www.cambridge.org
Information on this title: www.cambridge.org/9781107155855
DOI: 10.1017/9781316659274

First published 2019

Printed in the United Kingdom by TJ International Ltd. Padstow Cornwall

A catalogue record for this publication is available from the British Library.

Library of Congress Cataloging-in-Publication Data
NAMES: Allan, Janice M., 1966– editor. | Pittard, Christopher, editor.
TITLE: The Cambridge companion to Sherlock Holmes / edited by Janice M. Allan &
Christopher Pittard.
DESCRIPTION: Cambridge, United Kingdom ; New York, NY : Cambridge University
Press, 2018. | Includes bibliographical references and index.
IDENTIFIERS: LCCN 2018037329 | ISBN 9781107155855
SUBJECTS: LCSH: Holmes, Sherlock. | Doyle, Arthur Conan, 1859–1930 – Criticism and
interpretation. | Detective and mystery stories, English – History and criticism. | Private
investigators in literature.
CLASSIFICATION: LCC PR4624 .C35 2018 | DDC 823/.8–dc23
LC record available at https://lccn.loc.gov/2018037329

ISBN 978-1-107-15585-5 Hardback
ISBN 978-1-316-60959-0 Paperback

CONTENTS

CONTENTS

ILLUSTRATIONS

NOTES ON CONTRIBUTORS

JANICE M. ALLAN is Associate Dean within the School of Arts and Media at the University of Salford. Her research interests are focused on nineteenth-century popular fiction and she has published widely on sensation fiction and nineteenth-century constructions of deviance and literary value. Her most recent publications have explored the use of false hair in the Victorian period and the representation of private investigators in the fiction of Mary Braddon. She is the Executive Editor of *Clues: a Journal of Detection*.

CHRISTINE BERBERICH is Senior Lecturer in Twentieth- and Twenty-First Century English Literature at the University of Portsmouth. Her specialisms cover representations of national identity, popular culture and holocaust literatures. She is the author of *The Image of the English Gentleman in Twentieth-Century Literature: Englishness and Nostalgia* (2007), editor of *The Bloomsbury Introduction to Popular Fiction* (2014), and co-editor of *Land & Identity: Theory, Memory & Practice* (2011), *These Englands: Conversations on National Identity* (2012) and *Affective Landscapes in Literature, Art and Everyday Life* (2015). She is currently working on a popular history of P. G. Wodehouse and the prison camp at Tost, as well as preparing a monograph on perpetrator fiction.

MERRICK BURROW is Principal Lecturer in English Literature at the University of Huddersfield. He has published on a wide range of late Victorian and Edwardian writers of popular fiction, including H. Rider Haggard, Oscar Wilde, Erskine Childers, G. K. Chesterton and Arthur Conan Doyle. He is currently writing a monograph on Doyle and the cultural history of deception.

CLARE CLARKE is Assistant Professor of Nineteenth-Century Literature at Trinity College Dublin in Ireland. She has published widely on crime and detective fiction. Her first book, *Late Victorian Crime Fiction in the Shadows of Sherlock* (2014), was awarded the HRF Keating Prize in 2015. She is currently working on *The Rivals of Sherlock Holmes*, which will be published by Palgrave in 2019.

JONATHAN CRANFIELD is Senior Lecturer in English Literature and Cultural History at Liverpool John Moores University. He is the author of *Twentieth-Century Victorian: Arthur Conan Doyle and the* Strand Magazine, *1891–1930* (2016) and the co-editor of *Fan Phenomena: Sherlock Holmes* (2014). He has also published articles on H. G. Wells, Arthur Conan Doyle, the *Strand Magazine*, popular science and late-Victorian periodicals.

STACY GILLIS is Lecturer in Modern and Contemporary Literature in the School of English Literature, Language and Linguistics at Newcastle University. Her research interests reside in the intersections of feminist theory, theories of the body and popular cultural and intellectual histories. Her work extends across the long twentieth century, but her primary research focus is on British popular culture in the early twentieth century. She is the co-editor of *Women on Screen: Feminism and Femininity in Visual Culture* (2011) and *The Devil Himself: Villainy in Detective Fiction and Film* (2001).

STEPHAN KARSCHAY is Associate Professor of British Literature and Cultural Studies at the University of Hamburg. His main research interests are the relationship between literature and science in the nineteenth century and Gothic fiction, film and media from the eighteenth to the twenty-first centuries, as well as scandals in literature and culture. He is author of *Degeneration, Normativity and the Gothic at the* Fin de Siècle (2015).

STEPHEN KNIGHT is Honorary Research Professor in Literature at the University of Melbourne, having previously worked at the Universities of Sydney, Australian National, Melbourne, De Montfort and Cardiff. He has published widely on medieval and popular literature, notably on Robin Hood, and has long worked on crime fiction, beginning with *Form and Ideology in Crime Fiction* (1980). His most recent book is *Towards Sherlock Holmes: A Thematic History of Crime Fiction in the 19th Century World* (2017). Currently he is researching a book on G. W. M. Reynolds, provisionally titled *The Man Who Outsold Dickens*.

NEIL MCCAW is Professor of Victorian Literature and Culture at the University of Winchester. His publications include *Writing Irishness in Nineteenth-Century British Culture* (2004), *How to Read Texts* (2013) and *Adapting Detective Fiction: Crime, Englishness and the TV Detectives* (2012). He recently edited and wrote the introduction for a facsimile edition of Doyle's 'The Adventure of the Creeping Man', and is currently writing *The Historical Dictionary of Sherlock Holmes*. In addition to these publications he has written several museum exhibitions, including one award-winning display about Sherlock Holmes that toured to France, Germany, and Japan, and has been the Academic Director of The Arthur Conan Doyle Collection, Lancelyn Green Bequest, the largest archive of its kind in the world, since 2005.

BRAN NICOL is Professor of English Literature at the University of Surrey, where he is Head of the School of Literature and Languages. He has published extensively on crime fiction and 'crime culture' and on modern and contemporary British and American fiction. His many books include *Stalking* (2006), *Postmodern Fiction: An Introduction* (2009) and *The Private Eye: Detectives in the Movies* (2013), as well as the collection, *Crime Culture: Figuring Criminality in Fiction and Film*, co-edited with Patricia Pulham and Eugene McNulty (2010).

ROBERTA PEARSON is Professor of Film and Television Studies at the University of Nottingham. Among her most recent publications are the co-authored *Star Trek and American Television* (2014), and the co-edited *Many More Lives of the Batman* (2015) and *Storytelling in the Media Convergence Age: Exploring Screen Narratives* (2015) and *Contemporary Transatlantic Television Drama* (2018). She is the author, co-author, editor or co-editor of numerous works, including several on Sherlock Holmes.

CHRISTOPHER PITTARD is Senior Lecturer in English Literature at the University of Portsmouth, specialising in Victorian literature. He has published widely on Victorian literature and culture and on detective fiction, including articles for *19: Interdisciplinary Studies in the Long Nineteenth Century, Studies in the Novel, Victorian Periodicals Review, Women: A Cultural Review* and *Clues: A Journal of Detection*. He is the author of *Purity and Contamination in Late Victorian Detective Fiction* (2011) and editor of *Alternative Dickens* (*Victoriographies*, 2018). He is currently working on the book *Literary Illusions: Secular Magic and Victorian Literature*.

CAROLINE REITZ is Associate Professor of English at John Jay College of Criminal Justice and the City University of New York Graduate Center. She is the author of *Detecting the Nation: Fictions of Detection and the Imperial Venture* (2004), as well as articles on Victorian literature and culture and twentieth-century detective fiction. She is currently at work on a book manuscript about fiction serialised in Charles Dickens's journals and is a co-editor of *Dickens Studies Annual*.

JEREMY TAMBLING was formerly Professor of Literature at Manchester University and Professor of Comparative Literature at the University of Hong Kong. He has published extensively on all aspects of literary and cultural theory, and on urban studies. His latest book is *Histories of the Devil: From Marlowe to Mann and the Manichees* (2017).

CATHERINE WYNNE is Senior Lecturer in English at the University of Hull. She is the author of *The Colonial Conan Doyle: British Imperialism, Irish Nationalism and the Gothic* (2002) and several journal articles and book chapters on Doyle.

A scholarly edition of Doyle's *The Parasite* and Stoker's *The Watter's Mou'* was published in 2009 and, with Sabine Vanacker, she co-edited a collection of essays on Doyle's afterlife, *Sherlock Holmes and Conan Doyle: Multi-Media Afterlives* (2012). She has also published extensively on Bram Stoker and her latest work is the biographical *Lady Butler: Painting, Travel and War* (2018).

ACKNOWLEDGEMENTS

Christopher Pittard and I are most grateful to Linda Bree, Bethany Thomas and Tim Mason at Cambridge University Press for the help, support and encouragement they have offered in bringing this book to press. The editorial guidance of Jennifer Diann Jones has also been invaluable.

I owe a debt of gratitude to my colleagues at the University of Salford, especially Nigel Howe, Hannah Greaves and Iván García, for their tireless support, encouragement and interest in this project. Andrew Mangham, Anne-Marie Beller and Nadine Muller have continued to shape and sharpen my thinking, as have my students. Many thanks are due to my parents, John and Catie Allan and, most especially, Andy and Sophie, who have made Sherlock Holmes a welcome guest in our home and seldom grumbled when he interfered with our plans.

Janice M. Allan

Many thanks to those colleagues past and present at the University of Portsmouth who have been helpful in numerous ways: Páraic Finnerty, Julian Wolfreys, Kate Brombley, Rachel Smillie, Bran Nicol, Bronwen Price, Jessica Dyson, Mark Frost, and Rosie Paice. At Portsmouth City Council, thanks to Jane Mee, Laura Weston, and particularly to Michael Gunton, head archivist at the Arthur Conan Doyle Collection (Lancelyn Green Bequest). I am especially grateful for the friendship and advice of Lawrence Frank, who passed away in September 2018 just before this book went to press. The influence of his monumental readings of Holmes is felt throughout both my own work and many of the chapters in this volume.

Thanks to my friends and family: Chris Wellings, Gareth Edwards, Andrew Bickerstaffe, Adam Dodd (an invaluable resource on all things Holmesian), my parents Geoff and June, my brother Matthew, and of course Maggie. Thanks, most of all, to my wife Jennifer, for her support, patience and understanding.

Christopher Pittard

TEXTUAL NOTE

The Sherlock Holmes canon has a complex publishing history, with a number of variants in titles and content. Three of the most obvious examples of this complexity are the re-naming of the second *Strand Magazine* series of *The Adventures of Sherlock Holmes* (1892–3) as *The Memoirs of Sherlock Holmes* on publication in volume form in 1894; the variation in title between the US and UK publications of *The Sign of Four* (the novel first appearing in *Lippincott's Monthly Magazine* in 1890 as *The Sign of the Four*, a title retained by many US editions) and the positioning of 'The Cardboard Box' within the canon. Originally published in the second series of *Adventures* in the *Strand*, Doyle felt its slightly more sensationalist tone made it unsuitable for inclusion in the *Memoirs*, and it did not appear in volume collections until the later collection *His Last Bow* (1917). Its status is further complicated by the fact that early scenes from 'The Cardboard Box' were transferred to the beginning of 'The Resident Patient' as published in *Memoirs*. Later editions of the stories can therefore vary considerably from their first appearances in magazines such as the *Strand* and the identification of a definitive text becomes a matter of textual choice.

For ease of reference, all citations from the Holmes stories are taken from *The Penguin Complete Sherlock Holmes* (London: Penguin Books, 2009), as the most widely available single-volume edition of the canon. Readers should be aware, however, that this edition incorporates various textual oddities (for instance, giving 'The Reigate Squires' the American title of 'The Reigate Puzzle' (under which it was published in *Harper's Magazine*)); breaking the chronology of the stories' publication by including *The Return of Sherlock Holmes* (1905) before *The Hound of the Baskervilles* (1901–2); and including the revised opening of 'The Resident Patient'. More scholarly editions of the canon are available; these include the Oxford University Press editions of *A Study in Scarlet*, *The Memoirs of Sherlock Holmes*, *The Hound of the Baskervilles*, *The Case-Book of Sherlock Holmes* and *Selected Stories*;

Penguin Classics editions of *A Study in Scarlet, The Sign of Four, The Adventures of Sherlock Holmes, The Memoirs of Sherlock Holmes, The Hound of the Baskervilles, The Valley of Fear* and *His Last Bow* and *the Case-Book of Sherlock Holmes*; and Broadview's editions of *The Sign of Four* and *The Hound of the Baskervilles*. However, these are incomplete selections of Doyle's Holmesian work; the most comprehensive recent collected edition is Norton's two volume *The Complete Annotated Sherlock Holmes* (ed. Leslie S. Klinger), which divides the canon into short stories and novels.

The Penguin Complete Sherlock Holmes also omits the illustrations that accompanied the original publication of nearly all of the stories. Where it is necessary to refer to these (most prominently in Chapter 10 on Sidney Paget's illustrations for the *Strand*), page numbers will be given for the original magazine appearance of the stories. While a number of modern editions include the original illustrations, the demands of repagination often require the resizing or shifting of the images in relation to the accompanying text (a trend set as early as Newnes's republication of *The Adventures of Sherlock Holmes* in single volume form in 1892, where the dual-column layout of the *Strand* was replaced with a more conventional single-column book page and thus necessitated the movement of illustrations that had been previously integrated into the print). Even where modern editions are reprints of the *Strand* pages (as in the three volume Wordsworth Classics edition of 1992) these can sometimes reverse the original recto-verso ordering of the pages, thus obscuring the visual echoes across page openings set up by the *Strand's* illustrators and art editors.

The frequent title prefix of 'The Adventure of . . . ' has been dropped when referring to the short stories. The only other text to be cited parenthetically in the *Companion* is Doyle's autobiography *Memories and Adventures* (1924), which is cited throughout as *Memories*; all page numbers in this case refer to the 2012 Cambridge University Press edition.

CHRONOLOGY

1859   Arthur Ignatius Conan Doyle born at 11 Picardy Place, Edinburgh, on 22 May, son of Charles Altamont Doyle and Mary Doyle (*née* Foley).

1860   Sidney Paget, Doyle's illustrator for the *Strand Magazine*'s Holmes stories, born 4 October.

1868   Doyle moves to England and attends a Roman Catholic preparatory school, Hodder House, in Stonyhurst.

1870   Doyle attends Stonyhurst College, a Catholic school run by Jesuits (–1875)

1874   Jean Leckie, Doyle's second wife, born at 3 Kidbrook Terrace, Kidbrook, Kent, on 14 March.

1876   Doyle begins medical studies at the University of Edinburgh (completed in 1881).

1877   Doyle meets Dr Joseph Bell, whom he identifies as the intellectual model for Sherlock Holmes.

1879   Doyle's first publications, 'The Mystery of Sasassa Valley' and 'Gelsenium as a Poison' appear in *Chamber's Edinburgh Journal* and the *British Medical Journal* respectively, in September and October.

1880   Doyle is employed as ship's surgeon on the Greenland whaler *Hope* (February–September).

1881   Doyle graduates from Edinburgh University with Bachelor of Medicine and Master of Surgery; makes second voyage as ship's surgeon on *S. S. Mayumba*, sailing to West Africa.

1882   Doyle sets up medical practice at 1 Bush Villas, Elm Grove, in Southsea, a suburb of Portsmouth, in June; writes first novel, *The Narrative of John Smith* (lost and published posthumously in 2011).

1885   Doyle receives MD from University of Edinburgh (dissertation entitled, 'On Vasomotor Influences in Tabes Dorsalis'); marries Louisa Hawkins ('Touie') on 5 August, in St Oswald's Church in Thornton, North Yorkshire.

1886 Doyle drafts *A Study in Scarlet*; the novella, introducing Sherlock Holmes, is rejected by three publishers before Ward, Lock and Company buy the copyright for £25 and agree to publish it the following year.

1887 UK publication of Fergus Hume's *The Mystery of a Hansom Cab* (first published in Melbourne in 1886); *A Study in Scarlet* appears in *Beeton's Christmas Annual*.

1888 First volume edition of *A Study in Scarlet* published by Ward, Lock and Company, including six illustrations by Charles Doyle.

1889 Doyle and Oscar Wilde commissioned by Joseph Stoddart to write for *Lippincott's Magazine*; Wilde contributes *The Picture of Dorian Gray*.

1890 *The Sign of the Four* appears in *Lippincott's Magazine* in February; Doyle studies ophthalmology in Vienna and travels within Europe; George Newnes launches the *Strand* in December.

1891 Doyle contributes an anonymous story to the *Strand*, 'The Voice of Science', followed by the first series of Adventures (July 1891 to June 1892); moves to London to practice as an eye specialist at 2 Upper Wimpole Street; in August, decides to give up medicine and make his living as an author.

1892 The first set of Adventures is published in volume form as *The Adventures of Sherlock Holmes*; a second set appear in the *Strand* (December 1892 to December 1893).

1893 Doyle visits Reichenbach Falls; Louisa is diagnosed with tuberculosis; Charles Doyle dies. 'The Final Problem', in which Holmes 'dies', appears in December, initiating the period known as the 'Great Hiatus' (–1894: within Holmesian chronology his death occurs in May 1891 and his 'resurrection', in 'The Empty House', in April 1894). *Under the Clock*, the first Holmesian theatrical adaptation opens at Royal Court Theatre, London, in November.

1894 Second set of Adventures published in volume form as *The Memoirs of Sherlock Holmes*.

1895 Doyle travels to the front to witness the Sudan War first hand; publication of *The Stark Munro Letters*.

1897 Doyle moves with Louisa to Undershaw, Surrey; meets Jean Leckie.

1899 William Gillette portrays Holmes on stage in *Sherlock Holmes, or the Strange Case of Miss Faulkner*, at Garrick Theatre, New York, in November.

1900 Doyle serves as a volunteer during the Boer War at the Langman Field Hospital; stands unsuccessfully for Parliament.

1901   Holmes reappears in *The Hound of the Baskervilles*, a retrospective adventure serialised in the *Strand* (August 1901 to April 1902).

1902   Doyle is knighted.

1903   A new series of thirteen stories appear in *Collier's Weekly* (September 1903 to January 1905) and the *Strand* (October 1903 to December 1904); 'The Empty House' explaining the events at the end of 'The Final Problem'.

1905   Latest series of Holmes stories published in volume form as *The Return of Sherlock Holmes*.

1906   Louisa Doyle dies on 4 July; Doyle becomes involved in the case of George Edalji, wrongly accused of cattle mutilation.

1907   Doyle marries Jean Leckie.

1908   Sidney Paget dies on 24 January; Doyle and Jean move to Windlesham, Crowborough, East Sussex.

1910   *The Speckled Band*, a theatrical adaptation written and produced by Doyle, is performed at the Adelphi Theatre, London in June.

1912   Ronald Knox publishes 'Studies in the Literature of Sherlock Holmes'.

1914   *The Valley of Fear* serialised in the *Strand* (September 1914 to May 1915)

1915   Frank Richards's parodic series *Herlock Sholmes* first appears, published until 1954 in boys' magazines including *Greyfriars Herald*, the *Magnet* and *Gem*; *The Valley of Fear* published in volume form.

1917   *His Last Bow* published, comprising a preface, seven stories published in the *Strand* between 1908 and 1913, and the delayed volume publication of 'The Cardboard Box' (originally from the first series of *Adventures*).

1921   Stoll Picture Productions produce 47 film adaptations (–1923; two of which are feature length). Mary Doyle (mother) dies.

1924   Publication of *Memories and Adventures*.

1927   *The Case-Book of Sherlock Holmes* published, comprising twelve stories published in the *Strand* and various US magazines between 1921 and 1927; 'Shoscombe Old Place' is the last Holmes story published by Doyle.

1928   *Sherlock Holmes – The Complete Short Stories* published by John Murray.

1929   *Sherlock Holmes – The Complete Long Stories* published by John Murray; Basil Dean, director, *The Return of Sherlock Holmes*, the first Holmes film to feature sound.

1930   Doyle dies on 7 July at Windlesham Manor in Crowborough, East Sussex.

1934   Baker Street Irregulars founded in New York by Christopher Morley; the Sherlock Holmes Society founded in London by A. G. Madconell, Dorothy Sayers and others.

1939   Basil Rathbone portrays Holmes in fourteen films (and numerous radio plays), updating Holmes to contemporary settings, starting with *The Hound of the Baskervilles* and concluding with *Dressed to Kill* (–1946).

1940   Jean Conan Doyle dies 27 June.

1946   *The Baker Street Journal* launched by the Baker Street Irregulars.

1951   Holmes's Baker Street rooms recreated for display at the Festival of Britain, and subsequently transferred to the Sherlock Holmes pub, Northumberland Street, London.

1954   Publication of John Dickson Carr and Adrian Conan Doyle's *The Exploits of Sherlock Holmes*.

1964   BBC series *Sherlock Holmes*, starring Douglas Wilmer and Nigel Stock (–1968).

c.1967 Adventuresses of Sherlock Holmes founded by Evelyn Herzog, Linda Patterson, Pat Moran, Lisa Jones, Mary Ellen Ebeling and M. E. Couchon.

1970   Billy Wilder, director, *The Private Life of Sherlock Holmes*.

1974   Nicholas Meyer, *The Seven Per-Cent Solution* (film adaptation in 1976).

1978   Michael Dibdin, *The Last Sherlock Holmes Story*.

1979   Bob Clark, director, *Murder by Decree*.

1984   Granada Television series *Sherlock Holmes* (with nine series varying in title according to the source material), starring Jeremy Brett (–1994).

1985   Barry Levinson, director, *Young Sherlock Holmes*.

1986   Ron Clements, Burny Mattinson, Dave Michener and John Musker, directors, *The Great Mouse Detective*, based on Eve Titus's book series *Basil of Baker Street* (1958–82).

1988   Thom Eberhardt, director, *Without a Clue*.

1990   Opening of the Sherlock Holmes Museum on Baker Street.

1994   Laurie R. King's *The Beekeeper's Apprentice* starts the Mary Russell series of novels featuring Holmes.

1999   Animated television series, *Sherlock Holmes in the 22nd Century* (–2001).

2000   The last of Doyle's Holmes stories enter the public domain.

2004   Michael Chabon, *The Final Solution*; Holmesian collector and editor Richard Lancelyn Green dies 27 March.

2005 Mitch Cullin, *A Slight Trick of the Mind,* adapted for film as *Mr Holmes* (2015).

2009 Guy Ritchie, director, *Sherlock Holmes.*

2010 Official opening of the Arthur Conan Doyle Collection (Lancelyn Green Bequest), Portsmouth City Library.

2010– The BBC series *Sherlock,* written and produced by Mark Gatiss and Steven Moffat, featuring Benedict Cumberbatch as Holmes.

2011 Anthony Horowitz's *The House of Silk,* endorsed by the Arthur Conan Doyle estate as an authorised pastiche; Guy Ritchie, director, *Sherlock Holmes: A Game of Shadows;* the Baker Street Babes established by Kristina Manente.

2012– CBS series *Elementary* starring Jonny Lee Miller as Holmes and Lucy Liu as a female Dr Watson.

2014 *Sherlock Holmes: The Man Who Never Lived and Will Never Die,* a major exhibition at the Museum of London (–2015).

2015 A 'lost' Holmes story, 'Sherlock Holmes: Discovering the Border Burghs and, by deduction, the Brig Bazaar', is discovered in Selkirk and reprinted in the *Daily Telegraph;* the story's attribution to Doyle is largely dismissed.

2016 Confirmation of a *Sherlock Holmes 3* with Robert Downey Jr.

2018 Etan Cohen, director, *Holmes and Watson,* comedy starring Will Ferrell as Holmes and John C. Reilly as Watson.

I

JANICE M. ALLAN AND
CHRISTOPHER PITTARD

Introduction

Sherlock Holmes has a fair claim to being the most immediately and widely recognisable fictional character in English literature, even if this recognition often depends on mythologised versions of Doyle's texts. Holmes's cape and deerstalker are country wear that would appear appropriate in the rural settings of 'The Boscombe Valley Mystery' and *The Hound of the Baskervilles*, but would be out of place in *fin de siècle* London; the phrase 'Elementary, my dear Watson' appears nowhere in the canon of Doyle's fifty-six short stories and four novels. Yet whereas Holmes's closest competitors in the cultural recognition stakes – Frankenstein's creature and Count Dracula – are more popularly imagined in terms of particularly iconic cinematic adaptations rather than their literary originals, Holmes exceeds the totalising grasp of any single adaptation or representation, including Doyle's own. Whereas Mary Shelley's monster retains Boris Karloff's face in the popular imagination, the popular Holmes is a mixture of Doyle's writings, the illustrations of Sidney Paget (and, to a lesser extent, Frederic Dorr Steele), William Gillette's theatrical adaptation, the televisual rendering of Jeremy Brett and the cinematic portrayal of Basil Rathbone. Different generations will have their preferred image of Holmes, but with the sense that no one of these excludes the others, or is somehow definitive. It looks likely, however, that the current televisual post-modern Holmeses of Benedict Cumberbatch (in BBC's *Sherlock* (2010–)) and Jonny Lee Miller (in CBS's *Elementary* (2012–)) will exercise a significant impact on this composite image for the generations to come.

Part of Holmes's success lay in the serial nature of his adventures. Doyle's first two novels, *A Study in Scarlet* (1887) and *The Sign of Four* (first published as *The Sign of the Four* in 1890) were only modest successes; it was only with the move to the monthly short-story format of the *Strand Magazine* in 1891 that Holmes's popularity took off. The repetitive nature of monthly episodes had both contextual and structural significance. In terms of the criminological context, the knowledge that there would be a new Holmes story each month not only questioned the finality of each adventure, but also signalled a late Victorian concern that crime itself was inherently repetitious; in the 1890s, about 55 per cent of prisoners were repeat offenders, a figure rising to 75 per cent in the Edwardian period.[1] While Doyle's fiction tends to avoid featuring repeat offenders within its fictional universe, it is one of the ironies of the Holmesian canon that the story that sought to definitively end the series – 1893's 'The Final Problem' (Doyle's titular adjective is significant) – introduced modern culture's paradigmatic image of the repeat offender, the criminal mastermind Professor James Moriarty. Moriarty's comparatively sparse appearances in Doyle's stories – he is referenced in several but appears in person only once – have since been compensated for by his use in a wide variety of Holmesian re-imaginings. It is as if readers realised that Moriarty represented a principle of criminalistic repetition left understated by Doyle.

In structural terms, the repetition of the Holmes stories also served to liberate Holmes from the strictures of a set plot. If the original visions of Frankenstein's creature and Dracula were confined to the definitive narratives set out for them by Mary Shelley and Bram Stoker, the variety of Holmes's sixty adventures encouraged the idea that Holmes and Watson could be transplanted into other and diverse textual settings. In this reading, the familiar narrative structures of the stories (formalised in 1912 by Ronald Knox in 'Studies in the Literature of Sherlock Holmes') became generative rather than restrictive; prospective writers of Holmes stories could take the broader structures of Doyle's texts (the opening in Baker Street, the initial display of deductive power, the client's statement of the case and so on) and alter the details to make new narratives. This innovative combination of formal familiarity with variety of content made Holmes particularly amenable to an emerging fandom in the 1890s. It is no surprise that one early manifestation of such fandom, in the so-called 'great hiatus' following Holmes's 'death' in 1893, was a contest in the *Strand*'s sister publication, *Tit-Bits*, inviting readers to write their own Holmesian adventures.[2] Of course, such competitions also acted as advertising for what George Newnes saw as one of his greatest publishing assets, but while in the 1890s Holmes was the commodity being advertised, by the twentieth century he had shifted to become the advertisement itself. Just as enthusiastic readers of Doyle had transplanted Holmes into their own stories, his visibility was consolidated by his frequent appearance in advertising for companies and commodities too diverse to list in full; a representative sample, drawn from Amanda J. Field's survey of Holmesian advertising in the United Kingdom, includes New Golden Glow Beer, Teachers' whisky, the Yellow Pages, Canon typewriters, Kellogg's Crunchy Nut Cornflakes and Kodak. Paradoxically, while Holmes represents specific forms of masculinity, Englishness and epistemological method, in the context of (post-)modern capitalism, he is a surprisingly flexible figure. Field notes that Holmes is 'a floating signifier that can be applied at will to different advertising campaigns in different historical situations'.[3]

Holmes's status as a 'floating signifier' raises further questions of genre. The *Companion* focuses primarily on Holmes as a crucial figure of detective fiction, but while this approach may seem self-evident or beyond question, Holmes's appearance in other genres and modes should not be overlooked. One might claim that Holmes is just as much a figure of science fiction in a twofold argument that both reclaims Doyle's texts as science fiction and notes that Holmes has been an attractive figure for that genre. In the first half of this analysis, it might be noted (as by Neil McCaw) that a story such as 'The Creeping Man' constitutes science fiction in the way that it extrapolates fantastic results from existing scientific discourses (in this case, of degeneration anxieties).[4] The other half of this argument would be to note the frequency with which Holmes is deployed by more immediately recognisable science fiction texts. A recurrent trope of late twentieth-century revisions of Doyle was the resuscitation of a (cryogenically or otherwise) suspended Holmes in the future, whether ours or his. Such a plot occurs in the television films *The Return of Sherlock Holmes* (1987) and *Sherlock Holmes Returns* (1993) and more strikingly in the animated series *Sherlock Holmes in the 22nd Century* (1999–2001), where the revivified Holmes is paired with a robot Watson. Hologramatic representations of the Holmesian universe play a crucial role in episodes of *Star Trek: The Next Generation* ('Elementary, my Dear Data' (1988) and 'Ship in a Bottle' (1993)), raising questions of perception and of the extent to which literary worlds constitute virtual realities in themselves.

Even more complex intertextual parallels exist between Holmes and *Doctor Who* (1963–89; 1996; 2005–). Both heroes meet in novels such as Andy Lane's *All-Consuming Fire* (1994). The 1977 *Doctor Who* story *The Talons of Weng-Chiang*, set in the world of London's popular theatres at the *fin de siècle*, has the Doctor donning an inaccurate deerstalker and cape to track down a killer (and, not coincidentally, a giant rat, recalling Watson's reference to the giant rat of Sumatra, 'a story for which the world is not yet prepared' ('The Sussex Vampire' 1034)). Such crossovers are not solely intertextual, but paratextual; the Holmesian Doctor of *Talons* was played by Tom Baker, who would go on to portray Holmes in the BBC's *Hound of the Baskervilles* in 1982 (a casting double also achieved by Peter Cushing); more recently, *Sherlock* is produced by two writers with a prominent role in *Doctor Who*'s modern revival, Mark Gatiss and Steven Moffat. But the close relationship between Holmes and *Doctor Who* reveals a further dimension. British culture, rooted in a Christian tradition, needs its heroes to be resurrected, from the promised return of King Arthur to the modern regenerations of *Doctor Who*. Doyle might have sought to kill off Holmes in 1893, but the very act of his resurrection in 'The Empty House' only served to cement Holmes's place as a truly mythic figure of British culture.

The other generic context that stands in a complex relationship to the Holmes canon is that of comedy. Again, such an argument is twofold: although it is not often recognised, Doyle's texts qualify as comic writing while Holmes has been deployed as a figure of parody. With regard to the first part of this analysis, there is a considerable critical tradition which sees detective fiction as an inherently comedic form, most famously George Grella's argument that detective fiction 'remains one of the last outposts of the comedy of manners in fiction'.[5] Just as comedy resolves its problems into a harmonious whole, so too does detective fiction transform its epistemological mystery and social ruptures into a resolution. For our purposes, however, there are two limitations to such an argument. The first is that such an analysis tends towards a conservative model of detective fiction that emphasises resolution and narrative closure: aesthetically conservative in that it promotes formula; politically conservative in that it characterises detective fiction as a narrative of the restoration of polite middle-class norms following social rupture. The second is that while all detective fiction may be comedic, not all detective fiction is necessarily funny; we should not blur the comedic with the comic. Coming back to Doyle, the popular image of Holmes as the ascetic model of rationality tends to obscure the frequency with which he laughs and makes verbal jokes, and the extent to which the stories consciously employ the language of the absurd. When, in 'The Red-Headed League', Jabez Wilson follows up the address of the mysterious League only to find 'a manufactory of artificial knee-caps' (182), we are expected to react to the case in the same way as Holmes and Watson have already done in the preceding paragraphs: with laughter. Doyle's success in comparison to his detective fiction contemporaries (including no-less ingenious writers such as Grant Allen and L. T. Meade) partially lies in his astute recognition of the inherent comedy of the genre. The excessive absurdity of the situations animating stories such as 'The Red Headed League' and 'The Blue Carbuncle' needs to be read through the *Strand*'s conscious policy of mitigating the sensationalist elements in crime fiction and downplaying the risk of disgust prompted by more explicit forms of crime narrative. There is also something about the comic absurdity of the Holmes stories that recalls the parallel Freud draws between jokes and the working of the unconscious and, in particular, the often humorous juxtapositions of dreams. The argument that Freud found a parallel between psychoanalysis and Holmesian methods of detection is a familiar one; the idea that it is comedy that links the two is less well explored.

Yet there is a gap at the centre of Doyle's comedic vision, which laid the path for parodic reinterpretations from the 1890s onwards: Holmes himself. In Doyle's stories Holmes is rarely, if ever, the explicit butt of the joke. On occasions where Holmes fails ('A Scandal in Bohemia' and 'The Yellow Face'), the humorous potential of such scenes is ironic or understated (indeed Watson explicitly notes that the ending of 'Scandal' causes Holmes to make fewer jokes about the abilities of women (175); merry, if sexist, humour is replaced with serious respect). Yet Holmes would quickly find himself a rich subject for satirists and parodists, representing as he did a perfect model for theories of laughter emerging in the late nineteenth and early twentieth centuries. In Henri Bergson's argument that laughter is prompted by the perception of the mechanical in the organic (that the 'attitudes, gestures and movements of the human body are laughable in exact proportion as that body reminds us of a mere machine'),[6] it is difficult not to hear the echo of Watson's disbelief ten years earlier in *The Sign of Four* when Holmes fails to recognise Mary Morstan as an attractive woman: '"[Y]ou really are an automaton – a calculating machine ... There is something positively inhuman in you at times"' (96). Doyle stops short of making Holmes a figure of fun, but the potential for Bergsonian humour is implicit from the start.

Later visions of Holmes have picked up on this comedic subtext. A curious reversal occurs in the careers of Holmes and Watson over the course of the twentieth century. By the mid-twentieth century, Watson had become the foolish target of laughter, most notoriously in Nigel Bruce's cinematic portrayal alongside the competence and control of Basil Rathbone's Holmes. There is a sense in which Bruce's bumbling Watson bears little resemblance to Doyle's original, although the acerbic interchange that opens *The Valley of Fear* hints at this development ('"I am inclined to think—" said I. "I should do so," Sherlock Holmes remarked impatiently' (769)). By the late twentieth-century and early twenty-first, however, it would be Holmes that would gradually become the figure of humour. Harvey O'Brien notes that 1970s and 1980s Holmes adaptations tend to diminish the detective by animalising him, making him the victim of trauma, or regressing him to adolescence. More recent adaptations have pathologised Holmes's intellect by, in part, making it a source of comedy.[7] In Guy Ritchie's two *Sherlock Holmes* films, it is Jude Law's Watson who provides the model of imperial masculine competence, while Robert Downey Jr's Holmes offers laughs with his campy performance and ludicrous inventions. The BBC's *Sherlock* takes a slightly different route in repeatedly characterising the detective as a 'high functioning sociopath' who, in episodes such as 'The Six Thatchers' (2017), is too distracted by the business of detection to pay attention to details such as his duties at the christening of John Watson's child. Such adaptations bring out the comedy inherent in Doyle's text, but they also run the risk of creating a perversely anti-intellectual model of Holmes whereby the values of the intellect are no longer heroic.

Yet one can still find manifestations of the mid-century comedically dumb Watson. In 2001, the *Guardian* reported on LaughLab, a year-long University of Hertfordshire project to find the world's funniest joke. The *Guardian* reported that, in the first three months of the project, 'more than 100,000 people from seventy countries have visited the laughlab.co.uk website, submitted a total of 10,000 jokes and rated them on a specially designed "laughometer"'.[8] At the time of reporting, the leading joke (with 47,000 votes) featured familiar figures from literary history:

> Sherlock Holmes and Dr Watson are going camping. They pitch their tent under the stars and go to sleep. In the middle of the night Holmes wakes Watson up: 'Watson, look up at the stars, and tell me what you deduce.'
>
> WATSON: 'I see millions of stars and even if a few of those have planets, it's quite likely there are some planets like Earth, and if there are a few planets like Earth out there, there might also be life.'
> HOLMES: 'Watson, you idiot, somebody's stolen our tent!'

The joke works at a number of levels. Those with only the briefest acquaintance with Holmes and Watson will immediately understand the archetypes represented by those characters. Others who know the canon inside out will perceive nods to Holmes's own camping expedition in *The Hound of the Baskervilles* and his supposed ignorance of the workings of the solar system in *A Study in Scarlet*. For more immediate purposes, the joke neatly crystallises many of the concerns of the *Companion*: from the Holmesian method to neo-Holmesian adaptation.

The *Companion* is organised into three parts: 'Contexts', 'Case Studies' and 'Holmesian Afterlives'. Despite the enduring appeal of Doyle's detective, the canon stands in a particular relationship to the late Victorian and modernist periods in which it was originally produced and consumed. On the one hand, it bears the imprint of a range of *fin de siècle* anxieties and preoccupations while, on the other, it helped to shape popular conceptions of criminality, the power of science and constructions of Englishness and empire. The eight chapters contained within Part I offer contextual readings that set the scene, as it were, by offering clear and concise analyses of a range of relevant contexts, from the importance of serial publication through to constructions of gender and sexuality to new forms of surveillance and power. The three case studies that constitute Part II combine sustained textual analyses of key works with an investigation of broader themes that dominate the canon as a whole: nation, empire and otherness, the problematics of vision and the role of Paget's illustrations, and the uneasy relationship between scientific positivism and its other, the uncanny ambiguity of the Gothic.

In addition to interrogating the appeal of Holmes for literary theory and fandoms, the final part of the *Companion* turns to the afterlife of Doyle's most famous creation in order to explore the many and varied adaptations, re-workings and re-inventions that sustain the Holmesian myth, as well as exploring issues relating to authenticity and originality as source texts and adaptations become increasingly difficult to distinguish. As Neil McCaw persuasively argues in his chapter on adapting Holmes, the BBC's *Sherlock* is best seen as 'a celebration of the rich tapestry of the Sherlockian franchise past and present, in all its shapes and colours' and thus we do it little justice 'if we insist on reading back from this series to Doyle's founding works'. For this reason, the *Companion* is largely silent on this particular manifestation of Holmes's ongoing popularity and readers are referred to the dedicated sources included in the Further Reading. In what follows, we offer a brief account of the contents of each chapter to help readers navigate through the volume as a whole.

The *Companion* opens with Merrick Burrow's lively discussion of the place and importance of Sherlock Holmes within the history of detective and crime fiction, both explaining and challenging popular teleological readings that construct Doyle's detective as a 'Victorian giant who eclipses his literary forebears and peers alike'. Drawing inspiration from Dr Joseph Bell, one of his lecturers at the University of Edinburgh, where Doyle studied medicine between 1867 and 1881, Doyle was determined to create a new type of detective, one able to transform the act of detection into 'something nearer to an exact science' (*Memories* 75). Having examined the precursors and contemporaries against which Doyle defined this new detective, Burrow explores a range of Holmes's contemporaries, including Fergus Hume, whose *Mystery of a Hansom Cab* (1886) far eclipsed the rather meagre sales of *A Study in Scarlet*, Holmes's first outing, published the following year. The chapter surveys Doyle's competitors, who were all too willing to step into the gap left by Holmes's 'death' in 1893, as well as his influence on the Golden Age whodunits and the hard-boiled thriller. It concludes, finally, by acknowledging the global legacy of Holmes's influence, a topic which dominates Part III.

As Clare Clarke asserts in Chapter 3, 'Doyle, Holmes and Victorian Publishing', Sherlock Holmes 'was the progeny of a fortuitous marriage between a new type of author, publication and reading public that emerged at the end of the nineteenth century'. Having traced the technological, social and cultural changes that contributed to the death of the triple-decker novel and the concomitant rise of a new periodical market and readership, Clarke offers an extended analysis of the *Strand* and, more specifically, how George Newnes's mission to offer 'cheap, healthful literature'[9] influenced Doyle's presentation of Holmes at the same time that Holmes's popularity influenced the fate of the *Strand* (and its sister-publication, *Tit-Bits*). It is worth noting that the tension between art and commerce, which Clarke identifies in Doyle's dealings with Newnes and others, was a keynote of his literary career as he struggled to balance the public demand for Holmes with his own literary ambitions.

Tracing the centrality of urban spaces to crime narratives, Stephen Knight posits that 'there can be little doubt that a word-association test of the terms "city" and "detective" would most often, all around the world, generate two names: London and Sherlock Holmes'. As Knight goes on to argue, however, the relationship between Holmes and London was initially problematic and consistently more complex than this universal association suggests. In addition to exploring the relationship between Holmes's encyclopaedic spatial knowledge, detection and authority, the chapter allows twenty-first century readers to view London from a late-Victorian perspective, shedding light on the connotations of the various settings of the canon. Adopting one of the best-known stories, 'The Man with the Twisted Lip', as a case study, Knight explores what this narrative reveals about Doyle's understanding of urban space, class and epistemology.

Turning from the urban to the rural, Christine Berberich's 'Englishness and Rural England' reads the canon against the rise of New Imperialism in order to explore how the canon's traditional English, rural settings – particularly the country house – are juxtaposed with, or threatened by, foreign 'Others'. According to this reading, such spaces are consistently Orientalised and 'contaminated' by returned colonials (having been themselves contaminated by their travels) or actual foreigners. In the process, these homely, English spaces are rendered *unheimlich* (uncanny), thereby destabilising normative national identity. Against this threat, Berberich argues, stands the figure of Sherlock Holmes: 'the quintessential Englishman, the seemingly perfect representative of a stable and permanent Englishness'. Fulfilling a national desire for stability in a period of political volatility was just one of the many ways in which Doyle was involved in a two-way dialogue with his public: his work shaped by as well as shaping the attitudes of his contemporaries.

In Chapter 6, 'Gender and Sexuality in Holmes', Stacy Gillis offers a two-part discussion of the detective as 'the embodiment and arbiter of absolute masculine authority'. Gillis first explores how Doyle's emphasis on logic, reason and rationality helped to establish Holmes's masculinity, as well as how it was re-enforced through a network of cross-textual references across a range of early twentieth-century detective and mystery fiction. The second half of the chapter then traces how the rise of gender and queer studies led to new ways of analysing Doyle's narratives. Focusing on 'A Scandal in Bohemia' as a case study to illustrate the destabilising powers of disguise, Gillis demonstrates the value of re-reading the canon through recent and varied methodological approaches – a topic that Bran Nicol picks up in Chapter 13 in Part III.

Chapters 7 and 8 are best read in tandem, with Jonathan Cranfield's concise introduction to the key scientific concepts and controversies of the period paving the way for Stephan Karschay's more focused exploration of criminal anthropology as a specific field of scientific research during the *fin de siècle*. Doyle's scientific detective demands to be read against the 'durable reference points' provided by Charles Lyell, Charles Darwin and Cesare Lombroso – all of whom, according to Cranfield, share an emphasis 'on everyday empirical observation allied to deductive and abductive reasoning' – and the chapter is essential reading for those not familiar with their ideas. At the same time, Cranfield offers a necessary corrective to those who accept, without question, Doyle's characterisation of Holmes's method as a '*science of deduction*' (*A Study in Scarlet* 19, emphasis added). Referring to a wide range of stories, Cranfield reveals the scientific status of both Doyle and Holmes to be far more ambiguous and ambivalent than they first appear. Ambivalence is also a feature of Doyle's engagement with the deterministic tenets of criminal anthropology as espoused by its founding father, Cesare Lombroso. In addition to offering a clear account of Lombroso's key ideas relating to inborn criminality, together with its visible signifiers, and the principles of atavism, whereby the criminal is conceived as a primitive evolutionary throwback, Karschay explores how such ideas are deployed and challenged by Doyle. Of particular interest are the discussions of infant criminality and the connection between the atavistic criminal and so-called primitive races within the canon, the latter providing further evidence of the jingoistic anxieties explored by both Berberich and, in Part II, Caroline Reitz.

The final chapter of Part I, Jeremy Tambling's Foucauldian reading of 'Holmes, Law and Order', traces the rise of a panoptical society where law is inextricably bound up with violence. Tambling's wide-ranging discussion explores the relationship between crime and guilt and the uncanny alignment of criminal and detective. Focusing on 'The Abbey Grange', Tambling also offers a fascinating analysis of the mechanisms by which texts persuade readers into accepting their ideological presuppositions – even when these go against extratextual objections and moral codes – including the various criminal acts committed by Holmes himself.

The first of the three case studies that constitute Part II is Caroline Reitz's 'The Empires of *A Study in Scarlet* and *The Sign of Four*'. Adopting a narratological approach to these 'formally messy' novels, Reitz offers a compelling analysis of boundaries – bodily, textual and national – in order to explore 'what constitutes the jurisdiction of the English detective and the boundaries of the detective story in a violent, messy world'. Although Doyle has been labelled 'one of the great Victorian apologists of empire',[10] the picture that emerges from Reitz's reading is more nuanced and complex than such a statement suggests. Like the volume as a whole, the intention is to defamiliarise – to render queer or strange through the adoption of varied perspectives – what has often been taken for granted about Doyle and his detective.

Building on existing discussions of visuality within the canon, Christopher Pittard's chapter breaks new ground by focusing on the stories' treatment of the visual in the context of their material production, illuminating the interplay between Sidney Paget's illustrations and Doyle's words in the pages of the *Strand*. Moving from Paget's method to a detailed compositional analysis of key illustrations from the first two series of adventures, Pittard explores a range of visual tropes, the imagistic chains within and between stories and the role of Paget's illustrations in shaping the meaning of Doyle's narratives. In the final of the three case studies, 'Gothic Returns: *The Hound of the Baskervilles*', Janice Allan explores the very different topographies – geographical, psychological and symbolic – that dominate Doyle's most famous and successful novel. Exploring the extent to which the novel destabilises the various binaries – science/superstition, legible/illegible, definite/amorphous – on which it also depends, Allan's discussion focuses on the moor as a site of Gothic undecidability that resists the principles of circumscription on which Holmes's method depends.

In the first chapter of Part III, 'Holmes and Literary Theory', Bran Nicol explores the appeal that Sherlock Holmes – and detective fiction more generally – holds for literary theory. Having established that Holmes 'embodies the kind of "suspicious logic" which literary study in the twentieth and twenty-first centuries, informed by theory, demands', Nicol offers a wide-ranging discussion of both Holmes's method and the extent to which it is illuminated by – as well as illuminating – a range of critical approaches, including formalism, Marxism, psychoanalysis and post-structuralism. Reading theory and fiction through and against each other, Nicol's chapter serves as a salient reminder that Holmes's influence and afterlife is not limited to multimedia fictions.

Holmes's multimedia afterlife is the focus of the concluding chapters of the volume by Neil McCaw, Catherine Wynne and Roberta Pearson. Travelling the distance from *Under the Clock* (1893), the first publicly performed Holmesian adaptation, to China's current obsession with the BBC's *Sherlock*, McCaw traces more than a century's worth of the global re-imaginings – across every conceivable media – of Doyle's character. Despite such diversity, issues relating to fidelity and authenticity are central to the discussion, as are trends for pastiche and/or parody and, more generally, the need for re-invention as adaptors move beyond the familiar ground of the canon in a bid to capture new and extended audiences. The Holmes that emerges from McCaw's discussion is a 'multi-dimensional and multi-platform brand, universally recognisable and thus an essentially global popular-cultural figure'. Following McCaw's concise overview of the history of Holmesian adaption, Wynne offers a focused discussion of neo-Holmesian fiction. As re-inventions of the great detective began to appear within Doyle's own lifetime, they constitute, she argues, an early instance of neo-Victorian fiction, albeit *avant la lettre*. In addition to exploring how such fictions constitute both an 'imagined and imaginative space' that allows historical and fictional worlds to converge, Wynne engages in an extended analysis of the neo-Holmesian fictions of Michael Chabon and Mitch Cullin, exposing how such texts mine 'the repressed trauma of the canon'.

In the final chapter of the *Companion*, 'Sherlockian Fandom', Roberta Pearson explores the distinctions in class, gender and cultural hierarchy that have shaped Sherlockian fandom since the establishment of the Baker Street Irregulars (BSI) in 1934. Pearson's reading offers a fascinating account of how the BSI's decision to exclude women – the first female members were inducted only in 1991 – was intimately bound up with a range of anxieties tied to cultural prestige as well as the challenge posed first by the Adventuresses of Sherlock Holmes (ASH) and, more recently, The Baker Street Babes: an all-female fandom that privileges a female point of view. While recent years have seen a move towards integration as fandom goes mainstream, Pearson ensures that we do not forget its contested history.

It has been our intention that this *Companion* cater for both new and experienced readers of Sherlock Holmes, exploring and explaining key issues that illuminate the canon but also offering readings that challenge and defamiliarise. In the same way that Doyle renders strange and uncanny the familiar world of his readers – be that the security of the home or the stability of gender and nation – so too does this volume encourage readers to view an old friend in a new light.

Notes

1. Martin J. Wiener, *Reconstructing the Criminal: Culture, Law and Policy in England 1830–1914* (Cambridge: Cambridge University Press, 1990), 342.
2. Ann K. McClellan, '*Tit-Bits*, New Journalism, and Early Sherlock Holmes Fandom', *Transformative Works and Cultures* 23 (2017), [http://dx.doi.org/10.3983/twc .2017.0816, accessed 9 October 2017].
3. Amanda J. Field, 'The Case of the Multiplying Millions: Sherlock Holmes in Advertising', in Sabine Vanacker and Catherine Wynne (eds.), *Sherlock Holmes and Conan Doyle: Multi-Media Afterlives* (Basingstoke: Palgrave Macmillan, 2013), 19–35 (33).
4. Neil McCaw, 'Introduction', in Arthur Conan Doyle, *The Adventure of the Creeping Man: A Facsimile Edition* (Winchester: Winchester University Press/ Portsmouth City Council, 2017), 6–27.
5. George Grella, 'Murder and Manners: The Formal Detective Novel', *Novel* 4:1 (1970), 30–48 (33).
6. Henri Bergson, *Laughter: An Essay on the Meaning of the Comic*, 1900, trans. Cloudesley Brereton and Fred Rothwell (New York: Macmillan, 1914), 29. Original emphasis.
7. Harvey O'Brien, 'The Curious Case of the Kingdom of Shadows: The Transmogrification of Sherlock Holmes in the Cinematic Imagination', in Vanacker and Wynne, *Sherlock Holmes*, 64–79 (73–7).
8. Tim Radford, 'Scientists close in on the world's funniest joke', *Guardian*, 20 December 2001, [https://www.theguardian.com/uk/2001/dec/20/humanities .research, accessed 9 October 2017].
9. George Newnes, 'Introduction', *Strand Magazine* 1 (January 1891), 3.
10. Jon Thompson, *Fiction, Crime and Empire: Clues to Modernity and Postmodernism* (Urbana and Chicago: University of Illinois Press, 1993), 66.

PART I

Contexts

2

MERRICK BURROW

Holmes and the History of Detective Fiction

In the summer of 1927, shortly after publishing his final Sherlock Holmes story and just three years before his death, Arthur Conan Doyle recorded one of the first ever sound-on-film interviews. In it he recounts how he first came to write the Holmes stories, stressing the significance of his own scientific training as a medical doctor and his dissatisfaction with some of the 'old-fashioned' detective stories that he used to read for pleasure. In these, he suggests, 'the detective always seemed to get at his results either by some sort of a lucky chance or fluke, or else it was quite unexplained how he got there ... That didn't seem to me quite playing the game'. Beyond his sense of annoyance with these stories, Doyle explains, he saw a gap in the literary marketplace and 'began to think of turning scientific methods, as it were, onto the work of detection'. He describes how he drew inspiration from the example of Joseph Bell, one of the lecturers from his medical school, whose powers of observation enabled him not only to diagnose patients' diseases but also 'very often their nationality and occupation and other points'. It was the example of Bell, Doyle suggests, that gave him 'a new idea of the detective'.[1]

It is with a palpable sense of bemusement that Doyle describes how his 'new' detective subsequently developed from this 'comparatively small seed' into a 'monstrous growth' after Holmes began to appear in short story form in the *Strand Magazine* in 1891.[2] As Holmes's popularity took root, avid fans began to write him letters, applying for positions as domestic servants and even offering unsolicited advice on beekeeping when Holmes 'retired'. These were not the only ways in which the Great Detective outgrew Doyle's original conception. More significant from a literary perspective is the manner in which Holmes has come to be viewed as synonymous with nineteenth-century detective fiction in general, a Victorian giant who eclipses his literary forebears and peers alike, and whose influence has shaped the conventions of the detective genre, either by emulation or by dissent, ever since.

Doyle's reflections in the filmed interview suggest that the source of Holmes's success lay in the originality of his application of scientific methods to the 'work of detection' – thus allowing readers the chance of solving the mysteries themselves. But Doyle's comments on the 'old-fashioned detective' also highlight the fact that the genre began long before Holmes appeared in print. So too, in fact, did the type of fictional detective who employed scientific methods to solve mysteries. The extent of Holmes's dominance in our perceptions of late-Victorian detective fiction might lead to the conclusion that Doyle was the most successful practitioner of detective fiction, even if he did not invent the genre or the scientific method. But even this is not altogether correct. Why, then, does Holmes loom so large in the history of detective fiction? The first part of this chapter examines some of the late-Victorian detective fiction against which Doyle defined his 'new' detective, before exploring the influence of Edgar Allan Poe and Emile Gaboriau. It then surveys some of Holmes's competitors and considers the reasons why he eventually prevailed in shaping the direction that the genre would take. The final part of the chapter traces the course of Holmes's influence in the development of the whodunit and hardboiled American private eye thrillers as well as the wider field of crime writing.

Holmes's Precursors

The most successful detective story of the nineteenth century, judged by volume of sales at least, was not written by Doyle but by a New Zealand barrister named Fergus Hume, whose first novel *The Mystery of a Hansom Cab* (1886) sold over 300,000 copies in Britain alone during the first six months of publication. Hume had wanted to pursue a career as a playwright in Melbourne, where he moved shortly after being admitted to the bar in 1885. Finding it difficult to be taken seriously by theatre directors, he set about writing a novel that would raise his literary profile. Hume was aiming for maximum attention and, with that in mind, he consulted with a bookseller as to which were the most popular books:

> He replied that the detective stories of Gaboriau had a large sale; and as, at this time, I had never even heard of this author, I bought all his works – eleven or thereabouts – and read them carefully. The style of these stories attracted me, and I determined to write a book of the same class; containing a mystery, a murder, and a description of low life in Melbourne.[3]

Hume, up until that point a comparative stranger to the detective genre, rightly assumed that his imitation of Gaboriau's established formula would do well in the popular fiction market. Even so, he could not have anticipated the scale of his book's eventual success. The publishers he initially approached rejected his novel and Hume resorted to printing 5,000 copies at his own expense. Sales in Australia were brisk but still Hume did not appreciate the book's commercial potential, selling the rights to his novel for just £50 in advance of the first London printing in November 1887. By the following May, *The Mystery of a Hansom Cab* had sold 200,000 copies and its sales continued at the rate of around 3,000 copies per day.[4]

Doyle's first foray into detective fiction, *A Study in Scarlet*, was published in 1886, the month following *The Mystery of a Hansom Cab*. In contrast to Hume's bestseller, *A Study in Scarlet* had meagre sales and received scant critical attention. Stung by their contrasting fortunes, Doyle was scathing in his assessment of Hume's novel: 'What a swindle "The Mystery of a Hanson Cab" is. One of the weakest tales that I have read, and simply sold by puffing'.[5] Doyle's novel could hardly have been more different from *The Mystery of a Hansom Cab*. Unlike Holmes, Hume's detectives are either inept or corrupt, while the eventual solution of the crime arises from a chance discovery rather than scientific detection. It was perhaps with Hume's outrageously successful novel in mind that Doyle retrospectively bristled at the thought of the detective who was not 'playing the game'.

The Mystery of a Hansom Cab had demonstrated the spectacular commercial possibilities of crime fiction but Hume's detectives possessed none of Bell's analytical acumen. For this – and for the template for what would come to be known as 'classic' detective fiction – Doyle drew upon the 'tales of ratiocination' written in the 1840s by Edgar Allan Poe, in which enigmatic crimes are solved through the intellectual acuity of C. Auguste Dupin: 'The Murders in the Rue Morgue' (1841), 'The Mystery of Marie Rôget' (1841-2) and 'The Purloined Letter' (1845). Doyle remarked in his autobiographical *Memories and Adventures* that 'Poe's masterful detective, M. Dupin, had from boyhood been one of my heroes' (74). Dupin's tales follow Tzvetan Todorov's well-known typology of detective fiction, in which he argues that the genre is characterised by duality as the narrative is divided into two distinct stories: that of the crime and that of the investigation. In classic detective fiction of this type (including the Holmes stories) the narrative of the investigation centres on the detective and is typically narrated by a third party, such as Watson. The story of the crime, on the other hand, is usually recounted by the detective as the solution to the mystery. The figure of the detective thus became central in a way that was quite distinct from earlier crime fiction, in which the narrative was primarily focalised around the exploits of a criminal. In the classic detective story the crime is principally significant as the occasion for a demonstration of the detective's acumen. This is foregrounded in Poe's stories by the prefacing of the crime narrative with a miniature essay on some specific aspect of analytical reasoning, such as the discussion at the outset of 'The Murders in the Rue Morgue' of the qualities of analytical observation at work in games of chess, draughts and whist, which are then demonstrated by Dupin in the solution of the crime.

'The Murders in the Rue Morgue' is also a founding example of the locked room subgenre of detective fiction. The story concerns the discovery of the bodies of two women in a locked upper-storey apartment in Paris who have been murdered with extreme brutality. In addition to the mystery of how the murderer got in and out of the apartment the case presents other problems that baffle the official police, including the fact that no valuables had been taken and that witnesses reported hearing an extremely strange voice that no one could identify. Dupin solves the case by virtue of his skills in observation and analysis – concluding, for example, that witnesses' disagreement on the characteristics of the voice pointed to the fact that it was not a human voice at all. This inference also accounts for the other peculiar features of the case: the climbing agility required to scale the building, the indifference to valuables and the extreme violence of the crime. The perpetrator, Dupin concludes, was an escaped orang-utan.

The influence of 'The Murders in the Rue Morgue' upon the Holmes stories can be seen not only in the foregrounding of the detective's acumen but also in his pairing with a confidential narrator. Doyle even adapted the plot of Poe's story for his second Holmes novel *The Sign of Four*, in which Bartholomew Sholto is discovered murdered in a locked attic room; the murderer in this case being an Andaman Islander who could '"climb like a cat"' (156). In 'The Purloined Letter' Dupin seeks to recover a compromising document that has been stolen from the Queen by a government minister, who is using it to exercise power over her. Dupin, reflecting upon the bold character of the minister, speculates that he would be likely to adopt the principle of hiding the letter in plain sight, using excessive obviousness as a technique of misdirection. Dupin visits the minister upon some pretext and, after deducing that a crumpled letter dangling from the mantelpiece is the one stolen from the Queen, he uses a pre-arranged disturbance in the street outside to distract the minister's attention while he retrieves it. The plot of the first Holmes story to appear in the *Strand*, 'A Scandal in Bohemia', is a variation on the same plot, in which the Prince of Bohemia seeks Holmes's assistance to recover a compromising photograph, whose hiding place

Holmes also discovers with the aid of assistants who create a disturbance outside.

Dupin is also invoked in Doyle's 'The Fate of the *Evangeline*', published two years before his first Holmes story: '"Exclude the impossible," [Dupin] remarks in one of Poe's immortal stories, "and what is left, however improbable, must be the truth"'.[6] Dupin, in fact, never utters this dictum in quite such a pithy formulation. The phrase is Doyle's own, and it is one that Holmes adopts as his own in *The Sign of Four* (as well as in 'The Beryl Coronet', 'Silver Blaze', 'The Priory School', 'The Bruce-Partington Plans' and 'The Blanched Soldier'). Holmes's debt to Dupin is touched upon directly during the course of a disquisition upon the 'science of deduction' in the second chapter of *A Study in Scarlet*, in which Watson comments upon the similarity between Poe's detective and Holmes. Surprisingly, perhaps, Holmes rejects the comparison: '"Now, in my opinion, Dupin was a very inferior fellow. That trick of his of breaking in on his friends' thoughts with an apropos remark after a quarter of an hour's silence is really very showy and superficial. He had some analytical genius, no doubt; but he was by no means such a phenomenon as Poe appeared to imagine"' (24).

Holmes's churlishness here is perhaps best understood as the product of Doyle's own literary insecurity at a time when the manuscripts he sent out to publishers 'used to come circling back with the precision of a homing pigeon'. The problem, as Doyle acknowledged, was that these early works of fiction were 'too reminiscent of the work of others' (*Memories* 75, 74). However, with *A Study in Scarlet* Doyle felt that he was onto something and so 'when my little Holmes book began also to do the circular tour I was hurt, for I knew that it deserved a better fate' (*Memories* 75). Holmes did not find his niche until he began to appear in short stories in the *Strand* in 1891, which quickly established reader loyalty both to the character and the publication. Upon receiving the manuscript for 'A Scandal in Bohemia' Herbert Greenhough Smith, the magazine's editor, reportedly ran into the office of its owner, George Newnes, declaring that he had discovered the greatest writer of short stories since Edgar Allan Poe.[7]

This change in Doyle's literary fortunes, and the assurance of an established place of publication for Holmes, allowed for a more generous acknowledgement of Dupin and Poe. In 'The Cardboard Box' Holmes ascribes his former view of Dupin to Watson, remarking that '"some little time ago when I read you the passage in one of Poe's sketches in which a close reasoner follows the unspoken thoughts of his companion, you were inclined to treat the matter as a mere *tour-de-force* of the author"'. Holmes adds that he is '"constantly in the habit of doing the same thing"' as Dupin, a point which he practically demonstrates by breaking in on Watson's own internal thought processes (888). However, when it came to publishing the stories from the *Strand* in a single volume, Doyle left out 'The Cardboard Box' because he felt its subject matter was unduly gruesome (in the story a woman is sent a cardboard box containing two severed human ears). It is therefore a mark of the importance that Doyle placed upon paying tribute to Dupin that he transplanted the thought-reading episode into the opening scene of 'The Resident Patient' when it was re-published in *The Memoirs of Sherlock Holmes*.

In his preface to a 1902 edition of *The Adventures of Sherlock Holmes* Doyle went even further, giving Poe comprehensive credit for the entirety of the classic detective fiction genre:

> Edgar Allan Poe ... was the father of the detective tale, and covered its limits so completely that I fail to see how his followers can find any fresh ground which they can call their own. For the secret of the thinness and also of the intensity of the detective story is, that the writer is left with only one quality, that of intellectual acuteness, with which to endow his hero. Everything else is outside the picture and weakens the effect. The problem and its solution must form the theme, and the character-drawing be limited and subordinate. On this narrow path the writer must walk, and he sees the footmarks of Poe always in front of him. He is happy if he ever finds the means of breaking away and striking out on some little side-track of his own.[8]

Poe may have been the single most important influence upon Doyle in the early Holmes stories, but he was certainly not the only one. In *The Sign of Four*, Doyle incorporates motifs borrowed from Wilkie Collins's *The Moonstone* (1868), including a conspiracy originating from India, jewel theft, drug addiction, a dishonourable army officer and another estimable detective in the form of Sergeant Cuff. In the same passage from *A Study in Scarlet* in which Holmes ungraciously disavows comparison with Dupin he also rejects Lecoq, the detective made famous in Gaboriau's *L'Affaire Lerouge* (1865) and *Monsieur Lecoq* (1868), which enjoyed tremendous sales until Holmes eclipsed their popularity in the 1890s. Asked by Watson what he thinks of Gaboriau's detective, Lecoq, Holmes sardonically describes his French precursor as '"a miserable bungler"' (25). But here, too, Doyle betrays an anxiety of influence rather than genuine disdain. Holmes's methods of close observation and inference resemble to a remarkable degree those of Gaboriau's detective.

Lecoq was, in turn, modelled on a combination of Dupin (Gaboriau being another of Poe's literary admirers) and the real-life detective and sometime criminal Eugène François Vidocq, the first director of the *Sûreté Nationale* whose sensational *Mémoires de Vidocq* (1828) had themselves served as inspiration for literary policemen and criminals in Honoré de Balzac's *Le Père Goriot* (1834–5), Eugène Sue's *Les Mystères de Paris* (1842–3), Alexandre Dumas's *Les Mohicans de Paris* (1854–5) and Victor Hugo's *Les Miserables* (1862). Vidocq is also mentioned in 'The Murders in the Rue Morgue' by Dupin who, like Holmes, gives his progenitors short shrift, describing Vidocq as '"a good guesser, and a persevering man. But, without educated thought, he erred continually by the very intensity of his investigations. He impaired his vision by holding the object too close"'.[9]

This pattern of disavowal delineates a chain of influence connecting Holmes to Vidocq via Poe and Gaboriau. Poe's short stories provided direct inspiration for some of Doyle's plots. Likewise, the two-part structure of both *A Study in Scarlet* and *The Valley of Fear* is indebted to Gaboriau, whose novels are similarly divided into distinct parts dealing firstly with the narrative of the detective's enquiry into a crime and followed by a narrative that unfolds its back story. In Gaboriau's novels, however, the solution to the crime emerges from details that are not available to the detective or the reader within the narrative of the investigation. In Doyle's terms they are 'old-fashioned' detective stories that are not 'playing the game'. Gaboriau's stories also differ from the tales of Dupin and Holmes insofar as the boundary between Lecoq and his criminal quarry is relatively porous – as indeed it had been for Vidocq, who was recruited from the ranks of the criminal underworld. Holmes's identification with the criminal mind, on the other hand, is only ever a matter of intellectual interest; a point that is reinforced from time to time by Watson's reassuring observation that it was fortunate for society that Holmes had adopted the profession of the consulting detective rather than that of the master criminal – an alternative possibility that is projected instead into the figure of his nemesis, Professor Moriarty.

Holmes's Competitors

Doyle left the field wide open for imitators when, in December 1893, Holmes plunged with Moriarty into the chasm of the Reichenbach Falls. There was no shortage of candidates to replace him or to emulate his tremendous commercial success. Of these, the most immediate substitute for Holmes came in the form of Arthur Morrison's private investigator, Martin Hewitt, whose tales, starting with 'The Lenton Croft Robberies' (March 1894), graced the pages of the *Strand* in Holmes's wake. With Hewitt, Morrison followed fairly closely the formula that Doyle had adopted from Poe and developed around Holmes, producing a series of stories linked by the central character of the detective, an associate who narrates and a plot focused upon an investigation in which Hewitt uses observation and logic to solve enigmatic crimes. Morrison did not simply make a clone of Holmes, however; he gave Hewitt a more genial and down-to-earth persona that contrasted with Holmes's artistic hauteur. But Morrison was nevertheless plugging an obvious gap in the market that Doyle had recently vacated, as were a number of his contemporaries. These included L. T. Meade, whose *Stories from the Diary of a Doctor* began appearing in the *Strand* in July 1893, developing the subgenre of the medical mystery story that Doyle himself had pioneered in some of his early stories that were later collected under the title *Round the Red Lamp* (1894). Grant Allen, another of Doyle's contemporaries who also stepped into the space left by Holmes, published the majority of his detective fiction in the *Strand* during the interregnum between 'The Final Problem' and *The Hound of the Baskervilles*. Allen had already published occasional detective stories, such as 'The Great Ruby Robbery' (1892) but his major contribution to the genre came in three sets of interconnected stories: *An African Millionaire* (June 1896 and May 1897), *Miss Cayley's Adventures* (March 1898 to February 1899) and *Hilda Wade* (March 1899 to February 1900). Allen became terminally ill during the publication run of *Hilda Wade* and, in an act of professional friendship, Doyle undertook to complete the final two stories to relieve his fellow author's mind (*Memories* 261).

Doyle's readiness to pick up the baton suggests that both he and Allen felt there was a reasonable amount of common ground between them, at least in their manner of writing detective stories. Allen's radical views in respect of gender, marriage and sexuality were a world away from Doyle's own conservative attitudes. But both men accommodated themselves to the remit of the *Strand*'s offering of 'cheap, healthful literature'.[10] *Hilda Wade* is nonetheless a notable departure from the Holmes stories in its treatment of detection as a matter of interpretation of character as much as the analysis of material clues. Hilda Wade, the sleuth, is a nurse endowed with a particularly heightened capacity for female intuition. She is aided in her investigations by Dr Hubert Cumberledge, who is both her narrating Watson and eventual lover – a radical twist on the sidekick motif and a departure from the homosocial ethos of the Holmes stories.

Allen and Meade were not alone in the 1890s in their search for an alternative niche in the literary marketplace to that of the Holmesian detective story. Morrison, whose Martin Hewitt tales were widely viewed as inferior imitations of Holmes, attempted a bold departure with a series of detective stories gathered under the title of *The Dorrington Deed-Box* (1897). James Rigby, a young heir to a fortune narrates the first story of the series, in which he tells of how he met a detective named Dorrington, to whom he confided the information that Italian *Camorra* – a mafia-like organisation – had assassinated his father some twenty years previously. Soon afterwards Rigby notices that he is being followed and begins to fear the same fate when he finds the sign of the *Camorra* fixed to his hotel room door. He seeks advice and assistance from Dorrington, who suggests that they exchange identities in order to protect Rigby's safety. Rigby gives Dorrington documents that establish his identity, and which thereby provide legal access to his inheritance, soon after which he realises that he has been the victim of an elaborate and murderous deception. Rigby awakes from a drug-induced sleep to find that Dorrington has stolen his identity and left him to drown in an iron tank that is filling with water. After escaping from the tank Rigby goes in search of Dorrington, finding only a hastily abandoned office and a box of case files, which provides the framework for the remainder of the series of stories. Morrison's innovation combined the identities of criminal and detective, breaking with the Holmesian formula he had followed in the Martin Hewitt stories to produce something much more original. *The Dorrington Deed-Box* was, however, a commercial flop and for the next thirty years or so the mainstream of the detective genre continued to develop along the lines that Doyle had established with Holmes.

It is a testament to the reach and depth of Holmes's influence that the clear separation of detective from criminal, which Morrison attempted to break with in *The Dorrington Deed-Box*, became an unquestionable norm in the Golden Age of detective fiction, as did the idea of deploying clues. In the earliest stories Doyle foregrounds Holmes's remarkable aptitude for reading clues as a sign of his superhuman capacities. But in building the framework for Holmes's accounts of his processes of deduction, Doyle stumbled upon an approach that enabled readers to join in the game, turning the detective method into a technique of interpretation that they might themselves imitate. If this was indeed the key to Holmes's success and long-standing influence, however, it is remarkable how few of the stories make clues genuinely accessible to the reader. It was perhaps only with the benefit of hindsight, at a time when the whodunit was at the height of its popularity, that the importance of 'playing the game' with the reader suggested itself to Doyle as having been the key to Holmes's success. In the early days Doyle was primarily seeking recognition for originality and commercial success. Later, as he tired of writing the Holmes stories, he struggled to breathe life into a format he felt he had already exhausted. Thus, it fell to the next generation to formalise the principles of fair play to which writers were expected to conform in the Golden Age of the whodunit.

Holmes's Legacy

The rules for the writing of detective fiction became so firmly established in the Golden Age of the whodunit that Ronald A. Knox eventually formulated them (with playful irony, it should be noted) into the 'Ten Commandments' that he included in his introduction to *The Best Detective Stories of 1928–29*. In explaining the role of these commandments Knox explained that 'the detective story is a game between two players, the author of the one part and the reader of the other part'.[11] What had begun as an incidental (and decidedly variable) feature in the Holmes stories hardened in the inter-war years into a set of expectations for a subgenre of detective fiction that, at the same time, acquired distinctive markers of Englishness and an unmistakable upper-middle-class ethos:

> [W]hen we say that the detective story has rules, we do not mean rules in the sense in which poetry has rules, but rules in the sense in which cricket has rules – a far more impressive consideration to the ordinary Englishman. The man who writes a detective story which is 'unfair' is not simply pronounced guilty of an error in taste. He has played foul, and the referee orders him off the field.[12]

Knox evokes an image of the writer as an English gentleman amateur – even if she happened to be female. Indeed, many of the most significant and popular of the writers of whodunits were women: Agatha Christie, Margery Allingham, Dorothy L. Sayers, Ngaio Marsh and Josephine Tey, to mention only the most well-known. There were plenty of male authors of Golden Age murder mysteries too, including Michael Innes, A. A. Milne, Edmund Crispin and Cyril Hare, and fictional detectives of both sexes, of which the most famous are Hercule Poirot, Miss Jane Marple and Lord Peter Wimsey. In general, these stories tend towards insularity and nostalgia. They are typically set in rural English villages and aristocratic country houses from which the outside world of urban squalor, restless lower-classes, industrial spoliation and the rise of totalitarianism are largely excluded, and in which murder and detection are the elements of a game played between sporting amateurs. Knox's rules of fair play stipulate that the culprit must be introduced early on in the story and that the reader must see the same evidence as the detective. Likewise, the distinction between detective and criminal established by Doyle had to be maintained, and Knox was firm on the point that it was cheating if the detective turned out to be the murderer.

Knox's ten commandments captured both the conservatism and the self-consciously playful spirit of the Golden Age whodunit. But their reduction of detective fiction to the pure form of a game also set the seal upon its imminent stagnation. The deployment of twists, red herrings and so forth were considered legitimate tactics. But the scope for such variations was subject to the law of diminishing returns. The parallel game of clues played by reader and detective that had begun with Doyle eventually exhausted itself in the novels of Agatha Christie. This, perhaps, was reason enough to look for new modes of detective fiction. But there were other reasons to reject not only the baroque murder plots of the Golden Age detective stories, but also their narrow social milieu and their separation of the intellectual game of investigation from the sordid business of crime as a social reality.

When Raymond Chandler wrote 'The Simple Art of Murder' (1944) he was gunning for all three and praising instead Dashiell Hammett, who 'gave murder back to the kind of people that commit it for reasons, not just to provide a corpse; and with the means at hand, not with hand-wrought duelling pistols, curare, and tropical fish'.[13] Chandler was the most outspoken and, along with Hammett, the most significant of the writers of hardboiled crime fiction that flourished in America between the 1920s and the 1950s. This development in the detective genre was not only a reaction against the contrived enigmas of the whodunit. It grew out of the quintessentially American late-nineteenth century genre of the Western, in which gunslinging cowboys dispatched frontier justice, but transposed it to the urban context of Prohibition-era racketeering and gangsterism. The principal representatives of hard-boiled style were the so-called '*Black Mask* boys' – Hammett, Chandler, Carroll John Daly, Horace McCoy and Paul Cain – all of whom published in *Black Mask* and other cheap pulp magazines such as *Dime Detective* and *Black Aces*.

Chandler credits Doyle as a key pioneer of the detective genre but, unsurprisingly, given his disdain for the artifices of the whodunit, gives him little credit for his role in developing the intellectual games of classic detective fiction. For Chandler, Holmes figures as 'mostly an attitude and a few dozen lines of unforgettable dialogue'.[14] This might not sound like much, but attitude and dialogue are amongst the most vital components of hardboiled fiction. Chandler's remarks about Holmes clearly demonstrate that there was more than one trajectory to his influence on subsequent developments in crime fiction. The hardboiled detective had become a vulnerable figure in the narrative. He (and it is invariably 'he' in Hammett's and Chandler's stories) does not arrive on the scene of the crime after the moment of danger has passed. The hardboiled detective is an embattled protagonist who is routinely double-crossed, beaten up, drugged and shot at, and whose main objective is to survive rather than to restore social order. Holmes's intellectual showmanship may have been jettisoned, but his physical courage, mental toughness and dogged pursuit of the truth persists in Chandler's famous description of the attitude of his ideal protagonist:

[D]own these mean streets a man must go who is not himself mean, who is neither tarnished nor afraid. The detective in this kind of story must be such a man. He is the hero, he is everything. He must be a complete man and a common man and yet an unusual man. He must be, to use a rather weathered phrase, a man of honor, by instinct, by inevitability, without thought of it, and certainly without saying it. He must be the best man in his world and a good enough man for any world.[15]

Chandler's romantic vision restored a quality of moral integrity to the detective story that Hammett had largely dispensed with in his tales of gangsters and corrupt lawyers such as *The Maltese Falcon* (1930) and *The Thin Man* (1934). Hammett's detective protagonists were flawed, even corrupt; as much gangsters as detectives, and with a matching capacity for brutality. But in novels such as *The Big Sleep* (1939), *Farewell, My Lovely* (1940) and *The Long Goodbye* (1954) Chandler's most famous detective figure, Philip Marlowe – though similarly exposed to danger – is ironic, intellectual and romantic; as much inclined to respond to an antagonist with sarcasm as with violence. Marlowe is often viewed as a twentieth-century American revision of the medieval knight errant. But he is also channelling a romantic conception of masculine integrity whose place in detective fiction derives from Holmes. Likewise, Chandler's evocation of the 'mean streets' down which his detective must travel also has Victorian echoes, harking back – consciously or otherwise – to the gritty slum fiction of Morrison's *Tales of Mean Streets* (1894). With the exposure of the detective to jeopardy, hardboiled fiction merged the two narratives of the classic detective story into one, immersing the detective directly into the story of the crime itself and transforming it into a thriller in which the chief source of interest is no longer simply the question of who committed a crime in the past but whether the detective will manage to survive the investigation at all – a narrative device that Doyle pioneered in 'The Final Problem'.

In addition to classic and hardboiled detective fiction (both of which have remained popular), Holmes's post-war influence can be seen in police procedural narratives such as the *Inspector Gideon* series by J. J. Marric, beginning with *Gideon's Day* (1955–90) and, in America, Ed McBain's *87th Precinct* series (1956–2005). These stories shift the focus away from a single detective to represent the workings of investigative teams across multiple crimes. But in their focus upon narratives of investigation and interpretation of material evidence they retain many aspects of the Holmesian model. Continental European writers also built upon the tradition of classic detective fiction, with Georges Simenon's Maigret series of novels (1930–72) retaining a strong focus upon the central detective. Maj Sjöwall and Per Wahlöö likewise followed in Doyle's (and Poe's) footsteps with their series of Martin Beck novels between 1965 and 1975, as did Josef Škvorecký with the Prague-based detective Lieutenant Boruvka in a series of stories published between 1966 and 1981.

Looking beyond Western traditions, Holmes's influence made a significant impact in both China and Japan. The first translations of Holmes stories appeared in China as early as 1896 and they continued to be the most commonly translated Western texts up to the end of the late Qing dynasty in 1911, when the traditional feudal social order gave way to a wider influx of Western influences. As Chinese ways of life changed during the early twentieth century, Holmes acquired a new kind of significance. The emphasis upon scientific reasoning in Doyle's stories was seen as a welcome harbinger of modernity and the Holmesian type of detective story quickly began to displace traditional Chinese *Gong-an* tales, in which revered feudal officials solved crimes. In Japan, too, a tradition of crime and detective fiction developed during the twentieth century under the influence of Western classic detective fiction, whose most notable exponent was Edogawa Rampo (a witty Japanese rendering of the name Edgar Allan Poe that served as the pen name of Tarō Hirai), whose debut work of detective fiction 'Ni-sen dōka' ('The Two-Sen Copper Coin') was published in 1923.

Holmes has been significant to the history of detective fiction not only in the extent of his influence upon the crime writers that came afterwards but also in the manner in which his figure has cast a shadow over both his precursors and peers as well. He has become a seemingly permanent fixture in the landscape not only of crime writing, but also of television and film adaptation, fan fiction and graphic novels. Furthermore, his significance has always been multifaceted, as is illustrated by the different ways in which Holmes influenced both the Golden Age whodunit and the American hardboiled thriller. This variety also shows up in the different possibilities that Doyle's peers explored in their efforts to fill the niche in the market that Holmes vacated in December 1893, many of which (though not all) were very successful at the time on their own terms. It is tempting to look for a single continuous narrative that would neatly explain Holmes's overwhelming success and dominance of the field. Doyle himself, when reflecting back on Holmes's 'monstrous growth', put it down to the importance of inserting clues into the Holmes stories as the key to the 'game' that would take centre stage with the emergence of the Golden Age whodunit. But Doyle's pronouncement – made at the height of the whodunit's popularity – perhaps only serves to obscure the extent to which Holmes's appeal has in fact always been based upon a range of different features – including style, attitude, moral vision and cultural distinctiveness. It is this plurality that has, in different ways and for different reasons, continued to attract readers and to inspire new writers to engage with and reinvent Holmes.

Notes

1. Fox Film Corporation, *Arthur Conan Doyle* 1927, [http://archive.org/details/SirArthurConanDoyleSpeaks_272, accessed 10 May 2017].
2. Ibid.
3. Fergus Hume, 'Preface', in *The Mystery of a Hanson Cab*, 1886 (Sydney: Sydney University Press, 2010), xi–xiv (xii).
4. Christopher Pittard, *Purity and Contamination in Late Victorian Detective Fiction* (Farnham: Ashgate, 2011), 29.
5. Jon Lellenberg, Daniel Stashower and Charles Foley (eds.), *Arthur Conan Doyle: A Life in Letters* (London: Harper Perennial, 2008), 250.
6. Arthur Conan Doyle, *Uncollected Stories: The Unknown Conan Doyle*, ed. John Michael Gibson and Richard Lancelyn Green (London: Secker & Warburg, 1982), 193.
7. Lellenberg et al., *Arthur Conan Doyle*, 293.
8. Arthur Conan Doyle, 'Preface', in *The Adventures of Sherlock Holmes* (New York: D. Appleton and Company, 1902), v–viii (vi).
9. Edgar Allan Poe, *Tales of Mystery And Imagination*, 1902 (London: Everyman, 1993), 425.
10. George Newnes, 'Introduction', *Strand Magazine* 1 (January 1891), 3.
11. Ronald Knox, 'Introduction', in Ronald Knox and Henry Harrington (eds.), *The Best Detective Stories of the Year: 1928* (London: Faber & Gwyer, 1929), vii–xxiii (x).
12. Ibid., x–xi.
13. Raymond Chandler, 'The Simple Art of Murder', 1944, in *Pearls Are a Nuisance* (London: Penguin Books, 1964), 181–99 (195).
14. Ibid., 185.
15. Ibid., 198.

3

CLARE CLARKE

Doyle, Holmes and Victorian Publishing

In 1921, close to end of his career and life, Arthur Conan Doyle wrote to Herbert Greenhough Smith, the literary editor of the *Strand Magazine*, about the collaborative nature of the birth of his most famous creation: 'if I am his father, you were the "accoucheur"'.[1] Indeed, Sherlock Holmes was the progeny of a fortuitous marriage between a new type of author, publication and reading public that emerged at the end of the nineteenth century. The Victorian *fin de siècle* was truly the age of the periodical press. The expensive and bulky triple-decker novel was dying; by 1897, the number of three-volume novels published annually in Britain had fallen to just four.[2] Publishing costs were dropping as taxes on paper and advertising were repealed, at the same time as paper production and printing technology advanced. Typesetting, which at the start of the nineteenth century had been done by hand, was revolutionised by the invention of the linotype machine, allowing multiple lines of text to be run at once. The commercialisation of half-tone technology as a means of producing low-cost, high-quality illustrations meant that photographs and drawings could be incorporated with basic linotype printing. Growing train networks also enabled fast and wide distribution of print material. The existence of over 800 W. H. Smith railway bookstalls, established in the second half of the nineteenth century, meant that the middle-class commuter could not only buy good quality reading material for their journey but even borrow it at one station and return it at another.

Perhaps most importantly of all, Forster's 1870 Education Act made elementary education compulsory for those between the ages of five and twelve in England and Wales as well as setting up board schools for the children of the working classes for the first time. Literacy rates rose and, by the time the first generation of children to benefit from the Act became adults in the late 1880s, new forms of cheap media were springing up to cater for their reading tastes and preferences. Periodicals were born of this combination of social change and new technology and catered to this new mass literate reading public. By 1900 there were over 50,000 periodicals in circulation in Britain and the colonies; magazines catering to every taste, budget, every professional or political organisation. It was not in novels but in these ephemeral publications that most Victorian fictional detectives first appeared.

Periodicals were sold primarily at newsagents and railway bookstalls, providing perfect light reading for leisure time – serialised fiction, interviews with celebrities, factual articles on science, society or politics and puzzles – things for men to read on the journeys to and from work, for their wives to read later at home and for their children to look at after the day's lessons were finished. Michael Wolff emphasises the importance of these ephemeral publications as mirrors of Victorian social concerns, claiming that 'the years that we call Victorian are best mirrored in serial publications – literature, argument, the tastes and preoccupations of just about every level and sort of society, all display themselves in newspapers and journals'. Not only did these magazines reflect the tastes of readers, they also helped shape and guide them: 'One might almost claim that an attitude, an opinion, an idea, did not exist until it had registered itself in the press, and that an interest group, a sect, a profession, came of age when it inaugurated its journal'.[3]

Sir George Newnes (1851–1910), perhaps the most famous media baron of late-Victorian Britain, was a man acutely attuned to the new periodical market, to its role in both reflecting and shaping the opinions of readers and to its potential as a money-making enterprise. Newnes was the epitome of the Victorian self-made man, founding a vast and hugely lucrative publishing empire from nothing and establishing some of the most successful magazines of the 1880s and 1890s, including the *Strand* and *Sunday Strand, Tit-Bits, The Westminster Gazette, The Wide World Magazine* and *Woman's Life*. With his first successful periodical publication, the weekly penny paper *Tit-Bits*, launched in 1881, Newnes demonstrated that he understood how to target and poach the readers of lowbrow penny papers. Nineteenth-century penny papers contained lurid content about crime and gambling, alongside sensational stories. The 'tit-bits' referred to in the title of Newnes's new publication, by contrast, were wholesome snippets of information: sixteen pages of short stories, jokes, correspondence and advertisements. The editorial rule was that no column could be longer than an inch and a half; no story could be too complicated.

Tit-Bits also sought to foster a sense of community with its readers, encouraging them to contribute items, participate in contests and write to the newspaper for advice. Features such as the 'Inquiry Column' and 'Answers to Correspondence' invited readers to become part of a dialogue with the publication. Reader competitions also offered the possibility of genuinely life-changing financial rewards. One of the most famous of these, which took place at Christmas 1883, offered a prize of a suburban London villa for the best short story submitted. This strategy kept sales at an impressive 500,000 copies per week and developed a readership of what Newnes called 'loyal Tit-Bitites'.[4]

Newnes saw his publications as improving literature that would elevate readers' tastes and do them good. This was the sort of publication that Newnes himself wanted to read but which did not yet exist. He firmly believed that his own humble beginnings helped him understand the types of topics that ordinary people wanted to read about – as he put it, 'I am the average man. I don't have to put myself in his place. I am in his place. I know what he wants'.[5] Nowhere was this more evident than with his next publication, the *Strand*. The sixpenny magazine, launched at Christmas 1890, was aimed at a prosperous readership – members of the established and aspiring middle and upper-middle classes. With this new publication, Newnes hoped to reconfigure the middle ground of the magazine market, as he had done with the penny paper market. This time, he would target white-collar urban commuters, as well as the sizeable number of British citizens scattered throughout the empire. The *Strand* was available by mail order or at railway bookstalls for sixpence, and provided a cheap, entertaining assortment of light, short articles and stories perfect for a journey. Thanks to Newnes's reputation, the popularity of *Tit-Bits* and extensive advertising in *Tit Bits* and billboards across the country, the *Strand*'s first issue sold over 300,000 copies.

The publication's name, shared with the location of its offices in Victorian London's main East–West thoroughfare, was a geographical metaphor for its modern, urban content. As Newnes put it, 'it is through the Strand itself that the tide of life flows fullest and strongest and deepest'.[6] Lavishly produced and boasting at least one illustration on every opening page, its content combined biographies of famous and important men, entertaining short stories, factual articles on science, professions and the empire, as well as pictures of celebrities and puzzles for children. To read the *Strand*, then, was to experience the 'tide of life' at the heart of the British Empire. The first issue included factual articles on the Metropolitan Fire Brigade and the Royal Veterinary College, several stories in translation and 'Portraits of Celebrities at Different Times of their Lives', which reproduced photographs of eminent Victorians alongside a few lines of biography. The first celebrities to feature were literary luminaries Alfred, Lord Tennyson, Algernon Swinburne and H. Rider Haggard. Just a few months later, following the publication of the first six Holmes stories, the magazine's biggest success, Arthur Conan Doyle, would join this list.

An integral part of late-Victorian 'urban life' covered by Newnes and the *Strand* was crime. The late 1880s and 1890s witnessed a dramatic fall in the numbers of criminals at large in London, as new Metropolitan Police stations and frequent foot patrols began to take effect. Nonetheless, public interest in crime remained unabated and the print media was central to the British consumption of crime narratives. Nineteenth-century British readers loved to read about crime in all its gory detail – as a *Pall Mall Gazette* review explains: 'Scratch John Bull and you find the ancient Briton who revels in blood, who loves to dig deep into a murder, and devours the details of a hanging. If you doubt it, ask the clerks at Mr. Smith's book stalls, ask the men and women who sell newspapers in the street. They will tell you'.[7]

As the nineteenth century progressed, narratives of crime began to evolve. At the beginning of the nineteenth century, the most popular forms of crime narrative were criminal broadsides – penny newspapers sold at the gallows, providing sensational accounts of the criminal and their acts – and lurid penny dreadfuls about murder, such as *The String of Pearls* (1846–7) featuring the killer barber Sweeney Todd. As the century progressed, these were replaced by less prurient and picaresque narratives about crime – sensation novels and detective fiction featuring crime in respectable society, cases where the criminal is caught and where the detective is a new kind of hero. The marriage of the politically conservative periodical format and the crime genre was a key factor in this formal and ideological change.

This move towards the celebration of the fictional detective as hero arrived at a time when the Metropolitan Police were not viewed in a particularly positive light. The years preceding the birth of Holmes and the *Strand* constituted a challenging time for the reputation of London's police force and detective branch, as both suffered sustained attacks in the national press, with coverage drawing attention to a number of embarrassing and worrying failures. One prong of attack concerned the Metropolitan Police force's inability to prevent repeated bomb attacks on the British mainland carried out during the 1880s by supporters of Irish Home Rule, including one daring bomb attack upon the offices of the Irish Branch of Scotland Yard. The press, particularly left-leaning papers such as T. P. O'Connor's *Star* and W. T. Stead's *Pall Mall Gazette*, interpreted these attacks as worrying indicators of police inefficiency. The force's reputation suffered further owing to accusations of brutality at a number of public demonstrations held by Socialists and the working classes, in particular a protest about coercion in Ireland held in November 1887. During the demonstration, police charged protesters; violence broke out, with hundreds injured and three deaths. In the press this event was referred to as Bloody Sunday. The most intense and sustained press criticism of the Metropolitan Police, however, was precipitated by the perceived failures of the investigation into the 1888 Whitechapel Ripper murders. When the police had failed to identify a viable suspect after the murders of five women, the left-wing press poured forth its outrage about the force's inefficiency, reading the lack of investigatory progress as a lack of concern for low-status citizens of London's impoverished East End. As the *Star* trumpeted, 'The police, of course, are helpless. We expect nothing of them'.[8]

From its inception in 1891, just two years after the still-unsolved Ripper murders, the *Strand* devoted many of its features to matters of crime and detection. The first issue contained an article on the Thames River Police, while the second featured Grant Allen's 'Jerry Stokes', a story about a hangman, setting in train the magazine's relationship with crime fiction. However, Newnes's editorial policy regarding crime exhibited contradictory impulses. He wanted to capitalise on readers' interest in crime – and thus included multiple articles and stories about crime and criminals – but also to 'purify' crime narratives, removing their sensationalism.[9] Newnes spoke about his desire to 'improve his readers' cultural health'; to provide them with 'cheap, healthful literature'.[10] This purifying approach is evident in the magazine's factual features on crime and detection. In issues of the *Strand* published between 1891 and 1900, there is not one mention of the unsolved Ripper murders or the pressing late-nineteenth-century problems of police brutality or inefficiency.

'Policemen of the World' (February 1897), for instance, opens with the benign and paternalistic view that policemen (there would be no police-*women* until 1915) are 'a necessary evil' – there 'to hunt down rascals and to help women across the street'.[11] Indeed, the article focuses not on the international approach to crime control, but rather on the various uniforms worn by international officers. Almost entirely absent from the magazine's discussion of policing in Ireland, for instance, is the fraught topic of Anglo-Irish politics. Instead the article glosses Ireland's 'Emergency trouble' with a cheery platitude about officers' 'good temper under difficulties and danger', immediately refocussing on a description of the constabulary's 'dark green uniforms'.[12]

An article in the *Strand*'s first issue, which follows the Thames River Police on their nightly patrol, illustrates the magazine's ideological move towards the celebration of, and trust in, the police. The article repeatedly stresses the industriousness and professionalism of the officers. The correspondent informs readers that when the *Princess Alice* sank in 1878, 'the men of the Thames river police were on duty for four or five nights at a stretch'.[13] Similarly, the 1902 article, 'Making a Policeman', emphasises the moral character of London's police. The article opens with the cheery observation that 'the Metropolitan Policeman – *he is worthy of the capital letter* – is a living monument of civility, kindliness and good temper', adding 'every policeman in London is a gentleman'.[14] In 1886, aspiring author Arthur Conan Doyle had decided to set about creating a new kind of scientific detective story, inspired by the methods of his old University of Edinburgh mentor Dr Joseph Bell, alongside his enjoyment of the work of Emile Gaboriau, Robert Louis Stevenson and Edgar Allan Poe. Doyle's self-imposed set of rules for detective fiction – that the criminal should not be heroic, that the number of legally punishable crimes should be kept to a minimum and that sensationalism should be suppressed – meant that his attitude aligned itself neatly with the *Strand*'s conservative editorial approach to crime and thus constituted a key factor in the success of the union between the two.

Sherlock Holmes made his first appearance in *A Study in Scarlet* in *Beeton's Christmas Annual* 1887, published by Ward, Lock and Co., after being rejected by three of the other big publishing firms. Surprising as it may now seem, this first Holmes story caused barely a ripple of interest with either critics or the reading public. Indeed, Holmes might have remained a one-book novelty had it not been for a luncheon hosted by the American publishing house Lippincott's in September 1889. The managing editor of the publishing house, Joseph Stoddart, invited Doyle and Oscar Wilde to each submit a crime story for the first English edition of *Lippincott's Magazine*. Wilde's contribution was *The Picture of Dorian Gray* (1891); Doyle's offering was *The Sign of Four*, a second outing for Holmes. Once again, however, his detective fiction failed to cause a stir. The view of the *Athenaeum* coldly conceptualises reviewers' estimation of the novel's throwaway nature: 'Dr. Doyle's admirers will read the little volume through eagerly enough, but they will hardly care to take it up again'.[15]

Doyle's diaries and letters for the years following the publication of his first two Holmes novels frequently turn to his disappointment with their meagre sales and critical reception. As he wrote to his mother, 'Verily, literature is a difficult oyster to open'.[16] In March 1891, Doyle's relationship with the newly-established *Strand* began with the publication of 'The Voice of Science', a light-hearted comedic short story. Later that year, still largely untroubled by literary success, Doyle approached the *Strand*'s literary editor, Herbert Greenhough Smith, with two sample stories and a proposal to revive Holmes in a series of interconnected stories that would 'engage the attention of the reader' and 'bind that reader to that particular magazine' (*Memories* 95). Doyle had astutely observed that a serial created problems for the reader who happened to miss an episode. Self-contained stories with strong recurring characters, he proposed, would keep the reader loyal to the publication and coming back for more as they would not be at sea if they missed an episode. After reading the two sample stories – 'A Scandal in Bohemia' and 'The Red-Headed League' – Greenhough Smith reportedly ran to Newnes to tell him that he had discovered 'the greatest short-story writer since Edgar Allan Poe'.[17]

Doyle's offer of six Holmes stories was snapped up and the ensuing relationship between author and publication was to become one of the most mutually profitable in literary history. In turn, the relationship between Doyle and the *Strand* was to inaugurate one of the nineteenth century's most successful marriages of form and genre – that of periodical publication and the short-story detective series. Doyle would go on to publish fifty-six Holmes stories and two novels in the *Strand* over a period of more than thirty years. The Holmes stories to which *Strand* readers were introduced were notably less bloody, less sensational and featured a notably less bohemian detective than the earlier novels, doubtless a strategy to ensure that the series was palatable to the *Strand*'s socially conservative editors and readers. The strategy worked and, following the publication of 'A Scandal in Bohemia' in July 1891, the magazine's already impressive sales figures soon boomed at well over 500,000 copies per issue.[18]

Not only did the Sherlock Holmes stories have an immediate impact on the publication's sales, they also necessitated structural changes in the publication process and even in the library lending system. In the wake of Holmes's appearance, libraries were soon obliged to stay open late on the magazine's publication day, the third Thursday of every month, to cater for clamouring fans.[19] In her biography of Newnes, Hulda Friedrichs also outlines the changes to the magazine's printing process precipitated by the popularity of Doyle's stories: 'with the arrival of Sherlock Holmes, it [the *Strand*] entered the period where it had to be sent to press a month before the date of publication, keeping the machines working till the day it was put upon the bookstalls'.[20]

Doyle dispatched his second Holmes adventure, 'A Case of Identity', to his agent A. P. Watt on 10 April 1891; he sent 'The Red-Headed League' on 20 April, followed by 'The Boscombe Valley Mystery' on 27 April. On 4 May, Doyle was struck down by a serious case of influenza, which delayed his sending the fifth Holmes story, 'The Five Orange Pips', until 12 May. The sixth story, 'The Man with the Twisted Lip', was delayed until Doyle had fully recovered and was not received by Watt until August. The illness precipitated a decision by Doyle to quit his ill-paying medical career and devote himself to full-time writing: 'I saw how foolish I was to waste my literary earnings in keeping up an oculist's room in Wimpole Street, and I determined with a wild rush of joy ... to trust for ever to my power of writing'.[21] By September he had given up his unprofitable practice and moved to suburban South Norwood to work from home as a full-time writer.

No sooner had Doyle delivered the sixth Holmes story than Greenhough Smith implored him for a further six. Less than four months after the first of the Holmes stories had been published, however, Doyle was already tiring of detective fiction. He wrote to his mother: '"*The Strand*" are simply imploring me to continue Sherlock Holmes ... The stories brought me in an average of £35 each, so I have written ... to say that if they offer me £50 each, irrespective of length I may be induced to reconsider my refusal'.[22] This request was quickly and easily granted by the editors at the *Strand* who were aware of the stories' vital impact upon the magazine's booming sales figures. The editors' relief at Doyle's agreement to provide further Holmes stories is palpable in the magazine's 'Portraits of Celebrities at Different Times of Their Lives' feature on Doyle in the December 1891 issue. Alongside pictures of Doyle, the copy breathlessly exclaims: 'There are few better writers of short stories than Mr. Conan Doyle, and it gives us great pleasure to announce the extraordinary adventures of Sherlock Holmes, which have proved so popular with our readers during the past six months, will be continued in the new year'.[23]

In November 1891, however, when only the fifth Holmes story, 'The Five Orange Pips', was running in the *Strand*, Doyle's personal papers again make clear the nature of his feelings about Holmes's place in his personal literary hierarchy. He was concerned that periodical fiction was demeaning, detract-ing from his 'higher work', his historical romance novels (*Memories* 81). In a letter to his mother, he outlines that he has written the first five stories of the new collection – 'The Blue Carbuncle', 'The Speckled Band', 'The Noble Bachelor', 'The Engineer's Thumb' and 'The Beryl Coronet'. He also wrote the now famous lines, 'I think of slaying Holmes in the sixth [story] & winding him up for good & all. He takes my mind from better things'.[24] In response, Doyle's mother counselled her son to postpone Holmes's death. Arthur relented; however, from this date he continued to plan the character's demise.

Nonetheless, the second set of six *Adventures* followed – published in the *Strand* from January to June 1892 and concluding with 'The Copper Beeches'. Ever the canny businessman, Doyle was correct in his assumption that the twelve Holmes adventures would make 'a rather good book'.[25] Therefore, in October 1892, the twelve stories were published in a large run of 10,000 copies as the first volume of Newnes's new 'Strand Library'. The volume cover – with gilt lettering and a light blue bevelled cloth, featuring a miniature sketch of the *Strand* – deliberately marketed the *Adventures of Sherlock Holmes* as 'a *de luxe* book-version of the *Strand Magazine* itself'.[26]

Newnes and Greenhough Smith persuaded Doyle to keep Holmes alive for a second series of twelve stories, for which they paid £1,000, a huge sum at the time. These stories were published in the periodical between December 1892 and 1893 and in volume form by the Strand Library as *The Memoirs of Sherlock Holmes* (1894). Doubtless keen to placate and maintain the magazine's large number of Holmes fans in the period between July 1892 and the detective's return in December, Newnes engaged in several strategies to keep Doyle and Holmes in the forefront of his readers' minds. First, the magazine featured several distinctly Holmesian detective stories by established authors J. E. Preston Muddock (writing as Dick Donovan) and Grant Allen; secondly it advertised the imminent return of Sherlock Holmes; and thirdly, it ran a number of features and interviews with Doyle himself. Harry How's 'A Day with Dr Conan Doyle' (July 1892), not only maintains Doyle's profile within the magazine until Sherlock's return, its entire first page effuses over Doyle's contribution to the magazine and the genre. In so doing, the article self-reflexively underlines the links between the detective genre, the author, the reader and the publication itself.

With Holmes as a key component of the magazine, sales of the *Strand* boomed; Doyle enjoyed financial security coupled with literary celebrity and the name Sherlock Holmes soon entered the public consciousness as synonymous with skilled detection. Such was the clamour for more of Doyle's detective fiction that his two earlier Holmes novels reversed the usual journey from periodical to volume form and were retrospectively serialised in Newnes's *Tit-Bits* in 1893. The same year, *A Study in Scarlet* was reissued multiple times – by Lippincott's, Lever Brothers' Sunlight Library and Ward, Lock and Bowden – and advertised in prestigious venues such as *The Times*, with the strapline: 'everything that prince of amateur detectives, Mr Sherlock Holmes, says is worth hearing'.[27] In November 1893, capitalising upon notoriously weak late-Victorian copyright laws, what is thought to be the first play starring Holmes, *Under the Clock*, a musical satire penned by Charles Brookfield and Seymour Hicks, debuted at London's Royal Court Theatre, where it ran for seventy-eight performances. The following July, *The Times* reported an incident in which a thief who had stolen an MP's gold watch and chain was apprehended by a member of the public with the words 'I am Sherlock Holmes the second'.[28] A little more than two years after his first appearance in the *Strand*, it appears that Holmes was very much a household name.

But, at the very height of his fame, in 'The Final Problem', published in the *Strand* in December 1893, Doyle fulfilled his promise to kill off Sherlock Holmes. During a struggle with master-criminal Professor Moriarty (never previously mentioned in a Holmes story), the detective disappeared over the

Reichenbach Falls. The full-page Sidney Paget illustration facing the story's opening page left readers in no doubt about the detective's fate, depicting Holmes toppling off the side of the waterfall and emblazoned with the title 'The Death of Sherlock Holmes'.[29] Although Holmes was later (and frequently) resurrected, at the time of the story's publication Doyle firmly believed that the hero was dead and that this would be the last Holmes story.

While there is little or no evidence to support many Doyle biographers' favourite claim that thousands of Londoners wore black armbands to mourn the death of Holmes, the *Strand* and its readers were nonetheless dismayed at his demise. Newnes referred to the detective's death as 'the dreadful event'.[30] Some 20,000 *Strand* readers are reported to have cancelled their subscriptions to the magazine. Newnes and Greenhough Smith clamoured to install a fitting successor to Holmes, commissioning short detective stories from such *Strand* favourites as L. T. Meade and Grant Allen. Rival periodicals like *Windsor Magazine* hoped to poach bereft readers by commissioning Holmesian detective stories of their own. Canny advertisers lost little time in capitalising upon this sad event; immediately after Holmes's death, Beecham's Pills launched a campaign for their medicine under the heading, 'The Last Letter from Sherlock Holmes', in which the detective appears to be alive and in hiding, but writes to Watson to request a box of the 'indispensable' pills.[31]

Seven years later, however, with William Gillette's wildly successful stage adaptation *Sherlock Holmes* about to open in London, Doyle began to consider Holmes's resurrection, pitching the novel *The Hound of the Baskervilles* to the *Strand*. It was serialised in the magazine in 1901–2, and set in train the rekindling of the relationship between Doyle, Holmes and the *Strand* that would last for almost another thirty years. In 1903, still torn between the commercial potential of detective fiction and his aesthetic preference for historical romance, Doyle was persuaded once again to resurrect Holmes. The catalyst for this decision, as so often in Doyle's career, was money. This time, however, it was not Greenhough Smith and the *Strand* that persuaded Doyle to bring back his detective. Rather, it was the astronomical sum of $45,000 promised by the US magazine *Collier's Weekly*. As Doyle put it in a letter to his mother: 'I have done no Sherlock Holmes Stories for seven or eight years, and I don't see why I should not have another go at them and earn three times as much money as I can by any other form of work'.[32] And so, Doyle conjured a scenario in which Holmes had been alive and in hiding since his dramatic tumble into the Reichenbach Falls in 1893. Doubtless owing to his lengthy personal and commercial investment in Doyle and Holmes for the *Strand*, Greenhough Smith was understandably displeased that Doyle only agreed to resurrect his detective after the promise of a huge payment from the American magazine. Nonetheless, the British rights were sold to Holmes's home, the *Strand*, for another large sum. Thus, in the *Strand*'s September 1903 edition, ten years after Holmes's purported death in 'The Final Problem', the editors ran a huge banner for the next issue, emblazoned 'THE RETURN OF SHERLOCK HOLMES'. Beneath it, they triumphantly exclaimed: 'Fortunately the news [of Holmes's death], though based on circumstantial evidence which at the time seemed conclusive, turns out to be erroneous'.[33]

This announcement heralded the return of Holmes to the magazine and thirteen stories starring the resurrected detective featured in the *Strand* between October 1903 and December 1904. It is important to note, however, that they had their first publication a month earlier in *Collier's*, the magazine that had proffered such a large sum to secure them (from September 1903 onwards). The collection was soon released in volume form as *The Return of Sherlock Holmes*, by US publisher McClure, Phillips and Company, as well as by George Newnes in the United Kingdom. A group of seven stories followed in the period 1908–17 and were published in volume edition as *His Last Bow* (1917). During this period, the final Holmes novel *The Valley of Fear* was serialised in the *Strand* from September 1914 to May 1915. The final twelve Holmes stories, later collected as *The Case-Book of Sherlock Holmes*, were published in the magazine from 1921–7. The final Holmes story, 'Shoscombe Old Place', was published by the *Strand* in April 1927.

The twentieth-century Holmes stories were marked by an increasing frustration on Doyle's part about the old tensions between art and commerce and an attendant cooling in relations with the editors at the *Strand*. His correspondence with Greenhough Smith, while still civil, became increasingly fractious. In a letter to the literary editor accompanying the stories that would be collected as *The Return of Sherlock Holmes*, Doyle suggests that 'The Norwood Builder' is 'in the very first rank of the whole series for subtlety and depth' but concedes, 'As to the [Solitary] Cyclist, I did not like it so well nor was I satisfied with it & yet I could make no more of it', adding 'You will appreciate more fully now my intense disinclination to continue these stories which has caused me to resist all entreaty for so many years. It is impossible to prevent a certain sameness & want of freshness'.[34] Indeed, in many ways, Doyle's twentieth-century Holmes stories demonstrate a desire or need to break new ground, to forego some of his old dictums about decorum and the 'healthful' focus which had aligned him so closely with the *Strand*; the later tales constitute something of a formal and thematic departure from his earlier work, becoming bloodier and less conservative, more morally ambiguous and less concerned with resolution. The '"striking and bizarre"' '"little problems"' of the earlier Holmes *Adventures* ('The Blue

Carbuncle' 244, 'The Red-headed League' 190) give way to more baroque tales of domestic abuse, forced marriage, blackmail and murder. Holmes dabbles in house-breaking, musing that he might have become '"a highly efficient criminal"' ('Charles Augustus Milverton' 577) if he had chosen to do so.

Despite the tensions between the author and magazine, the end of the *Strand*-Holmes era was ever-focused on the dialectical relationship between author, reader and text. Thus, it was marked by an article by Doyle in which he invited readers to enter a competition (with prize money of £100) to match his choice of the twelve best Holmes stories (Doyle eventually choosing 'The Speckled Band', 'The Red-headed League', 'The Dancing Men', 'The Final Problem', 'A Scandal in Bohemia', 'The Empty House', 'The Five Orange Pips', 'The Second Stain', 'The Devil's Foot', 'The Priory School', 'The Musgrave Ritual' and 'The Reigate Squires').[35] In the note to Greenhough Smith, which accompanied his choices and the manuscript of his final story, Doyle seemed happy to finally bring a close to the Holmes era, writing: 'It's not of the first flight, and Sherlock, like his author, grows a little stiff in the joints, but it is the best I can do. Now farewell to him for ever!'[36] Although the detective would live on in many cultural forms over the next hundred years, this marked the end of the relationship between Doyle, Holmes and the *Strand*.

Notes

1. Quoted in Cameron Hollyer, 'Author to Editor: Arthur Conan Doyle's Correspondence with H. Greenhough Smith', *ACD: The Journal of the Arthur Conan Doyle Society* 3 (1992), 11.

2. Peter Keating, *The Haunted Study: A Social History of the English Novel 1875–1914* (London: Secker and Warburg, 1989), 26.

3. Michael Wolff, 'Charting the Golden Stream: Thoughts on a Directory of Victorian Periodicals', *Victorian Periodicals Newsletter* 4:3 (1971), 23–38 (26–7, 26).

4. Quoted in Kate Jackson, 'George Newnes and the "loyal Tit-Bitites": Editorial Identity and Textual Interaction in *Tit-Bits*', in Laurel Brake, Bill Bell and David Finkelstein (eds.), *Nineteenth-Century Media and the Construction of Identities* (Basingstoke: Palgrave, 2000), 11–26 (11).

5. Quoted in Reginald Pound, *Mirror of the Century: The Strand Magazine 1891–1950* (London: Heinemann, 1966), 20.

6. Raymond Blathwayt, 'Lions in their Dens: George Newnes at Putney', *The Idler* (March 1893), 161–73 (170).

7. Unsigned, 'The Nightmare at the Lyceum', *Pall Mall Gazette* 5 (7 August 1888).

8. Unsigned, 'What We Think', *Star* 1 (1 October 1888).

9. Christopher Pittard, *Purity and Contamination in Late Victorian Detective Fiction* (Farnham: Ashgate, 2011), 76.

10. Ibid., 68.

11. C. S. Pelham-Clinton, 'Policemen of the World', *Strand Magazine* 13 (February 1897), 214–24 (214).
12. Ibid., 224.
13. Unsigned, 'A Night with the Thames Police', *Strand Magazine* 1 (January 1891), 124–32 (125–6).
14. H. J. Holmes, 'Making a Policeman', *Strand Magazine* 23 (April 1902), 386–91 (386). Original emphasis.
15. Unsigned, 'Novels of the Week', *Athenaeum* (6 December 1890), 773–4 (773).
16. Jon Lellenberg, Daniel Stashower and Charles Foley (eds.), *Arthur Conan Doyle: A Life in Letters* (London: Harper Perennial, 2008), 247.
17. Ibid., 293.
18. Laurel Brake and Marysa Demoor (eds.), *Dictionary of Nineteenth-Century Journalism in Great Britain and Ireland* (Gent: Academia Press, 2009), 604.
19. Pound, *Mirror of the Century*, 92.
20. Hulda Friedrichs, *The Life of Sir George Newnes* (London: Hodder and Stoughton, 1911), 122.
21. Lellenberg et al., *Arthur Conan Doyle*, 294.
22. Ibid., 296. Original emphasis.
23. Unsigned, 'A. Conan Doyle', *Strand Magazine* 2 (December 1891), 606.
24. Lellenberg et al., *Arthur Conan Doyle*, 300.
25. Ibid.
26. Peter D. McDonald, *British Literary Culture and Publishing Practice, 1880–1914* (Cambridge: Cambridge University Press, 2002), 119. Original emphasis.
27. Unsigned, 'Publications', *The Times* 2 (18 July 1893).
28. Unsigned, 'Police', *The Times* 3 (9 July 1894).
29. Arthur Conan Doyle, 'The Adventure of the Final Problem', *Strand Magazine* 6 (December 1893), 558.
30. Quoted in Pound, *Mirror of the Century*, 45.
31. Unsigned, 'The Last Letter from Sherlock Holmes', *Fun* 30 (16 January 1894).
32. Lellenberg et al., *Arthur Conan Doyle*, 512.
33. Unsigned, 'The Return of Sherlock Holmes', *Strand Magazine* 26 (September 1903), 360.
34. Lellenberg et al., *Arthur Conan Doyle*, 514.
35. Arthur Conan Doyle, 'The Sherlock Holmes Prize Competition: How I Made My List', *Strand Magazine* 73 (June 1927), 32.
36. Quoted in Andrew Lycett, *Conan Doyle: The Man Who Created Sherlock Holmes* (London: Phoenix, 2008), 440.

4

STEPHEN KNIGHT

Doyle, Holmes and London

One of crime fiction's most notable achievements is to have reimagined certain cities at crucial times in their development. Think, for example, of Raymond Chandler's booming Los Angeles, the uncertain post-war London of John Creasey's Gideon and the independent and criminal Edinburgh of Ian Rankin. In the work of such writers, the city is central to the criminographical narrative, but there can be little doubt that a word-association test of the terms 'city' and 'detective' would most often, all around the world, generate two names: London and Sherlock Holmes. Arthur Conan Doyle's canon presents us with, as Watson comments in 'The Resident Patient', a crime fiction account of 'the ever-changing kaleidoscope of life as it ebbs and flows through Fleet Street and the Strand' (424) and across the great city.

Difficulties stood in the way of this dynamic development. Doyle started by writing action adventures and then historical fiction, with the American short story writer Bret Harte and his own fellow-countryman, Walter Scott, as respective models, and his quickly developed distaste for Holmes threatened to bring an early end to the city-detective pairing. A less familiar challenge was Doyle's limited knowledge of London, both at the start and throughout the saga. He grew up and studied medicine in Edinburgh; after being a ship's surgeon for about a year, travelling to South Africa, he briefly joined a classmate's medical practice in Plymouth. The first Holmes narrative, *A Study in Scarlet*, was written in 1886 while he and his new wife, 'Touie' were living on site at his own practice at 1 Bush Villas in Southsea, a suburb of Portsmouth on the Hampshire coast. Although the couple did move briefly to north London, when Doyle set up practice as an eye specialist in March 1891, ill-health, a lack of patients and the success of the Holmes stories within the *Strand Magazine*, led to a move to Norwood in distant south-west London, where they stayed until 1897 when Doyle built Undershaw, a large house in southern Surrey, an hour's travel from the city.

The decision to situate his detective in London was influenced by Edgar Allan Poe's imaginary Paris and Emile Gaboriau's realisation of the same city for Inspecteur Lecoq – Doyle mentions both early in *A Study in Scarlet* (24–5) – but he was also responding to his artist/illustrator uncles John and Richard, who lived and worked among the excitements of the capital. Richard designed the long-running cover of *Punch* in 1849, illustrated the works of some of the most important writers of the day, including Charles Dickens, William Makepeace Thackeray and John Ruskin, and led a busy social life amongst artists and the gentry. In 1874 the fifteen-year-old Doyle visited London for three weeks and they showed him around energetically, including Madame Tussaud's, then located in Baker Street: he wrote to his mother that he 'was delighted by the room of Horrors, and the images of the murderers'. Back at school, he confessed to 'enjoy[ing] my 3 weeks in London immensely. I saw everything and went everywhere. In one walk I thoroughly saw St Pauls, Westminster Abbey and bridge, houses of parliament – The Tower – Temple Bar, the Guild Hall and other places of interest'.[1]

This early interest in London is evident in his first book, *The Narrative of John Smith*, written in 1883 but lost in the post on its way to a publisher (a re-written but incomplete version was published posthumously in 2011). Almost without event, the short novel chronicles the thoughts of a clever man lodging 'in a second-floor front in a quiet London thoroughfare'[2] – effectively Holmes without anti-criminal action. The first two Holmes novels, *A Study in Scarlet* and *The Sign of Four*, base their plots on overseas misdeeds, as in their key sources, Robert Louis Stevenson's *The Dynamiter* (1885) and Wilkie Collins's *The Moonstone* (1868), but the international threats are confronted at home: in *A Study in Scarlet*, before he meets Holmes, Watson, wounded and back from Afghanistan, is pleased to see 'a friendly face in the great wilderness of London' (16).

In marked contrast to the exhaustive research that Doyle undertook to ensure the accuracy of the settings of his historical fiction, his attempts to master London were decidedly more haphazard. In a March 1890 letter to Joseph Stoddart, editor of the American *Lippincott's Magazine*, Doyle remarked, 'It must amuse you to see the vast and accurate knowledge of London which I display. I worked it all out from a Post Office map'.[3] The 1888 London Post Office map, however, does not include the outer London settings Doyle at times employs, and inside its range he was highly selective. There were no numbers as high as 221B on Baker Street in 1886: its northward extension was then York Place. That said, the fictional address had credibility – Michael F. Harrison reports that by 1880 the area had changed 'from high-class residential to upper-middle-class-residential and commercial',[4] and it was very close to the prestigious medical specialist quarter focused on Devonshire Square.

But Baker Street had another meaning: the underground station on the new Metropolitan Railway (now part of the modern underground's Metropolitan line) had opened in 1863 and was a major interchange for commuters traveling from the rapidly expanding west and north-west suburbs into London, especially the City. This was the market of archetypal *Strand* readers that George Newnes would capture on launching the magazine in 1890. Baker Street was the right place for a modern professional problem-solver, and also made a distinct connection with the commuting, story-reading public at large. It is not surprising, then, that the canon thematises city travel from the outset. In *A Study in Scarlet* Holmes inspects cab-tracks outside the murder location, and it turns out that Jefferson Hope, the avenging American, has been pursuing his enemies as a cab-driver. A sense of mobility is also strong in *The Sign of Four*: Holmes and Watson cross the Thames by cab to Thaddeus Sholto's house, apparently in Wandsworth, which Sholto describes as '"the howling desert of South London"' (100), and then on to his brother's house in Upper Norwood, well south of the river. After they return north, the action climaxes in a melodramatic chase down the Thames, where the steam-launches of modern London engage with the exotic crimes of empire, including an Andaman islander with poisoned darts.

The great detective can master this adventurous London, but the stories also include a more relaxed city life. At the start of *A Study in Scarlet* Watson meets a friend at the Criterion Hotel at Piccadilly, surely in the American Bar, described by Harrison as of 'overpowering magnificence'.[5] They head off to lunch at what the historian Priscilla Metcalf calls 'the elaborate new Holborn restaurant'[6] in the busy area that would shortly become the site of the Aldwych development. Watson and his friend are not impoverished medical men: they are sharing the life of glittering London, not unlike Doyle's uncles (the Prince of Wales once invited Richard to dine at his club).[7] Such sophistication recurs. In *The Sign of Four*, the father of Mary Morstan, the future Mrs Watson, disappeared when he was at the Langham Hotel, one of the city's finest, and where the Hon Philip Green stays in 'Lady Frances Carfax' (947). The ubiquitous Prince of Wales opened it in 1865 and Stoddart, of *Lippincott's Magazine*, was staying there in August 1889 when Doyle travelled up from Portsmouth to dine and was commissioned to write *The Sign of Four*.

The modest reception of *A Study in Scarlet* had not committed Doyle to a London detective and, after *The Sign of Four*, he still planned historical fiction, as well as a medical career, spending several months in Vienna studying to be an eye specialist. Only then, as suggested above, did the Doyles move to London, renting rooms at 23 Montague Place, near the British Museum in Bloomsbury. Doyle, the new eye consultant, took rooms at 2 Upper Wimpole Street (then named Devonshire Place), in the medical area, not far from Baker Street. With very few patients and plenty of time to write, he surely saw early issues of the new *Strand* produced by Newnes in December 1890. Having done well with the sensational *Tit-Bits*, Newnes now wished to target middle-class urban and particularly suburban readers, offering fiction and journalism on national and international themes. The name was crucial: the Strand linked the twin spheres of English power, the business-focused City of London and the governing domain of Westminster. The Strand then had some ten theatres, close to a hundred cafes and public houses, and a firm link to modern media, being a continuation of Fleet Street where the London and national newspapers were located. The first issue of the magazine included a ten-page article, 'The Story of the Strand', claiming in its opening words that 'The Strand is a great deal more than London's most ancient and historic street: it is in many regards the most interesting street in the world'.[8]

London Life with Holmes and Watson

The great detective and his chronicler relish this busy London. In 'The Bruce-Partington Plans' they meet at Goldini's, an actual restaurant in Kensington; at the end of *The Hound of the Baskervilles*, before visiting the opera they dine at Marcini's, apparently invented – although there was a Marioni's in the Strand.[9] In 'The Greek Interpreter' they visit Mycroft at the Diogenes Club 'some little distance from the Carlton' (436), so they are in Pall Mall near the famous Carlton Club (Harrison suggests that the reference in 'The Greek Interpreter' is to the Carlton Hotel in the Haymarket but the hotel was not built until four years after the story's first appearance in 1893);[10] Holmes and Watson eventually visit the Club in 'The Illustrious Client'. They also attend fine restaurants: after posing as 'The Dying Detective' Holmes feels like '"something nutritious at Simpson's"' (941); in 'The Illustrious Client' he will brief Watson over dinner there, watching 'the rushing stream of life in the Strand' (988), and they return the following night; in 'His Last Bow', after Holmes defeats the German menace in East Anglia, he makes plans to dine the next evening at Claridge's, the grand Mayfair hotel (978).

From the start Holmes enjoys concerts – early in *A Study in Scarlet* he listens to the female violinist Norman-Néruda (34); in 'The Red-headed League' he and Watson attend another violinist, Sarasate y Navascues, at St James's Hall (184–5); at the end of *The Hound of the Baskervilles* Holmes has a box for Meyerbeer's opera *Les Huguenots* (766). Another London luxury emerges when, at the start of 'The Illustrious Client', they take a Turkish bath at the city's finest establishment, the Northumberland Avenue baths (984); on the same street, the Northumberland Hotel is the choice of the unostentatious select, like Sir Henry Baskerville in *The Hound of the Baskervilles* (685). Northumberland Street features in two more stories ('The Greek Interpreter' and 'The Noble Bachelor'); only Baker Street is more frequently mentioned in the canon.

Holmes's urban knowledge is part of his arsenal of crime-solving capabilities: as early as *The Sign of Four* Watson says that, in comparison to his own 'limited knowledge of London', Holmes 'was never at fault' (99) in identifying the streets of the city in thick fog, implying that his geography and his criminal insights work together. This ability is, as if to re-assert Holmes's authority, made explicit from the *Return* stories onwards. In the opening narrative, 'The Empty House', Watson boasts that 'Holmes's knowledge of the byways of London was extraordinary' (489), and he links this with his vigilance against crime – 'I knew not what wild beast we were about to hunt down in the dark jungle of criminal London' (488). Triumph against the surviving Moriarty forces seems to relax the tension: Holmes's last words in the story are '"once again Mr Sherlock Holmes is free to devote his life to examining those interesting little problems which the complex life of London so plentifully presents"' (496). Such triumph, however, has its price. Reminiscing about the heyday of Moriarty's influence at the start of the following story, 'The Norwood Builder', Holmes notes that, '"[t]o the scientific student of the higher criminal world no capital in Europe offered the advantages which London then possessed"'. And yet, for Holmes, whatever pleasures London may offer, in the absence of a worthy adversary, it '"has become a singularly uninteresting city"' (496). Fortunately, both for the detective and his readers, London once again becomes a site of criminality and mystery.

Although modern imaginings of Holmes, especially in film and television, are almost always drenched in fog, this is – with the exception of *The Hound of the Baskervilles*, where fog contributes to the Gothic atmosphere of the non-London moors – actually a rare and unstressed occurrence in the stories. In *A Study in Scarlet*, as they drive to Brixton it is 'a foggy, cloudy morning' (27) and in *The Sign of Four* they ride south in a cab while 'a dense, drizzly fog lay low upon the great city' (98), but the characters seem untroubled by it. While Watson briefly implies that the fog is partially responsible for his failure to cognitively map the city, the more significant cause of his disorientation is his uninterrupted and excitable conversation with Miss Morstan. When, earlier in the novel, Holmes notes '"how the yellow fog swirls down the street and drifts across the dun-coloured houses"' he continues, '"[w]hat could be more hopelessly prosaic and material?"' (93). Urban fog is

46

mentioned in three stories ('The Copper Beeches', 'The Bruce-Partington Plans' and 'The Dying Detective') and implied in a fourth (if the 'gray curtain' of 'The Red Circle' is in fact fog (907)), but it is far from the emotive avatar of urban mystery created by modern interpretations of the Holmes myth.

Settings in the Short Stories

The mythic link between Holmes's detection and the urban space of London is so strong that the largest surprise in this context is that of the fifty-six short stories only twenty-one are substantially set in the city itself, and three of these ('The Greek Interpreter', 'The Final Problem' and 'The Illustrious Client') are only partially set in London, moving to outer suburbs or overseas. In fact, Doyle located more than half the Holmes stories in non-urban areas well outside London. However, there usually remains some connection with the capital and only a few locations are really distant from the city, like the Dartmoor of 'Silver Blaze', the Hereford/Somerset context of 'The Boscombe Valley Mystery' and others set in Cornwall, Derbyshire and Norfolk. Most of the non-London locations are easily reached by train from the city and can be seen as part of the capital's national out-reach, with a south-eastern emphasis; in *The Sign of Four*, Watson comments upon 'the monster tentacles which the giant city was throwing out into the country' (99). There are two visits to Winchester and one to Aldershot, but several stories are set in Kent and Sussex and Harrison names eight locations in Surrey.[11] Helping to shape the image of a 'national London', almost all the stories that are not centred on London (including *The Hound of the Baskervilles* and *The Valley of Fear*) nevertheless start and end in the city.

The *Adventures* has more inner London stories than any other collection, with six, while the *Memoirs* only has one fully in the city and two half set there. These nine London stories focus on three key domains. Cases that involve the upper classes are located in the West End. In 'A Scandal in Bohemia', for example, the king is at the Langham and Irene Adler has 'a bijou villa' (168) in St John's Wood, planned as the first elite suburb and also notorious as a base for the mistresses of the wealthy.[12] Even more grandly, 'The Noble Bachelor' lives in Grosvenor Mansions, an imaginary address evidently in hyper-elite Mayfair, and something of the same style is accorded to 'The Resident Patient' who chooses Brook Street, also in Mayfair. In 'The Red-Headed League' less elite figures are found closer to the city centre, in what might be called the inner north: somewhere '"near the City"' (178) is Jabez Wilson's vacated office, conveniently near a bank, in the fictional Saxe-Coburg Square (at times called Coburg Square), within walking distance of Aldersgate station. Action in 'The Blue Carbuncle' is a little further north and west, between a pub near the British Museum and Tottenham Court Road where the goose is originally lost. But the jewel-bearing goose was from Brixton Road, which points to the third domain of inner London activity, south of the river.

This is the most surprising area, a region never mentioned in G. W. M. Reynolds's wide-ranging *The Mysteries of London* (1844–8) and hardly referenced by Dickens, although *Dombey and Son*'s (1848) malign industrial manager James Carker lives in Camberwell. Doyle would have passed through south London regularly on train and road journeys from and to Norwood and, before that, Portsmouth. It was a strongly developing region in the later nineteenth century, as more and more bridges crossed the river (the last being Wandsworth in 1873), and the toll-gates were removed on the roads into the city from the south by the 1860s. South London was unfashionable – a sociological analysis found it had fewer people in the highest social classifications than the much wealthier north and west[13] – but Doyle was, from the start, interested in it. *A Study in Scarlet*'s villains, Enoch Drebber and Joseph Stangerson, are based in Camberwell, but so is the charming Miss Morstan in *The Sign of Four*. In 'A Case of Identity' the Sutherland family live in this busy and fairly respectable area with lively theatres and a medium-distance walk from the city – the father was a plumber working in Tottenham Court Road and the dubious stepfather claims to work for a wine merchant in Leadenhall Street. Another partly south London story is 'The Greek Interpreter', where the titular figure is abducted and taken to Beckenham, then returned, still south of the river, to Wandsworth Common. He was captured in North Kensington which, like the neighbouring Lisson Grove and especially Notting Hill, had a very poor reputation at the time. Selden, the escaped convict in *The Hound of the Baskervilles* is '"the Notting Hill murderer"' (701) and, in 'The Red Circle', Gregson treats the troubled Italian wife of Gennaro Lucca as if she were 'a Notting Hill hooligan' (910).

The stories often posit a Holmes who has total spatial knowledge of the city. This is, perhaps, most striking in the panoptic reverie at the beginning of 'A Case of Identity':

> If we could fly out of that window hand in hand, hover over this great city, gently remove the roofs, and peep in at the queer things which are going on, the strange coincidences, the plannings, the cross-purposes, and wonderful chains of events, working through generations, and leading to the most *outré* results, it would make all fiction with its conventionality and foreseen conclusions most stale and unprofitable. (190–1)

If London, as this passage suggests, is a criminally generative space – a prolific source of mystery and crime as well as its narratives – Holmes puts himself forward as an all-seeing agent of control. The potentially disturbing quality of this pervasive surveillance is, however, disarmed in the wider stories by the realisation that Holmes's coverage of London has substantial gaps. 'The Yellow Face' and 'The Three Gables' are, for example, the only two stories set in north-west London. This seems odd, as that is the area from which people travelled in to Baker Street station on the Metropolitan railway which, by the 1890s, reached out as far as Verney Junction in Buckinghamshire. Perhaps those readers wanted to hear about areas grander than – or more distant from – their own suburban reality; the *Strand*, in its fascination with an emergent celebrity culture (most clearly in the ongoing 1890s series *Portraits of Celebrities at Different Times in their Lives*) and stories regularly featuring higher strata of society, certainly cultivated a fascination among its readership with social 'betters'.

There is a more significant absence in the Holmes settings, with one notable exception: 'The Man with the Twisted Lip' is the only case where both Holmes and the narrative venture for substantial periods into the East End, that poor and dangerous area of London, well-known as threatening, but rarely mentioned in other stories (references to Rotherhithe in 'The Dying Detective', the Commercial Road in 'The Creeping Man' and Shadwell in 'The Cardboard Box' aside). It is in this respect that the story becomes an important case study for Doyle's understanding of urban space, class and epistemology. The story finds Watson, to aid his wife's friend, venturing into an East End opium den – the conflation of the East End with the Far East hinting at how the dangerous foreign other can encroach on the civilised space of the west – where he finds Holmes already at work on a case. In describing this primitive, even hellish, space, located at the bottom of 'a steep flight of steps leading down to a black gap like the mouth of a cave' (230), Doyle relied on an anonymous piece the *Strand* had published in June 1891, 'A Night in an Opium Den' which, in turn, relies on Orientalist representations of such establishments in Ratcliff Highway. The central action of the story, however, takes place on Upper Swandam Lane, 'a vile alley lurking behind the high wharves which line the north side of the river to the east of London Bridge' (230). Doyle's model for this fictional street is usually taken to be the locale near the real Lower Thames Street (other readings that favour Swan Lane overlook the fact that this is to the west of London Bridge). The foreign otherness of the opium den that opens the story is continued in the international inhabitants of the fateful house: in addition to the strange appearance of Hugh Boone, the house is

49

occupied by a Dane and a Lascar vividly illustrated by Sidney Paget. The Lascar, while fairly quickly acquitted of involvement in the crime, is nonetheless found to be '"a man of the vilest antecedents"' (235), the adjective connecting him to the geography of Upper Swandam Lane.

The Orientalism of 'The Man with the Twisted Lip' is of a piece with a broader east/west divide in Victorian London. As noted above, the Strand connected the realms of Parliament and the financial City, but just beyond lay the East End, a space increasingly defined in opposition to a West End represented by affluence and entertainment. The late-Victorian modernisation of the West End involved the construction of Charing Cross Road and the clearing of notorious slums around Seven Dials and St Giles, creating new centres of moneyed entertainment. By contrast, the East End became the subject of a series of investigations into the effects of slum-living and poverty: Andrew Mearns's pamphlet *The Bitter Cry of Outcast London* (1883) was followed by George R. Sims's books *How the Poor Live* (1883) and *Horrible London* (1889), journalistic enquiries mirrored in 'Twisted Lip' by Neville St Clair's initial intention of writing undercover pieces on the condition of the East End. While some slum clearance and redevelopment did take place – most famously the demolition of the Old Nichol slum (between Shoreditch and Spitalfields), immortalised in Arthur Morrison's *A Child of the Jago* (1896) – there was a sense in which East London was portrayed as a space that was simultaneously static and decaying. But further, the division of London into east and west replayed a similar division at the global level; the language of social investigators frequently adopted the terminology of colonialism in order to suggest that the centre of London itself contained the uncivilised other. Mearns referred to the eastern slums as 'the great dark region of poverty, misery, squalor, and immorality';[14] Margaret Harkness suggestively titled her 1890 slum fiction (with a murder subplot) *In Darkest London*. Most famously, Sims referred to 'a dark continent that is within easy walking distance of the General Post Office'.[15]

Doyle's reliance on 'A Night in an Opium Den' in writing 'The Man with the Twisted Lip' makes the slum experience literary, rather than experiential, and this may be true in deeper ways concerning Doyle and this story, which may express in fictional form the unease Doyle was feeling about earning so much and being praised for work so far beneath his conscious and elevated ambitions. Indeed, he may have felt that he, like the gentlemanly journalist Neville St Clair, was now shamefully earning money in the streets with his embarrassingly popular stories. That may also be why this is the only case that occurs in London where Holmes does not operate out of Baker Street: he has effectively moved to Lee in Kent, staying during his inquiries in the home of the missing, apparently murdered, man. The unique location of this story may be the writer's way of projecting the feelings he expressed to his mother in a letter after five stories saying, 'I think of slaying Holmes in this sixth' as '[h]e takes my mind from better things'.[16] Her horrified response led him to write 'The Man with the Twisted Lip' as the sixth story, and keep Holmes going for another eighteen.

Kaleidoscopic Techniques

There are enough slippages between Holmes's fictional London and the late Victorian reality to make us wary of simply mapping one on to the other, or even suggesting such a thing as a coherent idea of London. In a striking urban expedition in 'The Six Napoleons', Holmes and Watson (evidently in a cab) travel right across London from Kennington to Stepney and pass through a kaleidoscopic array of city spaces: in 'rapid succession we passed through the fringe of fashionable London, hotel London, theatrical London, literary London, commercial London, and, finally, maritime London' (588). They take a longer route than necessary, crossing the Thames early to admire the city's variety rather than going more directly through south-of-the-river London. The implications of the scene are twofold. Firstly, it provides a handy reminder that any singular conception of London must be a construct, an ordering of a variety of different and competing zones. Holmes may know his way around London, but any sense of it as a totality must be as idiosyncratic as Holmes's own bizarre indexing system back at Baker Street. Secondly, Holmes and Watson's leisurely route emphasises that city space is not merely something to be passed through on the way to a predetermined goal; the journey itself has value.

This kaleidoscopic view of London, and the difficulties in mapping fictional space on to existing geography, can also be found in moments where the canon's mapping does not agree with that of reality. At times, Doyle alters the names of London streets, apparently to avoid issues with residents who, understandably, might not wish to see crimes foisted upon their neighbourhood. The possible underground train murder site of Caulfield Gardens, Kensington, becomes Cornwall Gardens in 'The Bruce-Partington Plans'; the creation in 'The Red-Headed League' of the fictional 'Saxe-Coburg Square' may be to protect any real bank from the idea of being tunnelled into. The idea of a threat to highly-placed people may generate the non-existent address of Whitehall Terrace in 'The Second Stain': in a similar mode the Hotel Cosmopolitan, from which the blue carbuncle was stolen, appears to represent Claridge's ('The Blue Carbuncle' 248). Some changes might be read as simple errors: Barclay Square for Berkeley Square in 'The Bruce-

Partington Plans' and Campden House Road rather than the actual Campden Hill Road in 'The Six Napoleons', for instance.

Other changes, however, hint at more complex relationships with the past, both of the city and of Doyle personally. The references to 'Regent's Circus' rather than Piccadilly Circus in 'The Greek Interpreter' and 'Charles Augustus Milverton' imply a nostalgic attachment to the old-fashioned name, though in the latter story the older name is a subtle way of indicating the retrospective quality of the account (Watson begins his narration with the disclaimer that 'It is years since the incidents of which I speak took place' (572)); time becomes mapped onto space. More personal acts of spatialised memory occur in subtler ways. In 'The Red Circle', Great Ormond Street, very close to where the Doyles lived in Bloomsbury, becomes Great Orme Street, conceivably linked to the decision to change the story's title from 'The Bloomsbury Lodger'. 'The Norwood Builder' provides a more tangible link to Doyle's past, being set at a large house in south-west outer London at South Norwood rented by the Doyles in the summer of 1891, following Doyle's serious bout of influenza and his decision on recovery to give up the medical profession and rely entirely on his literary powers. This sense of personal presence in the story becomes especially significant in the context of the suggestive qualities of the title of the story that immediately precedes it, 'The Empty House'. In 'The Musgrave Ritual' Holmes says he first lived in London in Montague Street, very near the Doyles's starting-point in Montague Place; Montague Place itself had already featured in 'The Copper Beeches' as the address from which Violet Hunter writes to Holmes.

Conclusion

Despite Holmes's eventual retirement to the South Downs, and some elements of variation as the story-sequence continues in time (there are more European and fewer imperial villains, a rise in melodrama as well as in the social level of the stories), the pattern of the settings does not vary significantly overall. Of the final sets of collected stories, in *The Return* eight of the thirteen stories are non-urban, but only three of the eight in *His Last Bow* (including 'The Cardboard Box', delayed from *The Memoirs)*, while in *The Case-Book* six of the twelve stories are fully non-urban and one, 'The Illustrious Client', is half set in the city. In these last three collections inner London settings are still common. Of these stories, two are basically at Baker Street ('The Empty House' and 'The Dying Detective') and two in elite Westminster ('The Second Stain' and much of 'The Illustrious Client'). Others like 'The Three Garridebs' and part of 'The Mazarin Stone' innovatively explore the residential and semi-commercial mix of inner western

London, which goes as far north as Hampstead in 'Charles Augustus Milverton', but the blackmailer's activities are city-oriented, not in any way suburban, and Harrison comments that the area was, by the 1880s, 'full-urban',[17] so these are not late ventures into the almost absent suburban north-west. South London appears rather less than before, with a full presence as South Brixton in 'The Veiled Lodger', a limited role in 'Lady Frances Carfax', which mixes genteel South Kensington (and parts of Europe) with Brixton, and a larger one in 'The Six Napoleons', which links South Kensington to south-of-the-river Kennington.

The Sherlock Holmes settings belong, like the crimes he investigates, to the world of magazine-buying respectable Londoners, where the dominant criminal activities arose from the lower-classes – notoriously the numerically dominant misdemeanours were mugging and baby-farming, right across the city. The stories all focus on the crimes to which *Strand* readers felt vulnerable, especially if they became wealthy enough to move out into the comfortable country areas not far from the city – and perhaps even the crimes they could, if only unconsciously, feel themselves capable of committing.

The locations of Holmes's London activity, and so the city Doyle recounts for his readers, are highly selective. There are no doubt casual elements at times, like the recurrent variation in where Watson lives and works, but while more than half of the stories are in fact outside London, that can be seen as part of the national, indeed international, impact of the great capital, of which its magazine-reading citizens were strongly aware. Whether in the city streets or further afield, Doyle's criminographical realisation is never fully separated from the interests, aspirations and reach of the urban residents, in most instances by train, and at all times by imaginative projection. The man from Edinburgh created a potent system for exposing the threats of criminality felt by, even occasionally shared by, the respectable London-based readers of the *Strand*, both a magazine of – and a symbolic focus for – the kaleidoscopic city.

Notes

1. Jon Lellenberg, Daniel Stashower and Charles Foley (eds.), *Arthur Conan Doyle: A Life in Letters* (London: Harper Perennial, 2008), 66, 67.
2. Arthur Conan Doyle, *The Narrative of John Smith*, ed. Jon Lellenberg, Daniel Stashower and Rachel Foss (London: British Library Publishing, 2011), 22–3.
3. Arthur Conan Doyle, letter to Stoddart, quoted in Russell Miller, *The Adventures of Arthur Conan Doyle: A Biography* (London: Harvill Secker, 2008), 120.
4. Michael F. Harrison, *In the Footsteps of Sherlock Holmes*, rev. edn. (Newton Abbot: David and Charles, 1971), 82.

5. Harrison, *In the Footsteps*, 63.
6. Priscilla Metcalf, *Victorian London* (London: Cassell, 1972), 50.
7. Daria Hambourg, *Richard Doyle: His Life and Work* (London: Art and Technics, 1948), 23.
8. Unsigned, 'The Story of the Strand', *Strand Magazine* 1 (January 1891), 4–13 (4).
9. Arthur Conan Doyle, *The Hound of the Baskervilles*, 1902, ed. W. W. Robson (Oxford: Oxford University Press, 1994), note to 168, see 188.
10. Harrison, *In the Footprints*, 149.
11. Ibid., 167.
12. Jerry White, *London in the Nineteenth Century* (London: Vintage, 2008), 73.
13. David R. Green, 'The Metropolitan Economy: Continuity and Change, 1800-1939', in Keith Haggard and David Green (eds.), *London: A New Metropolitan Geography* (London: Arnold, 1991), 8–33, see figure on page 23.
14. Andrew Mearns, 'The Bitter Cry of Outcast London', 1883, in Peter J. Keating (ed.), *Into Unknown England, 1866–1913: Selections from the Social Explorers* (London: Fontana, 1976), 91–111 (92).
15. George R. Sims, 'From How the Poor Live', 1883, in Keating, *Into Unknown England*, 65–90 (65).
16. Lellenberg et al., *Arthur Conan Doyle*, 300.
17. Harrison, *In the Footprints*, 156.

5

CHRISTINE BERBERICH

Englishness and Rural England

In '"Englishness" and National Identity', Krishan Kumar argues that 'English culture, at its deepest level, is seen as created by a series of "national poets", dramatists and novelists. Their writing embodies values, whole ways of life, which express the aspirations of the national culture at its best and highest.'[1] In his reading, nineteenth-century writing made an especially significant contribution towards establishing an idea of a united English national identity, a cultural Englishness, so to speak, that is still influential to this day. Although Kumar specifically refers to national poets and writers, by which he presumably means canonical authors, this notion needs to be expanded to include popular writers of the time and none more so than Arthur Conan Doyle and his iconic character Sherlock Holmes.

Since his first relatively low-key appearance in 1887, Sherlock Holmes has acquired quasi-mythological status. Holmes has become not only the quintessential detective but the quintessential Englishman, the seemingly perfect representative of a stable and permanent Englishness. Holmes's silhouette is recognised all over the world; pubs across the country and even abroad, have been named after him. He has also been used to advertise a variety of products ranging from shoes to beer to tobacco.[2] But, most importantly for the argument of this chapter, Holmes has been and is still being used to market and boost tourism across England. A quick internet search of Holmes and tourism shows just how intimately linked the fictional detective has become not only to London, where countless bus and walking tours in search of Holmes are offered, but also to other English locations that can claim a link, no matter how tenuous, to either Doyle, or to one of Holmes's adventures. The *Visit England* website invites users to 'Investigate the Origins of Sherlock Holmes at Portsmouth Museum';[3] Devon brands itself as 'Baskerville Country';[4] Bristol markets itself as a Holmes location simply on the strength of having hosted the production team of the BBC series *Sherlock*;[5] the sleepy village of East Dean in East Sussex calls itself the retirement home of Holmes, offering its visitors a map of a 'Sherlock

Holmes Walk' around the village and proudly displaying a commemorative Blue Plaque announcing that 'Sherlock Holmes, Consulting Detective and Bee Keeper, retired here 1903–1917'.[6] The magazine *British Heritage Travel* went to particular lengths in 2009, listing iconic Holmes locations that start, predictably, at 221B Baker Street, London but then extend across the country, taking in Groombridge Place Gardens and Enchanted Forest in Kent, which Doyle visited often and which appears as Birlstone Manor in *The Valley of Fear*; *The Hound of the Baskerville*'s Dartmoor; and Doyle's beloved Sussex countryside that features in many of his stories.[7]

Particularly noteworthy is the American *aficionado* David L. Hammer's series of travel books dedicated to Holmes locations that include *The Travelers' Companion to the London of Sherlock Holmes* (2001), *The Game is Afoot: A Travel Guide to the England of Sherlock Holmes* (1983), and *The Worth of the Game: Being a Final Travel Guide to the England of Sherlock Holmes* (1993). In the blurb to *The Game is Afoot*, Hammer sketches out his aim: 'to go on quests to locate as many actual geographical places as possible associated with Mr. Holmes and his life'.[8] The geography of real England is thus used to authenticate a fictional character, blurring the lines between fact and fiction. Crucially, this plethora of publications linking the land with the character show that Holmes has become a cultural icon that is inseparable from England and, in particular, a specific nineteenth-century Englishness that survives to the present day.

This chapter focuses on the notion of Englishness in the Sherlock Holmes novels and stories. Given Doyle's personal background – he was born in Scotland to parents with Irish origins – this very focus on English national identity in his work stands out. Doyle was always fiercely proud of his family ancestry – yet he created one of the most, if not the most celebrated Englishman of all time. More than that, though, Doyle consciously created, celebrated and upheld an Englishness that further popularised political attitudes towards national identity at the time. In particular, the focus is on the use of rural England and traditional English spaces such as the country house in the Holmes stories. During Doyle's lifetime, Britain considerably expanded her empire but also saw related changes to English national identity that simultaneously appeared to become both more embattled and more rigorously enforced. This imperial expansion brought with it international strife and armed conflict, ranging from the Indian Mutiny of 1857 and the Siege of Khartoum of 1885 to the Anglo-Boer War (1899 to 1902) and culminating in the First World War. At the home front, and in particular under the four Liberal governments of William E. Gladstone, there had been a more cautious approach towards imperial policy and more tolerance of left-wing criticism. But by the time of the first Holmes publication in 1887, the tone was changing again: dissenting voices were increasingly silenced, and a 'New Imperialism' was steadily emerging, more forcefully advocating renewed imperial expansion, especially to protect British interests against newly rising colonial powers such as the United States, France and Germany.

Artists, scientists and writers alike took up the call of New Imperialism, propounding theories of British superiority, of which Doyle was an avid proponent. Ellen Burton Harrington outlines 'a body of late-nineteenth-century literature and scientific discourse that helped to promote the continued need for imperialism to an increasingly divided nation'.[9] As such, the Holmes stories take a two-pronged – and highly ideological – approach to the construction of national identity: traditional English, rural settings are juxtaposed with – or threatened by – an influx of foreign 'Others'. In particular, the country house or ancestral manor house is repeatedly 'Orientalised' in Holmes's cases: brought to quasi-ruin by descendants of old English families who have lived abroad and acquired strange and foreign ways, or inhabited by actual foreigners whose different and generally devious behaviours threaten the status quo of England. Doyle thus utilises homely spaces his readers would have instantly recognised and associated with traditional Englishness – but then turns them into *unheimlich* (uncanny) spaces that threaten to destabilise a normative national identity. Steadfastly standing against this threat is the figure of Holmes, the *English* detective who, by solving crimes and mysteries, upholds not only law and order but also reinstates a supreme Englishness in a space almost or briefly contaminated by the foreign Other.

Detection, Englishness and Imperial Ideology

Fredric Jameson, in a discussion of Raymond Chandler's work, suggests that the detective story is 'a form without ideological content, without any overt political or social or philosophical point [which] permits … pure stylistic experimentation'.[10] This point is refuted by Laura Marcus who, although stressing the importance of detective fiction for narrative theories and experimentation, emphasises the importance of understanding the social and historical context of the genre. As such, she explains, 'the centrality of detective fiction [especially in the nineteenth century] is seen as both aesthetic and ideological, as it mediates a culture in which crime and punishment are both profoundly internalised in ever more elaborate forms of discipline and surveillance'.[11] The ideological content and messages of detective fiction should, consequently, not be underestimated – and especially not when it comes to the Holmes stories, written during particularly volatile political times. The late nineteenth and early twentieth century required a stable counter-discourse to political insecurity, and this manifested itself in an increased demand for narratives highlighting national stability, with the home nation as a safe space, strongly policed and guarded against infiltrators. Doyle's writing repeatedly suggests that the security of this homely space is under threat from outsiders, both imperial Others and European immigrants.

As Ronald R. Thomas has shown, this attitude was part of a wider political drive for increased control over the individual in order to safeguard national security, as 'criminal deviance became increasingly understood as an issue of national security'.[12] Scientific writing – for instance by Cesare Lombroso, Francis Galton or Havelock Ellis – suggested that criminal tendencies could be detected in physical features, and crudely linked this to a person's racial background. New developments in policing and, in particular, surveillance (such as Galton's fingerprint classification system, which allowed prints to be compared and thus used to identify criminals) began to permeate society, even down to its youngest members, brought together in Robert Baden-Powell's popular Boy Scouts Movement whose motto was to 'Be Prepared'. As Simon Featherstone explains, the Boy Scouts' motto 'was a personal and political injunction' to be 'alert to the possibility of enemy attack',[13] and thus impressionable young boys were trained constantly to look out for illegal activities or suspicious signs of an impending invasion.

Popular culture fed such fears through the widely read genre of invasion anxiety literature – the first notable text was George Tomkyns Chesney's *The Battle of Dorking* (1871) but other, and probably better-known examples include Erskine Childers' *The Riddle of the Sands* (1903) and John Buchan's *The Thirty-Nine Steps* (1915). In all of this writing – political tracts, scientific discourse, and fictional narratives alike – foreigners were eyed with suspicion and unfavourably distinguished from the English norm. This norm is associated with both traditional Englishness (fair play, gentlemanliness, honour) and rural England (unspoilt villages, ancestral homes, peaceful landscapes) as the ultimate representative of the homely, safe haven. The formulaic approach to detective fiction – a crime is committed, the detective investigates, the detective solves the case, the culprits are punished, peace is established – lends itself particularly well to this ideological affirmation of English core values: Englishness is under threat; the detective solves the case; Englishness emerges victorious. The Holmes stories thus reassured their readers that England might, temporarily, be under threat, but that rigorous surveillance and the vetting of all Others would safeguard its future. Detective fiction in the cases of Sherlock Holmes thus becomes an ideological tool, meant, as Harrington puts it, to '[consolidate] a normative national':[14] a national identity that is considered the one everybody has to aspire to, and that aims to actively exclude those who do not fit in – as will be demonstrated in the following case studies.

The Green and Pleasant Land and the 'Foreign' Threat

Holmes's cases generally start in his chambers at 221B Baker Street in London, and much has been written about Doyle's use of its cityscapes. Yet many of Holmes's investigations almost immediately see him leave London behind and travel to more rural areas in a quest to solve crime. The novels and stories are full of evocative landscape descriptions and asides referring to traditional settings: 'It was nearly four o'clock when we at last, after passing through the beautiful Stroud Valley and over the broad gleaming Severn, found ourselves at the pretty little country town of Ross' ('The Boscombe Valley Mystery' 207); '[we] drove for four or five miles through the lovely Surrey lanes' ('The Speckled Band' 265); 'we found ourselves in the pretty Surrey village of Esher' ('Wisteria Lodge' 877). With locations such as these, Doyle is setting the tone: these settings are the familiar, homely landscapes generally associated with a traditional, safe Englishness. Importantly, the rural places Doyle predominantly depicts are synonymous with the Southern English scenery of the Home Counties, with a slight extension into Hampshire and Gloucestershire. It is only rarely that Holmes ventures further West – to Devon or Cornwall, say – and his landscape depictions then generally vary, becoming darker and more threatening.

Most prominent here are his Gothicised depictions of Dartmoor in *The Hound of the Baskervilles* and the 'sinister semicircle of Mounts Bay' with its 'black cliffs and surge-swept reefs' (955) in the Cornwall of 'The Devil's Foot'. These places, however, are shown to be on the fringes of the far more traditional English countryside to be found in Kent, Surrey or Sussex. For Doyle and his readers at the time, the South-East represented the most recognisable of English core values, and these are also the locations that have become popularised through the many different Sherlock Holmes adaptations over the decades. Yet Doyle cleverly uses the familiar settings of the English countryside as sites of mystery and murder to unsettle his readers; Watson himself comments on the contrast between bucolic idyll and crime investigation in 'The Speckled Band':

> It was a perfect day, with a bright sun and a few fleecy clouds in the heavens. The trees and wayside hedges were just throwing out their first green shoots, and the air was full of the pleasant smell of the moist earth. To me at least there was a strange contrast between the sweet promise of the spring and this sinister quest upon which we were engaged. (265)

Landscape and crime are thus consciously juxtaposed as mutually exclusive; crime cannot be allowed to contaminate the innocence and purity of the land.

The Valley of Fear offers another pertinent example illustrating Doyle's use of landscape. Early on in the novel, there is an unusually lengthy description of both the village of Birlstone as well as the adjacent Manor House. The village is described as:

> a small and very ancient cluster of half-timbered cottages on the northern border of the county of Sussex. For centuries it had remained unchanged; but within the last few years its picturesque appearance and situation have attracted a number of well-to-do residents, whose villas peep out from the woods around. These woods are locally supposed to be the extreme fringe of the great Weald forest, which thins away until it reaches the northern chalk downs. A number of small shops have come into being to meet the wants of the increased population; so there seems some prospect that Birlstone may soon grow from an ancient village into a modern town. (779)

Here, Doyle conjures up a rural setting steeped in tradition ('very ancient', 'unchanged' and 'picturesque'). With this short passage, he both expresses his admiration of the village of bygone days and his potential fear at the onward march of modernity that might change places such as Birlstone forever. The ancient Manor House of Birlstone is similarly described as a place with a long history, unchanged and – as yet – largely untouched by time: 'The Manor House, with its many gables and its small diamond-paned windows, was still much as the builder had left it in the early seventeenth century' (779). For Doyle, places such as this expressed a quintessential Englishness that needed to be protected. But in *The Valley of Fear*, Doyle gives his country house an even stronger ideological emphasis: Birlstone Manor metaphorically comes to stand for all of England when he describes the lovingly renovated drawbridge mechanism of the moated house, concluding that '[b]y thus renewing the custom of the old feudal days the Manor House was converted into an island during the night' (780). The reintroduction of the tradition of raising and lowering a drawbridge to protect the house's residents and keep out unwanted intruders might seem romantic or even whimsical. Yet it needs to be read in the context of late nineteenth- and early-twentieth-century invasion fears and the associated political attempts to, if not limit then at least, stringently police incomers to England to reduce the risk of crime. More than that, though, it also hints at the very real dangers facing England at the time of publication of *The Valley of Fear*: published on 22 November 1914, the novel appeared fewer than four months after the outbreak of the First World War, a war that brought with it a very realistic threat of a foreign invasion of the British Isles.

A large number of Holmes stories involve such a traditional, quintessentially English manor house or rural farm initially connoting prosperity, ancestry and tradition. They provide a seemingly safe and protected space – but by repeatedly making these places the sites for inexplicable mysteries and crime, Doyle again and again feeds into contemporary fears of the unknown, the uncanny, the Other. For Sigmund Freud, the uncanny (or *unheimlich*) signifies an event that disturbs the peace of something that has long been familiar, homely or cosy,[15] and Doyle largely follows two different approaches in presenting his traditional English locations as sites of unsettlement: he either turns the rural house into a quasi-Gothicised site of mystery and intrigue, or he shows this quintessentially English location as being inhabited by foreign Others. In 'The Boscombe Valley Mystery', for instance, the old and generally idyllic house at Hatherley Farm is depicted with 'drawn blinds and … smokeless chimneys … [that] gave it a stricken look' (211). Instead of an inviting trail of smoke from the chimney, or gleaming windows, this particular house appears neglected, uninhabited, dark; and this immediately suggests that this formerly homely English safe haven has become corrupted, shrouded in a mystery that endangers its status as a symbol of secure Englishness. Similarly, the 'isolated and ancient farmhouse' at the heart of 'The Sussex Vampire' is characterised by 'an odour of age and decay' that 'pervaded the whole crumbling building' (1039), an immediate harbinger of the drama and mystery within.

Other country estates are suspicious due to their foreign owners or occupants. In 'The Engineer's Thumb', the house, occupied by mysterious Germans, presents an unwelcoming facade that does not bode well. It is described as 'pitch dark inside', 'a labyrinth of an old house, with corridors, passages, narrow winding staircases, and little low doors' (280, 281) that all but disorientate the unfortunate engineer ensnared within. Wisteria Lodge, in the story of the same name, has been rented by a Mr Garcia of South American origin who is soon found murdered – by another South American, as it turns out; the lady of the house in 'The Sussex Vampire' is from Peru – and an immediate suspect of occult vampirism. Familiar settings are thus defamiliarised; the homely is turned into the *unheimlich*; and English values are shown to be intrinsically endangered by the foreign Other who has settled in the heartland of Englishness with the aim to undermine and deconstruct it from within.

Many of Holmes's mysteries thus combine the Gothicising of the house with the threat of the foreign and unknown in a process of Gothicising Orientalism, an intermingling of the uncanny with the imperial Other. Different from the Gothic tales of the late eighteenth century, where such uncanny sites as ruined castles or labyrinthine houses were usually located abroad to feed their readers' fear of the foreign unknown, Doyle's stories bring the foreign 'home', thus emphasising its potentially even greater danger. The houses are shown to be confusing, dispiriting places, victims of destabilising foreign influences. Two particularly prominent examples that ought to be discussed at some length can be found in the stories 'The Speckled Band' and, especially, 'Wisteria Lodge'.

In 'The Speckled Band' Holmes and Watson are called to the aid of Miss Helen Stoner who fears for her life living in the old house of Stoke Moran with her stepfather Dr Roylott, who has spent many years as a doctor in India. Doyle initially delineates a traditional setting – the heir of the family finally returning to his ancestral manor after many years away and to the joy of the villagers, glad to 'see a Roylott of Stoke Moran back in the old family seat' (260); the two young women – Helen and her twin sister Julia – in his care; enough money to sustain the family. Yet, this setting is immediately defamiliarised: years in India have turned Roylott into a choleric man who quarrels with everybody around him; the manor house is crumbling and the doctor is uninterested in maintaining the estate in the way he should. On the arrival of Holmes and Watson, the house is described to be 'of gray, lichen-blotted stone, with a high central portion and two curving wings . . . In one of these wings the windows were broken and blocked with wooden boards, while the roof was partly caved in, a picture of ruin' (266). The Gothic setting is thus provided immediately.

Most importantly, Julia dies under very mysterious circumstances. The night of her death is described in suitably Gothic tones: only one wing is inhabited, with the rest of the house lying empty; the 'wind was howling outside, and the rain was beating and splashing against the windows' until the night is disrupted by 'the wild scream of a terrified woman' (261). Helen Stoner also describes other noises in the house: mysterious whistling and a clanging sound. Gone is the traditional, safe English space. Instead, there is now a threatening, Gothic semi-ruin, with the second young woman seemingly left to her fate with the choleric stepfather. But Doyle further subverts the homely by Orientalising it – the doctor has acquired strange, foreign ways during his time in India and surrounds himself with exotic animals, such as a baboon and a dangerous cheetah. Much to the detriment of his relations with the rest of the village, he allows gypsies, ever the stock figures of Otherness, on to his grounds and, predictably, they are immediate suspects in Julia's death. The murder weapon eventually turns out to be a deadly Indian swamp adder that has been trained by Roylott to slip through the vent into his stepdaughters' room to kill them with a quick bite – a very real foreign danger in England's green and pleasant land, and one to boot that is consciously set against its innocent victims, the English damsel in distress in a ruined house.

In 'Wisteria Lodge' Doyle defamiliarises the familiar English space of the house into an exotic, *unheimlich* space full of mystery and danger. Like many of the other country houses in the Holmesian canon, Wisteria Lodge is an 'old tumble-down building in a crazy state of disrepair'. Add to this the fact that Wisteria Lodge is inhabited by two South Americans and a 'half-breed' cook and there is enough material to label the establishment 'a queer household ... to find in the heart of Surrey' (872). A household consisting of an English gentleman, his English secretary and English cook would, undoubtedly, not have attracted the label 'queer', nor aroused suspicion; but, once again, it is the foreignness of its inhabitants that turns Wisteria Lodge into a liminal space that sharply distinguishes it from its more normative neighbours. When Holmes and Watson visit Wisteria Lodge to investigate Garcia's murder and clear the innocent Englishman Scott Eccles from suspicion, they find the house hidden behind a 'high wooden gate' and at the end of 'a gloomy avenue of chestnuts'. The 'high wooden gate' emphasises the house's seclusion; the 'gloomy avenue' suggests a dark mystery that needs to be illuminated. The house itself is similarly described as desolate and uninviting, 'a low, dark house, pitch-black against a slate-coloured sky' (877) – yet another Gothic space, further tainted by the crime committed within its confines. The country constable guarding the house finds himself unnerved by '"the queer thing in the kitchen"', his fear of a '"devil"' at the window hinting at the supernatural (877, 878).

It is this very '"queer thing"' that further Orientalises and exoticises the space of the English country house: in the kitchen, Holmes and Watson find themselves confronted with 'an extraordinary object ... so wrinkled and shrunken and withered that it was difficult to say what it might have been ... black and leathery and ... [bearing] some resemblance to a dwarfish, human figure' (878). Additionally, they find the 'limbs and body of some large, white bird, torn savagely to pieces with the feathers still on' (878), 'a zinc pail which contained a quantity of blood' and 'a platter heaped with small pieces of charred bones' (879). Accessories such as these are soon identified by Holmes to be utensils for voodoo worship – and with this, Doyle not only presents his readers with foreign influences but, even more strongly, with exotic practices and black magic. The traditional space of the English country house has, through 'savage practices', been thoroughly Othered and defamiliarised; under cover of a traditional English setting, the South American criminals – Holmes finds out that Mr Garcia was a victim of the 'Tiger of San Pedro', a feared South American dictator – have contaminated the countryside.

'Wisteria Lodge' is a particularly important story in the Holmes canon, as it not only upholds English values (the English detective uncovers the plot) against foreign infiltration (the South American criminals have to flee the country) but simultaneously appears to critique British foreign policy: '"What does the law of England care for the rivers of blood shed years ago in San Pedro, or for the shipload of treasure which this one man has stolen?"' exclaims Miss Burnet (885). This implicitly suggests that English politicians, as well as the general public, are not interested in crimes against humanity committed in far-flung places. Only when foreign crime comes closer to home does English law and order try to react. Ironically, Doyle thus seems to challenge the very political stance that he simultaneously upholds and reinforces in the majority of his stories.

There is another glimpse of this slightly more ambivalent attitude in 'His Last Bow', first published on 22 October 1917 at the height of the First World War. This story has an entirely unusual perspective: it starts with a focus on the high-ranking German spy, Von Bork, who has settled in a 'long, low, heavily gabled house', above a 'broad sweep of the beach at the foot of the great chalk cliff' (971) that clearly denotes a rural Sussex or Kent setting. Once again, there is a foreign enemy who has infiltrated rural England and who fits seemingly perfectly into English rural society. Holmes himself is only revealed quite late in the story, having disguised himself – convincingly – as an Irish-American spy in the pay of the Germans. But what is important about this story is its narrative approach with regards to Englishness: told in a distanced third-person voice, the tone throughout the story is pensive and melancholy, with an overarching sense of foreboding.

The story starts with a specific date, 'nine o'clock at night upon the second of August [1914] – the most terrible August in the history of the world', with a sense that 'God's curse hung heavy over a degenerate world', and with 'an awesome hush and a feeling of vague expectancy in the sultry and stagnant air' (970). This time it is the date, far more than the location, that sets the tone for Doyle's readers: on the first of August 1914, Germany had declared war on Russia, on the third of August a declaration of war against France and a threat of invasion of Belgium followed, and on the fourth of August, Britain declared war on Germany, honouring her treaties with France and Belgium. Doyle uses this specific date – with a historical hindsight of over three years of devastating warfare – to paint a picture of England as a nation under acute threat, but also a nation largely ignoring this threat and still steeped in mediaeval notions of honour and fair play that might, ultimately, cost them the war. Although Holmes in his successful disguise eventually unmasks and defeats the German spy, his victory is not triumphant. Instead, the story ends on the warning note that '"[t]here's an east wind coming all the same, such a wind as never blew on England yet"', a wind that '"will be cold and bitter ...and a good many of us may wither before its blast"' (980). As Tom Ue has pointed out, this story 'was one of [Doyle's] contributions to Britain's war effort' that was suitably advertised, in the *Strand Magazine*, as 'Sherlock Holmes Outwits a German Spy'.[16] Yet here there is none of the formerly jingoistic and oversimplified presentation of foreign danger and English superiority. Instead, Doyle offers a more mature dialogue about nations, identities and the dangers of stagnation in the face of an unstoppable modernity.

Conclusion: 'Till we have built Jerusalem, in England's Green and Pleasant Land'

The novelist W. Somerset Maugham believed that Holmes's success was due to Doyle's persistence in reminding his readers of the detective's attributes again and again, with 'the same pertinacity as the great advertisers use to proclaim the merits of their soap, beer or cigarettes'.[17] These attributes take in Holmes's logic and his typically British, 'unflappable' attitude. By extension, though, they could also take in Doyle's presentations of rural England: a traditional bucolic Englishness that is, time and time again, shown to be under threat from foreign influences but that is, always, rescued by Holmes. His enemies are almost always either foreigners – colonial Others such as the Andaman islander Tonga in *The Sign of Four*, Australians in 'The Boscombe Valley Mystery', Americans in *The Valley of Fear*, but also, increasingly, European Others from new imperial competitors: Germans, most regularly, but also Italians, French and Russians. Supported by a growing canon of scientific writing on racial differences and racially motivated predispositions to criminality, the Holmes stories use clearly recognisable foreign Others to contrast unfavourably with English core values, showing them to endanger English locations and values. In a move typical of nineteenth-century Orientalism, the Other is thus used repeatedly to further cement a perceived notion of national identity – the norm can only be seen if it is demarcated sharply from that which is *other*. If Doyle's criminals are not outright foreigners, then they are Englishmen who have lived in – and been tainted by – foreign lands that have led them to forget English values. But the fact that Holmes is usually victorious hammers home the message of English superiority over other nations.

Thus, the Holmes canon, in particular through its depiction of an endangered rural English national identity, not only supported the predominant political discourse of New Imperialism but, through its far-reaching popularity, further popularised it, turning it from a predominantly *political* into a *popular* discourse that celebrated exclusivity and conservatism. With a few notable exceptions – such as the brief dissenting passages in 'Wisteria Lodge' and 'His Last Bow'– Doyle's writing has a clear ideological message about Englishness that allows a return to the opening quotation by Kumar about 'writing [that] embodies values, whole ways of life, which express[es] the aspirations of the national culture' of the time. Holmes's adventures are not merely stories to entertain, but also stories that were meant to edify, to reassure their nineteenth- and early twentieth-century readers at home, and to safely position them in a world where British power might be challenged but is, ultimately, always reinstated. As Thomas writes so succinctly: 'Doyle's works, along with those of Galton and others [such as Ellis and Lombroso], offer narratives of scientific justification for many of the racial, national, and gender prejudices that formed the political justification for New Imperialism'.[18] The result is a body of writing that has created a cultural myth, repeatedly showing a dangerous outside world encroaching on England's green and pleasant land – but one that is constantly defeated or held at bay by the quintessential Englishman in the figure of Sherlock Holmes.

Notes

1. Krishan Kumar, '"Englishness" and National Identity', in David Morley and Kevin Robins (eds.), *British Cultural Studies, Geography, Nationality and Identity* (Oxford: Oxford University Press, 2001), 41–55 (42).
2. Amanda J. Field, 'The Case of Multiplying Millions: Sherlock Holmes in Advertising', in Sabine Vanacker and Catherine Wynne (eds.), *Sherlock Holmes and Conan Doyle: Multi-Media Afterlives* (Basingstoke: Palgrave Macmillan, 2013), 19–35.
3. 'Investigate the origins of Sherlock Holmes at Portsmouth Museum', *Visit England*, [https://www.visitengland.com/experience/investigate-origins-sherlock-holmes-portsmouth-museum, accessed 4 May 2017].
4. 'Baskerville Country, Dartmoor, Devonshire', *Country File Magazine*, [www.countryfile.com/days-out/baskerville-country-devon, accessed 4 May 2017].
5. 'Sherlock', *Visit Bristol*, [http://visitbristol.co.uk/about-bristol/all-about-bristol/film-and-tv-in-bristol/sherlock, accessed 4 May 2017].
6. 'Did Sherlock Holmes Retire Near Beachy Head?', *Beachy Head*, [https://www.beachyhead.org.uk/latest/2012/01/did-sherlock-holmes-retire-near-beachy-head/, accessed 4 May 2017].
7. 'On the Trail of Sherlock Holmes', *British Heritage Travel*, [http://britishheritage.com/on-the-trail-of-sherlock-holmes-2/, accessed 4 May 2017].
8. *Sherlock Holmes Bookstore and Café*, [www.sherlock-holmes.com/genbooks.htm#afoot, accessed 4 May 2017].
9. Ellen Burton Harrington, 'Nation, Identity and the Fascination with Forensic Science in Sherlock Homes and CSI', *International Journal of Cultural Studies* 10:3 (2007), 365–82 (371).

10. Fredric Jameson, 'On Raymond Chandler', in Glenn W. Most and William W. Stowe (eds.), *The Poetics of Murder: Detective Fiction and Literary Theory* (San Diego: Harcourt, Brace, Jovanovich, 1983), 122–48 (124).
11. Laura Marcus, 'Detection and Literary Fiction', in Martin Priestman (ed.), *The Cambridge Companion to Crime Fiction* (Cambridge: Cambridge University Press, 2003), 245–68 (246).
12. Ronald R. Thomas, 'The Fingerprint of the Foreigner: Colonizing the Criminal Body in 1890s Detective Fiction and Criminal Anthropology', *ELH* 61:3 (1994), 655–80 (659).
13. Simon Featherstone, *Englishness: Twentieth-Century Popular Culture and the Forming of English Identity* (Edinburgh: Edinburgh University Press, 2009), 29.
14. Harrington, 'Nation, Identity', 366.
15. Sigmund Freud, 'The "Uncanny"', in *Art and Literature*, trans. James Strachey. In *The Penguin Freud Library*, vol. 1 (London: Penguin, 1990), 335–76 (337).
16. Tom Ue, 'Holmes and Raffles in Arms: Death, Endings, and Narration', *Victoriographies* 5:3 (2015), 219–33 (227).
17. W. Somerset Maugham, 'The Decline and Fall of the Detective Story', *Essays on Literature* (London and Toronto: New English Library in association with Heinemann, 1967), 151–73 (160).
18. Thomas, 'Fingerprint', 662.

6

STACY GILLIS

Gender and Sexuality in Holmes

The notion of the detective who, in solving crimes, provides the absolute truth of the solution – and, in so doing, offers restoration to the community of affected individuals – is a compelling one, with a long history. More often than not, in the early years of the detective fiction genre, this detective figure, imbued with authority over both the crime and the narrative, was male. In his seminal essay 'The Guilty Vicarage' (1948), W. H. Auden argues that the 'job of the detective is to restore the state of grace in which the aesthetic and the ethical are as one'. In his discussion of the resolution of the narrative arc in detective fiction, Auden selected Sherlock Holmes as one of a small group of '[c]ompletely satisfactory detectives', alongside the slightly later Inspector French (introduced in Freeman Wills Croft's *Inspector French's Greatest Case* in 1924) and Father Brown (introduced in G. K. Chesterton's 'The Blue Cross' in 1910). Auden characterises Holmes as an 'exceptional individual who is in a state of grace' because he is a 'genius' for whom 'scientific curiosity is raised to the status of a heroic passion'.[1] While there have been recent challenges to the notion of exceptionality, this reading of the (usually male) detective continues to impact both on representations of the detective in contemporary detective fiction and also on scholarship about the genre. This chapter considers the ways in which Holmes has been read as both the embodiment and arbiter of absolute masculine authority, before considering how recent work in queer and gender studies has opened up critiques of the reification of masculine authority in the canon.

Authority: Reason and Rationality

In 1923, Dorothy L. Sayers published the first of the Lord Peter Wimsey detective novels, *Whose Body?* In this novel, the amateur detective Wimsey is presented as effete, nervy and with a tendency for verbal incontinence. A veteran of the First World War, he often needs to rely on the care of his valet and mother when he experiences episodes of shell shock, which are triggered by his detecting activities and his growing awareness of the moral turpitude of the criminal. These episodes, combined with his juxtaposition with the criminal – the physically dominant and publicly successful Sir Julian Freke (a well-respected surgeon who counts mountaineering amongst his hobbies) – effectively feminise Wimsey. This feminisation is strongly accentuated through the meta-textual references in the novel to the logic and rationality of Sherlock Holmes: '"If ever you want to commit a murder"', Wimsey advises a gathering of friends and family, '"the thing you've got to do is to prevent people from associatin' their ideas"'. He goes on to observe that '"it's only in Sherlock Holmes and stories like that, that people think things out logically"'. Later, when Wimsey has stumped his police friend Parker, he says that doing so '"[m]akes me feel like Sherlock Holmes"' and '"gives me confidence in myself"'.[2] The references to the logical and rational masculine authority of Holmes act as a particularly forceful counterpoint to the feminisation of Wimsey in Sayers's early novels. These are, however, only a few of the multitude of references to Holmes that litter early twentieth-century detective, crime and mystery fictions: in texts from E. C. Bentley's detective satire *Trent's Last Case* (1913) to John Buchan's spy thriller *The Thirty-Nine Steps* (1915), the multiple references to Holmes secure his masculine authority. These references to Holmes are certainly evidence of the early popularity of the figure, but should also be understood as speaking to a particular model of masculinity: one predicated upon logic, rationality and exceptionality.

The cross-textual re-enforcement of Holmes's masculine authority is justified in part, as, from the outset, he is represented as a genius: focused and unique. As Auden suggests, 'his knowledge is absolutely specialized'.[3] In the first Holmes story, *A Study in Scarlet*, Watson meets Stamford, his former dresser at St Bart's Hospital who, in suggesting that Watson move in with Holmes, describes the latter as having '"a passion for definite and exact knowledge"' (17). Later in the novel Watson notes that Holmes 'would acquire no knowledge which did not bear upon his object' (21). Holmes's authority is further substantiated through his demonstration of knowledge: he has written a number of monographs, including one on the analysis of tobacco ash, and another on enigmatic writing. Holmes describes himself as a '"consulting detective"' and laconically states that '"in London we have lots of government detectives and lots of private ones. When these fellows are at fault, they come to me, and I manage to put them on the right scent"' (24). Here Holmes emphatically positions himself as exceptional, an assessment that Watson (admittedly sometimes grudgingly) works to secure in his narration of Holmes's investigations.

Thus, from the opening pages of the first Holmes story, his association with facts and knowledge imbues him with authority. This authority is confirmed by his relationship with all the other police detectives in London: as the individual to whom they repeatedly turn, he has control over their work in solving crimes, and thereby over the criminals of London. He is thus in control of both justice and crime and endowed with a substantial social mandate. This figuration of Holmes as a model of masculine authority can be found in many of the other Doyle stories, from his masterful appearance on the moors in *The Hound of the Baskervilles*, 'brooding over that enormous wilderness of peat and granite which lay before him' (726) to his account of himself in 'The Bruce-Partington Plans'. In comparing himself to Mycroft, who possesses the '"tidiest and most orderly brain, with the greatest capacity for storing facts, of any man living"', he implicitly claims '"the same great powers"' for himself (914). Unsurprisingly then, a focus on masculine authority has been a hallmark of many critical readings of the Holmes canon.

Sayers's meta-textual lineal linking of Wimsey with Holmes has its precedence in the Holmes stories: Watson says that Holmes reminds him of '"Edgar Allan Poe's Dupin"', remarking that he '"had no idea that such individuals did exist outside of stories"' (*A Study in Scarlet* 24). This meta-textual lineage promulgates a seductive history of the male detective and his authority – Dupin to Holmes and onwards – that is common to much scholarly work on detective fiction. Even T. S. Eliot, one of the few critics not to endorse this lineage, does so only to position Holmes as wholly unique: Eliot 'cannot think of anything with which to compare Sherlock Holmes' and posits that he does not 'seem to be descended from either Sergeant Cuff [from Wilkie Collins's 1868 novel *The Moonstone*] or Monsieur Dupin'. Eliot does, however, speak to the impact of Doyle's detective in terms of lineage, stating that Holmes, like Professor Moriarty, has had 'a numerous progeny'.[4] This masculine authoritative lineage – notwithstanding that, when Watson makes the comparison between his friend and Dupin, Holmes's sole comment is that Dupin is 'a very inferior fellow' (*A Study in Scarlet* 24) – has been remarked upon by many critics of detective fiction. For example, T. J. Binyon, in his early study of the genre, argues that Holmes is 'recognizably, like Dupin, a product of the Romantic tradition'. This similarity works to reinforce his masculine authority: Holmes, like Dupin, is 'another proud, alienated hero, superior to and isolated from the rest of humanity; a sufferer from *spleen* and *ennui*'.[5] Holmes is here positioned as heroic, certainly, but more crucially as exceptional, and separated from all others through his heroic masculine authority.

The notion of exceptionality has even been extended to the readers of Holmes. In Christopher Redmond's study of sex in the Holmes canon, for example, he apologises for 'any apparent implication that all readers of Sherlock Holmes stories are [heterosexual and] male' but still goes on to argue that they are committed to a model of heterosexual masculine authority which, for Redmond, is the reason for the canon's tremendous popularity with male readers (the appeal of Holmes to female readers is often linked to the film and television adaptations, rather than the original stories, and to the star persona of the actor playing Holmes: be it Basil Rathbone, Jeremy Brett or Benedict Cumberbatch).[6] The notion of a community of male readers of Holmes was identified by Doyle himself at the end of his writing career. In the Preface to *The Case-Book of Sherlock Holmes* (1927) he notes that Holmes had begun 'his adventures in the very heart of the later Victorian era, carried it through the all-too-short reign of Edward, and has managed to hold his own little niche even in feverish days'.[7] While not all the stories in *The Case-Book* were originally published in the *Strand Magazine* (some, for example, were first published in *Collier's* before being reprinted in its pages), Doyle used the magazine as a means of uniting the male readership of the stories: 'it would be true to say that those who first read of [Holmes] as young men have lived to see their own grown-up children following the same adventures in the same magazine'.[8] Christopher Pittard's exploration of the *Strand* and reading communities speaks to the politics of this grouping of readers: it 'was a magazine meant to be *read* by the family, but bought by the man, affirming the gendered aspect of domestic economy'.[9] Addressing this group of putative readers, Doyle hopes that the stories have been a distraction from 'the worries of life' and goes on to thank his readers for their 'past constancy'.[10] Here a community of readers is posited, one which is both cross-generational and male. This notion of a community of readers has marked the cultural afterlife of Holmes for close to a century: a community of readers committed to Holmes's masculine authority within the stories.

Challenge: Disguise and Deception

While the fervour for Holmes has not abated, the rise of gender studies from the 1980s onwards has shifted the focus of some detective fiction criticism. New ways of reading the relationship between masculinity and authority in the Holmes canon first appeared in the late 1990s. In his 1997 study of Holmes and masculinity, Joseph Kestner proposed that the detective's first appearance in *A Study in Scarlet* in a scientific laboratory is significant as the laboratory is a 'space signifying not only rationality and logic but also linking these traits with masculinity'. Kestner also notes that Holmes's use of such expressions as 'I perceive' or 'don't you see' aligns 'him not only with masculinity but also with dominance' through the conflation of sight with knowledge, and then with control.[11] However, Kestner also points to the threat of transgression in the stories, a threat not to be found in the figure of Holmes himself, but rather in other characters. In addition to 'an attempt to police and patrol society', the Holmes narratives, for Kestner, 'also must police and patrol masculinity' itself. As men within the texts 'defect' from a 'normative masculinity', Holmes works to contain these transgressions.[12]

In 'The Man With the Twisted Lip', for example, Holmes deduces that the middle-class Neville St Clair is not, in fact, drugged and/or murdered in an opium den, as his wife fears but, instead, uses the den as a space to change his clothes as he is, in fact, working as the beggar Hugh Boone, making more than £700 per annum (close to £90,000 in contemporary terms). The secret of this ungentlemanly behaviour (far better to work for less money as a journalist, the narrative implies) is maintained with the curious statement that if '"the police are to hush it up, there must be no more of Hugh Boone"' (244). This containment of transgressions against cultural expectations relating to men's behaviours and actions features in a number of the early Holmes stories and Kestner argues that, despite a conflation of Holmes with masculine authority, the stories often 'present conflict which remains unresolved, resolutions which remain inconclusive, and masculinity which remains under siege rather than secure'.[13] Yet while such conflict serves to threaten the normative modes of late Victorian and Edwardian middle-class masculinity that Holmes embodies, the stories have been read as confirming – through the narrative resolution of each mystery – and reifying these normative modes. There has been a long-standing popular, as well as early critical, perception of the detective as the one who, in deducing the story of the crime, provides the truth of the narrative, which thereby enforces the detective's narrative and moral authority. More recent critical work on detective fiction challenges this reading of narrative and moral authority, and its relationship with masculinity.

Late Victorian and Edwardian middle-class masculinity can be dismantled through queering – or re-calibrating readings of emotional and sexual politics – the stories' focus on masculine authority. Andrew Smith, for example, points to how the Holmes stories can be read as challenging 'the idea of rationality' and examining 'the expectations and limitations associated with dominant masculine scripts'. Holmes's rationality is, in fact, 'compromised by encounters with seemingly unconventional forms of masculine conduct', such as with St Clair in 'The Man with the Twisted Lip'.[14] Focusing largely on the relationship between Holmes and the urban, how London 'becomes a site within which gender debates are determined by a form of political geography', Smith touches upon the transgressive confusions created by the use of disguise in the stories. It is fruitful to consider how the disguises adopted by others can be read through the lenses of queer and gender theories, as speaking to a fluidity of gendered – as well as raced and classed – subjectivities.[15]

A number of individuals deploy disguise in the Holmes stories: from St Clair's disguise as a beggar to Violet Hunter's unwitting disguise as Alice Rucastle in order to deceive the latter's fiancé in 'The Copper Beeches', to Rodger Baskerville and his wife masquerading as the Stapleton siblings in *The Hound of the Baskervilles*. This interest in disguise continues through to the last of the Holmes stories: from the disguised (and disgraced) Russian former political activist Sergius in 'The Golden Pince-Nez' to Holy Peters's disguise as the Rev Dr Shlessinger in 'Lady Frances Carfax' and then even Watson's disguise as Dr Hill Barton, collector of Ming china, in 'The Illustrious Client'. Disguise is thus used by criminals, by detectives and even practiced upon victims. What is important to note is that in texts which foreground an authoritative masculinity, disguise can be read as operating a challenge to a normative mode of gender politics: that is, disguise challenges the expectations and limits of late Victorian and Edwardian middle-class masculinity through demonstrating the precarity and performativity of gender.

It is telling that in a sequence of stories that foreground the disruptive potential of disguise, it is Holmes who is represented as both excelling in the act of disguise and also, quite simply, as having a penchant for dressing up. Indeed, he has written a monograph on disguises, so his expertise is secured both through his prowess in dressing up, but also in his accumulation of knowledge about the subject. In a number of stories, including 'Charles Augustus Milverton' and 'The Empty House', Holmes so excels at his disguise as, respectively, a plumber (going so far in his quest to gain information about the Milverton household that he becomes engaged to a housemaid) and a querulous book-collector, that Watson does not recognise him. Similarly, in 'The Dying Detective', Holmes, in feigning near-death illness to capture the criminal, also deceives Watson, both in his capacity as a close friend and as a medical professional. Holmes, then, is presented as exceptionally skilled at physically and emotionally preparing these disguises, and also as a very good actor. As Watson notes in 'A Scandal in Bohemia', it is not just that Holmes changes his appearance, but that his 'expression, his manner, his very soul seemed to vary with every fresh part that he assumed'; as he goes on to claim, the 'stage lost a fine actor, even as science lost an acute reasoner, when he became a specialist in crime' (170). Holmes is here presented as having the emotional nuances of an actor as well as the rational deductive powers of a scientist and these distinctions – which would, in the late nineteenth-century context, be gendered as feminine and masculine respectively – are emphasised by Watson as making Holmes particularly well-suited to solving crime.

In 'A Scandal in Bohemia', the reader is introduced to Irene Adler who, according to Watson, 'eclipses and predominates the whole of her sex' for Holmes, although we quickly learn that Holmes does not feel 'any emotion akin to love' for her. Emotion, says Watson, despite his claims for Holmes's emotional nuances as an actor, is particularly 'abhorrent to his cold, precise but admirably balanced mind' (161). While it may be that Watson doth protest too much about Adler's lack of emotional impact on Holmes, it is evident that, in a story about desire and deception both in and out of marriage, the focus is ostensibly on heteronormative authority. As we learn, the King of Bohemia must recover an incriminating photograph of himself and Adler, as his fiancée, who is '"the very soul of delicacy"', cannot have a '"shadow of a doubt as to [his] conduct"' (166). Adler, in turn, wishes to marry Geoffrey Norton, who knows about her past, but wants to retain the photograph as a 'weapon' against 'any steps which [the King] might take in the future' (175). Holmes believes he has identified the hiding place of the incriminating photograph when he was in disguise as a clergyman who is attacked by guardsmen outside Adler's house and was brought in to her living quarters. The feminising of Holmes here – in disguise, attacked by soldiers in public, being carried inside to a couch – is countered by his behaviour when he wants to take the photograph. He aggressively violates Adler's hiding space which, as the photograph is in a 'recess behind a sliding panel' and bearing in mind the story's focus on sexuality and desire, renders this private hidden space as vaginal. Holmes is physically aggressive: he 'rushed' at the bell pull, 'tore back' the shutter, and 'plung[ed]' in his hand. There are overtones of rape here, and it is significant that the picture is revealed not to be the desired incriminating photograph, but rather a picture of 'Irene Adler herself in evening dress' (174). It is appropriate that she is in evening dress, as the story, with its focus on disguise and deception, hinges on the similar capacities for disguise and deception that both Holmes and Adler possess.

In this story, Holmes deploys a number of disguises to solve the case, and his expertise at so doing is much admired by Watson. In addition to the above-discussed scene in which Watson praises Holmes – he knows it is Holmes only because he has seen him go into the bedroom and return as 'an amiable and simple-minded Nonconformist clergyman' (170) – there are other instances of Holmes's capacity for deception: when a 'drunken-looking groom, ill-kept and side-whiskered' appears in Holmes's rooms, Watson has 'to look three times before [he is] certain it was him', despite being accustomed to what he describes as Holmes's 'amazing powers in the use of disguises' (167). Holmes's great talent in disguise – together with his strong desire to dress up – can be read as a queering of authoritative masculine authority. This is particularly clear in the passage in 'A Scandal in Bohemia' when Holmes, having clarified the location of the photograph, is greeted outside his door by a 'slim youth in an ulster' (173) who passes quickly on. This 'slim youth' is, in fact, Adler, who has followed Holmes and Watson home, largely to demonstrate her authority both over Holmes and over the narrative: for Elizabeth Miller, 'Holmes, the expert eye, finds his visual acumen continually thwarted by the female body's resistance to interpretation'.[16] It is significant that Adler, for whom, we are told, '[m]ale costume is nothing new' as she often takes 'advantage of the freedom which it gives', is dressed as a man in her 'walking-clothes' to follow Holmes home (174–5). While Holmes declares that '"I've heard that voice before"' (173) he is unable to penetrate the male disguise she is wearing. Disguise thus operates queerly to challenge Holmes's masculine authority.

Anxiety: Control and Coercion

While some early critical readings of the Holmes stories noted these challenges to male authority, it has only more recently become the sustained focus of Holmes criticism. Stephen Knight posited early on that the stories are marked by male anxiety, which has its roots in both a loss of masculinity and a fear of patriarchal power being supplanted. In 'The Speckled Band', for example, Knight describes how Dr Roylott attacks his stepdaughter with a snake 'forced through a hole he has pierced in her wall'. While he does not probe the reading he provides too far, he does admit that 'a close analysis would chart the meaning more fully'.[17] These psychosexual tensions pivoting on male anxiety have, more recently, been investigated with much greater force. The male-on-female threat of violence or actual violence – including, but not limited to, physical and/or emotional abuse, sexual coercion, robbery, rape, murder, imprisonment and sex trafficking – is a hallmark of many of the Holmes stories, and men within many of the families are actively pursuing violence against their female family members. In her discussion of the play *The Speckled Band: An Adventure of Sherlock Holmes* (1912) – which Doyle adapted from the short story of the same title – Catherine Wynne argues that the 'stepfather's desire for the continued appropriation of his stepdaughters' money causes him to sexually, emotionally and physically control them in an environment replete with imperialistic resonance'.[18] This desire for control over women's financial, emotional and sexual lives is visible in many of the stories with their Gothic threats against women: from the threat of rape by Mary Sutherland's stepfather in 'A Case of Identity' to the murder of Mary Cushing (followed by the sending of her ear through the post to her sister) in 'The Cardboard Box' and Violet Smith's forced marriage to secure an inheritance in 'The Solitary Cyclist'.

In such stories, Holmes's authority is derived, in part, by saving women from various threats to their financial, emotional and sexual lives, and this brings us back to Auden's notion of the detective as being exceptional. Holmes's saving of these women takes two forms: one is the physical act of rescuing the women, and the other is as the producer of the truth in terms of the solution. But his response to the women and their situations varies. Racing to rescue Smith from a forced marriage, Holmes ignores a wounded groom as '"we can't do him any good, but we may save her from the worst fate that can befall a woman"' (535). His arrival precipitates the murder of one of the members of the gang who had '"played cards for her"' so that one '"was to marry her, and the other have a share of the plunder"' (537), knowing that she was, unknown to herself, going to inherit a fortune from her uncle. It is Holmes who saves Smith both physically – from the implied rape that would follow the marriage – and socially – as it is implied that her fiancé in the Midlands would not marry someone who had been previously married. Holmes airily confirms that '"a forced marriage is no marriage"' (536). Lisa Surridge has compellingly argued that 'Holmes upholds and supports bourgeois marriage' and invites 'readers to participate with him in penetrating and investigating the private home' and Holmes's actions in entering Adler's house to find the picture can fruitfully be placed alongside the gang threatening Smith in 'The Solitary Cyclist'.[19] It is telling that Watson silences Smith from this point onward in that story – previously articulate and verbose, she does not speak again.

Indeed, it is significant that this story ends with Watson drawing attention to this narrativising of the event. Acknowledging that it is often difficult 'to round off [his] narratives, and to give those final details which the curious might expect', he then states that Smith did inherit the fortune and marry her fiancé who became the senior partner of 'famous Westminster electricians' ('The Solitary Cyclist' 538). While Watson is not able to recognise this, not only is Smith silenced, but this passage also confirms that her fiancé employed her money to move to London and secure his career prospects, in many ways precisely what the criminal gang intended to do with Smith's fortune. Masculine authority is asserted here, both in terms of physically rescuing Smith, as well as in terms of narrativising *her* story, which becomes, in effect, *his* story. While Watson's gesture to the 'curious' reader in the final lines of 'The Solitary Cyclist' can be read as part of the creation of the community of readers discussed above, it also draws attention to the constructedness of the story. This can be read as obliquely acknowledging the possibilities for other solutions and other narratives. Tzvetan Todorov's well-known formulation of the duality of 'the story of the crime and the story of the investigation' at the heart of the whodunit opened up narratological discussions about the possibilities of the detective's solution being only one among others.[20] The detective's solution is, however, believed, because of his/her (although usually his) authority within the narrative. The possibility of other solutions – and with the Holmes stories this also must take into account the added layer of Watson's narrative – works to disrupt this authority.

Was Watson a Woman?

In 1941, just over a decade after the publication of the final Holmes story, the crime writer Rex Stout published 'Watson Was a Woman' in *The Saturday Review of Literature*, an essay based on a talk he had given earlier that year to the Baker Street Irregulars. Stout's interest in Holmes was long standing: as well as his investiture in the Baker Street Irregulars as a member in 1949, his own detective, Nero Wolfe, bears a notable resemblance to Mycroft Holmes (Wolfe is a corpulent armchair detective whose assistant does the legwork) and there is a painting of Holmes over his assistant's desk. The lineage of the male detective is vital here: the similarities between Wolfe and Mycroft speak to the possible relationship between Wolfe and Holmes, something John Clark noted in 1956 when he posited, in the *Baker Street Journal*, that Wolfe was the offspring of Holmes and Irene Adler.[21] This is apparently corroborated by the fact that the same vowels appear in the same order in both Sherlock Holmes and Nero Wolfe (an observation which has been named by Ellery Queen as 'The Great O-E Theory').[22] In 'Watson Was a Woman', Stout argues, tongue-in-cheek, that that there is, in fact, no Doctor Watson:

> Right at the very start, on page 9 of 'A Study in Scarlet', I found this:
> ... it was rare for him to be up after ten at nights, and he had invariably breakfasted and gone out before I rose in the morning.
> I was indescribably shocked. How had so patent a clue escaped so many millions of readers through the years? That was, that could only be, a woman speaking of a man.[23]

A number of other examples are discussed, including Holmes's breakfasting habits, his violin playing – 'Imagine a man asking another man to play him some of Mendelssohn's *Lieder* on a violin!'[24] – Watson's pointed comments about Holmes's smoking in *The Hound of the Baskervilles* and Watson's faint when Holmes returns, apparently from the dead, in 'The Empty House'. Stout then posits that the clues to Watson's true identity are contained in the titles of the stories and infers, through speciously complicated numerological reasoning involving the number of stories and Holmes's and Watson's ages, that Watson is, in fact, *the* woman' ('A Scandal in Bohemia' 161; emphasis in original): that is, Irene Watson, *née* Adler (Stout then queries the parentage of Wimsey, implying Holmes might be his father, as Wimsey 'was born, I believe, around the turn of the century – about the time of the publication of "The Adventure of the Second Stain"').[25]

This sort of humorous analysis is a well-trodden hallmark of parts of Sherlockiana and a queering of Watson and Holmes's relationship is at the heart of much of it: whether Watson is working to persuade Holmes, with the help of Mycroft and Sigmund Freud, that Professor James Moriarty is not his archenemy, but rather his childhood mathematics tutor who is one of the few to know a terrible family secret, in Nicholas Meyer's pastiche *The Seven-Per-Cent Solution* (1974), to the multitude of slash fan fictions (a genre that focuses on sexual relationships between fictional characters) which describe, often in graphic detail, the sexual relationship between Holmes and Watson. This emotional frisson is both referenced and parodied in the BBC's *Sherlock* series (2010–), with Watson having to deny repeatedly to Mrs Hudson that he and Holmes are in a physically intimate relationship, and with her expectation, when he announces his engagement in 'The Empty Hearse' (2014), that he is marrying a man. Stout's humorous reading of Holmes and Watson's relationship in 1941, then, should be understood as flagging up the potential for other readings of the gender politics in the Holmes canon.

It is challenging to provide a definitive account of a character who appears in fifty-six short stories and four novels over a period of forty years, particularly when the internal consistencies of this fictive world vary across the texts. Without delving into the details of speculation about the nature of the relationship between Watson and Holmes, Stout's essay does illustrate how Holmes can be understood as an exemplar of late Victorian and Edwardian middle-class masculinity, with a Henry Higgins-like attitude to his domestic and professional partner. Holmes can be read, as he was for many decades, as representing an absolute masculine authority, despite his occasional failures or mishaps; an authority that works to counter and disrupt other examples of transgressive masculinity. Women are often protected by Holmes: but while this can be read as firmly positioning him within the heroic mode identified by Binyon and others, it also speaks to the precarity of middle-class women's position at the turn of the nineteenth century.

The silencing of women in the Holmes canon is pervasive. In 'The Crooked Man' and 'The Dancing Men', wives of murdered men have nervous breakdowns and are voiceless in Watson's account, while in *The Hound of the Baskervilles*, Stapleton's wife is literally silenced by her husband:

> [t]o this post a figure was tied, so swathed and muffled in the sheets which had been used to secure it that one could not for the moment tell whether it was that of a man or a woman. One towel passed around the throat and was secured at the back of the pillar. Another covered the lower part of the face.　　(758)

While the Holmes stories do reify reason and order through the figure of the detective, the number of plot and character devices borrowed from the Gothic, with specific relevance to women, speaks to the anxieties about their role in both public and private, as well as to the complexities of the male response. These anxieties and complexities are often, however, the focus of the staggering number of global multimedia adaptations that have populated the cultural afterlife of the world's first consulting detective over the past century. It is in these adaptations, that this authority, and the focus on reason and logic, is refracted as well as reflected, and in many of these texts, an ambiguity about gender and sexuality is found, an ambiguity that complicates the positioning of Holmes as that doyen of logic, reason and rationality in the original stories.

Notes

1. W. H. Auden, 'The Guilty Vicarage', *Harper's Monthly* 196:1176 (1948), 406–12 (409, 410).
2. Dorothy Sayers, *Whose Body?* (London: Hodder & Stoughton, 2003), 120, 150.
3. Auden, 'Guilty Vicarage', 410.
4. T. S. Eliot, review of The Complete Sherlock Holmes Short Stories, *The Criterion* 8: 32 (April 1929), 552–6 (552).
5. T. J. Binyon, '*Murder Will Out*': *The Detective in Fiction* (Oxford: Oxford University Press, 1990), 10.
6. Christopher Redmond, *In Bed with Sherlock Holmes: Sexual Elements in Arthur Conan Doyle's Stories of the Great Detective* (Toronto: Simon and Pierre, 1984), 15.
7. Arthur Conan Doyle, 'Preface', in *The Case-Book of Sherlock Holmes* (London: John Murray, 1952), 5–7 (6).
8. Ibid.
9. Christopher Pittard, *Purity and Contamination in Late Victorian Detective Fiction* (Farnham: Ashgate, 2011), 67. Original emphasis.
10. Conan Doyle, 'Preface', 6, 7.
11. Joseph Kestner, *Sherlock's Men: Masculinity, Conan Doyle, and Cultural History* (Farnham: Ashgate, 1997), 42, 43.
12. Ibid., 45.
13. Ibid.

14. Andrew Smith, *Victorian Demons: Medicine, Masculinity and the Gothic at the Fin-de-Siècle* (Manchester: Manchester University Press, 2004), 118.

15. Ibid., 119.

16. Elizabeth Carolyn Miller, *Framed: The New Woman Criminal in British Culture at the* Fin de Siècle (Ann Arbor: University of Michigan Press, 2008), 26.

17. Stephen Knight, *Form and Ideology in Crime Fiction* (Basingstoke: Macmillan, 1980), 96.

18. Catherine Wynne, 'Philanthropies and Villainies: The Conflict of the Imperial and the Anti-Imperial in Conan Doyle', in Philippa Gates and Stacy Gillis (eds.), *The Devil Himself: Villainy in Detective Fiction and Film* (Westport: Greenwood, 2002), 69–80 (71).

19. Lisa Surridge, *Bleak Houses: Marital Violence in Victorian Fiction* (Athens: Ohio University Press, 2005), 239.

20. Tzvetan Todorov, 'The Typology of Detective Fiction', in *The Poetics of Prose*, trans. Richard Howard (Ithaca: Cornell University Press, 1977), 42–52 (44).

21. John D. Clark, 'Some Notes Relating to a Preliminary Investigation into the Paternity of Nero Wolfe', *Baker Street Journal* 6:1 (1956), 5–11.

22. Ellery Queen, *In the Queens' Parlor* (New York: Simon & Schuster, 1957), 4–5.

23. Rex Stout, 'Watson Was a Woman', *The Saturday Review of Literature* 23:19 (1 March 1941), 3–4, 16 (3).

24. Ibid., 16.

25. Ibid.

7

JONATHAN CRANFIELD

Doyle and Evolution

This chapter focuses on the relationship between the Sherlock Holmes stories and important strains of radical nineteenth-century science: the geological studies of Charles Lyell, the evolutionary biology of Charles Darwin and Alfred Russel Wallace and, finally, their post-Darwinian mutations in the eugenics of Francis Galton and the criminology of Cesare Lombroso. These are by no means the only scientific discourses that can help us to understand Sherlock Holmes but they share some key distinguishing qualities, not least a methodological emphasis on everyday empirical observation allied to deductive and abductive reasoning. These discourses also left particularly strong footprints on literary and popular culture during the second half of the nineteenth century. Their significance has been subsequently reinforced by their use as durable reference points in the burgeoning field of 'literature and science' criticism since the early 1980s.

This field has reached a shared consensus that the Sherlock Holmes stories are enmeshed in discourses of science, though there are long-running disputes over the precise nature of the relationship. In an influential 1989 essay, Gillian Beer cautioned against the predominance of either 'causal' or 'casual' relationships between literature and science.[1] The first type of relationship would view science as the cause and literature as the effect. According to this view, scientists initiate new ways of understanding the world which then trickle down through other forms of culture including literature. A 'casual' relationship, by contrast, implies much looser ties and suggests that scientists and authors came to share language and ideas in a more diffuse way through cohabiting within the same culture. These different approaches yield very different results when analysing the Holmes canon. This chapter outlines some of the key scientific concepts and controversies from this period and then explores how they can be mapped onto the Holmes stories in different ways.

Deep Time and Evolution

Lyell's *Principles of Geology* was first published in 1830 and exerted a substantial influence over later generations of scientists across multiple fields. His work and that of his disciples helped to precipitate radically changing perceptions of the world during the Victorian period. Darwin later wrote, 'I always feel as if my books came half out of Lyell's brain' and, moreover, that he always saw natural phenomena 'partially through his eyes'.[2] Lyell's assiduous analysis of geological strata and stratification (stratigraphy), allowed him to enlarge substantially earlier notions of historical time and of humanity's reduced place within it. Based upon his analysis of rock strata, coastal erosion patterns and delta formations, he was able to offer a view that was gradualist rather than catastrophist. Influential catastrophists such as George Cuvier had argued that the Earth's landscape could only have been shaped by a series of violent upheavals that could fit within a short biblical timeline. According to this view the history of the Earth had been nasty, brutish and short. Lyell demurred and argued that only slower, longer, more stable and uniform processes could have shaped the Earth as he saw it.[3] His new model of gradualist consistency opened up huge vistas of unrecorded history (what Robert Hutton had previously termed 'deep time') but he also emphasised the power of everyday observation. Lyell argued that extraordinary varieties of animal life could only have thrived on a relatively 'tranquil' landscape and that the divide between biological and geological observation could be bridged through 'deduction'.[4] Lyell thus made the past seem further away in time but empirically closer in terms of how it could be recovered and understood.

Lyell also played a key role as Darwin and Wallace independently reached their initial conclusions about the theory of evolution. These conclusions about species mutability (disappearance), speciation (multiplication) and adaptation would coalesce into the theory of evolution by natural selection. Evolutionary theories implicitly posited a closer relationship between humans and animals than many had hitherto been comfortable with. Religious orthodoxies specifically distinguished humans from other animals over which the God of the Old Testament had granted them dominion. In its simplest terms, the work of Darwin and Wallace called this primacy into question. Darwin later wrote that 'the mode of origin, and the early stages of the development of man, are identical with those of the animals immediately below him'.[5]

In an 1855 article Wallace compared all life to 'a branching tree', metaphorically bringing all species into one overarching taxonomical flow.[6] He later sent a more detailed manuscript for Darwin to pass on to Lyell. Both

Lyell and Darwin were struck by the similarity of the younger man's work to Darwin's. In retrospect, though, Darwin and Wallace approached their subject in different ways. Wallace used a top-down perspective to think about species in the aggregate whilst Darwin focused more closely on the minutiae of individual organisms and their development. Lyell solved the apparent conflict of interest and effectively enshrined Darwin's principal claim to the ideas by reading Wallace's manuscript *after* Darwin's unpublished notes for *On the Origin of Species* at a Linnean Society meeting in July 1858. The ensuing furore and debates over the scientific status of evolution lasted for many decades and reached into every area of public life. They converged with rising tides of religious scepticism, outright atheism and nonconformist believers who rejected the dogmas and institutions of organised religion which had previously regulated public life.

Scientists were given an increasingly prominent public platform throughout the nineteenth century. As such, they helped to shape the intellectual climate within which many fiction writers like Arthur Conan Doyle were raised. Lyell, Darwin and Wallace expanded their influence beyond traditional scientific circles and institutions by seeking new readerships and exploiting different approaches to popularise their ideas. Lyell and Wallace avidly used the periodical marketplace, writing in magazines and journals to explain their own ideas, attack those of their rivals and air their opinions more freely. In this way they helped to curate the more intellectual corners of the periodical writing boom that would accelerate in the 1860s after the repeal of the 'taxes on knowledge'.

The controversy attending the spread of their ideas was not solely limited to the status of humans in relation to animals but also to tensions that centred on questions of race. In 1863, Lyell used his enlarged sense of history to argue that all the human races had descended from a single breeding group: 'if the various races were all descended from a single pair, we must allow for a vast series of antecedent ages'.[7] Polygenic (multispecies) racial science had often insisted on much clearer distinctions between the races as opposed to monogenists (single species) who argued that all races shared a common root. The polygenist view, Lyell argued, was a product of historical shortsightedness in surveying superficial differences between 'civilised' and 'barbaric' nations in the modern day.[8] Darwin, too, took up this argument in his *Descent of Man* (1871): 'Those naturalists ... who admit the principle of evolution, and this is now admitted by the majority of rising men, will feel no doubt that all the races of man are descended from a single primitive stock'.[9] Though these ideas were generally expressed in soft, Eurocentric language, they also opened up potential challenges to preconceived notions of white racial supremacy.

Later in the century, new strains of post-Darwinian science emerged that sought to close down these challenges. In the work of Francis Galton and Cesare Lombroso, the conceptual complexities of evolution were often boiled down to a binary struggle between the forces of progression and those of regression or degeneration. This work found a huge audience in popular science writing and in the re-emergence of Gothic and horror fiction. Both were reflective of a new populism that cut against some of the polygenic nuance of Lyell and Darwin. Degeneration was a scientific term used to describe the simplification of complex organisms but which became reactionary shorthand for the cultural decline of Europe and its empires.[10] Though Galton and Lombroso worked in different disciplines they tended to draw hard, taxonomical dividing lines between races, between classes and the sexes.

Galton's speculations in *Hereditary Genius* (1869) helped to shape his eugenic movement based on evolutionary ideas spiced with nationalism, racial idealism and sexual selection. If positive or negative characteristics could be passed on through the generations, he mused, could humans not be bred for their 'natural qualities' in the same way as pedigree dogs? This outlook could also influence geopolitical thinking, for example when considering 'what races should be politically aided to become hereafter the chief occupiers of [Africa]' after European colonisation.[11] Lombroso applied a biological, evolutionary view to the question of crime and criminality. In his 1876 book *L'Uomo Delinquente* (translated and abridged as *Criminal Man* in the 1890s) he argued that predispositions towards transgressive behaviour were echoes of humanity's brutal, animalistic past. The criminal's 'atavistic character' was, he argued, held in common with 'animals and lower or prehistoric human races'.[12] Such genetic taints could thus be passed on through the generations and be detected by an expert 'reader' of bodies. His work fed high levels of interest in biometric approaches to criminology where dimensions of ear length and nose thickness, for example, could be considered damning indictments of criminal propensity. His most famous disciples, the English criminologist and sexologist Havelock Ellis and the sociologist Max Nordau, became hugely significant cultural figures in 1890s Britain. Indeed, it could be said that the emergence of culturally totemic detectives such as Sherlock Holmes in the period was made possible by the popular spread of this new criminology.

Sherlock Holmes and Science

The work of these men, and the debates that raged in their wake, came to exert a profound influence upon the writing of literature. An early and striking example of direct literary engagement may be found in Alfred Tennyson's long elegiac poem *In Memoriam* (1849). The poem dramatises the existential confusion of a speaker whose soul craves the certainty of a benign God but whose rational mind finds only the uncertainty of the vast, unknowable prehistory opened up by geologists, archaeologists and paleontologists. The rigorous self-criticality and aesthetic beauty of Tennyson's poetry enacted the psychological consequences of a collision between a fixed worldview and new scientific ideas. Yet such unequivocal moments of engagement were relatively rare and distinguished by the psychological depth and symbolic openness encouraged by long form poetry. Detective fiction with its demands for resolution, closure and explanation, was not a natural home for deep, existential questions or radical uncertainty.

As a young man Doyle acquired a deep appreciation of Darwin, Wallace and Tennyson; he later wrote that *In Memoriam* 'sprang into full flower fifty years before its time'.[13] However he drew a clear distinction between Tennyson's artistic process and his own, observing that 'even a moderate faculty for imaginative work seems to me to weaken seriously the ties between the soul and the body'.[14] His appreciation of science and scientists was based as much on their manly personal attributes as upon the specific nuances of their work. He vividly remembered Darwin's *The Voyage of the Beagle* (1839) and Wallace's *The Malay Archipelago* (1869), both written for general readers. They exhibited for him 'the romance of travel and the frequent heroism of modern life'.[15] Darwin's greatness for Doyle lay partly in his 'comprehensive mind' and partly in his 'fine contempt for danger'.[16] Wallace, meanwhile, impressed both with his 'complete investigation' of the local fauna and his casual allusion to living amongst cannibals for eight years. 'Science', Doyle concluded, had 'its heroes no less than Religion'.[17]

Whilst it would be odd if Doyle had remained in total ignorance of Lyell's work, he never referred to him, or the broader swathe of Lyell's ideas, in his letters or published writing. He does, however, refer explicitly to Darwin and Wallace at several points. They helped to shape his youthful religious attitudes which waxed from nonconformism to outright agnosticism. Doyle reacted against both the strict Jesuitism of his schooling and the Roman Catholicism of the London branch of his family from whose patronage he could easily have profited. He remembered these days in his autobiography *Memories and Adventures*:

> the foundations not only of Roman Catholicism but of the whole Christian faith, as presented to me in nineteenth century theology, were so weak that my mind could not build upon them. It is to be remembered that these were the years when Huxley, Tyndall, Darwin, Herbert Spencer and John Stuart Mill

were our chief philosophers, and that even the man in the street felt the strong sweeping current of their thought. (32)

Doyle was styled as a medical man in his early press appearances and the prefix Dr appeared frequently in his advertisements. His public statements about Sherlock Holmes also emphasised the scientific components of the character: 'I tried to build up a scientific detective who solved cases on his own merits and not through the folly of the criminal' (*Memories* 26). In an interview for *Strand Magazine* in 1892 he explained that Holmes had been based upon an Edinburgh surgeon, Joseph Bell, for whom he had clerked during his studies. Bell's 'powers of intuition were simply marvellous' and he was capable of blending medical diagnoses with astonishing insights into patients' careers and personal histories.[18] This suggests that Doyle may be a useful candidate for a 'causal' analysis of his fiction as someone well placed to understand and respond to science explicitly.

Yet upon closer inspection Doyle's scientific status is more ambiguous. He sought to preserve the prestige of his medical background whilst leaving the work behind him as soon as his literary output achieved success. He found his education at the University of Edinburgh to be somewhat arduous and his degree was consequently mediocre. In *The Firm of Girdlestone* (1890) he described the university as 'a great unsympathetic machine'.[19] He felt that his work as a general practitioner was only tenuously connected with cutting edge research and he became quickly dissatisfied. An 1890 advice manual for young GPs warned against the 'attrition of mind' that could occur in practice and encouraged them to join local scientific societies where 'the Professor, the specialist and the General Practitioner all meet'.[20] Many of these issues found their way into the portrayal of Dr Watson as an honest, curious but unspectacular mind. In 'The Dying Detective', for example, Holmes simulates a virulent Asiatic fever and purposefully offends Watson to keep him ignorant of the charade: '"after all, you are only a general practitioner with very limited experience and mediocre qualifications"' (933).

Doyle's later specialisation in oculism was somewhat spurious. He established himself in his Wimpole Street practice upon the flimsiest possible training obtained at the famed Krankenhaus during a short stay in Vienna in 1890. He attended few lectures and absorbed very little scientific knowledge with his 'conversational' German (*Memories* 94). This dilettante approach was certainly not uncommon amongst his peers; the ranks of medicine were thought to be filled with inferior practitioners because of its reputation as a cheap profession. However, it does suggest that Doyle was not animated by an enduring interest in medical and scientific matters. He would later caution young men not to 'choke' themselves 'with the dust of the pedants' and to instead 'cultivate that popular science which attracts'.[21]

In the eyes of some critics, Sherlock Holmes represents the embodiment of a worldview derived from Lyell and Darwin. In *Detective Fiction and the Nature of Evidence* (2003), Lawrence Frank argues that Holmes's method was a route through which radical theories depicting the world as godless and driven by chance were made palatable to an otherwise censorious middle-class readership.[22] Holmes's status as an intellectual iconoclast and bohemian outsider might make him an ideal candidate to popularise these ideas and he certainly acknowledges these influences in various ways. In 'The Five Orange Pips', he discusses his view of the '"ideal reasoner"' (224): '"As Cuvier could correctly describe a whole animal by the contemplation of a single bone, so the observer who has thoroughly understood one link in a series of incidents should be able to accurately state all the other ones, both before and after"' (225). Cuvier, alongside his geological work, had also been an influential early practitioner of paleontology. In this capacity he helped to popularise the image of prehistoric animals such as the Mastodon, the Pterodactyl and the Mosasaurus. The discovery of the remains of these animals presented further fuel for radical refashionings of the past.

Holmes's observation resembles not just Cuvier but Lyell's later work *The Antiquity of Man* (1863). Lyell took Cuvier's fossil findings and mapped them onto his longer, gradualist timeline, urging his readers to step 'beyond the reach of history' and to realise that 'man and the mammoth coexisted'.[23] Like both men, Holmes, in the words of an admiring client in 'The Red Circle', can '"read great things out of small ones"' (903). Even if the constraints of middlebrow short fiction sharply limited the radical conclusions that Holmes might draw from these clues, there are still some striking similarities, not least the fact that Holmes pays minutely close attention to the ground beneath his feet.

In *A Study in Scarlet* Holmes asserts that '"to my trained eyes every mark ... has a meaning"' (84) and in *The Hound of the Baskervilles* he refers to what can be read from '"the gravel page"' (680). There certainly appears to be a superficial comparison between Holmes and Lyell's ways of viewing the world. Both look to everyday landscapes in order to unpack the densely coded information imprinted upon them. In *Principles*, Lyell shows how geological strata could unfold 'as clearly as a written chronicle, the ... sequence of events' which led to its formation.[24] Holmes is certainly able to reconstruct the past from the soil in this way. His interest, by comparison though, extends only as far as the preceding few days and he pursues specific, local details with little interest in generalisable principles. This is where the doubled nature of Holmes's character comes into play: his outsider pose stops short of ever disturbing the satisfied religious contentment of the clients that most closely reflected Doyle's real-life readers. Soil for Holmes was not necessarily a route into Lyell's 'deep past' but rather a metaphor for a secure iteration of middle-class British identity. Watson refers to Hilton Cubitt in 'The Dancing Men' as 'a fine creature . . . of the old English soil' (513) and in *A Study in Scarlet* '"British soil"' (86) stands in for the nation state in need of preservation from the invasion of undesirable peoples and substances.

It is also salient that both the stories and the character of Holmes changed substantially over the years in somewhat contradictory ways. Doyle evidently found it necessary to flesh out the initial picture of Holmes as a kind of intellectual magpie focused solely on crime. In *A Study in Scarlet*, Watson remarks that Holmes's interest in geology is '[p]ractical, but limited'. The clear irony of this is to contrast Holmes with the average late-Victorian polymath: 'Literature.—Nil' 'Philosophy.—Nil' (21). For Holmes at this point, science is not part of an omnivorous desire to learn; he is, in Stamford's derogatory term 'an enthusiast' (16). He needs to understand soil variations across the country in order to identify stains on trouser legs and residues on shoe soles. He is relatively incurious, though, about the long geological upheavals that lead to their underlying formation. Similarly, he understands astronomy only inasmuch as it can help to predict the movements of the tide and changes in weather. He famously affects to be unaware of the heliocentric model of the universe (21).

In *The Sign of Four* Holmes recommends that Watson read Winwood Reade's controversial book *The Martyrdom of Man* which, in 1872, had outlined a Darwinian and largely secular view of world history. In the novel Holmes also adopts a cartoonishly reductive version of early sociology, arguing that '"the individual man is an insoluble puzzle, in the aggregate he becomes a mathematical certainty. You can, for example, never foretell what any one man will do, but you can say with precision what an average number will be up to"' (137). This panoptic view of society recalls the top-down methodology of Wallace, as well as the evolutionary sociology of thinkers like Herbert Spencer who grappled with measuring what he called 'the social aggregate'.[25] This was, at the very least, careless writing since Holmes is frequently shown to be able to codify and index every square inch of skin, hair, dress or manner in a way that directly challenges notions of autonomy and individualism. As Rosemary Jann has noted, Holmes's method adopts the approaches of nascent criminology but applies them to the whole of society: 'it is not just the criminal body, but the entire social body that must be coded'.[26] Holmes thus strips the characters of some of the aura of individualism that characterised late nineteenth-century bourgeois consumer culture. This also suggests that Doyle was not particularly interested in endowing the character with clear, consistent scientific values. Holmes's pose of implied atheism and dispassion would not survive the character's transition to the *Strand* short stories in 1891. In 'The Naval Treaty', for example, Holmes remarks to Watson that '"there is nothing in which deduction is so necessary as in religion . . . Our highest assurance of the goodness of Providence seems to me to rest in the flowers"' (455). This revelation is not depicted as an aberration but as a moment of truth that is usually concealed beneath a scientific, rationalist veneer.

Indeed, Holmes generally works to underpin a catalogue of core bourgeois values: nationalism, property rights, the laws of exchange, the sanctity of wedding vows and the inviolability of the middle-class home. Holmes might seem an odd choice to defend these values: he is apparently asexual, a drug user, evinces deeply impolite and antisocial behaviour and refined aesthetic tastes in the arts. References to science within the stories are thus piecemeal and sometimes contradictory. They emerge in different stories in different ways and establish heterogeneous, often contradictory meanings. Rigorously 'causal' readings of the stories in relation to science are often limited by this fact. 'Casual' readings, though, can yield significant results especially in relation to post-Darwinian science.

In the later stories both Holmes and Watson make more frequent recourse to the language of deep time. In 'The Devil's Foot', Holmes's mental health is damaged to such an extent that he and Watson leave for remote Cornwall 'to avert an absolute breakdown' (955). The landscape there is riven with 'traces of some vanished race which had passed utterly away, and left as its sole record strange monuments of stone, irregular mounds which contained the burned ashes of the dead, and curious earthworks which hinted at prehistoric strife' (955). Holmes finds respite from his everyday occupations by burying himself in the deep past and in the abstruse historical study of the Cornish language. This kind of framing had long been a part of the popular Gothic tradition but in this story it allows Watson to depict Holmes in his later career, nearing retirement and weighing the great cost of his labours. It also ennobles Holmes's efforts on behalf of civilisation in general against the great historical tides that might one day sweep it away entirely with all the other 'forgotten nations' (955). Each defeated criminal represents a potential threat to the order and stability of that civilisation. Lyell had described the great possibilities of his new geology by quoting Barthold Niebuhr, historian of the ancient world: 'he who calls what has vanished back into being, enjoys a bliss like that of creating'.[27] Holmes in this way sublimates his artistic instincts into his work and derives his satisfaction from improbable feats of recovery and re-narration.

Other stories elaborate upon this idea and depict society and its institutions as a fragile assemblage built atop a Darwinian jungle. Holmes's role is to think in clear biological terms about the people that he encounters and about the genetic depredations that might hasten a general reversion to animal laws. In 'The Bruce-Partington Plans', Holmes surveys the foggy London streets from his window: '"See how the figures loom up, are dimly seen, and then blend once more into the cloud-bank. The thief or the murderer could roam London on such a day as the tiger does the jungle, unseen until he pounces"' (913). The story pits Holmes against the spy, Hugo Oberstein, who attempts to steal the secret British plans for a new submarine and sell them to European rivals. The Darwinian framing of the story broadens this individual encounter to incorporate an evolutionary struggle between rival European powers. This evolutionary language recurs notably in 'The Illustrious Client' where Watson encounters the villainous Baron Gruner: 'If ever I saw a murderer's mouth it was there – a cruel, hard gash in the face, compressed, inexorable, and terrible ... [I]t was Nature's danger-signal, set as a warning to his victims' (996).

Doyle's language is instantly evocative of several passages from Darwin's *Descent of Man* that discuss sexual selection and the shared instinct for preservation amongst a community. Darwin argues that breeding groups ensure their long-term survival with signs of 'warning' and 'recognition'.[28] The story tasks Holmes with detaching Gruner from the unshakeable devotion of his English fiancée, Violet de Merville. Violet is '"young, rich, beautiful, accomplished"' and the inheritor of a noble imperial lineage; her father is '"General de Merville of Khyber fame"'. The General, though, has become a '"weak, doddering old man"' in the face of a '"brilliant, forceful rascal like this Austrian"' (986). The plot may simply describe the saving of a vulnerable young woman from an undesirable marriage but the story's descriptive and metaphorical language casts Holmes as nothing less than the preserver of his race and nation against a foreign incursion. His methods supplement and amplify nature's 'warning signal' on behalf of an increasingly fragile Anglophone world order.

In 'The Empty House' Watson writes, 'I knew not what wild beast we were about to hunt down in the dark jungle of criminal London' (488). This metaphorical language is a useful example of the ways in which evolutionary ideas were safely encoded into the stories. London could be depicted as a jungle and its inherent dangers exploited for fictional purposes, but the wilder, more radical implications of the theory were tamed by the imposition of hunting iconography. Holmes makes this slippage clear in 'The Man with the Twisted Lip': '"I [came] to find an enemy ... one of my natural enemies, or, shall I say, my natural prey"' (232). Humans may be part of the evolutionary struggle but they participate by playing the role of a super-predator.

In 'The Blanched Soldier' Holmes takes over narration from the absent Watson and muses that his method 'is but systematized common sense' (1011) while in 'The Lion's Mane' he acknowledges that 'I hold a vast store of out-of-the-way knowledge without scientific system' (1090). As such, the stories establish Holmes as the idealised image of the amateur, self-taught polymath. Indeed, a not insignificant number of stories pit Holmes against villains for whom specialisation has exerted a perverting influence: beetle-browed unfortunates such as James Moriarty, Professor Presbury in 'The Creeping Man' and especially Culverton Smith in 'The Dying Detective'. Smith is a Sumatran plantation owner who becomes an expert in Asiatic diseases and uses this expertise to murder his nephew and attempt to murder Holmes. According to this reading of the stories, Holmes and his work remain tethered to the real world because they are employed in the service of his clients and the interests that they embody on behalf of the readers. In *A Study in Scarlet* Holmes explains that he chooses to focus on '"practical"' areas of knowledge because his '"trade"' depends upon them (24). This keeps him away from abstruse avenues of enquiry with limited application to everyday life.

Though the theories of Lyell, Darwin and Wallace were built upon everyday observation, post-Darwinian science was more likely to suggest that it was built upon everyday common sense. Galton provided scientific legitimation for pervasively racist attitudes and Lombroso described his work as supporting prejudices based on class, dress and appearance. He wrote that his father 'once placed before forty children twenty portraits of thieves and twenty representing great men, and 80% recognised in the first the portraits of bad and deceitful people'.[29] As such, their work was less likely to offend contemporaneous middlebrow sensibilities than to tacitly support them as proof of their veracity.

By the time that post-Darwinian strains of evolutionary and sociological thought were emerging in the 1880s, new magazines like the *English Illustrated Magazine* (1883), the *Strand* (1891) and its imitators, like the *Idler* (1892), were well-placed to popularise them. These magazines would often intersperse short stories by the likes of Doyle, Grant Allen and H. G. Wells with non-fiction articles by the same authors on subjects as diverse as tuberculosis cures (Doyle), natural history studies of spiders and aphids (Allen) and speculations about the military deployment of tanks (Wells). Doyle was receptive to post-Darwinian ideas as they satisfied his relatively superficial interest in science as well as his deep-lying ideological commitment to Empire, race and nation. In 'The Creeping Man', for instance, Holmes disentangles the strange case of the elderly Professor Presbury who injects himself with monkey serum in a doomed attempt to rejuvenate himself. Holmes reflects that scientific attempts to prolong life could have extremely deleterious effects upon society: '"the material, the sensual, the worldly would all prolong their worthless lives ... It would be the survival of the least fit. What sort of cesspool may not our poor world become?"' (1082–3). The story stages a confrontation between the forces of degeneration and those that guard against it. Presbury's fall shows that, in Holmes's words, '"the highest type of man may revert to the animal"' (1082). Holmes thus becomes the watchdog of genetic and moral propriety. The passage plays with the phrase 'survival of the fittest' which had been coined by Spencer in the early 1860s and enthusiastically adopted by Darwin and Wallace. Holmes inverts the meaning to describe his fears about a society overtaken by 'worldly' sensualists and criminals. His every-day actions are thus encased in service to this wider narrative: '[s]uddenly the dreamer disappeared, and Holmes, the man of action, sprang from his chair' (1083).

'The Creeping Man' is a relatively benign example of this discourse in the Holmes stories but there are also some glaring instances of racially charged language that directly recall the polygenic worldviews of Galton and Lombroso. In his essay on 'Restrictions in Marriage', Galton warned against the dangers of both miscegenation (inter-racial breeding) and incestuous intra-familial breeding. He wrote in terms of disgust and 'loathing' at both prospects which he saw as linked threats: 'close likeness, as between the members of a thorough-bred stock, causes some sexual indifference: thus highly bred dogs lose much of their sexual desire for one another, and are apt to consort with mongrels'.[30] In 'Wisteria Lodge' a suspect is described as being '"a huge and hideous mulatto, with yellowish features of a pronounced negroid type"' (880). The suspect's mysterious return to the crime scene is ultimately explained by a helpful text of Eurocentric anthropology: '"Here is a quotation from Eckermann's *Voodooism and the Negroid Religions* ... our savage friend was very orthodox in his ritual"' (887). In 'The Three Gables' Watson evinces a racialised disgust in describing the 'hideous mouth' (1023) of Steve Dixie, a 'negro prize-fighter' (1028). Holmes, meanwhile, taunts Dixie saying '"I won't ask you to sit down, for I don't like the smell of you"' and pretending to reach for his '"scent-bottle"' (1028). In *The Sign of Four* ethnographic studies offer Holmes a better understanding of Tonga, the aboriginal antagonist from the Andaman Islands. Holmes's volume describes the people as '"fierce, morose"', '"naturally hideous"' and '"[s]o intract-able"' that they resist even the benign blandishments of British colonialism

(128). In so doing, it also affirms some of post-Darwinian science's base conflations of criminality with poverty and racial otherness.

Conclusion

It is possible broadly to identify three stages of Doyle's relationship with evolution and deep time. First, as a young man, he embraced materialist thinking (as opposed to the idealism of religious explanations of the world) and allowed it to shape a radical and iconoclastic view both of the world and of the significance of humanity within it (*Memories* 69). Later, he demurred from this and preferred to accentuate Darwin and Wallace's roles as masculine explorers and virile progenitors of ideas. Finally, in his middle age, he fully accepted spiritualism as truth and saw materialists as cases 'stuck in arrested development' (*Memories* 32).

The Holmes stories belong to the middle phase of this progression. They carry imaginative echoes of these grand, sweeping ideas. Like glacial erratics, isolated tropes dot the stories as evidence of the author's former interests. The Holmes stories sit easily alongside Doyle's autobiographical fiction where he began to find a new accommodation between science and religious niceties. The young couple at the centre of *A Duet, with an Occasional Chorus* (1889), for example, visit Westminster Abbey: 'Here was Darwin who revolutionized zoology, and here was Isaac Newton who gave a new direction to astronomy. Here were old Ben Jonson, and Stephenson the father of railways, and Livingstone of Africa, and Wordsworth, and Kingsley, and Arnold'.[31] There is no sense that the philosophical consequences of evolutionary ideas might warp either the fiction itself or its underlying middlebrow values. Darwin was valuable only inasmuch as he represented the continuity of national prestige rather than the disruption of revolutionary change. The Holmes stories fit into this part of Doyle's career by exploiting fragments of scientific insight to exaggerate the threats of individual antagonists and to valorise Holmes's endeavours against them. By writing in this way, Doyle also expressed far greater affinity for post-Darwinian thinkers than Darwinian ones.

This impression is reinforced by another piece of autobiographical fiction, *The Stark Munro Letters* (1895): 'Is it not glorious to think that evolution is still living and acting – that if we have an anthropoid ape as an ancestor, we may have archangels for our posterity?' This consoling mixture of evolution with soft-focus sermonising was blended seamlessly with a crude reading of racial progress: 'Nature, still working on the lines of evolution, strengthens the race in ... the killing off and extinction of those who are morally weak. This is accomplished by drink and immorality.'[32] Doyle retreated from the openness and uncertainty at the heart of mid-century radicalism and found himself more confident once those ideas had mutated into more reactionary forms. He was able to disregard detailed scientific specifics and focus on larger narratives about race and nationhood. He was in no danger, to use his own words, of 'los[ing] himself in the subdivisions of the Lepidoptera'.[33] A sentence buried at the end of his literary essay *Through the Magic Door* (1907) suggests that he imagined Holmes as an open, generalisable signifier of science which could be loosely applied to any field or withdrawn at will: 'The mere suspicion of scientific thought or scientific methods has a great charm in any branch of literature, however far it may be removed from actual research'.[34]

Notes

1. Gillian Beer, 'Discourses of the Island', in Frederick Amrine (ed.), *Literature and Science as Modes of Expression* (London: Kluwer Academic Publishers, 1989), 1–27 (8).
2. Frances Darwin (ed.), *The Life and Letters of Charles Darwin* (London: John Murray, 1887), 55.
3. Charles Lyell, *Principles of Geology* (London: John Murray, 1837), 311.
4. Ibid., 182.
5. Charles Darwin, *The Descent of Man* (London: John Murray, 1874), 11.
6. Alfred Russel Wallace, 'On the Law which has Regulated the Introduction of New Species', *Annals and Magazine of Natural History* 12 (1855), 184–96 (192).
7. Charles Lyell, *The Geological Evidence of the Antiquity of Man* (London: John Murray, 1868), 356.
8. Lyell, *Geological Evidence*, 79.
9. Darwin, *Descent of Man*, 176.
10. Edwin Ray Lankester, *Degeneration: A Chapter in Darwinism* (London: Macmillan, 1880), 29.
11. Francis Galton, *Hereditary Genius* (London: Macmillan, 1914), 323, 58.
12. Cesare Lombroso and Gina Lombroso Ferrero, *Criminal Man According to the Classification of Cesare Lombroso* (London: G. P. Putnam's Sons, 1911), 18.
13. Arthur Conan Doyle, *Through the Magic Door* (New York: McClure, 1908), 256.
14. Ibid., 45.
15. Ibid., 244.
16. Ibid., 246.
17. Ibid., 247.
18. Harry How, 'A Day with Dr. Conan Doyle', *Strand Magazine* 4 (August 1892), 182–8 (188).
19. Arthur Conan Doyle, *The Firm of Girdlestone* (New York: H. M. Caldwell, 1890), 31.
20. Jukes De Styrap, *The Young Practitioner* (London: H. K. Lewis, 1890), 55.
21. Doyle, *Through the Magic Door*, 249.

22. Lawrence Frank, *Victorian Detective Fiction and the Nature of Evidence: the Scientific Investigations of Poe, Dickens, and Doyle* (Basingstoke: Palgrave Macmillan, 2003), 7.
23. Lyell, *Geological Evidence*, 16, 62.
24. Lyell, *Principles of Geology*, 263.
25. Herbert Spencer, *The Principles of Sociology*, vol. 1 (New York: D. Appleton and Company, 1897), 11.
26. Rosemary Jann, 'Sherlock Holmes Codes the Social Body', *ELH* 57:3 (1990), 685–708 (687).
27. Lyell, *Principles of Geology*, 74.
28. Darwin, *Descent of Man*, 312.
29. Lombroso and Lombroso, *Criminal Man*, 50–1.
30. Francis Galton, *Essays in Eugenics* (London: The Eugenics Education Society, 1909), 53–4.
31. Arthur Conan Doyle, *A Duet, with an Occasional Chorus* (London: Grant Richards, 1899), 53.
32. Arthur Conan Doyle, *The Stark Munro Letters* (London: Smith, Elder and Company, 1912), 44, 101.
33. Conan Doyle, *Through the Magic Door*, 249.
34. Ibid., 254–5.

8

STEPHAN KARSCHAY

Doyle and the Criminal Body

'It is your commonplace, featureless crimes which are really puzzling, just as a commonplace face is the most difficult to identify.' ('The Red-headed League' 183)

The steady rise of detective fiction in Victorian Britain, which reached a high point in the iconic figure of Sherlock Holmes at the end of the nineteenth century, is closely bound up with two important developments: the evolution of criminal anthropology as a field of scientific research and the establishment of a professional national police force. While officers of the law focussed on the act of crime and its possible prevention, criminologists investigated the nature of criminality in order to identify its origins and causes. The figure of the literary detective partakes in both of these endeavours: Sherlock Holmes investigates criminal acts by drawing on theories of criminality that help him to *apprehend* (in both senses of the word) criminals and their crimes. Just like nineteenth-century criminological discourse, Arthur Conan Doyle's Holmes stories search for the unique characteristics of crime and construct criminality in distinctive ways which interrogate and, at times, destabilise scientific assumptions about the nature of the criminal offender: are the seeds of crime to be found in social conditions, or is criminality predetermined by evolutionary biology? What is the relative significance of nature and nurture in the development of crime? And is criminality only visible in the results it wreaks or can it be detected on the face of the criminal offender?

Different criminologists answered these questions in different ways, and the dominance of Cesare Lombroso (1835–1909) as the founding father of criminal anthropology in the popular imagination should not gloss over the fact that his deterministic theories were met with considerable criticism from continental as well as British commentators. This chapter attempts to do justice to the broad spectrum of responses to Lombrosian criminology by reading a wide variety of Doyle's stories through the multifaceted prisms offered by nineteenth- and early-twentieth-century debates on crime and the nature of the criminal. The Holmes stories – and detective fiction more generally – reflect these disciplinary arguments and contribute to their complexity in creative and entertaining ways. While often mobilising the sensational language employed by Lombroso and incorporating ideas of atavistic reversion and infant criminality into their plots, the Holmes stories also reveal an ambivalent stance towards questions of biological and social determinism, as well as a generically motivated distrust about the supposed stigmatic visibility of criminality.

Criminal Beginnings: Inborn Criminality and Atavistic Reversion

At the beginning of 'The Greek Interpreter', Holmes and Watson discuss 'the question of atavism and hereditary aptitudes' to determine 'how far any singular gift in an individual was due to his ancestry and how far to his own early training' (435). Considering the great emphasis that the detective puts on honing his observational skills and his method of deduction, it may come as a surprise to the reader that his estimation about the relative influence of heredity and the environment – i.e. nature versus nurture – comes firmly down on the side of the former. He assures Watson that his intellectual prowess as a detective runs in the family, with his brother Mycroft possessing the same ability '"in a larger degree"' (435) than Holmes himself. That the determining influence of heredity can act in favour of beneficial qualities as much as criminal ones is made evident in the conclusion of the mystery that Holmes and Watson are about to solve. The story's central villain, Wilson Kemp, a violent kidnapper and blackmailer, proves to be 'a man of the foulest antecedents' (446). Similarly, in 'The Final Problem', Holmes's archenemy Professor James Moriarty – despite being '"of good birth and excellent education"' – is characterised as having '"hereditary tendencies of the most diabolical kind"' with a '"criminal strain . . . in his blood"' (470–1).

The understanding of criminality as an inborn quality was the central paradigm around which the Italian psychiatrist Lombroso built his science of criminal anthropology in the second half of the nineteenth century with his multi-volume compendium *Criminal Man* (*L'uomo delinquente*, 1876–97). By understanding crime as 'a product of any organism's physical constitution', Lombroso tried to shift criminological attention away from the criminal act to the agent of crime in order to make plausible the high rates of recidivism, i.e. the conspicuous number of repeat offenders amongst the criminal class.[1] For Lombroso, the recognition of a biological predisposition to crime was 'not merely an idea, but a revelation'.[2] Reminiscing about the development of his scientific convictions towards the end of his career, Lombroso describes the post-mortem examination of the notorious Italian felon Giuseppe Villella, in which he claims to have exposed a curious structure at the base of the criminal's skull (the 'median occipital fossetta') commonly found in lower animals such as rodents.[3] This anatomical curiosity prompted Lombroso to characterise the criminal as 'an atavistic being who reproduces in his person the ferocious instincts of primitive humanity and the inferior animals'.[4] To Lombroso, crime constituted what Daniel Pick has usefully labelled a 'bio-historical anachronism', committed by individuals whose anatomy and physiology were arrested at an earlier developmental stage than that of modern man.[5] The technical term for this phenomenon, used by Lombroso and referenced by Holmes and Watson in 'The Greek Interpreter', is atavism, from the Latin *atavus* for 'ancestor' and described by the evolutionary biologist Charles Darwin (albeit without using the word) as 'the principle of reversion, by which a long-lost structure is called into existence'.[6] In this understanding, criminals were conceptualised as degenerate throwbacks to an earlier stage in humanity's evolutionary development so that the violent transgressions of the criminal offender became signs of his animalistic nature.

From the moment of its inception, criminal anthropology was anything but uncontroversial, particularly with French criminologists like Alexandre Lacassagne (1843–1924) and Gabriel Tarde (1843–1904) advocating a stronger focus on the social milieu of crime as opposed to the dominant biological determinism of Lombroso. Even though the first English translations of *L'uomo delinquente* only became available posthumously in 1911, many of Lombroso's articles had appeared in British periodicals throughout the 1890s, including an extensive summary of his main ideas under the title 'Criminal Anthropology: Its Origin and Application' in the journal *Forum* in 1895. Britain also witnessed the most famous endorsement of Lombroso's criminological theories in Havelock Ellis's *The Criminal* (1890) and their most comprehensive repudiation in Charles Goring's *The English Convict* (1913). Ellis's popular account summarised and celebrated the tenets of criminal anthropology as much as it relativised Lombroso's emphasis on atavism, while stressing the importance of social factors in the aetiology of crime (an influence the Italian criminologist had, in fact, never fully rejected). Despite these critical reservations, Lombroso's name took a peculiar hold in the popular imagination as is evident in Mina Harker's classification of the eponymous vampire in Bram Stoker's *Dracula* (1897) as 'a criminal and of criminal type'.[7] It was the identification of criminals by their telltale 'stigmata' that tapped into a popular earlier fascination with phrenology and physiognomy, which transformed criminological practice into something of a pastime for amateur detectives – what William Greenslade described as 'a game that anyone could play'.[8]

Throughout the Holmes canon, Watson consistently colours his language with the sensationalist expressions used by scientists like Lombroso, who characterises the 'born criminal' (a term he adopted from his student Enrico Ferri) as a creature relishing 'the terrible pleasure of blood' and driven by an 'irresistible craving for evil for its own sake'.[9] In 'The Reigate Squires', a tale of burglary and murder, Watson detects in the eyes of one of the two culprits '"the ferocity of a dangerous wild beast"' (406) and, sure enough, young Cunningham proves to be '"a perfect demon"' (409). When Watson is reunited with Holmes after the detective's resurrection in 'The Empty House', the doctor proves as reliable as ever, following Holmes on a dangerous mission without knowing 'what wild beast [they] were about to hunt down in the dark jungle of criminal London' (488). When they have safely arrested Colonel Sebastian Moran, Moriarty's second-in-command, the ex-soldier appears to Watson 'wonderfully like a tiger' with 'his savage eyes and bristling moustache' (492). The language of atavistic reversion is pervasive in the Holmes stories, and at least one criminal offender uses it in his self-characterisation during the closing confession. In 'The Cardboard Box', the jealous husband who has killed his wife and her lover, recalls how he '"was like a wild beast . . . that had tasted blood"' on that fateful night and admits to '"a kind of savage joy"' (900, 901) in his macabre plan to send his meddling sister-in-law the gory parcel that contains the severed ears of his victims.

In explaining crime as the result of an inborn predisposition to criminality, Lombroso employed a curious discursive strategy that successively linked criminals, the members of non-white races and children in an extended racist analogy, thus foregrounding their supposedly common anatomical and behavioural features. Apart from physical characteristics such as 'thinness of body hair', 'overdeveloped jaws and cheekbones' and 'thick and curly hair', criminals and the 'colored races' supposedly share a whole roster of temperamental deficiencies: 'insensitivity to pain, lack of moral sense, revulsion for work, absence of remorse, lack of foresight . . . vanity, superstitiousness, self-importance, and . . . an underdeveloped concept of divinity and morality'.[10] Underpinning these indiscriminate juxtapositions is a concept first formulated by the German Darwinist Ernst Haeckel as the biogenetic law of evolutionary recapitulation, according to which ontogeny (the evolution of an individual organism during gestation) repeats phylogeny (the evolutionary development of the species as a whole).

This notion is obliquely referenced in *The Sign of Four* when Watson gazes at 'the prints of a naked foot' in Bartholomew Sholto's attic, which are 'clear, well-defined, perfectly formed, but scarce half the size of those of an ordinary man'; his whispered response to Holmes shows how disconcerted the doctor is by the implication of the footmarks: '"a child has done this horrid thing"' (112). Holmes himself admits to having been '"staggered for the moment"', but after a little reflection, the solution appears '"quite natural"' to the detective (112). Sholto's murder was not the deed of a child but committed by Tonga, an inhabitant of the Pacific Andaman Islands, whose inhabitants are judged by the gazetteer that Holmes consults as possibly '"the smallest race upon this earth"' (127). Watson's troubling descriptions of Tonga as an 'unhallowed dwarf' and a 'savage, distorted creature' (139, 138) are in line with the racist assumptions of nineteenth-century criminological and anthropological discourse. Lombroso's perceived analogy between the criminal, the savage and the child, furthermore, can be harnessed to explain why Holmes thinks the solution of the case 'quite natural'. The savage islander is criminal by nature and in respect of his underdeveloped moral sense, which is signalled by his stunted growth: he is just like a child.

Criminal Heirs: Heredity and the Transmission of Criminality

Not only were criminals likened to children, but children were understood by Lombroso to be, by default, of a criminal nature. After all, if ontogeny is accepted to repeat phylogeny, then infant criminality is the necessary consequence of that formula. In the third edition of *Criminal Man* (1884), Lombroso locates the 'seeds' of criminality 'in man's early life', convinced that children 'lack moral sense' and show all manner of behavioural and emotive patterns otherwise found in adult criminals such as anger, vengefulness, jealousy, mendacity, cold-heartedness, cruelty, laziness, vanity and a penchant for alcohol, gambling, obscenity and masturbation:[11] 'In general, the child prefers bad to good. He is more cruel than kind because he experiences strong emotions and has a sense of unlimited power.'[12] Inspired by Lombroso, Havelock Ellis wrote that the 'child is naturally, by his organisation, nearer to the animal, to the savage, to the criminal, than the adult'.[13] At the same time, criminologists like Lombroso and Ellis sought to reassure potentially disquieted readers that children would outgrow their criminal characteristics and develop into morally aware adults.

At least one Holmes case, 'The Sussex Vampire', supports this understanding of infant criminality as a 'natural' stage in the ontogenetic evolution of humankind. When, in this story, Holmes deflates the threat of vampirism by identifying the teenage half-brother of the assaulted baby as the real culprit ('"I saw such jealousy, such cruel hatred, as I have seldom seen in a human face"'), the shock to the boy's father could hardly have been greater in the case of a supernatural explanation: '"Good God! It is incredible!"' (1043). Holmes's recommendation of '"a year at sea ... for Master Jacky"'

(1044) suggests that the detective deems the boy's criminal tendencies remediable, and in this he is thoroughly in line with Lombroso's criminological advice: 'Better than punishment in the training of children are preventive measures such as good air, light and space, a diet of vegetables rather than meat, avoidance of alcohol, and sexual abstinence'.[14] Holmes's counselling of the boy's father is steeped in the masculinist discourse of imperial ideology that holds up the values of hard work and military discipline to throw off the traces of a biologically programmed criminality and develop into a fully formed and morally upright human being.

A more substantial and creative treatment of criminological theories of infant criminality is offered in 'The Copper Beeches', in which a young governess begs Holmes to help her determine whether it is safe to accept a position that has been offered to her in the Rucastle household under the most bizarre of conditions: shorn of her beautiful long hair and clad in a dress of a particular shade of electric blue, she is regularly required to sit on a chair in the drawing room and listen to her employer's humorous tales without ever being allowed to look out of the window. The case gradually becomes more sinister, and Holmes manages to expose a Gothic plot of female dispossession, incarceration and madness, which threatens to engulf the governess. However, Holmes finds the clue to resolving the mystery to lie with little Edward, the six-year-old son of the villain Rucastle: '"The most serious point in the case is the disposition of the child"' (329). Described by the governess as '"utterly spoiled and so ill-natured a little creature"', who is '"small for his age, with a head ... quite disproportionately large"' and who succumbs to '"savage fits of passion and gloomy intervals of sulking"' (324), little Edward appears like the stereotypical child of Lombroso's criminological textbook. Far from having '"little to do with [the governess's] story"' (324), the pronounced criminality of the boy points Holmes towards the hereditary strain of criminality running in the Rucastle household. As he explains to Watson: '"I have frequently gained my first real insight into the character of parents by studying their children. This child's disposition is abnormally cruel, merely for cruelty's sake, and whether he derives this from his smiling father, as I should suspect, or from his mother, it bodes evil for the poor girl who is in their power"' (330).

Criminal Careers: Nature, Nurture and the Evolution of Crime

The Hound of the Baskervilles is Doyle's most sustained engagement with the hereditary transmission of criminal tendencies, a concern neatly inscribed in its Gothic plot of manorial usurpation and supernatural persecution. This novel of familial inheritance opens with questions about the teleological directedness of evolution and subsequently provides an illustration of hereditary processes through an analysis of family portraits that, at first glance, seems to support Lombroso's belief in the determining influence of heredity by identifying the villain Stapleton as an atavistic descendant of the wicked Hugo Baskerville. Holmes explains the former's criminality as the natural consequence of his paternal descent; after all, Stapleton is the son of Sir Charles's youngest brother Rodger, who holds the dubious distinction of being '"of the old masterful Baskerville strain"', rendering him '"the black sheep of the family"' (681).

Yet this determinist narrative is undercut by the novel's depiction of the other male members of the Baskerville family: Sir Charles, the murdered squire, and his next-of-kin Sir Henry, who may possess 'the fiery temper' of his ancestors but is nonetheless a 'gentleman' of generally 'quiet assurance' (689, 685). This suggests, however, that the criminality of an individual is not necessarily the inevitable outcome of a diseased genealogy (nature) but is much more susceptible to chance, and that other factors – climatic, social, educational – can have a mitigating or indeed exacerbating influence. In 'The Empty House', Holmes says as much when he attempts an explanation of the workings of heredity: '"I have a theory that the individual represents in his development the whole procession of his ancestors, and that ... a sudden turn to good or evil stands for some strong influence which came into the line of his pedigree"' (494). This point is underscored in *The Hound of the Baskervilles* by the depiction of the Notting Hill murderer Selden who, on the surface, appears as a prime example of Lombroso's atavistic born criminal with his 'terrible animal face' and 'the peculiar ferocity of [his] crime' (725, 701). Despite Selden's branding as an incorrigible criminal offender whose presence in the neighbourhood constitutes a real danger to the community, he comes of an upright, hard-working family. Watson finds it difficult to believe that Selden's sister, Mrs Barrymore, 'this stolidly respectable person', is 'of the same blood as one of the most notorious criminals in the country' (722). It is clear from Mrs Barrymore's account of her brother's childhood that the loving attentions lavished on Selden fostered a strong sense of entitlement in the boy, and '"wicked companions"' (723) started him on the spiral of violence and crime that nearly landed him on the scaffold.

Scepticism about criminal anthropology's biological determinism was often compounded by a disapproval of Lombroso's general methodology: the construction of analogies between widely differing groups of people, the use of anecdotes, proverbs and examples drawn from literary history, together with the lack of sufficient control groups for his statistical calculations were all marked out for criticism at one point or another in Lombroso's career. In the early twentieth century, the statistician Charles Goring offered the most rigorous challenge to Lombroso's methodology with the publication of *The English Convict* (1913), which dismisses his 'unscientific methods' and 'superstitious belief' as little more than an 'imaginative luxury'.[15] Lombroso had frequently harnessed popular Italian proverbs (such as 'Red men or bearded women are best greeted from afar') to prove the visibility of criminality, suggesting that his study of the criminal only confirmed what had long been inscribed in popular wisdom and folk songs.[16] Goring, by contrast, pursued his investigation in the most careful statistical fashion to offer an explanation of the proclivity for criminality (what he called 'the criminal diathesis') by paying equal attention to biological and environmental factors, the former indeed suggesting a higher correlation with criminality than the latter.[17]

That environmental factors might be at least as important as biology in the genesis of crime and the evolution of a criminal nature had already been conceded by Lombroso's greatest populariser in Britain, Havelock Ellis. Despite his evident admiration for the founder of criminal anthropology, Ellis shows reservations about some of Lombroso's most fundamental convictions such as the prominent role of atavism in the development of criminality. In *The Criminal*, Ellis attempts to do justice to the complexity of his subject by reminding his readers that criminal heredity was comprised of two factors: 'the element of innate disposition' and 'the element of contagion from social environment'. One of these alone would not be sufficient 'to determine the child in the direction of crime'; in other words, criminality needed to be understood as the product of a combination of both biological and social influences.[18] The perpetrators of crime in the Holmes canon are only rarely the product of a diseased constitution on its own. Even the atavistic Notting Hill murderer is merely predisposed to crime by his biological make-up, and it is only through the malignant influence of his peers that Selden's descent into vice and crime is triggered.

Criminal Bodies: Visibility and Invisibility

Holmes's interpretive strategy is strikingly akin to the methodology of the medical practitioner, thus causing (in Maria Cairney's phrase) a 'category slippage between "criminal" and "patient" and ... "doctor" and "detective"'.[19] In *The Sign of Four*, Holmes himself establishes the link between the science of detection and medical diagnosis by appropriating the language of Watson's profession as he acknowledges that the discovery of new evidence '"confirms my diagnosis, as you doctors express it"' (118). This association of crime and disease is a recurring feature of the Holmes stories throughout the canon. In 'The Blanched Soldier', for instance, Holmes does not uncover a real crime at all but instead diagnoses a debilitating case of leprosy, which forces the afflicted patient into a self-imposed quarantine at his family's estate and compels the soldier's parents to adopt a suspicious inhospitality towards a visiting friend.

Lombroso himself founded the discipline of criminal anthropology on the conviction that criminality would be readily discernible to the diagnostic gaze of the medical expert, who could 'read' the traces of inborn depravity on the body of the criminal offender. With the help of a wide range of anthro-pometrical devices (such as the craniometer to determine the circumference of the skull) and algometrical instruments (such as the algometer to gauge sensitivity to pain), Lombroso and other nineteenth-century criminologists attempted to identify, measure and catalogue the physical 'stigmata' of the criminal in order to develop a scientific methodology for the identification of criminality. To record results and provide evidence for his theory, Lombroso created a photographic atlas from diverse sources designed to convey the baffling variety of criminal features as well as the physical characteristics common to all criminals. In a series of 219 photographs of thieves, pickpock-ets, murderers, assaulters, swindlers, forgers, sex offenders and bigamists, the Italian criminologist identified a long list of stigmata that marked the criminal as abnormal and underdeveloped: large jaws, a 'scanty' beard, enlarged sinus cavities, a 'shifty gaze', thick hair, 'jug ears', jutting cheek-bones, strabismus (or 'wandering eye'), sloping foreheads, prognathism and a 'feminine physiognomy' contributed to 'an almost family resemblance' that distinguished the physiognomy of the criminal type, while at the same time aligning it with stereotypical representations of non-European races.[20] The parallel between the medical criminologist and the literary detective is striking: both treat bodies like texts that can be subjected to a rigorous process of decoding and interpretation. Physical markers become signifiers that point to an underlying meaning: the criminologist reads them as con-firmation of a criminal nature, the detective as clues to the solution of a mystery. In both cases, physical bodies become bodies of evidence.

Given this close association of disease and crime, it is only logical that the medical doctor Watson performs the most extensive physiognomic readings throughout the Holmes canon. In 'A Scandal in Bohemia', Watson attempts to determine their masked client's personality in the exposed lower part of his face: 'he appeared to be a man of strong character, with a thick, hanging lip, and a long, straight chin suggestive of resolution pushed to the length of obstinacy' (164). When the doctor first meets Mary Morstan in *The Sign of Four*, he vows never before to have seen 'a face which gave a clearer promise of a refined and sensitive nature' (94). By the same reading strategy that allows him to evaluate characters of untainted integrity, Watson time and again identifies inward depravity in the stories' villains. In *A Study in Scarlet*, he offers a Lombrosian reading of the murdered Enoch J. Drebber that highlights the dead man's atavistic nature. Drebber's features 'bespoke vice of the most malignant type' (36): a 'low forehead, blunt nose, and prognathous jaw' all contribute to the man's 'singularly simious and ape-like appearance' (29). Significantly, however, Drebber is the victim rather than the culprit in this case, and Watson's recording of the actual perpetrator's features is, by comparison, far less detailed and more opaque: Jefferson Hope's is a 'dazed, savage face' (51), which bespeaks the assassin's surprise at being arrested and his passionate hatred of his victims – but none of Drebber's inborn proclivity to crime.

While accepting the deterministic certainties of criminology's positivism to a certain extent, therefore, this first Holmes story displaces them onto the victim of the case for obvious generic reasons. If criminals were always easily recognisable through a cataloguing of their atavistic characteristics, the Holmes stories' appropriation of criminological theories would severely limit the genre's potential to surprise its readers. Detective fiction, in other words, is less interested in the criminal *type* (as Lombroso was) but in criminal *identity* – as in 'whodunit'. In *A Study in Scarlet*, then, the typing of Drebber as criminal does not resolve the mystery, and the extended second half of the novel ('The Country of the Saints'), in which Watson's first-person account is superseded by an authorial third-person narration, provides the backstory that motivates the first half's plot of persistent persecution and assassination. By assigning the detection of criminality through visible stigmata a secondary importance at best, the Holmes stories oscillate between the alternating positions of endorsement and disavowal of Lombrosian criminology's entrenched positivism.

This uncertainty about the ready visibility of criminality becomes increasingly pronounced in the later Holmes stories. In 'The Illustrious Client', for instance, Watson provides a detailed reading of Baron Adelbert Gruner that emphasises the Austrian aristocrat's physical merits: Baron Gruner is 'a remarkably handsome man', whose 'European reputation for beauty was fully deserved' given his 'graceful and active lines', his 'large, dark, languorous eyes' and his 'regular and pleasing' features (996). The baron's pleasant appearance is so deceptive that it apparently requires the expertise of the medical man to isolate Gruner's single stigmatic marker, 'his straight, thin-lipped mouth', well-hidden behind a carefully groomed moustache: 'If ever I saw a murderer's mouth it was there – a cruel, hard gash in the face, compressed, inexorable, and terrible' (996). In Lombrosian fashion, Watson here perceives 'Nature's danger-signal' (996) – a phrase lifted from the title of a criminological article by J. Holt Schooling published in 1898 and also used in a description of Moriarty's companion, Colonel Moran, in 'The Empty House' (492). However, only at first glance does this suggest the story's unquestioning endorsement of criminal anthropology's reading strategies. Watson does not deduce Gruner's criminal nature *from* the latter's features but reads meaning *into* one of several facial characteristics. The result of this operation is to highlight both Watson's *a priori* assumptions (he already knows Gruner to be a murderer) and criminology's largely arbitrary identification of criminal stigmata. It is telling, then, that Watson is a more devoted physiognomist than Holmes, who admonishes his companion in 'A Scandal in Bohemia' to observe rather than merely see, and to be wary of '"twist[ing] facts to suit theories, instead of theories to suit facts"' (163). In this respect, Holmes's cautionary remarks anticipate the findings of Charles Goring, who in 1913 provided statistical data to reject Lombroso's stigmatically marked 'born criminal' as fictional: 'The physical and mental constitution of both criminals and law-abiding persons … are identical. There is no such thing as an anthropological criminal type.'[21]

'The Norwood Builder', a case of feigned murder, wrongful incrimination and fraud, playfully negotiates the question of criminality's ready visibility. A young lawyer, John Hector McFarlane, must defend himself against the accusation of murdering Jonas Oldacre, and the defendant's handsome appearance makes Watson hopeful that the jury might exonerate him – a position Holmes considers '"dangerous"', quoting the past case of a '"mild-mannered, Sunday-school young man"' who turned out to be a '"terrible murderer"' (504). When it emerges that the crime was staged by the supposed victim, the narrative at first seems to endorse the usefulness of physiognomy in the identification of criminality. Oldacre has 'an odious face – crafty, vicious, malignant, with shifty, light-gray eyes and white lashes' (508), a clear variation of Lombroso's typical criminal offender. Since Oldacre's ex-fiancée further characterises him as '"more like a malignant and cunning ape than a human being"' (503), criminal anthropology's discursive strategy of reading physical stigmata as indexical signs of an individual's atavistic nature seems to be corroborated as sound. Yet the pivot on which the plot hinges is precisely that appearances are deceptive and prone to be misread. In the end, the man who appeared guilty (despite his good looks) is acquitted against all odds, while the *invisible* victim is brought to light as the real (stigmatically marked) culprit in a double reversal that simultaneously corroborates and undermines the semiological certainties of criminal anthropology. Holmes's warning to Lestrade about '"how deceptive appearances may be"' (506) is highly ambiguous in light of the case's solution, as it can be read both ironically and literally. In this sense, the Holmes stories treat physiognomy as, at best, circumstantial evidence which, as Holmes reminds Watson in 'The Boscombe Valley Mystery', '"may seem to point very straight to one thing, but if you shift your own point of view a little, you may find it pointing in an equally uncompromising manner to something entirely different"' (204).

Criminal Apprehension: The Detective and/as Forensic Technology

The deceptiveness of appearances is nowhere more evident than in detective fiction's fascination with the entire arsenal of identity obfuscation: disguises, masks, multiple identities and alibis. The dangerous possibility – not so much of misreading bodies of evidence – but rather of subjecting forged evidence to the scrutiny necessary for the successful identification of criminal individuals, energised literary detection. It also produced two competing developments in the history of forensic technology: the system of measuring, documenting and storing anthropometrical data developed by the French criminologist Alphonse Bertillon (1853–1914) and the ultimately more successful technique of recording and decoding fingerprints (dactyloscopy) as pioneered by Charles Darwin's cousin, the polymath Francis Galton (1822–1911). While both strategies realised the importance of photography for modern forensics, Bertillon's 'signaletics' (later labelled 'Bertillonage') relied on the compilation and archivisation of a much wider body of information to be used for the correct identification of recidivistic criminals. Allan Sekula has described how Bertillon in the 1880s used frontal and profile pictures of repeat offenders (taken with meticulously calibrated cameras to allow for instant visual comparisons) and combined them with detailed shorthand descriptions of physical peculiarities, and a numeric code that recorded eleven measurements of the suspect's body (including height, length of arm, foot and spine as well as cranial circumference) to produce an early type of mug shot – the *portrait parlé* that would figuratively spell out an individual's criminal history.[22]

By contrast, Galton's *Finger Prints* (1892) attempted to establish the papillary ridges of the human hand as 'in some respects the most important of all anthropological data',[23] which could be used to supplement the Bertillon system with physiological details that would remain persistent 'from birth to death' and provide 'an incomparably surer criterion of identity than any other bodily feature'.[24] Galton admitted that his method of classifying ridges into arches, loops and whorls was, at best, of auxiliary importance for searching the registers and archives of criminal intelligence bureaus, which – in this respect – were better served by Bertillon; yet with regard to the unequivocal identification of individuals, Galton's conviction about the use-value of his system was unshakeable: 'There can be no doubt that the evidential value of identity afforded by prints of two or three of the fingers, is so great as to render it superfluous to seek confirmation from other sources'.[25] While Bertillonage originally enjoyed wide success from its implementation in the 1880s, particularly in France, Galton's research on fingerprinting triggered an at times rancorous debate between the two researchers on the relative merits of their methods. Ronald R. Thomas has shown how opinions on this argument were divided along national boundaries, and the Metropolitan police in London adopted Galton's methodology as early as 1901, while their French counterparts in law enforcement only accepted fingerprint identification in 1914.[26] Ultimately, Bertillon's storage of data proved too unwieldy for the practicalities of police work, and dactyloscopy supplanted anthropometry in the field of criminal identification on an international scale.

Even though the Holmes stories only reference Bertillon (not Galton) by name, the developments in fingerprinting proved at least as relevant for detective fiction, and Bertillonage seems to have been only initially endorsed by Doyle without reservation. While Holmes still expresses 'enthusiastic admiration of the French savant' (460) in 'The Naval Treaty', nine years later in *The Hound of the Baskervilles*, he is somewhat nettled by Dr Mortimer's personal ranking that places him merely as '"the second highest expert in Europe"' (672) with Bertillon taking pride of place. It is telling, however, that Bertillon figures so prominently only in Mortimer's '"precisely scientific mind"'; as '"a practical man of affairs"', Holmes's standing is unimpeachable (672, 673). After all, the practicalities of establishing the identities of victims and perpetrators, of producing witnesses and eliminating suspects are the detective's primary business, rather than the archival indexing and storing of criminal data. It is true that Holmes's encyclopaedic knowledge of past criminal cases and his metaphorical 'brain-attic' are of invaluable help in several cases; yet Holmes's insistent warning that this mental space cannot simply '"distend to any extent"' (21) and should thus only be stacked with tools that are of direct practical help to the detective's line of work, could also be read as a warning against Bertillon's overfraught archive. The correct decoding of physical traces such as partial handprints and footmarks, by contrast, are of crucial importance to the correct solution of a case from the beginning of the series, when in *A Study in Scarlet* the murderer uses his finger to write a gory message onto a wall at the crime scene. Similarly, footprints and their correct interpretation are a recurring feature of the canon, and Holmes himself has written a monograph on '"the tracing of footsteps"' (91). Ronald R. Thomas has convincingly demonstrated how Holmes's strategies as 'an expert interpreter of the *language* continually being written by the body' even pre-date those later developed in the field of forensic technology.[27]

In the same way that the Holmes stories support and question determinist theories of criminality, their engagement with advances in forensic technology are equally ambiguous. In 'The Norwood Builder' a bloody thumbprint seems to unequivocally condemn the young lawyer McFarlane of having murdered the vanished builder Oldacre. To Watson, the fingerprint seems to render the young lawyer's guilt 'evident' (506). Holmes, however, sees through Oldacre's ruse and correctly identifies the print as forged. Yet had it not been for Holmes's extraordinary powers of observation and deduction, the thumbprint would have incriminated the innocent suspect more severely than any of the circumstantial evidence found on Oldacre's estate (which includes the charred remains of an animal carcass and the suspect's walking stick). Even though the print ultimately leads Holmes to the real culprit, it cannot serve as an irrefutable index of an individual's guilt – a warning about the potential dangers of a forensic technology that promised to provide a 'surer criterion of identity than any other bodily feature'.[28] To read the features of criminality correctly and to solve those 'featureless' crimes that are most difficult to decode, it takes nothing less than the deductive powers of Sherlock Holmes, 'the most perfect reasoning and observing machine . . . the world has seen' (161). Possessed of preternatural powers of observation and deduction, Holmes is a forensic technology in himself, a veritable machine of detection, which cuts through detective fiction's thicket of false identities and red herrings to produce seemingly simple narratives that are nonetheless capable of negotiating the fascinating mystery of crime and criminality in complex and multi-layered ways.

Notes

1. Cesare Lombroso, *Criminal Man*, ed. and trans. Mary Gibson and Nicole Hahn Rafter (Durham: Duke University Press, 2006), 174.
2. Cesare Lombroso, 'Introduction', in Cesare Lombroso and Gina Lombroso Ferrero (eds.), *Criminal Man: According to the Classification of Cesare Lombroso* (New York: The Knickerbocker Press, 1911), xi–xx (xiv).
3. Lombroso, *Criminal Man*, 47.
4. Lombroso, 'Introduction', xv.
5. Daniel Pick, *Faces of Degeneration: A European Disorder, c.1848-c.1918* (Cambridge: Cambridge University Press, 1989), 126.
6. Charles Darwin, *The Descent of Man and Selection in Relation to Sex*, ed. and intro. Adrian Desmond and James Moore (London: Penguin, 2004), 57.
7. Bram Stoker, *Dracula, 1897*, ed. Maud Ellmann (Oxford: Oxford University Press, 1998), 342.

8. William Greenslade, *Degeneration, Culture, and the Novel, 1880–1940* (Cambridge: Cambridge University Press, 1994), 100.
9. Lombroso, *Criminal Man*, 66; Lombroso, 'Introduction', xv.
10. Lombroso, *Criminal Man*, 91.
11. Ibid., 188.
12. Ibid., 190.
13. Havelock Ellis, *The Criminal* (London: Walter Scott, 1901), 258.
14. Lombroso, *Criminal Man*, 197.
15. Charles Goring, *The English Convict: A Statistical Study* (London: His Majesty's Stationery Office, 1913), 18, 13, 11.
16. Lombroso, *Criminal Man*, 311.
17. Goring, *English Convict*, 26.
18. Ellis, *Criminal*, 103–4.
19. Maria Cairney, 'The Healing Art of Detection: Sherlock Holmes and the Disease of Crime in the *Strand Magazine*', *Clues: A Journal of Detection* 26:1 (2008), 62–74 (63).
20. Lombroso, *Criminal Man*, 204.
21. Goring, *English Convict*, 370.
22. Allan Sekula, 'The Body and the Archive', in Richard Bolton (ed.), *The Contest of Meaning: Critical Histories of Photography* (Cambridge: The MIT Press, 1992), 342–88 (357–62).
23. Francis Galton, *Finger Prints* (London: Macmillan, 1892), 1–2.
24. Ibid., 10, 2.
25. Ibid., 12.
26. Ronald R. Thomas, *Detective Fiction and the Rise of Forensic Science* (Cambridge: Cambridge University Press, 1999), 204–8.
27. Ibid., 225.
28. Galton, *Finger Prints*, 2.

9

JEREMY TAMBLING

Holmes, Law and Order

Several points may be taken as axiomatic about the detective in fiction: first that he is a mythological culture-hero in his ability to oversee and read the city, that rapidly expanding sphere which, in the nineteenth century, newly necessitated and challenged police competence to map and solve the social problems it posed. However intractable the problems of the city, and however impossible to solve by one all-knowing person, the detective gave the sense of being able to do so, of being able to 'mount a high tower in his mind', as Charles Dickens says of Inspector Bucket, and survey the city from a central and superior vantage point.[1] The second point is that like the police (or when acting *as* the police, in the examples of Dickens's Inspector Bucket or Wilkie Collins's Sergeant Cuff in *The Moonstone* (1868)), the detective stands for a panoptical surveillance of not just the city, but of the English landscape as well. Holmes in 'The Copper Beeches', for example, shows himself more suspicious of the country than the city, just because it is unknowable. Travelling through the countryside, he admonishes Watson to '"[t]hink of the deeds of hellish cruelty, the *hidden* wickedness which may go on, year in, year out, in such places, and none the wiser"' (323, emphasis added).

Michel Foucault's *Discipline and Punish* (1975) was a landmark study, about far more than the birth of the prison, in showing that, in its ideal form, the Panopticon – a form of prison initially proposed in 1791 by Jeremy Bentham, in which cells are organised around a central watchtower – offered a blueprint for institutions to exercise continuous silent control over people. In this model, prisoners know that they are subject to surveillance but never exactly when this gaze might be directed towards them; as a result, they regulate their own behaviour, as if *always* under surveillance. For Foucault, the implications of this are twofold. Firstly, this surveillance helps to construct subjectivity itself. Secondly, and more importantly for detective fiction, the Panopticon not only creates the 'docile body' of the prisoner, but also produces a demand on that body to confess the guilty secrets that accompany the conceiving of the self as a single discrete subject.[2] Thus, for Foucault, subjects were brought into the discipline of having to give a narrative account of themselves, narrative being held in the power of the state's disciplinary force, most obviously embodied in the police.

Such surveillance historically increased in Britain with new prisons such as Millbank (1816) and Pentonville (1842) and with the creation of the Metropolitan Police in 1829, putting those novels where police appear – and all realist novel-writing by implication, since realism is committed to seeing society as a whole, and not allowing any detail to be accidental, or not to fit – onto the side of the police. Narrative, as inherently committed to explanation and wholeness, must ultimately confirm the judgments made by the police in the way they regarded deviants, criminals or mental instability. With the power to secure and regulate people's narratives, all potential suspects, the police are on the side of normalisation. Holmes, like the police, suspects what is not normal: in 'Wisteria Lodge', for example, he notes '"how often the grotesque has deepened into the criminal"' (869). He too belongs to the panoptical society, putting everything and everyone under observation. Here nothing is accidental; everything that happens is symptomatic, to be treated as a clue which may be used as evidence. Blackmail, which seems to acquire a new significance in the nineteenth century, shows how the past may be opened up, nothing from it being trivial; everything becomes a trace, actions read as indexical to a character potentially criminal.

Law and Violence

The detective works secretly, because confidentially (being privately hired), and undermines societal and family structures before replacing them. In this, he is like the criminal. The alignment of detective with criminal is a twist deriving from Sophocles's *Oedipus* (*c*.429 BC), in which the detective Oedipus discovers himself as the patricide; in this tale, the criminal is revealed to be engaged in a detective-like deepening of self-knowledge. In detective fiction more broadly, this alignment of the detective mind with the criminal mind may even create both as guilty. The criminal transgresses in uncovering hidden knowledge (in which the detective follows him) to access what Sigmund Freud calls the 'primal scene', that hidden source of everything – the origin of the criminal's being – and of all action. In psychoanalytic terms, this necessitates a fantasmatic unveiling of the mother's body, infringing the incest-taboo which (for Freud) is the basic prohibition, imposed by the father, who stands as the agent of law. The prohibition, or taboo, as Freud calls it in 'Totem and Taboo' (1913), is a source of ambivalence because the tabooed object is also desired; furthermore, the person who infringes the taboo becomes taboo himself, a special object, sacred and untouchable, as well as cursed. Freud thinks of the instantiation of the taboo as coming, paradigmatically, from a primal murder of the father by his sons, who then, Freud says, 'felt remorse for the deed', which gave it the character of crime and created a sense of guilt.[3]

Freud's sense of a founding act of violence necessitating and creating law to control tabooed sexual desire accords with Walter Benjamin's assertion that law is given to 'condemn not to punishment but to guilt'.[4] Law has its authority because it appeals to the so-called 'natural', so claiming a mythic status outside history. But, for Benjamin, what establishes law is violence: violence, given a mythic and unquestioned status, founds the law and sustains it. Law works through the threat of imposing violence on those who transgress, most obviously in the example of capital punishment. In turn, this violence is sanctioned by its authority, whether public or private. Hence, Benjamin notes the popularity of the 'great criminal', however fictional, whose violence is directed against the law and who lays bare the violence that underpins it.

But the guilt that is felt, if we follow Freud, relates to transgressive thoughts within the realm of the sexual. Hence the fascination of the crime inside a locked room (in psychoanalytic terms, the place where the tabooed sexual happens), access to which seems impossible, as in 'The Empty House' (such fascinations would culminate in the sub-genre of the 'locked room mystery', in which the very impossibility of access to the scene of the crime is what provides the mystery: 'The Speckled Band' is the clearest example of Doyle working in this mode). In 'The Norwood Builder', the villainous Jonas Oldacre has even built his own locked room, impregnable of access, within his house, in order to hide away while the world assumes he is dead: his attempt to frame John Hector McFarlane for murder is an act of revenge for having been sexually spurned years ago (and so deprived of access to what the locked room speaks of). In 'The Red-headed League', John Clay resembles Benjamin's great criminal in his subtlety in getting into Jabez Wilson's house and mind (these are synonymous), in his play-acting and powers of persuasion, and in the sheer ingenuity and daring of his plan: tunnelling from house to bank, devising a pathway for himself that keeps him concealed in traversing it. He accesses a locked cellar of the bank by coming up through the floor (his name, Clay, is therefore appropriate, and his deviance (from masculinity) is suggested by his 'almost womanly hand' and 'clean-cut boyish face' (188)). He recognises Holmes as an equal; he is only contemptuous – openly so – of the police. But so is Holmes.

Moriarty, in comparison, is not a great criminal in the sense that he works with an organisation, making him more of a parallel to state-power than a solitary worker acting transgressively against it. But Moriarty appeals to a myth that spokespeople for law and order often use: that there is a secret conspiracy against which the ignorant world must be protected. As Holmes says of Moriarty in 'The Final Problem', '"there's the genius and wonder of the thing ... the man pervades London and no one has heard of him. That's what puts him on a pinnacle in the records of crime"' (470). While Holmes and Moriarty are intellectual equals, the pleasure for the detective is working his way into the mind of an unknown criminal: as he says in 'The Musgrave Ritual', '"I put myself in the man's place, and having first gauged his intelligence, I try to imagine how I should myself have proceeded under the same circumstances"' (395). The phrasing of this statement is odd; instead of suggesting that the detective tries to follow or repeat the criminal's moves, it suggests an identification, where the criminal re-enacts and repeats the actions imaginatively performed by the detective. Thus, the emphasis subtly shifts onto the detective as the primary criminal. This complicates the construction of Holmes as a scientific or analytical detective. Holmes's claims to solve mysteries through the application of logic obscure the extent to which his method is, in fact, based more on empathetic identification with the criminal than abstract reasoning. In the late story 'The Problem of Thor Bridge', for example, all depends on Holmes's ability to read the ultimate locked room: the mind of the murdered Maria Gibson, and to work out that she actually committed suicide in order to frame a younger woman for the crime. Here, the apparent victim is the criminal; the apparent criminal, the younger woman, the would-be victim. While Watson focuses on the 'innate nobility' of the victim, Miss Dunbar (1065), Holmes's fascination is with the motives and methods of the criminal, and there is virtually no identification with the victim in the Holmes stories, unless the one doubles as the other.

I will return to the question of identification but, for now, it is important to note that the detective, while finding guilt pervasive, works to marginalise its existence by fastening it onto the single criminal who, like the detective, is nonetheless a culture-hero in challenging the prior existence of guilt by transgressing societal and sexual codes. This enables several points to emerge. In the first place, there are now two types of criminals that need to be distinguished: the common type, who may be the province of the police (significantly called the police *force*), and Benjamin's great criminal, which is what the detective works with. This opens up a gap between the police, who are unimaginative and seen as suited for such cases, because, like Lestrade, they are '"practical"' (507) and stand for law; and the detective who stands for justice. As Holmes says in 'The Three Gables': '"I am not the law, but I represent justice so far as my feeble powers go"' (1032). But he also enables the law to work, and his skill is his method, which is ambiguous in itself: both analysing scientifically, as he claims so frequently, and yet being empathetic, depending on a close identification with the criminal.

Law and Justice

What then are the differences between law and justice? Law exists as an institution; it is a matter of lawyers observing and following precedents. Before Doyle, Dickens had shown how law is never self-evident; it must rely on legal fictions, i.e. statements and assumptions and fictions that may be untrue or unproven but which, for legal purposes, no one can question and which thus prop up the law. One example of such legal fictions is the statement that ignorance of the law is no excuse, a statement that has no authority in itself – what could possibly be the evidence to support the proposition? – but which nonetheless has a binding effect. In the same way, a detective story is an instance of a legal fiction which supports the law and its authority: hence its largely conservative appeal to readers. Holmes must boost the law's authority, especially when the police are not quite up to things (see, for example, 'The Six Napoleons', where Inspector Lestrade fails to realise the significance of the titular busts). This suggests that law is always in a state of crisis, needing to be propped up and made self-evident.

In an excellent chapter on the relationship between Holmes and the police, Luc Boltanski shows the many ways in which Holmes has to help out the law because what is at stake is the state, which law supports and which, in the nineteenth century, was forming itself on panoptical lines as a system of covert surveillance rather than open violence and repression. Should the state lose legitimacy, the detective is the backstop to maintain it. Holmes for ever hushes up scandals, which the police could not do, because a scandal could lead, so Boltanski argues, to an *affaire*, like the Dreyfus affair, which shook the legitimacy of the French state (1894–1906: the parallel to Holmes's career in chronological terms is not coincidental). Thus, the detective must work underground to keep the state inviolate and Boltanski concludes his chapter by arguing that 'the detective is the state in a state of ordinary exception'.[5]

The idea of a 'state of exception' derives from Carl Schmitt (1888–1985) and is reflected in Benjamin's argument that the exercise of justice demands a suspension of ordinary legal procedures which could never come to a determination save by a decision being made which has the power of suspension. A judicial decision, then, has the force of the illegal, suspending the question of law being debated: the act of decision being the work of a sovereign power, beyond the law, as with Holmes. Derrida, following Benjamin, elaborates on these points in his essay 'Force of Law' (1990). He agrees with Benjamin that there is no foundation to law except the violence which sustains it, so that this absence of foundation makes *justice* always something yet to come.[6] And asking for justice, for Derrida, risks making the self into an absolute, forgetting that the self is not a fixed subject for all time, but exists in time: no self, or subject, can ask for an absolute justice which stands outside time.

If violence founds the law then it is relevant for the Holmes stories that the police do not just carry out the law, they make it, and do so by their violence. But that does not make the detective, by contrast, a man of peace. As Holmes says to Inspector Lestrade in 'Charles Augustus Milverton', '"I think there are certain crimes which the law cannot touch, and which therefore, to some extent, justify private revenge ... [In such cases, m]y sympathies are with the criminals rather than with the victim"' (582). It must be remembered that Holmes is personally compromised in this case as he and Watson have themselves broken into Milverton's home in an attempt to steal a set of incriminating letters – an act described by Holmes as '"morally justifiable, though technically criminal"' (576) – only to witness Milverton's murder by a ruined woman who could not pay the blackmailer's fee. Thus, what he says may be only for the occasion. It is also true that the ideological positions urged within the text drive the plot forward and compel the reader to agree, making Holmes's conclusion as he states it almost irresistible. Yet the justification of revenge is strange and, it would be hoped, impossible in real life: it enforces Holmes as reactionary, even though we would also characterise him as a man who believes in going beyond common ideological positions, as when he allows the thief to walk free in 'The Blue Carbuncle'.

This is the central contradiction which makes the stories so fascinating. It might be better to say that Holmes is anarchic, as when he asks Watson, in 'A Scandal in Bohemia', '"You don't mind breaking the law?"' to which Watson, an old soldier with the British in Afghanistan, and so well used to questionable colonial methods, replies '"Not in the least"' (169). In this story, it is satisfactory that the woman, Irene Adler, is no less anarchic than Holmes and she bests him in anarchy, exercising her own version of law: keeping an incriminating photograph 'only to safeguard myself, and to preserve a weapon which will always secure me from any steps which he [the king of Bohemia] might take in the future' (175). The woman has no more reliance on the police than Holmes, and she knows the power of evidence. It is important to note, more generally, that female criminals seem to evade the justice which falls on their male counterparts ('Thor Bridge' is an interesting partial exception): the point holds also for 'The Musgrave Ritual', and implies that women may be more dangerous than men, beyond the law. By contrast, in both *Bleak House* (1853) and

The Moonstone the law seems prejudiced against women (in the former, Lady Dedlock is suspected of murder while, in the latter, Sergeant Cuff thinks Rachel Verinder has been working with the ex-thief, Rosanna Spearman).

Boltanski's phrase 'ordinary exception' implies that there is no normal condition: everything is an exception and everything is a matter of working with semi-transparent legal fictions. The detective so works to ensure a conclusion before a legal issue gets to court. But this only confirms the detective's rapport with the criminal and his ambivalence in sharing features with both the criminal and the police, his relationships with both being complex. In 'The Abbey Grange', Holmes allows the policeman (Hopkins) to go his own way, and carries out his own form of justice for the murder of Sir Eustace Brackenstall. In 'The Man with the Twisted Lip', he overrides the policeman (Bradstreet). In the latter case, no crime is committed, though for half the story Holmes thinks Neville St Clair has been murdered. Only when Holmes realises what sort of case this is – a transgression against middle-class social codes rather than murder – is he able to interpret correctly.

This learning to see what the problem is, that it is not the way it is initially stated, is the clue to understanding Doyle – we have to start from the end, not from the beginning. By the end of 'The Man with the Twisted Lip', two separate husbands have been restored to their middle-class wives, one from drug-taking in the East End, the other from posing as a beggar: both have been enjoying themselves far too much. Holmes believes the 'murder' case is a continuation of the first but thinks more clearly when he learns not to follow narrative precedent, even though he has stayed up all night as if he was on an 'Eastern divan' (240) in an opium-den. The case becomes soluble only when he learns to distinguish elements in what seems to be a single story, and realises the husband was not murdered (just as no one was murdered in 'The Norwood Builder') but is, rather, a man with a double life needing to be re-codified back into the middle class, where husbands are permitted only one identity.

If Holmes keeps St Clair from the police and public scandal, it is because the case would expose middle-class domestic arrangements, based upon conventional class and gender roles such as having a profession, as a mere sham, and Holmes will not do this: he is on the side of order (as well as law in its weak state of requiring support). He is neither with the criminal, nor practising a law other than the police's: being '"more anxious to hush up private scandals than to give them publicity"' (635) in 'The Missing Three-Quarter', he recognises an inadequacy in the law which only he can resolve, being both the detective who is professional (hired by Mrs St Clair) and amateur (separate from the police). And if he learns to think doubly, discarding his previous ideas (the police never have such subtlety), double thinking enables him to codify society into single terms – those of the family as the indispensable prop of the state.

The Truth versus the True in 'The Abbey Grange'

'The Abbey Grange' turns on a more complex incident than 'The Man with the Twisted Lip', whereby what the case is – as opposed to what it seems to be – must be understood before it can be solved. As Holmes demands of Watson, '"if I had not taken things for granted, if I had examined everything with care which I should have shown had we approached the case *de novo* and had no cut-and-dried story to warp my mind, should I not then have found something more definite to go upon? Of course I should"' (642). The case revolves around the murder of Sir Eustace Brackenstall; Mary, his Australian wife, has been found tied up and attacked. Was this a burglary from outside by a Lewisham-based gang of three, Randall and his sons, who recently committed a similar crime in Sydenham? Hopkins, the investigating policeman, thinks yes (it is a case of common criminals), and Holmes is half-convinced, thus following the law's literality (and single-thinking), but then goes his own way when he realises that only two celebratory wine-glasses were used, not three, at the time of the murder. It was not, then, the Lewisham gang of three. In his investigations, he summons up a sailor (in an echo of Edgar Allan Poe's 'The Murders in the Rue Morgue' (1841)): Jack Croker, an Australian seaman. Visiting Mary one last time before embarking on a long sea voyage, the couple are surprised by the villainous and sadistic husband who attacks both of them and Croker kills Sir Eustace. Holmes – and Watson – acquit him.

The narrative's ideology is not anti-police, even though Holmes treats the matter as an adventure: '"[t]he game is afoot"' (636), he announces to Watson, quoting another national hero, Shakespeare's Henry V (*Henry V* 3.1.32), associated with youthful transgression but thoroughly part of the English ideology and its support. Texts persuade readers into accepting their presuppositions, even against ordinary objections. Roland Barthes has argued that such ideology is carried through in the text by a series of binary oppositions, some flagged up, some implicit, but which leave no room for a third position, persuading the reader, unconsciously, to follow the ideology within the tale's narrative drive.[7] In 'The Abbey Grange' we can note a series of oppositions that establish a groundwork whereby a law is established which must acquit Croker:

1. The 'bitterly cold night and frosty morning' (635) of the opening versus the warmth of South Australia;

2. The wife's blond and blue-eyed appearance versus the dark, bearded husband;

3. Croker as 'golden-moustached, blue-eyed, with a skin which had been burned by tropical suns, and ... [a] huge frame ... as active as it was strong' (647), trusting Holmes as a '"white man"' (648), gives the tale a colonial character, where justice is served differently (and exceptionally) versus the husband as a '"devil"' who, in death, retains a 'terribly fiendish expression' (645, 640);

4. The husband's violence as surreptitious and irrational (he stabs his wife's arm with a hatpin) versus the precision of the murder as committed by Croker (symbolised in the cutting of the bell-rope): hit with a single tremendous blow, the husband falls instantly;

5. Sir Eustace's night-attire is described as 'foppish' and he is described as having '"false London ways"' (640, 645) versus Croker's description as a 'fine ... specimen of manhood' as well as 'loyal, honest, and kind-hearted' (647, 646);

6. Conventional English life '"with its proprieties and its primness"' versus the '"freer, less conventional atmosphere of South Australia"' (638);

7. The '"truth"' versus the '"true"' (649);

8. The police as bound by convention versus Holmes as not; as Holmes explains to Watson, '"what I know is unofficial, what [Hopkins] knows is official. I have the right to private judgment, but he has none. He must disclose all, or he is a traitor to his service"' (647).

Most of these oppositions are obvious, but some demand comment. The truth which is hunted is what a 'will to truth' – a term from Friedrich Nietzsche – seeks and creates. Truth, for Nietzsche and Foucault, is not disinterested; it is what (state/police) power wants to discover in a person in order to exercise better control and keep that person under its surveillance; in that sense, truth only exists according to the conditions which allow certain things to be said and others not.[8] When Holmes meets Croker, he demands a '"true account"' of events (638) and after hearing '"the whole truth"' says, '"I know that every word is true, for you have hardly said a word which I did not know"' (649). He shows that he has made a thorough examination of the murder-room (having locked it on the inside) which has virtually repeated Croker's actions (arriving, unexpected, at night, climbing on the mantelpiece, placing his knee on the bracket, etc.). Here, the sense of law as state-power and directly apprehensible, discussed by Foucault and Boltanski, may be supplemented by Freud's sense of law as an unconscious structure within the life of the subject.[9] Inspecting the room has allowed Holmes into the mind of the criminal. These forms of knowing are almost identical and his prior knowledge of the room means that Croker's later version of the truth fits his; the criminal's narrative repeats an account of actions that Holmes, in the way the story is narrated, has already performed; 'truth' is the alignment of the criminal's account with the detective's. They follow and repeat each other, reversing normal chronologies. Holmes can go on to his next act because he has identified with Croker.

Being in 'the truth', in Nietzsche and Foucault's sense, means following the dominant, controlling, virtually omniscient discourse of truth embodied in Holmes (he already knew Croker's story), rather than the police. Holmes imposes a test upon Croker to see if he really loves Mary and Croker passes with ease, making Holmes declare, '"you ring true every time"' (650). Here, 'true' means honest, manly and 'white'; it fits a code of honour that the tale supports and which, indeed, it relates to the (Australian) colonies, where justice works differently from its conventional London modes. Holmes positions Croker inside a discourse of truth, distinct from the literality of what he did (murder). 'Truth' and 'the true' contrast as opposites. The tale vindicates both while aligning the first with conventionality, proprieties and primness. Love between the two figures from Australia contrasts with English law, as conventional as married love. Hopkins of necessity follows English law but Holmes follows only his own '"conscience"' (646) – as in his testing of Croker. Holmes embodies an order that even allows him to suggest that Croker should wait a year (observing the proprieties) before wooing the now-widowed Mary. The obstacle to their union has been killed, properly, because of his mistreatment of his wife. What is vindicated is Holmes's clarification of a point that the police cannot recognise: that Sir Eustace's death was a coming together of truth and the true; his death thoroughly exposed his character. It is significant that Croker had gone down to visit his '"people"' at Sydenham. The locale brings him into a symbolic relationship with the Lewisham gang who were there and establishes both his similarity and difference from these '"common"' criminals (648).

The crime, by implication, was not Croker's murder of Sir Eustace, but the husband's prior violent behaviour; this reversal of expectation and chronology produces a justice that Holmes and Watson endorse. Assuming the roles of judge and jury, Watson pronounces him not guilty, leading Holmes to say '"*Vox populi, vox Dei*"' (650) – the voice of the people is the voice of God. If Watson speaks for the reader, that reader has been constructed by the ideology of the text and so thinks that way automatically. But the voice of that ideology is actually endorsed as God's view, as the final authority. In psychoanalytic terms, this is the voice of Jacques Lacan's 'symbolic order', language as incarnating the law of the father, the law of patriarchy. It is the order that keeps language and identity in place. For Lacan, this order is the 'phallic metaphor' that makes meanings combine and unify (as metaphors have the power to connect language and make connections).[10] There is nothing higher than such a law for Lacan; the child comes into it in acquiring language, which means perforce accepting the differential terms which establish gender.

'The Abbey Grange' works out and justifies an ideology which has its place in relation to the state, for it demonstrates its phallic authority. In being 'true' (straight), Croker shows that he has such authority, as with his severing of the bell-rope, an act which casually establishes an authoritative masculinity. He did not, strictly, need to cut it, but that assertiveness, as his unconscious signature, attracts Holmes's attention while examining the room. The unconscious which connects them (and gives the detective phallic authority) is that both have an attraction to the rope, which was cut, not at all frayed (nothing of weakness is present); the imagery of the bell-rope recalls 'The Speckled Band', where a similar rope becomes the means for a snake to twist its way up and out of one room and into the next. The rope has snake-like characteristics, as well as supporting it and acting as a conduit, like the tunnel for John Clay in 'The Red-Headed League'.

'The Abbey Grange' vindicates the law as the patriarchal symbolic order, upon which rests all hope of holding people obedient to the law. The law assents to the people's choice, but that choice was not free: law first manipulated the people's decision, which accords with it. Holmes's methods have often been compared with psychoanalysis, but whereas Freud questions the ideology that supports patriarchal authority, Holmes accepts it, or at least works within it. Even readings which suggest Holmes's resistance to such patriarchal authority end up reinforcing it. For instance, if we add in Freud's analysis from 'Totem and Taboo', then the murder of Sir Eustace is akin to the father's murder, while the kinship of Croker with Holmes shows the secret alliance of the sons against patriarchy. In this analysis Holmes is established as criminal-like, standing against the authority of patriarchy, but taken a step further the murder now founds a more complete law which is the law of the father as God (echoed in the title's inclusion of the word 'Abbey', a word derived from the Greek for father). So the father dominates even on the basis of his death, which creates a new band of brothers. Holmes and Croker may form a secret partnership to challenge patriarchal authority, but in so doing reinforce that authority. If that reading casts Mary as the mother, this may receive support from the extraordinary reverence that Croker has for her, even kissing the deck where she had walked.

Holmes frees Mary from any imputation of being an accomplice in the murder of her husband. This makes two points: first, the elementary one that the woman stands free of the law, even though Holmes can see that she is lying to him; second, that the pact between Holmes and Croker, whereby he is saved because he will not let the woman be incriminated, makes for a union between the men which is founded on the law of the father, by virtue of which the woman can, in this case, actually be spoken for. She is both inside and outside the law and a figure of ambiguity that Holmes cannot quite control or account for. In thus distributing justice, it must also be noted how violent Holmes can be, or how much violence he can sanction in others. 'The Speckled Band' ends with the death of Dr Roylott, for which, Holmes says, he is '"indirectly responsible"', though '"I cannot say that it is likely to weigh very heavily on my conscience"' (273). He has driven the viper back up the bell rope through the ventilator into the other room from whence Roylott sent it, and the viper kills its master: '"[v]iolence does"', says Holmes, '"in truth, recoil upon the violent, and the schemer falls into the pit which he digs for another"' (272). There is symmetry between the dog whip which the doctor uses to hold and control the snake in his room and the bell rope down which the snake climbs in the other.

This equality extends to the criminal and to Holmes. The violence which Roylott inaugurates becomes the display of the crime by Holmes and, at the same time, his exercise of justice against Roylott. Justice is revealed in, and as, violence, as is the case with the murder in 'The Abbey Grange'. If Holmes is the guardian of law and order, it is because of the exercise of violence. The nineteenth century, as Foucault shows, moved from public exhibitions of violence in displays of capital punishment towards more private demonstrations: 1868 saw Britain's last public hanging. Before then, public hangings showed an atavistic attitude that purposefully identified justice with violence; after that, the connection was not lost but concealed, and it comes back in the detective novel, especially in the way in which the case closes before the accused gets to court. The principle that contemporary justice is rooted in violence – and may be no more than that – is what Benjamin and Derrida wrestle with; it means that justice can never end violence, and that justice always has the character of revenge. Having broken into the home of the blackmailer, Charles Augustus Milverton, Holmes and Watson stand by while a previous victim 'poured bullet after bullet into [his] shrinking body'. As Watson readies himself to interfere, he is restrained by Holmes's hand: 'I understood the whole argument of that firm, restraining grip – that it was no affair of ours, that justice had overtaken a villain' (581). Hence the pleasure of the text which gives the reader the vicarious sense of witnessing justice in witnessing violence.

Freud argues that criminals become such out of a sense of guilt: rather than crime producing guilt, criminals are trying to work off some sense of a prior repression – obviously violent – exerted in their lives.[11] Holmes's abstraction and his insistence on logic misleads, as when he says about Roylott, '"it's a wicked world, and when a clever man turns his brains to crime it is the worst of all"' (268). Law and order are maintained on the basis of crime emerging *ex nihilo*, able to be wrapped up by a detective as violent as the criminal. The equation of justice with revenge and violence, which sets such violence above all others, and allows Holmes such moral thinking as when he sees Roylott dead, is guaranteed by the Holmes stories, produced by the power of such an ideology. Since violence is more problematic in the case of women, she may escape Holmes's powers; but the side view that Doyle's narratives permit onto the workings of ideology convey two surprising things: that criminal and detective are equivalent creations, both anarchists, and that the re-imposition of order equals the working out of violence.

Notes

1. Charles Dickens, *Bleak House*, 1853, ed. Nicola Bradbury (London: Penguin, 2003), 864.
2. Michel Foucault, *Discipline and Punish: The Birth of the Prison*, trans. Alan Sheridan (London: Penguin, 1984).
3. Sigmund Freud, 'Totem and Taboo', in *Totem and Taboo and Other Works*, ed. and trans. James Strachey. *Standard Edition of the Complete Psychological Works of Sigmund Freud*, vol. 13 (London: Hogarth Press, 1955), 1–161 (159). This is discussed by Jacques Derrida, 'Before the Law', in Derek Attridge (ed.),*Acts of Literature* (London: Routledge, 1992), 181–220 (197–8).
4. Walter Benjamin, 'Fate and Character', in *Selected Writings 1: 1913–1926*, ed. Marcus Bullock and Michael W. Jennings (Cambridge: Harvard University Press, 1996), 201–6 (204).
5. Luc Boltanski, *Mysteries and Conspiracies: Detective Stories, Spy Novels, and the Making of Modern Societies*, trans. Catherine Porter (Cambridge: Polity, 2014), 72.
6. Jacques Derrida, 'Force of Law: The "Mystical Foundation of Authority"', in Gil Anidjar (ed.), *Acts of Religion* (London: Routledge, 2002), 228–98.
7. Roland Barthes, *S/Z*, trans. Richard Howard (New York: Hill and Wang, 1974).
8. Friedrich Nietzsche, *The Birth of Tragedy and The Genealogy of Morals*, trans. Francis Golffing (New York: Doubleday Anchor, 1956), 286–9.
9. Freud, 'The Ego and the Id', in *The Ego and the Id and Other Works*, ed. and trans. James Strachey. *Standard Edition of the Complete Psychological Works of Sigmund Freud*, vol. 19 (London: Hogarth Press, 1961), 28–39.
10. Jacques Lacan, 'The Function and Field of Speech and Language in Psychoanalysis', in *Ecrits*, trans. Bruce Fink (New York: W. W. Norton, 2002),

229–322 (230). The connection of phallic authority with metaphor appears in 'The Instance of the Letter in the Unconscious, or Reason since Freud', 412–41.

11. Sigmund Freud, 'Criminals from a Sense of Guilt', in *On the History of the Psycho-Analytic Movement, Papers on Metapsychology and Other Works*, ed. James Strachey. *Standard Edition of the Complete Psychological Works of Sigmund Freud*, vol. 14 (London: Hogarth Press, 1957), 332–3.

PART II

Case Studies

10

CAROLINE REITZ

The Empires of *A Study in Scarlet* and *The Sign of Four*

In his *Memories and Adventures*, Arthur Conan Doyle looks back on the marriage of form and content that resulted in the unprecedented popularity of Sherlock Holmes. He writes that:

> a single character running through a series, if it only engaged the attention of the reader, would bind that reader to that particular magazine. On the other hand, it had long seemed to me that the ordinary serial might be an impediment rather than a help to a magazine, since, sooner or later, one missed one number and afterwards it had lost all interest. Clearly the ideal compromise was a character which carried through, and yet instalments which were each complete in themselves, so that the purchaser was always sure that he could relish the whole contents of the magazine. I believe that I was the first to realize this and 'The Strand Magazine' the first to put it into practice. (95–6)

Doyle continues: 'I felt that Sherlock Holmes, whom I had already handled in two little books, would easily lend himself to a succession of short stories' (*Memories* 96). He did: the *Strand Magazine* more than doubled its circulation with the run of Sherlock Holmes stories that began with 'A Scandal in Bohemia' in July 1891. Doyle's 'two little books' are, of course, *A Study in Scarlet*, published in *Beeton's Christmas Annual* in 1887, and *The Sign of Four*, published in 1890 in the American *Lippincott's Monthly Magazine*. What, then, is the relationship between those 'two little books' and what followed, arguably one of the most effective innovations in literary publishing history?

One might imagine that the baggier novel form is shed like an old skin so that Holmes can be streamlined in the pages of the *Strand*. But that would ignore the fact that Doyle returned to that form with *The Hound of the Baskervilles* and that he wrote a Holmes novel quite similar to *A Study in Scarlet* with *The Valley of Fear*. Understanding the stories in the *Strand* as a departure from the novels might invite us to believe that the over-riding concerns and formal oddities of those first two books – what constitutes the jurisdiction of the English detective and the boundaries of the detective story in a violent, messy world – is also shed; Holmes can focus his considerable energies on clearing up the fog-bound streets of the late-Victorian London with which he is so strongly associated. However, as Watson explains in the first pages of *A Study in Scarlet*, London is 'that great cesspool into which all the loungers and idlers of the Empire are irresistibly drained' (15). While it is beyond the scope of this chapter to follow Holmes to the *Strand*, the aim is to show how these two books establish concerns about England's place in a borderless world that the frequent formal boundaries of the serial short story do not entirely resolve.

The worlds of *A Study in Scarlet* and *The Sign of Four* are messy and global. Brutal western expansion and ruthless consolidation of power in the Mormon community are the focus of the American half of *A Study in Scarlet*, while a good portion of *The Sign of Four* is given over to Jonathan Small's retelling of a plot to steal Indian treasure that leaves a long trail of murder. These crimes do not stay contained in America or India but, from the first pages, are woven into investigations of crime on English soil. American Jefferson Hope's quest for revenge brings him to London as a cabman so he can track down and kill those responsible for the deaths of his beloved, Lucy, and her father, John Ferrier, back in Utah. Holmes gets involved in the crimes detailed in *The Sign of Four* because the quintessentially English Mary Morstan comes to Baker Street to pursue the mysterious disappearance of her father and annual appearance of a valuable pearl. Before a day has passed, she (and the reader) will have discovered that her father, Captain Morstan, Major John Sholto, his fellow officer from the Indian army, and the major's son, Bartholomew, are dead (the latter poisoned by a foreign thorn). The boundaries of the main characters' bodies are similarly marked by a violently connected world. *A Study in Scarlet* begins with Watson's account of the bullet in his shoulder from his service in the war in Afghanistan. *The Sign of Four* famously begins (and ends) with Sherlock 'thrust[ing] the sharp point' of a 'hypodermic syringe' into his 'sinewy forearm' (89). Holmes's drug is cocaine, but critics often note an association of his drug use with opium, in part because of the exoticised connection with foreigners in London.

The novels themselves are formally messy. Ian Ousby considers *A Study in Scarlet* 'the weakest of the full-length novels' and Joseph McLaughlin writes that it is often misunderstood because of its 'formal peculiarity'.[1] It is told in two parts, the first being Watson's English crime story and the second the story of Mormon violence in the American west. The pivot from Watson's first-person narrative to a third-person narration about America is startling.

The Sign of Four is more tightly organised, but the final part of the text takes the reader all the way back in time and space to the Sepoy Rebellion of 1857 and Jonathan Small's subsequent tour of the British imperial justice system, from a convict settlement in the Andaman Islands to Scotland Yard. The *Strand* stories might be tidier from a narrative point of view, but they are no less full of the loungers and idlers – or logic – of empire. Critics such as Jon Thompson see in the stories 'an adherence to a particular ideology of empiricism', an ideology that combines with 'a general ideology of imperialism' to create a more orderly understanding of the world.[2] The regularity of the *Strand*'s formal borders affords a kind of order that the novels do not. However, multiple borders also enable the opportunity for multiple transgressions, and further musing over what it is that boundaries do or fail to do. It creates the productive tension of, in Doyle's words, something complete in itself and something carrying through. The formal boundaries of the stories keep alive the central idea of these first novels: we draw boundaries around stories and nations rather arbitrarily, often violently and never permanently.

The problem of boundaries is underscored by the fluid character of the British Empire at the point of publication. Empire, and the nationalism that underwrites it is, in some senses, a problem of form. Ronald R. Thomas discusses E. J. Hobsbawm's argument that it was in the last decade of the nineteenth century that the nation became a political entity and nationalism an ideological force; Thomas sees the Holmes stories of this period as 'popular agents in forging that new identity of the nation as apparatus'.[3] Holmes has been seen by critics as playing a valuable role in policing the borders of that emerging nation.[4] But Thomas also admits that this was not always possible: 'At the very moment when the English were being confronted by the accusation of acting less like the moral policemen of the world and more like its lawless economic exploiters ... these popular detective stories brought the nation face to face with the specter of its own criminal guilt, an impending colonial revenge.'[5] *A Study in Scarlet* and *The Sign of Four* are as much about guilt and revenge as the science of detection. Yumna Siddiqi points out that the Holmes stories are intensely concerned with the figure of the returned and potentially damaged colonial. The 'return from the colonies to the metropole was a routine phenomenon' and Siddiqi sees Doyle himself as a returned colonial of sorts.[6] The question of how to tell the story of this world concerned him from the beginning of his adult life.

There are several empires in Doyle's life as well as in his work. He has been called 'one of the great Victorian apologists of empire'[7] and, after volunteering as a medical officer in a field hospital in South Africa, he wrote in support of England's actions in *The Great Boer War* (1902), for which he was knighted. His friends included imperialist luminaries Rudyard Kipling,

Rider Haggard, Andrew Lang and Robert Baden-Powell and he writes in *Memories and Adventures* with a sure-footed belief in the nation-building talents of Anglo-Saxons abroad. Doyle was also, however, an advocate for justice in the contact zone of empire, coming to the defence of Roger Casement, whose work in exposing the atrocities in the Congo he supported, and Anglo-Indian lawyer George Edalji, who was falsely convicted of a crime largely because of suspicions against his mixed-race family.[8] While the empire is taken for granted in the Holmes stories, there is nothing ennobling about it. The stories that emerge from characters' imperial lives are almost entirely tales of greed, desperation and abuse of power. In *Memories and Adventures*, Doyle would wonder if 'the colonies were really worth the price we had to pay' (50).

Less well-known but perhaps more important to a sense of how Doyle saw England's empires was his work prior to inventing Sherlock Holmes. In 1880, Doyle served as a ship surgeon on a whaler with the name he would later bestow on the main character in *A Study in Scarlet: Hope*. In October of 1881, after he graduated from medical school in Edinburgh, he served for six months as ship medical officer on the African Steam Navigation Company's steamer S. S. *Mayumba* bound for West Africa. While he certainly saw some of the painful legacies of slavery, Doyle also saw a range of opportunities for apprehending anew the boundaries of the world. The best evidence we have of this are the essays he wrote for the *British Journal of Photography* as an amateur photographer in 1882: 'On the Slave Coast with a Camera' and 'Up an African River with the Camera'. Here, as in *A Study in Scarlet*, the writing strains at its generic borders; the essays combine travel writing, social commentary, technical information and narrative of national identity. There is a subtle processing of the world he is seeing with his own eyes, even if sometimes behind a camera. Sometimes he is frankly racist, commenting repeatedly on the 'ugliness' and smell of the natives. He writes in 'Up an African River with the Camera' that 'Dante might have made another circle in hell to rival the frozen stream and the burning marl, had he ever realized the horrors of an African swamp'.[9] He comments on the barren nature of the African landscape in ways that underwrite imperial exploration. At other times, Doyle can be more broad-minded, understanding what he sees as the effects of, rather than justification for, imperialist occupation. He describes the natives as 'demoralized by contact with the traders and by the brutality of the slave trade'.[10]

A Study in Scarlet and *The Sign of Four* address questions of how bodies relate to one another in this violent, global space. Actual bodies – American, English, Indian and Andaman – are poisoned, stabbed and drowned across a range of narrative bodies (letters, novels, newspaper stories, histories, first-person and third-person accounts). Negotiating in and around these bodies helps to shape the detective who will eventually take his talents to the *Strand*.

A Study in Scarlet

A Study in Scarlet almost never appeared. Doyle offered it to three publishers before Ward, Lock and Company accepted it, and then only on the condition that they waited a year to bring it out in *Beeton's Christmas Annual* for 1887. Before we even meet Holmes, we are located within a world of unfinished foreign violence. Watson tells us he was 'attached to the Fifth Northumberland Fusiliers as Assistant Surgeon' at the time of the second Afghan War. While his service and sacrifice shape our sense of Watson as a man, an Englishman and a sure-footed narrator, Doyle does not represent his military service with waving flags: 'The campaign brought honours and promotion to many, but for me it had nothing but misfortune and disaster'. A 'Jezail bullet' struck Watson's shoulder and his recovery at the base hospital in Peshawar is impeded by 'enteric fever, that curse of our Indian possessions' (15). The effects of warfare are broadened from the bullet of an enemy's gun to the country itself. The language of possession subtly hints that Watson and his fellow soldiers might be where they do not belong.

Watson repairs his broken self by going 'halves' with Sherlock Holmes, who is looking for a roommate and who remarks that the doctor has been in Afghanistan. These two halves come together across the empire to figure out how an American winds up dead in London. Watson and Holmes, newly ensconced in the rooms on Baker Street, are contacted about a body found in a room where there is blood but no wound and no apparent robbery. The *Daily Telegraph* reports on the crime and 'after alluding airily to the Vehmgericht, aqua tofana, Carbonari, the Marchioness de Brinvilliers, the Darwinian theory, the principles of Malthus, and the Ratcliff Highway murders' concludes by 'admonishing the Government and advocating a closer watch over foreigners in England' (41). Doyle winks at contemporary theories of crime, which also illustrate the 'heterogeneous, global unity'[11] of London.

Another body, that of Joseph Stangerson, turns up and Holmes sets a trap for and apprehends Jefferson Hope. Before Holmes can explain how he did it and before Hope tells his story, however, the novel lurches to the edge of the civilised world. From the first lines of Part Two, America is an 'arid and repulsive desert' which serves as a 'barrier against the advance of civilization' (52). As with Doyle's representations of the West African coast, nature is a powerful and unforgiving force. The 'swift-flowing rivers' and 'dark and gloomy valleys' all 'preserve ... the common characteristics of barrenness, inhospitality, and misery' (52). Echoing the imperialist tropes of his photography essays, Doyle depopulates the hostile landscape: 'there are no inhabitants of this land of despair. A band of Pawnees or of Blackfeet may occasionally traverse it in order to reach other hunting-grounds' (52). Violence 'done under the name of religion' (63) holds the land in an 'invisible network' of terror (68). One aspect of this violent religion is polygamy, and the crimes that end up in Baker Street begin when Lucy Ferrier, the adopted daughter of John Ferrier, is forced to become part of the 'harem' (73) of one of the sons of the Mormon Elders, Drebber and Stangerson. Father and daughter refuse and they escape with Jefferson Hope. But they are followed, John Ferrier is murdered and Lucy, captured, dies of a broken heart shortly after her wedding day. Hope, using his frontier tracking skills (he describes himself as a '"Washoe hunter"' (68)), follows Drebber and Stangerson: 'If there was nothing else left to him, he could at least devote his life to revenge' (73). In an image Doyle will use in the future to describe Holmes himself, Hope is likened to 'a human bloodhound, with his mind wholly set upon the one object to which he had devoted his life' (76). The search significantly spans the world: 'When he reached St. Petersburg, they had departed for Paris; and when he followed them there, he learned that they had just set off for Copenhagen' (76). Hunting skills honed in the American west can be applied all over the globe. Hope provides an account of the murders while in custody at Scotland Yard before conveniently dying from an aneurysm. Sounding like Holmes, who refers to himself in *The Sign of Four* as '"the last and highest court of appeal in detection"' (90), Hope declares that '"I should be judge, jury and executioner all rolled into one. You'd have done the same, if you have any manhood in you, if you had been in my place"' (78).

The natural death of the American murderer who shares the soon-to-be celebrated traits of the Great Detective raises questions about what role England plays in solving the world's mysteries. The country's association with law and order is complicated by the novel's ending. While the reader knows that Holmes is the one who solved the crimes, the public story is different. A local newspaper reports that the successful resolution of the investigation '"brings out in the most striking manner the efficiency of our detective police force, and will serve as a lesson to all foreigners that they will do wisely to settle their feuds at home, and not to carry them on to British soil"' (86). Official narratives that attempt to draw boundaries around nations are misreading the way the world works: there is not a single story. This is underscored in the generic identity crisis of *A Study in Scarlet* as well. Some critics see *A Study in Scarlet* as shifting between the western, the sensation and the detective story.[12] Ousby sees it as a kind of reworking of the 'eulogistic tradition of biography'[13] with Watson the Boswell to Holmes's Johnson.

Critics read the rise of the detective story as a consequence of scientific innovation at the turn of the century. The most important aspect of Holmes, argues Christopher Clausen, 'is that he is conceived – and conceives of himself – as a man who applies scientific methods to the detection of crime, and that his success as a detective is due to those methods'.[14] The role of science in establishing the borders of civilised society and the connection of scientific discovery to a kind of imperial mastery has been a central focus of critical treatments of the Holmes stories. Watson comes down to breakfast in *A Study in Scarlet* to find a copy of 'The Book of Life', an article written by Holmes, which argues that 'an observant man might learn by an accurate and systematic examination of all that came in his way' (23). Though Watson finds absurd the idea that '"[f]rom a drop of water ... a logician could infer the possibility of an Atlantic or a Niagara without having seen or heard of one or the other"' (23), this detail is provided as foreshadowing Holmes's method, which reads footprints, bloodstains and poison in his emerging portrait of Jefferson Hope. In response to Watson's scepticism, Holmes invokes Darwin and says that '"[o]ne's ideas must be as broad as Nature if they are to interpret Nature"' (37). This is a nod to the Darwinian theories of criminality that are both mocked and deployed in the story (Drebber has a 'low forehead, blunt nose, and prognathous jaw' which gives him 'a singularly simious and ape-like appearance' (29)) but also a sense of the authority that comes with scientific knowledge. Scientific discoveries in the late nineteenth century were bound up with concepts of power; both science as a methodology and law as a form provide a sense of order that justifies the role England wants to play in the world.

However, these forms are not unquestioned. As Lestrade leads Hope away, feeling that the murders may well be justified, he says '"the forms of the law must be complied with"' (83). We all know that the 'criminal' in the cell is acting on principles of justice and the 'form' of police effectiveness, the 'testimonial' which concludes the novel, is misleading. What England represents at this moment is a fluid culture attempting to be understood by professionals (scientists, detectives, philosophers, anthropologists). But it also has a history of violence which calls into question its ability to model justice. English lawlessness is nodded at with Doyle's reference to Charles the First early in the text. As Holmes informs Watson, he has picked up a copy of *De Jure inter Gentes*, published in Latin in 1642, when '"Charles's head was still firm on his shoulders"' (38), reminding English readers of their own history of civil war. Indeed, the novel Doyle wrote while *A Study in Scarlet* was making the rounds was *Micah Clarke* (1889), a story of the Monmouth rebellion, which pitted Protestants against Catholics, countrymen against one another in a bloody battle with even bloodier justice: thousands were killed and another thousand executed or transported. America is part of this bloody English history and there is no nostalgia for America in the Holmes stories, where it exists as a place of brutality. From the Ku Klux Klan behind the murders in 'The Five Orange Pips' to the organised terrorism of *The Valley of Fear*, emissaries from America do not generally mean well.

Doyle does see America as part of England's story, part of the canvas that affords opportunity for 'Anglo-Saxon tenacity': the Mormons of *A Study in Scarlet* triumph over 'every impediment which Nature could place in the way' (58). But he is ultimately critical of how, here describing the Mormons as 'victims of persecution [who] had now turned persecutors on their own account, and persecutors of the most terrible description' (62). Power corrupts, an important lesson for even an occasional critic of British Empire. Doyle sees violence as borderless and is careful to point out that organised crime is widespread: 'Not the Inquisition of Seville, nor the German Vehmgericht, nor the Secret Societies of Italy, were ever able to put a more formidable machinery in motion than that which cast a cloud over the state of Utah' (62). Ousby sees the early Holmes as morally neutral, outrage 'almost inconceivable on the lips of the cold-blooded scientist of *A Study in Scarlet* or the languorous Decadent of *The Sign of Four*' (163). I would argue that it is not so much that the early Holmes is morally neutral but that there is a scepticism about what formal laws and narrative borders can do to organise the experiences of those who, in 'A Case of Identity', '"hover over this great city"' (191); Holmes realises the world is bigger than he is.

The Sign of Four

The Sign of Four begins with another body marked by imperial experience. Watson begins with a detailed description of Holmes injecting cocaine into his veins and feels 'irritable at the sight'. He gives Holmes a mild rebuke about the '"cost"' of such habits, noting that drug use '"involves increased tissue-change and may at least leave a permanent weakness"' (89). Lawrence Frank, however, notes that the concern might express a more generalised anxiety: 'Both the late-Victorian physician and the general public', Frank explains,

> perceived such addicting drugs as contaminations emanating from alien and primitive lands. It made little difference that cocaine came primarily from the Peruvian coca leaf, while opium and morphine were derived from poppy plants grown in the Ottoman Empire, Persia, and India. Watson's disapproval simply

furthers the mythology that identified cocaine and morphine as a threat to all things British, rational, and normal.[15]

The Sign of Four concerns not only threats to British bodies but what actually constitutes the boundaries of the empire and the English detective's beat.

Doyle's second Holmes novel is not quite as dramatically divided as his first but it shares some of the odd organisation of a story casting about for its generic footing. Holmes and his method are more consistently the focus, but there are echoes of the American part of *A Study in Scarlet* in Jonathan Small's 'strange story' which begins with the Sepoy Rebellion. Nicholas Daly calls *The Sign of Four* 'a whittled-down version' of Wilkie Collins's *The Moonstone* (1868).[16] Insofar as *The Sign of Four* tells the story of violence in India over treasure that ultimately involves English homes and English criminals, Daly is correct. But there is a significant difference between the novels, one that tells us something about the late-Victorian problem of borders that Doyle is working through. *The Moonstone* begins with the 'family paper' that details the story of John Herncastle's criminal behaviour in the storming of Seringapatam in 1799.[17] His crime and the booty (the Moonstone diamond) follow the family back not only to the heart of the English estate but to the bosom of the young woman, Rachel Verinder, who receives it as a birthday present. The mystery requires an imperial adventurer, London detective and mixed-race doctor to figure out the solution. Collins's novel raises questions it does not entirely answer about the 'crime' of British imperial practice and its legitimacy as the embodiment of the rule of law. But it does neatly begin and end with India, formally relegating them to the margins of a largely English tale. In terms of the plot, *The Sign of Four* is similar: English crimes abroad return to haunt English soil. But formally, Doyle tells this story in a series of flashbacks, making the boundaries between the English story and the story of empire more interwoven.

The story moves between east and west, India and London. Along with the pearls, Mary brings a letter arranging a meeting with her mysterious benefactor. She sets off with Watson and Holmes and, in the cab ride, the reader begins to learn of a world connected by imperial misdeeds. Major Sholto is a friend of Mary's father because they commanded troops at the Andaman Islands; the paper of the mysterious letter is made in India; and Watson entertains Mary through a foggy and ghostlike London with tales of adventures in Afghanistan. The reader is again reminded of the fluidity of borders when the trio finally reaches the 'questionable and forbidding neighbourhood' of Thaddeus Sholto, newly existing because of 'the monster tentacles ... the giant city was throwing out into the country' (99). They are greeted at this English suburban house by Sholto's Indian servant. The story Sholto tells them takes them to another site,

Pondicherry Lodge, the home of his brother Bartholomew. Pondicherry is a city in India that was fought over by the French and English and changed hands several times. Doyle reminds us of the complexity of imperial experience in thus naming the Sholto estate. Major Sholto died from fright before he could tell his sons the location of the treasure, of which Mary's pearls are but a taste. After a considerable search, Thaddeus and Bartholomew discover it in the roof, literally hanging over their heads. Before it could be retrieved, however, Bartholomew is murdered by a poisoned thorn. Holmes tellingly says that this case '"breaks fresh ground in the annals of crime in this country – though parallel cases suggest themselves from India and ... Senegambia"' (111). The interweaving of England and its empires continues as the chase follows Small and his sidekick, the Andaman islander Tonga, in a chase on the Thames, the commercial heart of the British Empire and, eventually, the final resting place of both Tonga and the priceless Agra treasure. Small is captured and gives his 'strange story' (143).

While the novel's conclusion does not accord the same sympathy to Small as it does to Jefferson Hope, it is still not clear where Doyle comes down on responsibility for these crimes and what kinds of national boundaries Holmes polices. On the one hand the characterisation of Tonga is clearly racist and serves imperialist narratives about cultural superiority. He is described as a 'savage, distorted creature' with 'features ... deeply marked with all bestiality and cruelty' (138). It is easy to see Doyle working through ideas about evolutionary anthropology here, not least in the prehistoric presence of Tonga in modern Victorian London. Together, Watson the army doctor and Holmes, who attributes his methodology to evolutionary thinking at the start of the novel, become, Frank argues, 'representatives of Empire, perceiving events through those anthropological prejudices that were marshalled at the end of the nineteenth century to legitimize imperialism'.[18] There is no refuting such claims, but they should be examined. Doyle shares late-century ideas about primitive peoples and crime, but he uses those ideas in characterising white criminals as well. Recall Enoch Drebber's simian qualities and the 'terrible animal face' of Selden, the brutal killer loose on the Devonshire moors in *The Hound of the Baskervilles* (725). Tonga is likened to an animal that 'grinned and chattered at us with half animal fury' (138). Small, however, gives Tonga credit for his loyalty, one of the most cherished qualities in the Holmes stories (think of Watson): '"He was staunch and true, was little Tonga. No man ever had a more faithful mate"' (155).

If one of the things that Holmes, as an imperial policeman, is supposed to do is order everything, that does not entirely happen in this novel either. The whodunit questions are answered but things are not restored to their rightful place. The Agra treasure ends up in the Thames. Unjust deaths hang, unresolved, in the narrative air. In particular, Doyle has Small describe the murder of Achmet, the merchant carrying the rajah's treasure to safety in the Agra fort, in a way that does not treat un-English life lightly. Achmet does not go quietly or anonymously. He evades the first attempt on his life '"running like the wind, with a smear of blood across his face"'. Both Small and Watson attest to the particularly 'cold-blooded business' of killing this man (150), and the reader is not allowed to lose Achmet in the novel's body count. Small is unrepentant about his throwing the treasure into the Thames. When Inspector Jones tells him he would have had a '"better chance at your trial"' if he '"had helped justice"', Small exclaims, '"A pretty justice! Whose loot is this, if it is not ours. Where is the justice that I should give it up to those who have never earned it"' (144)? If Small has no real justification, neither does the idea of imperialism, which often in the Holmes stories comes down to money. There is no redeeming idea, to paraphrase Marlow who would so characterise it eight years later in Joseph Conrad's *Heart of Darkness* (1899). When Small is being inducted into the plot by Abdullah Khan, the latter says '"We only ask you to do that which your countrymen come to this land for. We ask you to be rich"' (147). Such greed is of the same kind that drew Doyle's ire about King Leopold's atrocities in *The Crime of the Congo* (1909). As Siddiqi has argued, the colonial return narrative is ambivalent, from Watson's partial recuperation to crimes committed overseas coming home to roost. As she explains, the 'detective narrative then has to manage the supplement or the unresolved residue of historical trauma. In this sense, Conan Doyle's stories are energized by the contradictions of Empire'.[19] If *A Study in Scarlet* is awkwardly constructed because it does not know where to draw boundaries around crime, *The Sign of Four* is ambivalent on where it wants to draw boundaries around guilt.

Doyle is less ambivalent in his treatment of women in these first Holmes novels. If both *A Study in Scarlet* and *The Sign of Four* raise questions about England's empires and what constitutes the jurisdiction of the English detective, they seem more certain about what women represent to the nation. Both novels contain love stories and, to some degree, women stand in for a kind of national ideal, a thing to be won over, to be protected. Lucy Ferrier is described in *Scarlet* as 'the flower of Utah' (as Doyle continues, 'the year which saw her father the richest of the farmers left her as fair a specimen of American girlhood as could be found in the whole Pacific slope' (59). Hope's tenacity in winning Lucy's love is described just pages after Doyle praises American tenacity conquering the rugged western terrain. About his courtship, Hope 'swore in his heart that he would not fail in this if human effort and human perseverance could render him successful' (61). Similarly, in

The Sign of Four Mary Morstan becomes identified with the Agra treasure, which she stands to inherit but which would cost her Watson, lest his attentions be mistaken for the same financial greed which characterises the novel's villains from Sholto to Small. Critics such as Catherine Belsey and Frank have discussed the ways in which Doyle's representation of women serves an imperialist ideology. Amidst the cesspool of empire, Mary is the centre of a radiant and reliable Englishness. When Watson drops her off after the dramatic visit to Pondicherry Lodge, she is received with motherly attention. 'It was soothing', Watson explains, 'to catch even that passing glimpse of a tranquil English home in the midst of the wild, dark business which had absorbed us' (116).

While Doyle's representation of this feminine ideal in these first novels underwrites a British imperialist self-fashioning around ideas of purity and protection, such representations are challenged by the stories that will surround Holmes's adventures in the *Strand*. Doyle moves from his 'two little books' into the heterogeneous unity of George Newnes's monthly magazine, and Sherlock Holmes will be surrounded by the *Strand*'s notable female detectives. In the years during Holmes's reign, several female detectives travel the world exactly as Doyle imagined it, borderless and shaped by often violent forces of the expanding empire and global capitalism. Grant Allen, a friend and neighbour of Doyle's, wrote the Miss Cayley series from 1898–99 and the Hilda Wade stories from 1899, dying during the final instalment (Doyle finished it for him). Miss Cayley, clearly a New Woman, travels the world solving relatively light-hearted mysteries; Hilda Wade's investigation, however, embroils her in an imperial war. One instalment finds her riding a bicycle, holding a baby and evading angry troops fighting in the Matabele uprising. She is also, like Watson, in the medical profession (she is a nurse) and so cements the detective's association with the scientific method while challenging any notion that this subject position is reserved for men alone. Richard Marsh's Judith Lee, featured in stories running in the *Strand* from August 1911 to 1912, is an unusual sleuth. Like Holmes she is quirky (her key talent is lip-reading) and single. Unlike Holmes she narrates the stories herself, challenging the Watsonian tradition of 'eulogistic biography'. The *Strand*'s boundaries might shore up some formal concerns as the stories become, in Doyle's words, 'complete in themselves'. But the magazine's pages, full of different kinds of detectives and different genres narrating an increasingly connected world, keep the Great Detective in the same complicated conversation that troubled the boundaries of those 'two little books'.

Notes

1. Ian Ousby, *Bloodhounds of Heaven: The Detective in English Fiction from Godwin to Doyle* (Cambridge: Harvard University Press, 1976), 151; Joseph McLaughlin, *Writing the Urban Jungle: Reading Empire in London from Doyle to Eliot* (Charlottesville: University Press of Virginia, 2000), 27.

2. Jon Thompson, *Fiction, Crime and Empire: Clues to Modernity and Postmodernism* (Chicago: University of Chicago Press, 1993): 66.

3. Ronald R. Thomas, *Detective Fiction and the Rise of Forensic Science* (Cambridge: Cambridge University Press, 1999), 238–9.

4. Rosemary Jann, *The Adventures of Sherlock Holmes: Detecting Social Order* (New York: Twayne Publishers, 1995).

5. Thomas, *Detective Fiction*, 220.

6. Yumna Siddiqi, *Anxieties of Empire and the Fiction of Intrigue* (Cambridge: Cambridge University Press, 2008), 63–4.

7. Thompson, *Fiction, Crime and Empire*, 68.

8. See Arthur Conan Doyle, *The Crime of the Congo* (Windlesham, Crowborough: Hutchinson and Company, 1909).

9. Arthur Conan Doyle, *Essays on Photography*, eds. John Michael Gibson and Richard Lancelyn Green (London: Secker and Warburg, 1982), 50.

10. Ibid., 27.

11. Siddiqi, *Anxieties*, 65.

12. Thompson, *Fiction, Crime and Empire*, 64.

13. Ousby, *Bloodhounds of Heaven*, 146.

14. Christopher Clausen, 'Sherlock Holmes, Order, and the Late-Victorian Mind', *The Georgia Review* 38:1 (1984), 104–23 (109).

15. Lawrence Frank, 'Dreaming the Medusa: Imperialism, Primitivism, and Sexuality in Arthur Conan Doyle's The Sign of Four', *Signs: Journal of Women in Culture and Society* 22:1 (1996), 52–85 (58).

16. Nicholas Daly, *Modernism, Romance and the* Fin de Siècle: *Popular Fiction and British Culture, 1880–1914* (Cambridge: Cambridge University Press, 1999), 101.

17. Wilkie Collins, *The Moonstone, 1868*, ed. J. I. M. Stewart (London: Penguin Books, 1966), 40.

18. Ibid., 69.

19. Siddiqi, *Anxieties of Empire*, 85.

II

CHRISTOPHER PITTARD

Sidney Paget and Visual Culture in the *Adventures* and *Memoirs of Sherlock Holmes*

In 'A Scandal in Bohemia' Holmes makes an infamous distinction between 'seeing' and 'observing'. '"You see, but you do not observe"' (162), he tells Watson, using the example of the Baker Street steps to distinguish between the acts of unengaged perception (seeing) and of fitting what is known into a model of the world (observing). Watson has seen the steps countless times, but does not know how many there are. This scene has formed the basis for numerous discussions of visuality in the Holmes stories, based on a wider historical connection between powers of surveillance and the nineteenth-century emergence of detective fiction, and new understandings of vision itself, moving from abstract theories of opticality to embodied models of the seeing eye. The visual and optical cultures of the Holmes stories have been extensively explored by Martin Willis, Srdjan Smajić and Elizabeth Carolyn Miller, amongst others. But while these discussions often focus on vision within the plots of Doyle's fiction, this chapter situates the stories' treatment of the visual in the context of their material production; that is, in the *Strand Magazine*. It focuses, in particular, on the interplay between Sidney Paget's illustrations and Doyle's words in the twenty-four short stories published in the *Strand* as *The Adventures of Sherlock Holmes* between 1891–3 (and subsequently in volume form as the *Adventures* and *Memoirs*). This emphasis on the first two series encompasses both Holmes's figurative rebirth in moving to the short-story format of the *Strand*, and his 'death' in what Doyle assumed would be the final Holmes story, tracing the ways in which Paget's images became instrumental in consolidating Holmes's popularity.

Sidney Paget was not the first artist to picture Holmes. D. H. Friston had provided four images for *A Study in Scarlet* in *Beeton's Christmas Annual* in 1887; on republication in volume form by Ward, Lock and Company in 1888, Friston's work was replaced by six somewhat indifferent illustrations by Charles Doyle, Arthur's father. A slightly more successful image of Holmes was the frontispiece that Charles Kerr provided for the Spencer Blackett republication of *The Sign of Four* (1890). By 1891 Paget was, therefore, at least the fourth artist to illustrate Holmes (and roughly contemporary with George Hutchinson's work for a Ward reissue of *Study* in late 1891), but his influence on the popular visual conception of the detective would only be matched by William Gillette's stage portrayal (premiering in 1899) and Frederic Dorr Steele's images for American publications. Yet rather than being supplements to Doyle's texts, Paget's illustrations play a crucial role in the narratives' creation of meaning. In a periodical setting that emphasised continuity and resolution, the illustrations in each month's episode established chains of repetition between themselves and, in referring back to previous stories, fashioned a sense of continuity that facilitated a reading community without excluding new readers. Breakages in these chains therefore also signal moments of crisis in the stories (most obviously in 'The Final Problem').

It is not my intention to repeat the critical truism that the Holmes stories privilege sight over the other senses. True, there are irresistible connections to be made between the two, not least the biographical circumstance of Doyle being an ocular specialist. When, in *A Study in Scarlet*, Holmes asks '"Why shouldn't we use a little art jargon?"' (36), he emphasises what would be the continued importance of visual art to the Holmesian canon, culminating in the portrait of Hugo Baskerville in *The Hound of the Baskervilles*. More abstract visuality is crucial to stories such as 'The Musgrave Ritual', which turns on questions of optics and observations of light, and in which Holmes describes his process of deductive empathy in terms of the personal equation problem originating in astronomical observation (395). The iconic image of Holmes with a magnifying glass (sparingly used in Doyle's texts) exemplifies a wider trend in late Victorian detective fiction equating the detective with the supposed mechanical objectivity of the camera lens. As Walter Benjamin argues, the invention of photography 'made it possible for the first time to preserve permanent and unmistakable traces of a human being. The detective story came into being when this most decisive of all conquests of a person's incognito had been accomplished'.[1] Benjamin may have overstated the photograph's permanence and unmistakability, but visual technologies and detective fiction have long been critically inseparable.

Yet the familiar argument that the Holmes stories privilege sight has two blind spots, so to speak. First, it risks limiting the sensorium of the canon, in which smells, sounds and textures also signify (the scent of white jessamine and the cry of the hound in *The Hound of the Baskervilles*; that other Devonian dog, silent, in 'Silver Blaze'). Secondly, it often downplays the manner in which (as Smajić notes) the stories focus on logical reasoning and encyclopaedic or taxonomic forms of knowledge, rather than on empirical visual perception.[2] Indeed, the stories often present vision as an obstacle to detection, rather than its tool; consider the number of times Holmes closes his eyes while listening to his clients. The problems of seeing are explicitly addressed in 'The Five Orange Pips':

> Sherlock Holmes closed his eyes, and placed his elbows upon the arms of his chair, with his finger-tips together. 'The ideal reasoner', he remarked, 'would, when he has once been shown a single fact in all its bearings, deduce from it not only all the chain of events which led up to it, but also all the results which would follow from it … We have not yet grasped the results which the reason alone can attain to. Problems may be solved in the study which have baffled all those who have sought a solution by the aid of their senses'. (224–5)

Holmes's closed eyes reflect a distrust of pure empiricism and of the deception of the senses. Deductive observation makes use of sight, but it is worthless without rational training. Yet as Holmes notes, direct observation is not always necessary; the detective can solve the crime simply by reasoning from his study (indeed, except for a brief reference to Watson's medical visits, the real time action of 'The Five Orange Pips' never leaves Baker Street).

Yet for all their insistence on the powers of mental visualisation over empirical sight, the Holmes stories as they first appeared in the *Strand* undercut this by including several illustrations that direct – or challenge – the way readers envisaged Doyle's scenes and characters. The rest of the chapter therefore considers Paget's influence in the success of Sherlock Holmes following the detective's relocation to the *Strand*.

Sidney Paget

Paget was born in 1860 in Clerkenwell, one of nine children, of whom three were artists (Sidney's younger brother Walter, and his elder brother Henry). He was educated at Cowper Street School, before spending two years studying at the British Museum, and then at Heatherly School of Fine Art. Paget entered the Royal Academy Schools in 1881; several biographical accounts report that it was here that he met his fellow student Alfred Morris Butler (supposedly the model for Watson), but correspondence from 1879 suggests that Paget already knew Butler, or at least a contemporary of the same name (and did not initially like him: 'He was very kind + Butleresque but I don't like him + never shall. He showed me sketches of Italy, they are not good').[3] Paget found some modest success at the Royal Academy, winning medals in the Armitage prizes of 1883, 1885 and 1886 with work that mostly partook of a mid-Victorian artistic tradition of drawing on literary sources; his most notable work in this vein was the Arthurian *Lancelot and Elaine* (1891) and

'The Broken Sheds Looked Sad and Strange' (1881), inspired by Tennyson's 'Mariana' (1830).

Paget's fame would come with the launch of the *Strand* in December 1890. From the outset, the proprietor George Newnes closely associated the new sixpenny monthly with the visual arts; the first issue included a colour print from the 1890 Royal Academy Exhibition, and Newnes appointed the artist William H. J. Boot as art editor. Newnes had aimed to include images on every page, eventually compromising for an illustration on every opening, with his offices on Southampton Street incorporating a public gallery featuring the original drawings. Boot had intended to commission Walter Paget, a more experienced artist, but merely addressed the request to 'Mr Paget' at the family home, where it was picked up in error by the elder brother (though this version of events is disputed, most famously by J. D. Milner in the 1912 *Dictionary of National Biography*). The story recalls the start of Doyle's writing career, when the manuscript of his first novel *The Narrative of John Smith* became lost in the post, prompting Doyle to move in different literary directions. The textual-visual Holmes was thus created at the intersection of two fortuitous postal errors.

Paget worked prolifically not only for the *Strand* (appearing in the magazine before Holmes himself), but also for *Cassell's Magazine*, *The Graphic*, *The Sphere* and the *Illustrated London News*, among many others. Yet his fame derives chiefly from the Holmes work, which extended to *The Return of Sherlock Holmes*. Relatively few of his 359 known Holmesian drawings exist today; twenty-six images are known to belong to a mixture of private collections and public archives (including the University of Texas at Austin, the University of Minneapolis, Toronto Public Library and Portsmouth City Council), with the location of a further four unknown.[4] Somewhat bizarrely, most of the original drawings stored in the Paget family attic were destroyed by marauding squirrels;[5] however, enough of his work for novels such as Max Pemberton's *The Puritan's Wife* (1896) exists to offer insight into Paget's working practices.

The first stage of the process of illustrating Doyle's stories was Boot's selection of scenes for illustration, following a first reading of the text for a sense of plot, and a second to identify key incidents. Paget himself may have helped in this selection of scenes, and was certainly responsible for their captioning. Once the episodes were chosen, Paget made preliminary sketches in pencil on brown paper and board, picking out highlights in white watercolour or gouache. These sketches tend to focus on the details of individual figures or on particularly challenging anatomical compositions (Paget's sketches for *The Puritan's Wife*, held by Portsmouth City Council, feature a macabre array of detached body parts). The final drawing would be about ten inches by seven, around twice the size of the final product in the *Strand*, and copied using a combination of halftone photomechanical engraving (*Adventures*), and a more traditional engraving method using lines and hatching (*Memoirs*). In the former technique, a screen placed between the image and the camera translated the image into a matrix of small dots as a guide for the engravers, who would adjust the plate for the press as necessary to preserve or accentuate detail (only one drawing in the first series of the *Adventures* – 'A Simple Minded Clergyman' from 'A Scandal in Bohemia' – was not produced in this way, instead being reproduced by line engraving).[6]

As a result, the various engravers and printers of Paget's work had a substantial influence on the look of the final image, with faulty engraving or uneven ink distribution occasionally causing details to be lost, while the transfer of the image to the plate tended to flatten out many of the shadings and details in the original. Most of the images of the first series of *Adventures* were engraved by Waterlow & Sons Ltd (indicated by a W. & S. Ltd signature); Hare, another engraving firm, appears slightly less frequently, and a handful of images were engraved by Paul Naumann, who provided all of the engravings for the *Memoirs*. Once the engraving was ready the page would be set, with Paget's images fully integrated into the text, sometimes cutting across columns and paragraphs. Occasionally, small blocks of type were isolated in a corner by the diagonal cut of an inserted illustration, or the dual columns of the *Strand* had to swerve apart to accommodate a centrally placed image (an effect lost by reprints, which often move Paget's images to the margins, as did Newnes's reprint of the *Adventures* in volume form).

Rather than the image serving the words, the placement of words could serve the illustration; as the *Strand*'s early twentieth-century art editor George W. Leech commented, 'A thoughtful arrangement of the type can also materially enhance the look of the illustration'.[7] Authors were sometimes unimpressed by the implications of this inversion; Doyle, while largely content with Paget's work, complained to Herbert Greenhough Smith (the *Strand*'s literary editor) about Amédée Forestier's illustrations for his horror story 'The Leather Funnel' (1902), arguing that '[i]t is not right to print such a story two words on a line on each side of an unnecessary illustration. It is bad economy to spoil a £200 story by the intrusion of a 3 guinea engraving'.[8] If, as Franco Moretti argues of the Holmes stories, 'Suspicion often originates from a violation of the law of exchange between equivalent values: anyone who pays more than a market price or accepts a low salary can only be spurred by criminal motives', then Doyle himself was not above similarly policing the relationship between word and image in terms of economic exchange, of both monetary payment and space on the page.[9]

Paget's Holmes

Paget's illustrations are almost entirely centred on people and portraiture, especially of Holmes, an image reputedly based on his brother Walter and considerably more handsome than Doyle's original conception of Holmes as having 'a thin, razor-like face, with a great hawk's-bill of a nose, and two small eyes, set close together on either side of it'.[10] Of the 201 illustrations Paget produced for the *Adventures* and *Memoirs*, 121 feature Holmes; eighty-two of these include Watson, particularly so in the early stories of the *Memoirs*. Holmes is often pictured alone; Watson only receives this honour twice ('The Boscombe Valley Mystery' and 'The Final Problem'), and in two stories does not appear at all ('A Case of Identity' and 'The "Gloria Scott"'). Yet Watson's authority as narrator is subtly illustrated in that both series close with his image, not Holmes's: 'The Copper Beeches' shows Watson shooting the crazed Rucastle dog, anticipating *The Hound of the Baskervilles*; 'The Final Problem' ends with Watson alone at Reichenbach. 'The Final Problem' aside, Paget's focus on portraiture means that his figures often hover in spaces whose setting is only indicated by a few key signifiers. The pervasiveness of this style is evident in the striking appearance of the few exceptions; in the *Adventures* and *Memoirs* it is only in the opening street scene of 'The Resident Patient' that Paget implies a crowded London that approaches G. C. Haité's famous magazine cover image of the Strand itself. Paget's illustrations employ a more modernist theatricality; a few well-chosen props stand in for a whole setting. Yet he did not comprehensively reject his earlier tradition of realist painting; an image such as 'Tell Me Everything, I said' from 'The Yellow Face', in which the weeping Effie Munro kneels beside her husband while he turns aside in dismay, recalls similar dynamics in Augustus Egg's *Past and Present No. 1* (1858) and George Elgar Hicks's *Woman's Mission: Companion to Manhood* (1863).

The often isolated quality of Paget's earlier illustrations reflects another aspect of the Holmes stories. Rather than providing a wider visual field which must be sifted by the viewer for relevant signifiers (in the tradition of, for instance, Victorian narrative painting), Paget's images frequently represent a perspective where extraneous information has *already* been excluded. This recalls Michel Foucault's distinction between two types of medical vision: the gaze and the glance. For Foucault, the gaze 'implies an open field, and its essential activity is of the successive order of reading; it records and totalizes'.[11] In this sense, realist narratives tend to gaze, to reconstruct a wider world by ranging over its surface. By contrast, the glance 'strikes at one point, which is central or decisive; the gaze is endlessly modulated, the glance goes straight to its object'.[12] Though Paget occasionally gazes, more frequently he glances, homing in on key images. This perceptual mode predominates in the stories; the term 'glance' recurs frequently: '"I shall glance into the case for you"' (195); 'It was clear to me at a glance that he was in the grip of some deadly and chronic disease' (215). Sometimes the term is used paradoxically, as in 'The Speckled Band': 'Sherlock Holmes ran her over with one of his quick, all-comprehensive glances' (258), a modality that combines Foucault's ranging gaze with the piercing glance; more counterintuitively still, in 'The Beryl Coronet' Holmes promises that he and Watson will '"devote an hour to glancing a little more closely into details"' (308).

In excluding the irrelevant, Paget's illustrations come close to embodying the detective's view itself. But this is not to say that the images provide us with Holmes's perspective, nor that they always include visual clues. The complexities of the glance, and the problematics of vision in the Holmes stories more broadly, are encapsulated in the image 'Holmes Lashed Furiously' from 'The Speckled Band' (Figure 1). The choice of this illustration as the paradigmatic Holmesian image may seem paradoxical: the image of Holmes kneeling on Helen Stoner's bed while he lashes at the snake trained by Grimesby Roylott may be of interest to psychoanalytic critics (the visible phallic imagery of the cane replacing the unseen snake), but the illustration is striking for what it does not contain. Most of the image is a black wash of darkness. Why, then, this illustration? For one, the image captures a frequently recurring visual trope in *Adventures* such as 'The Red-headed League' and 'The Engineer's Thumb': the darkened room penetrated by a growing point of illumination (indeed, 'Holmes Lashed Furiously' is echoed by Paget the following month in 'The Engineer's Thumb' when Victor Hatherley is trapped within the hydraulic press). In the darkness of Helen Stoner's room, a crack of light from the adjoining room marks the arrival of the deadly snake. Everything becomes clear once a beam of light has penetrated the darkened room, allowing Holmes to then cast more (literal) light on the situation, although matters of optics momentarily blind Watson: '"You see it, Watson?" he yelled. "You see it?" But I saw nothing. At the moment when Holmes struck the light I heard a low, clear whistle, but the sudden glare flashing into my weary eyes made it impossible for me to tell what it was at which my friend lashed so savagely' (271–2). Watson's failure to see reads metaphorically at first as a failure to understand; readers must perform their own shifts of perspective when Watson's movement to the language of optics rewrites his blindness as literal.

'The Speckled Band', in presenting observers waiting in a darkened room for a light source to provide an explanatory image, borrows the imagery of

ADVENTURES OF SHERLOCK HOLMES.

" HOLMES LASHED FURIOUSLY."

Figure 1: Sidney Paget, 'Holmes Lashed Furiously', 'The Speckled Band', *Strand Magazine* 3 (February 1892), 155.

the camera obscura: the darkened box or room into which an inverted image of the exterior world is projected by the passage of light through a small aperture. As Jonathan Crary argues, the camera obscura represents an Enlightenment model of vision in which the observer became 'isolated, enclosed, and autonomous within its dark confines', and in which the act of seeing was separated 'from the physical body of the observer ... The monadic viewpoint of the individual is authenticated and legitimised by the camera obscura, but the observer's physical and sensory experience is supplanted by the relations between a mechanical apparatus and a pre-given world of objective truth'.[13] The nineteenth century would supplant this mechanical model of vision with modalities of sight that interiorised perception, both in terms of the psyche of the observer and the physicality of the eye. Thus, the artist Paget and the oculist Doyle borrow the iconography of the camera obscura to undermine it: the beam of light from the adjoining room is immediately washed out by Holmes's match (and in Paget's image by another light source that appears to be behind Holmes). Rather than presenting the passive viewer, Holmes immediately springs into action to delete the image. Watson's eyes are not the abstract observers of the camera obscura model, but the 'weary' physical organs of later ophthalmological models of embodied viewing. The curve of Holmes's rod implies action, of movement in time, but light also seems to curve around it; Paget's brush strokes of darkness follow the line of the cane and its projected course. Here, Paget's image approaches what W. J. T. Mitchell calls the hypericon: 'figures of figuration, pictures that reflect on the nature of images'.[14] Paget's illustration certainly draws on the darkened room imagery that structures the most famous of these hypericons (Plato's cave in the *Republic*, John Locke's dark room in *An Essay on Human Understanding*), but also mediates between what is seen and unseen, what is perceived and what is understood; the snake remains unseen by both Watson and the reader. The real focus of the image is the interplay between darkness and light, making darkness visible, but also rendering light blinding.

Chains of Illustration

While Paget's images might be understood in and of themselves, they also encouraged readers to view them sequentially. If Doyle and Newnes conceived of the Holmes stories as a series that could both be entered at any moment by new readers, yet also act as an unfolding text for a regular audience, then Paget's images worked in the same way in that they established imagistic chains within, and between, stories. While not acting in the narratologically sequential way of (for instance) the comic strip, nevertheless the images potentially offered competing stories. When *Strand* readers initially browsed their new copies, the narratives presented by the sequence of Paget's illustrations would have been their primary experience of the Holmes stories, to be displaced by Doyle's words. Likewise, it was Paget's signature that appeared much more frequently within the stories than Doyle's (mentioned only once, on the title page). Doyle was well aware of this primacy of the illustrator; in a letter to Greenhough Smith referring to the illustrations for his non-Holmes story 'The Lost Special', he specified that Max Cowper's drawings 'be mysterious like the story so that the reader can't quite understand it until he has read it'.[15] This is partially a concern with avoiding spoilers, but also that the reading experience threatened to overturn the hierarchy established in the later nineteenth century of author over artist. A browser who first read Holmes through the sequence of Paget's illustrations might construct a different kind of narrative altogether.

Many of Doyle's stories are now so familiar that it becomes difficult to recover any sense of how Paget's images might provide an alternative narrative. What is traceable, however, is how the illustrations take an active role in shaping meaning. 'A Scandal in Bohemia', the first story to unite Paget and Doyle, provides an excellent example. In this tale of reversals and exchanges (most obviously between the external signifiers of male and female, of detective and detected), the composition and placement of Paget's ten illustrations demonstrate a similar movement. The opening image, of Holmes standing before the fireplace in Baker Street while Watson sits on the left of the picture (Figure 2), provides the *Strand*'s first vision of Holmes, but also demonstrates a tension between word and image. The illustration accompanies a passage in which Holmes gleans information from the firelight striking the inside of Watson's left foot. But, as Elizabeth Miller points out, it is Watson's *right* instep that faces the light source, and Paget 'has framed the image so that the reader cannot see the effect of the firelight on Watson's right step either. What is visually available to Holmes in the story is not available in the illustration, both because of the "error" in the picture and because of its perspective'.[16] Miller reads this not as simple miscommunication between text and image, but rather as paradigmatic of how the stories complicate vision: 'vision is not a transparent, unmediated, or direct process, but is "framed" by conditions both internal and external to the viewer'.[17] There is, however, another sense in which this image self-reflexively foregrounds the question of vision in the stories: Holmes's stance in front of the fire makes him the literal focus, playing on the Latin *focus*, meaning hearth.

This inaugural image of Paget's Holmes is echoed on the facing page (Figure 3), with Holmes sitting at the table while Watson stands to read the King's note. The reflective qualities of the images themselves are enhanced by the manner in which (presumably) Boot has composed the page: the two images form a diagonally placed compositional pair: the first image in the top right of the page, the second in the bottom left. Whereas the first image shows Watson sitting on the left and Holmes standing on the right, the second illustration offers Holmes sitting on the right while Watson stands on the left. This reflective pattern continues over the page: the third image (Figure 4) shows the single figure of the masked King of Bohemia, while the fourth shifts the angle slightly to show the King throwing the mask onto the floor, accompanied in the picture by Holmes and Watson (Figure 5). Once again, the diagonal echo across the opening is preserved (bottom centre to top right). The fifth and sixth illustrations also offer a pair, though this time that you have been getting yourself very wet lately, and that you have a most clumsy and careless servant girl?"

"My dear Holmes," said I, "this is too much. You would certainly have been burned, had you lived a few centuries ago. It is true that I had a country walk on Thursday and came home in a dreadful mess; but, as I have changed my clothes, I can't imagine how you deduce it. As to Mary Jane, she is incorrigible, and my wife has given her notice; but there again I fail to see how you work it out."

He chuckled to himself and rubbed his long nervous hands together.

"It is simplicity itself," said he; "my eyes tell me that on the inside of your left shoe, just where the firelight strikes it, the leather is scored by six almost parallel cuts. Obviously they have been caused by someone who has very carelessly scraped round the edges of the sole in order to remove crusted mud from it. Hence, you see, my double deduction that you had been out in vile

"THEN HE STOOD BEFORE THE FIRE."

weather, and that you had a particularly malignant boot-slitting specimen of the London slavey. As to your practice, if a gentleman walks into my rooms smelling of iodoform, with a black mark of nitrate of silver upon his right fore-finger, and a bulge on the side of his top-hat to show where he has secreted his stethoscope, I must be dull indeed, if I do not pronounce him to be an active member of the medical profession."

I could not help laughing at the ease with which he explained his process of deduction. "When I hear you give your reasons," I remarked, "the thing always appears to me to be so ridiculously simple that I could easily do it myself, though at

each successive instance of your reasoning I am baffled, until you explain your process. And yet I believe that my eyes are as good as yours."

"Quite so," he answered, lighting a cigarette, and throwing himself down into an armchair. "You see, but you do not observe. The distinction is clear. For example, you have frequently seen the steps which lead up from the hall to this room."

"Frequently."

"How often?"

"Well, some hundreds of times."

"Then how many are there?"

"How many! I don't know."

"Quite so! You have not observed.

Figure 2: Sidney Paget, 'There He Stood before the Fire', 'A Scandal in Bohemia', *Strand Magazine* 2 (July 1891), 62.

And yet you have seen. That is just my point. Now, I know that there are seventeen steps, because I have both seen and observed. By the way, since you are interested in these little problems, and since you are good enough to chronicle one or two of my trifling experiences, you may be interested in this." He threw over a sheet of thick pink-tinted notepaper which had been lying open upon the table. " It came by the last post," said he. " Read it aloud."

The note was undated, and without either signature or address.

" There will call upon you to-night, at a quarter to eight o'clock," it said, " a gentleman who desires to consult you upon a matter of the very deepest moment. Your recent services to one of the Royal Houses of Europe have shown that you are one who may safely be trusted with matters which are of an importance which can hardly be exaggerated. This account of you we have from all quarters received. Be in your chamber then at that hour, and do not take it amiss if your visitor wear a mask."

" This is indeed a

"I CAREFULLY EXAMINED THE WRITING."

mystery," I remarked. " What do you imagine that it means ? "

" I have no data yet. It is a capital mistake to theorise before one has data. Insensibly one begins to twist facts to suit theories, instead of theories to suit facts. But the note itself. What do you deduce from it ? "

I carefully examined the writing, and the paper upon which it was written.

" The man who wrote it was presumably well to do," I remarked, endeavouring to imitate my companion's processes. " Such paper could not be bought under half a crown a packet. It is peculiarly strong and stiff."

" Peculiar—that is the very word," said Holmes. " It is not an English paper at all. Hold it up to the light."

I did so, and saw a large *E* with a small *g*, a *P*, and a large *G* with a small *t* woven into the texture of the paper.

" What do you make of that ? " asked Holmes.

" The name of the maker, no doubt ; or his monogram, rather."

" Not at all. The *G* with the small *t* stands for " Gesellschaft," which is the German for " Company." It is a customary contraction like our " Co." *P*, of course, stands for " Papier." Now for the *Eg.* Let us glance at our Continental Gazetteer." He took down a heavy brown volume from his shelves. " Eglow, Eglonitz—here we are, Egria. It is in a German - speaking country—in Bohemia, not far from Carlsbad. ' Remarkable as being the scene of the death of Wallenstein, and for its numerous glass factories and paper mills.' Ha, ha, my boy, what do you make of that ? " His eyes sparkled, and he sent up a great blue triumphant cloud from his cigarette.

" The paper was made in Bohemia," I said.

" Precisely. And the man who wrote the note is a German. Do you note the peculiar construction of the sentence—'This account of you we have from all quarters received.' A Frenchman or Russian could not have written that. It is the German who is so uncourteous to his verbs. It only remains, therefore, to discover what is wanted by this German who writes upon Bohemian paper, and prefers wearing a mask to showing his face. And here he

Figure 3: Sidney Paget, 'I Carefully Examined the Writing', 'A Scandal in Bohemia', *Strand Magazine* 2 (July 1891), 63.

comes, if I am not mistaken, to resolve all our doubts."

As he spoke there was the sharp sound of horses' hoofs and grating wheels against the curb, follrwed by a sharp pull at the bell. Holmes whistled.

"A pair, by the sound," said he. "Yes," he continued, glancing out of the window. "A nice little brougham and a pair of beauties. A hundred and fifty guineas apiece. There's money in this case, Watson, if there is nothing else."

"I think that I had better go, Holmes."

"Not a bit, Doctor. Stay where you are. I am lost without my Boswell. And this promises to be interesting. It would be a pity to miss it."

"But your client ——?"

"Never mind him. I may want your help, and so may he. Here he comes. Sit down in that armchair, Doctor, and give us your best attention."

A slow and heavy step, which had been heard upon the stairs and in the passage, paused immediately outside the door. Then there was a loud and authoritative tap.

"Come in!" said Holmes.

A man entered who could hardly have been less than six feet six inches in height, with the chest and limbs of a Hercules. His dress was rich with a richness which would, in England, be looked upon as akin to bad taste. Heavy bands of Astrakhan were slashed across the sleeves and fronts of his double-breasted coat, while the deep blue cloak which was thrown over his shoulders

"A MAN ENTERED."

was lined with flame-coloured silk, and secured at the neck with a brooch which consisted of a single flaming beryl. Boots which extended half way up his calves, and which were trimmed at the tops with rich brown fur, completed the impression of barbaric opulence which was suggested by his whole appearance. He carried a broad-brimmed hat in his hand, while he wore across the upper part of his face, extending down past the cheek-bones, a black vizard mask, which he had apparently adjusted that very moment, for his hand was still raised to it as he entered. From the lower part of the face he appeared to be a man of strong character, with a thick, hanging lip, and a long straight chin, suggestive of resolution pushed to the length of obstinacy.

"You had my note?" he asked, with a deep harsh voice and a strongly marked German accent. "I told you that I would call." He looked from one to the other of us, as if uncertain which to address.

"Pray take a seat," said Holmes. "This is my friend and colleague, Dr. Watson, who is occasionally good enough to help me in my cases. Whom have I the honour to address?"

"You may address me as the Count Von Kramm, a Bohemian nobleman. I understand that this gentleman, your friend, is a man of honour and discretion, whom I may trust with a matter of the most extreme importance. If not, I should much prefer to communicate with you alone."

I rose to go, but Holmes caught me by

Figure 4: Sidney Paget, 'A Man Entered', 'A Scandal in Bohemia', *Strand Magazine* 2 (July 1891), 64.

the wrist and pushed me back into my chair. "It is both, or none," said he. "You may say before this gentleman anything which you may say to me."

The Count shrugged his broad shoulders. "Then I must begin," said he, "by binding you both to absolute secrecy for two years, at the end of that time the matter will be of no importance. At present it is not too much to say that it is of such weight that it may have an influence upon European history."

"I promise," said Holmes.

"And I."

"You will excuse this mask," continued our strange visitor. "The august person who employs me wishes his agent to be unknown to you, and I may confess at once that the title by which I have just called myself is not exactly my own."

"I was aware of it," said Holmes dryly.

"The circumstances are of great delicacy, and every precaution has to be taken to quench what might grow to be an immense scandal and seriously compromise one of the reigning families of Europe. To speak plainly, the matter implicates the great House of Ormstein, hereditary kings of Bohemia."

"I was also aware of that," murmured Holmes, settling himself down in his armchair, and closing his eyes.

Our visitor glanced with some apparent surprise at the languid, lounging figure of the man who had been no doubt depicted to him as the most incisive reasoner, and most energetic agent in Europe. Holmes slowly reopened his eyes, and looked impatiently at his gigantic client.

"If your Majesty would condescend to state your case," he remarked, "I should be better able to advise you."

The man sprang from his chair, and paced up and down the room in uncontrollable agitation. Then, with a gesture of

"HE TORE THE MASK FROM HIS FACE."

desperation, he tore the mask from his face and hurled it upon the ground. "You are right," he cried, "I am the King. Why should I attempt to conceal it?"

"Why, indeed?" murmured Holmes.

"Your Majesty had not spoken before I was aware that I was addressing Wilhelm Gottsreich Sigismond von Ormstein, Grand Duke of Cassel-Felstein, and hereditary King of Bohemia."

"But you can understand," said our strange visitor, sitting down once more and passing his hand over his high, white forehead, "you can understand that I am not accustomed to doing such business in my own person. Yet the matter was so delicate that I could not confide it to an agent without putting myself in his power. I have come *incognito* from Prague for the purpose of consulting you."

"Then, pray consult," said Holmes, shutting his eyes once more.

"The facts are briefly these: Some five years ago, during a lengthy visit to Warsaw, I made the acquaintance of the well-known adventuress Irene Adler. The name is no doubt familiar to you."

"Kindly look her up in my index, Doctor," murmured Holmes, without opening his eyes. For many years he had adopted a system of docketing all paragraphs concern-

F

Figure 5: Sidney Paget, 'He Tore the Mask from his Face', 'A Scandal in Bohemia', *Strand Magazine* 2 (July 1891), 65.

the visual echo is created by having the images appear on successive recto pages in similar central positions, as if the second were a retinal afterimage of the first; the picture of Holmes disguised as a groom (Figure 6) is echoed but again reversed by the image of Holmes at Adler's wedding, his back to the viewer (Figure 7). The technique is repeated identically when the following portrait of Holmes as a clergyman is paired with him among the crowd assembled outside Briony Lodge. Paget avoids a sense of visual repetition not only by reversing the angles of his subjects (the clergyman faces us in Figure 8, but is turned away in the next image (Figure 9)), but in alternating depth of field; images composed on a single plane (Holmes sitting at the table, and the portraits of the King and Holmes's disguises) alternate with images that depend on receding perspective or multiple planes (Holmes at the hearth; Holmes's chair nearer to the viewer than Watson's; the three rows of Adler's wedding; and the receding scenery of Serpentine Avenue).

So far, the 'Scandal' illustrations follow a pattern of doublings: a first image is reflected in composition by a second; the second, third and fourth pairings introduce a solitary figure who, in the following image, is inserted into a more populated and delineated scene. The placing of three of these pairs on opposite pages of the *Strand* reinforces the pattern. The cumulative effect of this technique is to suggest continuity while avoiding staleness; the alternation of compositions allows them to become familiar without being stultifying. This doubling of the images is, however, complicated by the end of the story. The ninth image continues the clergyman sequence, in the illustration of Holmes and Watson on the doorstep at 221B while Adler, dressed as a boy, wishes Holmes good night (Figure 10). This illustration has been discussed extensively: Miller, for instance, reads it as 'an allegory of imagistic ambiguity ... suggest[ing] the difficulty of interpreting the world through visual apprehension, or the fundamental inconsistency between imagistic and linguistic modes of representation'.[18] What appears on the imagistic level as an almost queer image becomes (when combined with Doyle's text) an image of a different kind of gender transgression, and Miller goes on to argue that, despite their seemingly optical ideologies, the Holmes stories are deeply ambivalent about the power of the visual to capture knowledge and (particularly female) identity. The ease with which Adler assumes a visual masculine identity provides a reflective twist on Holmes's earlier disguises: the masculine, semi-pugilistic groom and the effeminate curly-haired priest.

But while Adler's drag unsettles the Holmesian universe, its illustration similarly disrupts the play of visual binaries established by Paget. For one, the clergyman guise adopted by Holmes appears in a third consecutive

" And mademoiselle's address ? " he asked.

" Is Briony Lodge, Serpentine-avenue, St. John's Wood."

Holmes took a note of it. " One other question," said he. " Was the photograph a cabinet ? "

" It was."

" Then, good night, your Majesty, and I trust that we shall soon have some good news for you. And good night, Watson," he added, as the wheels of the Royal brougham rolled down the street. " If you will be good enough to call to-morrow afternoon, at three o'clock, I should like to chat this little matter over with you."

II.

AT three o'clock precisely I was at Baker-street, but Holmes had not yet returned. The landlady informed me that he had left the house shortly after eight o'clock in the morning. I sat down beside the fire, however, with the intention of awaiting him, however long he might be. I was already deeply interested in his inquiry, for, though it was surrounded by none of the grim and strange features which were associated with the two crimes which I

"A DRUNKEN-LOOKING GROOM."

have already recorded, still, the nature of the case and the exalted station of his client gave it a character of its own. Indeed, apart from the nature of the investigation which my friend had on hand, there was something in his masterly grasp of a situation, and his keen, incisive reasoning, which made it a pleasure to me to study his system of work, and to follow the quick, subtle methods by which he disentangled the most inextricable mysteries. So accustomed was I to his in-

variable success that the very possibility of his failing had ceased to enter into my head.

It was close upon four before the door opened, and a drunken-looking groom, ill-kempt and side-whiskered, with an inflamed face and disreputable clothes, walked into the room. Accustomed as I was to my friend's amazing powers in the use of disguises, I had to look three times before I was certain that it was indeed he. With a nod he vanished into the bedroom, whence he emerged in five minutes tweed-suited and respectable, as of old. Putting his hands into his pockets, he stretched out his legs in front of the fire, and laughed heartily for some minutes.

"Well, really ! " he cried, and then he choked ; and laughed again until he was obliged to lie back, limp and helpless, in the chair.

"What is it ? "

"It's quite too funny. I am sure you could never guess how I employed my morning, or what I ended by doing."

"I can't imagine. I suppose that you have been watching the habits, and perhaps the house, of Miss Irene Adler."

"Quite so, but the sequel was rather unusual. I will tell you, however. I left the house a little after eight o'clock this morning, in the character of a groom out of work. There is a wonderful sympathy and freemasonry among horsey men. Be one of them, and you will know all that there is to know. I soon found Briony Lodge. It is a *bijou* villa, with a garden at the back, but built out in front right up to the road, two stories. Chubb lock to the door. Large sitting-room on the right side, well furnished, with long windows almost to the floor, and those preposterous

Figure 6: Sidney Paget, 'A Drunken-Looking Groom', 'A Scandal in Bohemia', *Strand Magazine* 2 (July 1891), 67.

front of the altar. I lounged up the side aisle like any other idler who has dropped into a church. Suddenly, to my surprise, the three at the altar faced round to me, and Godfrey Norton came running as hard as he could towards me."

"Thank God!" he cried. "You'll do. Come! Come!"

"What then?" I asked.

"Come man, come, only three minutes, or it won't be legal."

I was half dragged up to the altar, and, before I knew where I was, 1 found myself mumbling re-

"I FOUND MYSELF MUMBLING RESPONSES."

sponses which were whispered in my ear, and vouching for things of which I knew nothing, and generally assisting in the secure tying up of Irene Adler, spinster, to Godfrey Norton, bachelor. It was all done in an instant, and there was the gentleman thanking me on the one side and the lady on the other, while the clergyman beamed on me in front. It was the most preposterous position in which I ever found myself in my life, and it was the thought of it that started me laughing just now. It seems that there had been some informality about their licence, that the clergyman absolutely refused to marry them without a witness of some sort, and that my lucky appearance saved the bridegroom from having to sally out into the streets in search of a best man. The bride gave me a sovereign, and I mean to wear it on my watch chain in memory of the occasion."

"This is a very unexpected turn of affairs," said I ; "and what then?"

"Well, I found my plans very seriously menaced. It looked as if the pair might take an immediate departure, and so necessitate very prompt and energetic measures

on my part. At the church door, however, they separated, he driving back to the Temple, and she to her own house. 'I shall drive out in the Park at five as usual,' she said as she left him. I heard no more. They drove away in different directions, and I went off to make my own arrangements."

"Which are?"

"Some cold beef and a glass of beer," he answered, ringing the bell. "I have been too busy to think of food, and I am likely to be busier still this evening. By the way, Doctor, I shall want your co-operation."

"I shall be delighted."

"You don't mind breaking the law?"

"Not in the least."

"Nor running a chance of arrest?"

"Not in a good cause."

"Oh, the cause is excellent!"

"Then I am your man."

"I was sure that I might rely on you."

"But what is it you wish?"

"When Mrs. Turner has brought in the tray I will make it clear to you. Now," he said, as he turned hungrily on the simple fare that our landlady had provided, "I must discuss it while I eat, for I have not much time. It is nearly five now. In two hours we must be on the scene of action. Miss Irene, or Madame, rather, returns from her drive at seven. We must be at Briony Lodge to meet her."

"And what then?"

"You must leave that to me. I have already arranged what is to occur. There is only one point on which I must insist. You must not interfere, come what may. You understand?"

"I am to be neutral?"

"To do nothing whatever. There will probably be some small unpleasantness.

Figure 7: Sidney Paget, 'I Found Myself Mumbling Responses', 'A Scandal in Bohemia', *Strand Magazine* 2 (July 1891), 69.

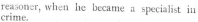

Do not join in it. It will end in my being conveyed into the house. Four or five minutes afterwards the sitting-room window will open. You are to station yourself close to that open window."

"Yes."

"You are to watch me, for I will be visible to you."

"Yes."

"And when I raise my hand—so—you will throw into the room what I give you to throw, and will, at the same time, raise the cry of fire. You quite follow me?"

"Entirely."

"It is nothing very formidable," he said, taking a long cigar-shaped roll from his pocket. "It is an ordinary plumber's smoke rocket, fitted with a cap at either end to make it self-lighting. Your task is confined to that. When you raise your cry of fire, it will be taken up by quite a number of people. You may then walk to the end of the street, and I will rejoin you in ten minutes. I hope that I have made myself clear?"

"I am to remain neutral, to get near the window, to watch you, and, at the signal, to throw in this object, then to raise the cry of fire, and to wait you at the corner of the street."

"Precisely."

"Then you may entirely rely on me."

"That is excellent. I think perhaps it is almost time that I prepared for the new rôle I have to play."

"A SIMPLE MINDED CLERGYMAN."

He disappeared into his bedroom, and returned in a few minutes in the character of an amiable and simple-minded Nonconformist clergyman. His broad black hat, his baggy trousers, his white tie, his sympathetic smile, and general look of peering and benevolent curiosity were such as Mr. John Hare alone could have equalled. It was not merely that Holmes changed his costume. His expression, his manner, his very soul seemed to vary with every fresh part that he assumed. The stage lost a fine actor, even as science lost an acute

reasoner, when he became a specialist in crime.

It was a quarter past six when we left Baker-street, and it still wanted ten minutes to the hour when we found ourselves in Serpentine-avenue. It was already dusk, and the lamps were just being lighted as we paced up and down in front of Briony Lodge, waiting for the coming of its occupant. The house was just such as I had pictured it from Sherlock Holmes' succinct description, but the locality appeared to be less private than I expected. On the contrary, for a small street in a quiet neighbourhood, it was remarkably animated. There was a group of shabbily-dressed men smoking and laughing in a corner, a scissors grinder with his wheel, two guardsmen who were flirting with a nurse-girl, and several well-dressed young men who were lounging up and down with cigars in their mouths.

"You see," remarked Holmes, as we paced to and fro in front of the house, "this marriage rather simplifies matters. The photograph becomes a double-edged weapon now. The chances are that she would be as averse to its being seen by Mr. Godfrey Norton, as our client is to its coming to the eyes of his Princess. Now the question is — Where are we to find the photograph?"

"Where, indeed?"

"It is most unlikely that she carries it about with her. It is cabinet size. Too large for easy concealment about a woman's dress. She knows that the King is capable of having her waylaid and searched. Two attempts of the sort have already been made. We may take it then that she does not carry it about with her."

"Where, then?"

"Her banker or her lawyer. There is that double possibility. But I am inclined to think neither. Women are naturally secretive, and they like to do their own secreting. Why should she hand it over

Figure 8: Sidney Paget, 'A Simple Minded Clergyman', 'A Scandal in Bohemia', *Strand Magazine* 2 (July 1891), 70.

"HE GAVE A CRY AND DROPPED."

Figure 9: Sidney Paget, 'He Gave a Cry and Dropped', 'A Scandal in Bohemia', *Strand Magazine* 2 (July 1891), 71.

illustration, unsettling the rhythm of the previous eight pictures. But whereas the reader might expect the following (and final) image of the story to close the series by offering a similar echo of its predecessor, the pattern is broken by instead offering the scene of the King, Holmes and Watson surveying the photograph of Adler (Figure 11). It is as if Adler's insertion into the previous image not only unsettles Holmes's acts of detection, but also the visual logic of the stories themselves, and inevitably the story ends on an image which reflects on the act of looking at an image (the picture is even exclamatorily titled 'This photograph!'). More importantly, while the status of Adler's photograph as fetishistic object has been extensively discussed (Holmes is left with the empty visual signifier of Adler), it has not been noted how the material form of the *Strand* renders this loss palpable. For, in turning the page to arrive at Paget's final image, readers

"GOOD-NIGHT, MR. SHERLOCK HOLMES."

Figure 10: Sidney Paget, 'Good-night, Mr Sherlock Holmes', 'A Scandal in Bohemia', *Strand Magazine* 2 (July 1891), 73.

have (if only momentarily) lost precisely what Holmes has gained – the image of Adler. Furthermore, first time readers realise that they have lost what they did not possess in the first place, since the revelation of Adler's identity only takes place on the following page, after the image of the disguised Adler is lost to view.

The interplay of Doyle's textual reversals with Paget's compositional inversions is particularly elegant in 'Scandal', as if Paget was aware that the

"THIS PHOTOGRAPH!"

Figure 11: Sidney Paget, 'This Photograph!', 'A Scandal in Bohemia', *Strand Magazine* 2 (July 1891), 74.

inauguration of a series that was far from guaranteed success needed to establish rapidly a formal continuity which could draw readers in, but also facilitate the surprises of the narrative. The technique is used more sparingly in subsequent stories. The first three illustrations of the 'The Red-headed League' form a triad centred on the image of a newspaper; later, the image of Holmes sitting in his chair at Baker Street is echoed on the turn of the page by that of Holmes at St James' Hall (Holmes's eyes are closed in both). 'A Case of Identity' culminates in two similar images of James Windibank, trapped at

Baker Street, and then escaping; the penultimate illustration of 'The Beryl Coronet' shows Arthur Holder struggling with Sir George Burnwell, an image restaged by the closing image of Holmes putting a gun to Burnwell's head. Imagery is repeated across stories: the image of Holmes and Watson sitting opposite each other in a train carriage that opens 'The Boscombe Valley Mystery' reappears as the opening to 'Silver Blaze', and again in 'The Naval Treaty' (a fourth variant, featuring Melas and his abductor, appears in 'The Greek Interpreter'). Returning to 'A Scandal in Bohemia', the composition of the opening image of Holmes in front of the hearth, or *focus*, is repeated in 'The Yellow Face' (this time with Grant Munro in Watson's position), reminding alert readers that Norbury was not Holmes's only failure.

Holmes's Death and Paget's Afterlife

If 'A Scandal in Bohemia' started the *Adventures* by foregrounding the regularity of image and composition in order to draw in an audience, then the closing story of the *Memoirs* – 'The Final Problem' – undermined visual expectations in the same way Doyle sought to kill off textual ones. The story's apocalyptic ending is subtly indicated by a shift in Paget's style whereby landscape becomes increasingly prominent, with portraiture becoming lost (indeed, landscape would similarly become more prominent in Paget's work for *The Hound of the Baskervilles*). The three page sequence 'It passed with a rattle and a roar', 'A large rock clattered down', and 'I saw Holmes gazing down', depicting the stages of Holmes and Watson's journey to Reichenbach, show human figures diminishing in proportion as the framed landscape materialises around them (Figures 12, 13 and 14). Likewise, whereas earlier images had often bled off into the page, those for 'The Final Problem' become increasingly detached from the typeset; 'It passed' still bleeds off at the edges, but the top half is framed by a prophetic black border; this border has extended by 'A large rock', showing three figures of medium size in the landscape; 'I saw Holmes' is an almost complete rectangle, with Holmes a tiny figure readers might struggle to spot. This is not to say that Paget's images did not use borders before (the first image of Holmes in 'Scandal' is a rare early example of a completely boxed image), but their use was sparing. In 'The Final Problem', however, the sense is of visual encroachment and containment, especially in 'It passed', where the wash of sky spills over the half border at the top, as if Paget's freer style strains against the frame.

Whereas in previous stories text and image intertwine, the illustration that opens 'The Final Problem', 'The Death of Sherlock Holmes' (Figure 15), was the first of the Holmesian *Strand* images to occupy its own page, with

"IT PASSED WITH A RATTLE AND A ROAR."

Figure 12: Sidney Paget, 'It Passed with a Rattle and a Roar', 'The Final Problem', *Strand Magazine* 6 (December 1893), 566.

a definite rectangular border (completing the sequence that would be suggested in the story). If earlier Paget images had subtly underscored their own means of production by often gradually shading off at their edges, the fully bordered image that opens 'The Final Problem' harks more towards photography. This is not simply the death of Sherlock Holmes, but also of Paget's early style, and later stories would increasingly separate text and image in this way. Indeed, the more photographic style that begins to appear in this story is reflected in the appearance of what Roland Barthes refers to as a photographic *punctum*: the incidental detail that 'overwhelms the entirety

"A LARGE ROCK CLATTERED DOWN."

Figure 13: Sidney Paget, 'A Large Rock Clattered Down', 'The Final Problem', *Strand Magazine* 6 (December 1893), 567.

of [a] ... reading' and redefines the image, hinting at an existence beyond its surface.[19] The *punctum* punctures not only the image, but also the viewer: 'A photograph's *punctum* is that accident which pricks me (but also bruises me, is poignant to me)'.[20] 'The Final Problem' indeed features an image of bodily puncture (Holmes's bleeding knuckles), though Paget's focus on this means it cannot act as a Barthesian *punctum*, being something that escapes the photographer's intention. For this reason, the concept does not easily

"I SAW HOLMES GAZING DOWN AT THE RUSH OF THE WATERS."

Figure 14: Sidney Paget, 'I Saw Holmes Gazing Down at the Rush of the Waters', 'The Final Problem', *Strand Magazine* 6 (December 1893), 568.

translate from photography to drawing, but the idea is nevertheless useful in understanding the shift in Paget's style in 'The Final Problem'. The *punctum* is necessarily subjective, dependent on the viewer's own context; in 'The Death of Sherlock Holmes' Holmes's hat falling into the precipice at Reichenbach, slightly off centre from the focus on Holmes and Moriarty, is

THE DEATH OF SHERLOCK HOLMES.

Figure 15: Sidney Paget, 'The Death of Sherlock Holmes', 'The Final Problem', *Strand Magazine* 6 (December 1893), 588.

one such incidental detail that potentially strikes at the reader in a way that Paget's images had not done before. The *punctum*, like the frame, suggests a wider world that cannot be represented within the image. Whereas before Holmes had inhabited a kind of privileged visual space penetrated only by those relevant to the story, in 'The Death' we see him within a universe that must be artificially contained by the frame.

This image also provides a particular example of Paget's robust cultural afterlife. Mark Tansey's painting *Derrida Queries De Man* (1990) borrows Paget's composition to depict the recently disgraced Paul de Man (discovered to have contributed antisemitic writings to the Belgian newspaper *Le Soir* during the Second World War) confronted by Jacques Derrida at a Reichenbach Falls-esque precipice, an appropriate tribute given the frequency with which the police dismiss Holmes as a mere 'theorist'. Yet it is not in the pictorial arts that Paget's influence has been most felt, but rather in filmic adaptation and fan culture. The *Strand* illustrations provided points of visual reference for several adaptations, ranging from the montage of Paget images that opens *The Seven Per-Cent Solution* (1976) to their influence on the Jeremy Brett television adaptations (1984–94), being overlaid on the closing titles and informing shot composition in deliberate homage. Neo-Victorian pastiche has similarly appropriated Paget's images, often recaptioning them (as in, for instance, Lewis Feuer's *The Case of the Revolutionist's Daughter* (1983) and David Hammer's *My Dear Watson* (1995)), while Edwardian translators who did not own the rights to the *Strand* images would conspicuously adapt Paget's work into 'new' illustrations (see, for instance, *La Cycliste Solitaire* (1910)), which often makes use of reversed angles in comparison to Paget's originals).

Paget died in 1908 from a mediastinal tumour, and subsequent Holmes stories were illustrated in the *Strand* by a range of artists including Arthur Twidle, Gilbert Holiday, H. M. Brock, Joseph Simpson, Alec Ball, Frank Wiles, Alfred Gilbert, Howard K. Elcock, and Paget's brother Walter. The final Holmes story to feature Paget's images, 'The Second Stain', encapsulates the shifts in the *Strand*'s tone as it entered the twentieth century: Paget's settings are more detailed (particularly in the image 'It hinged back like the lid of a box', showing Holmes and Watson discovering Lucas's hiding place under the drugget), and this move towards a more photographic realism is evident in the *Strand*'s increasing use of fully bordered and whole page images for the Holmes stories. But Doyle's story revisits the first narrative to feature Paget's vision of Holmes. Both 'Scandal' and 'Stain' focus on Holmes's employment by political authorities to locate an incriminating document in the possession of a transgressive woman; Holmes's ruse to find the hiding place used by Adler is echoed in Hilda Trelawney Hope's search of Lucas's rooms. Holmes's authority over Hope, and his decision to effectively pardon her, reads like an exorcism of anxieties at being outwitted by Adler. Fittingly, the story ends on a visual note: the prime minister asks how the missing letter came to be found in the dispatch box, and Holmes 'turn[s] away smiling from the keen scrutiny of those wonderful eyes' (666). The moment is unusual; the detective, frequently theorised as the agent of surveillance, becomes its subject. In future stories, Holmes would find himself under the illustrative gaze of less influential artists than Sidney Paget.

Notes

1. Walter Benjamin, *Charles Baudelaire: A Lyric Poet in the Era of High Capitalism*, trans. Harry Zohn (London: Verso, 1983), 48.
2. Srdjan Smajić, *Ghost-Seers, Detectives and Spiritualists: Theories of Vision in Victorian Literature and Science* (Cambridge: Cambridge University Press, 2010), 123–30.
3. Letter to Henry Paget, 8 November 1879. Arthur Conan Doyle Collection (Lancelyn Green Bequest), Portsmouth City Library. ACD1/G/10/6/1/2.
4. Randall Stock, 'Sidney Paget: Paintings by the Numbers', *Baker Street Journal* 59:1 (2009), 6–10 (8).
5. Ibid., 6.
6. Ibid.; Alex Werner, 'Sherlock Holmes, Sidney Paget, and the *Strand Magazine*', in Alex Werner (ed.), *Sherlock Holmes: The Man Who Never Lived and Will Never Die* (London: Ebury Press, 2014), 101–25 (115).
7. George W. Leech, *Magazine Illustration: The Art Editor's Point of View* (London: Pitman, 1939), 15.
8. Quoted in Cameron Hollyer, 'Author to Editor: Arthur Conan Doyle's Correspondence with H. Greenhough Smith', *ACD: The Journal of the Arthur Conan Doyle Society* 3 (1992), 11–34 (26).
9. Franco Moretti, *Signs Taken for Wonders: On the Sociology of Literary Forms*, trans. Susan Fischer, David Forgacs and David Miller (London: Verso, 1983), 139.
10. Quoted in Daniel Stashower, *Teller of Tales: The Life of Arthur Conan Doyle* (New York: Henry Holt and Company, 1999), 124.
11. Michel Foucault, *The Birth of the Clinic*, trans. A. M. Sheridan (London: Routledge, 2003), 149.
12. Ibid.
13. Jonathan Crary, *Techniques of the Observer: On Vision and Modernity in the Nineteenth Century* (Cambridge: MIT Press, 1992), 39–40.
14. W. J. T. Mitchell, *Iconology: Image, Text, Ideology* (Chicago: University of Chicago Press, 1986), 158.
15. Quoted in Hollyer, 'Author to Editor', 26.
16. Elizabeth Carolyn Miller, *Framed: The New Woman Criminal in British Culture at the* Fin de Siecle (Ann Arbor: University of Michigan Press, 2008), 45.
17. Ibid., 45–7.
18. Ibid., 26.
19. Roland Barthes, *Camera Lucida: Reflections on Photography*, trans. Richard Howard (London: Vintage, 1993), 49.
20. Ibid., 27.

12

JANICE M. ALLAN

Gothic Returns: *The Hound of the Baskervilles*

As early as November 1891, Doyle wrote to his beloved Ma'am to inform her that he was thinking 'of slaying Holmes . . . & winding him up for good & all', complaining that the work 'takes my mind from better things'.[1] While Mary Doyle's horrified response earned the detective a temporary reprieve, 'The Final Problem' saw Holmes, locked in the arms of Moriarty, plunge into the Reichenbach Falls. As Doyle confirmed to his mother, the intention was for Holmes 'never never to reappear' – 'I am weary of his name'.[2] For almost ten years, Doyle stayed true to his word and it was only in October 1903, with the publication of 'The Empty House' that he gave way to public pressure and financial temptation and brought his most famous creation back to life. It is, therefore, only appropriate that Doyle described *The Hound of the Baskervilles* as 'a real Creeper'.[3] Serialised between August 1901 and April 1902 (prior to Holmes's resurrection) but set in 1889 (pre-dating his death), Holmes is neither dead nor alive and thus occupies the liminal position of a ghost, as spectral as the titular hound. In bringing together the scientific detective and the supernatural beast of ancient legend, *The Hound* occupies a similarly liminal position, poised between the rational positivism of detective fiction and the uncanny ambiguity of the Gothic.

While these two genres appear, on the face of things, to be antithetical in method and intent, it is now widely recognised that they share a common ancestry, albeit one that was denied by early critics of detective fiction who wished to ground its 'literary status on its association with scientific method and highbrow literature'.[4] It is important to note, however, that Doyle's novel establishes, and indeed relies upon, a binary between science and superstition – the rational and the irrational – if only to reveal the boundary between them to be as slippery and permeable as the mire itself. This chapter, therefore, explores the interaction of the very different topographies – geographical, psychological and symbolic – that dominate Doyle's most famous and successful novel.

At Home in London

While it is the desolate landscape of Dartmoor that remains etched on the memory of readers, the familiar topography of London – captured in the opening five chapters and final retrospection – plays a crucial role in the novel. Structurally, these chapters represent an attempt, albeit never wholly successful, to circumscribe and delimit the uncanny world associated with the Gothic landscape of the moors. Paradoxically, however, they also help to constitute the very uncanniness they work to contain. For as Freud suggests, the production of the uncanny is very much 'an affair of "reality testing"'; it retains its character only 'so long as the setting is one of material reality; [and] where it is given an arbitrary and artificial setting in fiction, it is apt to lose that character'.[5] Thus the uncanny, as Nicholas Royle reminds us, 'is not simply an experience of strangeness or alienation . . . it is a peculiar commingling of the familiar and unfamiliar'.[6] London is, in more ways than one, the 'material' basis of all that follows.

Given Holmes's lengthy absence from the pages of the *Strand Magazine*, his re-introduction is surprisingly low key. '[S]eated at the breakfast table' at 221B Baker Street (669) with Watson by his side, the opening of the novel is, above all, recognisable. So too is the ensuing examination of James Mortimer's walking stick – a familiar demonstration of Holmes's observational and deductive prowess – that re-establishes the relationship between Holmes and Watson. Like the stick itself, the opening is 'solid, and reassuring' (669) and the intervening years melt away before the carefully crafted legibility of the tableau. Legibility is, in fact, the keynote of the London chapters and it is only appropriate that they are punctuated by what might be designated as multiple scenes of reading. In addition to Holmes's study of the stick, the list of 'texts' subject to scrutiny include: a Medical Directory, the phrenological reading of Holmes's skull, the 1742 manuscript of the Baskerville curse, the report of Sir Charles's death from the *Devon County Chronicle*, Sir Charles's footprints imprinted onto the 'gravel page' of the Yew Alley (680), an ordnance map, a warning letter, newspapers, a Hotel Directory, the register from the Northumberland, two telegraphs and, finally, the Official Registry of London cabmen. To drive the point home, the scrutiny of texts features in five of the first fourteen illustrations.

The multiplicity of texts within the opening chapters aligns closely with what Srdjan Smajić calls 'the genre's seeing-is-reading model' where the 'visible world is a text, [and] the detective its astute observer and expert reader'.[7] According to this paradigm, '[b]odies, dead or alive, are perfectly legible, unambiguous texts, but so are all other objects that enter the detective's field of vision . . . For the fictional detective, to see is to read – and to read is instantly to know, and know beyond a shadow of doubt'.[8] Holmes is not, of course, infallible – here, his 'indiscreet eagerness' leads him to lose Stapleton on Regent Street (691) – and Smajić immediately complicates his model by acknowledging the impact of erroneous inference. What is interesting, however, in the context of the London chapters of the *Hound*, is the ideal of legibility that they establish. Armed with his extraordinary observational skills, what is described in *A Study in Scarlet* as a 'passion for definite and exact knowledge' (17), as well as a vast array of reference sources, Holmes is, according to Smajić's argument, a master-reader and semiotician. In one of the novel's many instances of doubling discussed in this chapter, he appears to collect and pin down meaning in much the same way as Stapleton does butterflies. In so doing, he attempts to bring '"detection as near an exact science as it will ever be brought in this world"' (*A Study in Scarlet* 33). Such precision and legibility stand in stark contrast to the ambiguity and undecidability that is so closely associated with the Gothic, which is, as Victoria Margree and Bryony Randall suggest, characterised by 'an uncertainty as to what if any epistemological frame can make sense of the phenomena with which [it is] dealing'. In fact, this 'undecidability – at once epistemological and political – is key to the unsettling quality of Gothic *fin-de-siècle* literature'.[9]

Holmes's reading of the ordnance map of Dartmoor offers an interesting example of these two paradigms coming into contact. Having returned from a day at his club, Watson walks into the sitting-room to see 'a vague vision of Holmes in his dressing-gown coiled up in an armchair with his black clay pipe between his lips'. As the detective announces, '"I have been to Devonshire"':

> 'My body has remained in this armchair and has, I regret to observe, consumed in my absence two large pots of coffee and an incredible amount of tobacco. After you left I sent down to Stamford's for the Ordnance map of this portion of the moor, and my spirit has hovered over it all day. I flatter myself that I could find my way about'. (683)

This often cited passage has received a good deal of attention and critics have, quite rightly, stressed the extent to which it challenges the science/superstition binary that structures the novel. On the one hand, it is possible to associate it with what Christopher Pittard, building on the work of Lynda Nead, describes as a 'panoptic view from above, in which all is visible and immediately comprehensible'.[10] In the words of Nead herself, 'the viewpoint represented in the map and the plan' 'turns the heterogeneous world of the city into a text; it renders complexity legible and comprehensible'.[11] Thus the scene appears to conform to the 'seeing-is-reading' paradigm described above. At the same time, however, there is no doubt that the otherworldly vision of the 'coiled' Holmes – suggesting an animalistic, even reptilian creature – recounting an out-of-body experience, jars with the tenets of positivist rationalism and hints at Doyle's commitment to spiritualism. The 'vague' vision of Holmes also anticipates Watson's first view of the moor, 'dim and vague in the distance' (700). Thus, this is one of many indications of the extent to which the novel depends upon a binary only to call it into question.

Key to many readings of this scene is the question of perspective; it is 'the panoptic view from above' that is significant. And yet, this emphasis on the viewer says little about the map itself. Despite being of a very large scale, the map, by its very nature, frames and delimits the space it represents. This delimitation is emphasised, moreover, not only by Holmes confining his attention to the single section depicting '"the particular district which concerns us"' but also by focusing solely on its domesticated spaces: a '"few scattered dwellings"' rather than the space that '"extends"' beyond them (683–4). At the same time, the map reduces the moor's treacherous lows and jagged heights to so many concentric circles, transforming the unquantifiable depths of Grimpen Mire to a perfectly legible surface. In giving the indeterminate space of the moors a definite form, moreover, the map places the investigation on a metaphorically firm footing. In short, the map constructs the district as a contained and quantifiable space; a solid foundation upon which interpretation and meaning can be built.

Those familiar with the canon may well recognise a certain resemblance between the external topography of Dartmoor, as represented by Holmes's map, and the delimited inner topography of the detective himself. As he explains in *A Study in Scarlet*: '"a man's brain ... is like a little empty attic"' and it is '"a mistake to think that that little room has elastic walls and can distend to any extent"'. Thus only

> A fool takes in all the lumber of every sort that he comes across, so that the knowledge which might be useful to him gets crowded out, or at best is jumbled up with a lot of other things, so that he has a difficulty in laying his hands upon it. Now the skilful workman is very careful indeed as to what he takes into his brain-attic. He will have nothing but the tools which may help him in doing his work, but of these he has a large assortment, and all in the most perfect order.   (21)

The principle of circumscription that provides the foundation for Holmes's 'brain-attic' is all the more important when he is confronted with a mystery that is routinely associated with formlessness and depth – as Holmes admits to Watson, '"I am not sure that of all the five hundred cases of capital importance which I have handled there is one which cuts so deep"' (693).

Thus, it is not surprising that the 'seclusion and solitude' (683) – the thinking space, as it were – that is essential to Holmes's investigative process is here taken to an extreme. Upon his return to Baker Street, Watson opens the window to clear the haze of smoke in which Holmes is enveloped. And yet, immediately after he recounts his spiritual journey to Devonshire, Holmes announces: "'I think we'll shut that window again, if you don't mind. It is a singular thing, but I find that a concentrated atmosphere helps a concentration of thought. I have not pushed it to the length of getting into a box to think, but that is the logical outcome of my convictions"' (684). Situated within this metaphorical comfort zone, Holmes is confident not only in his ability to 'find [his] way about' but also in the belief that the 'thing takes shape ... It becomes coherent' (683, 685).

The Footprints of a Gigantic Hound

Chapter 6 marks a transition – always allowing for the ongoing slippage – between the novel's two very different physical and symbolic topographies: the legible terrain of modern London and the primitive Gothic landscape of Devon. As the argument in this chapter, thus far, has concentrated on the former, this is a timely moment to remind ourselves that *The Hound of the Baskervilles* is saturated with the familiar tropes of the Gothic. Amongst such features are a fragmented narrative (consisting of an ancient manuscript, letters, telegraphs and journal entries), a family curse, questions relating to lineage and inheritance, entrapment (physical and metaphorical), a persecuted woman and 'domestic tyrant' (715), doubles, a telltale portrait, aberrant and heightened states of mind and an ancient manor, Baskerville Hall, 'a place of shadow and gloom' (703). Travelling towards the Hall, Watson notes how, 'behind the peaceful and sunlit countryside there rose ever, dark against the evening sky, the long, gloomy curve of the moor, broken by the jagged and sinister hills' (700). In much the same way, a sense of unspecified dread looms over all the characters. As Sir Henry enters his ancestral home, 'long shadows trailed down the walls and hung like a black canopy above him'. Despite vowing to '"have a row of electric lamps up here inside of six months"' (702), shadows predominate, an apt metaphor for how the dark mysteries of the past intrude themselves into a supposedly enlightened present. Such intrusions are also marked in the novel's soundscape. From the first night at Baskerville Hall, when its 'deathly silence' is interrupted by 'the sob of a woman, the muffled, strangling gasp of one who is torn by an uncontrollable sorrow' (704) to the hound's 'last howl of agony' (757), the characters are haunted by the sounds of the moor.

Most memorable of the novel's Gothic features is the legendary hound itself: '"a huge creature, luminous, ghastly, and spectral"' which initiates '"a reign of terror"' in the district (681). The ontological impossibility of a 'spectral hound which leaves material footmarks' (727) – an uncanny blurring of the real and unreal – is a particularly clear example of Gothic undecidability. Such undecidability is evident when Holmes demands of Mortimer, '"you, a trained man of science, believe it to be supernatural?"' and Mortimer responds, '"I do not know what to believe"' (681). When Watson and Holmes finally encounter the creature on the moors, it is, even by today's standards, a wonderfully effective (and affective) moment.

> A hound it was, an enormous coal-black hound, but not such a hound as mortal eyes have ever seen. Fire burst from its open mouth, its eyes glowed with a smouldering glare, its muzzle and hackles and dewlap were outlined in flickering flame. Never in the delirious dream of a disordered brain could anything more savage, more appalling, more hellish be conceived than that dark form and savage face which broke upon us out of the wall of fog.   (757)

Although the first sight of the creature leaves Holmes, Watson and Lestrade 'paralyzed' with fear, the threat embodied by the hound – a threat both literal and ontological – is neutralised by the entirely material expedient of Holmes's pistol. Once dead, moreover, it becomes clear that there is nothing otherworldly about the creature, which is revealed to be nothing more than a 'gaunt, savage' mongrel. Although it is 'as large as a small lioness', its most disturbing aspects are reduced to mere trickery: a 'cunning preparation' of phosphorus to make the creature appear to glow and burn (757).

In offering a rational explanation for a purportedly supernatural event, Doyle is following the lead of conservative Gothic writers such as Ann Radcliffe (author of *The Mysteries of Udopho* (1794)) who relied on the so-called 'supernatural explained' as a means to moderate the more radical elements of the genre. And thus, paradoxically, the novel's most obviously Gothic episode is actually deployed in the service of what Catherine Belsey describes as the 'project' of the Holmes canon: 'to dispel magic and mystery, to make everything explicit, accountable, subject to scientific analysis'.[12] In killing the hound Holmes has not only saved Sir Henry but the concept of legibility itself. In order, therefore, to continue an exploration of the novel's Gothic undecidability, we must turn to the moor. For unlike the meaning of the legendary hound which, at the end of the day, can be pinned down like one of Stapleton's specimens, the moor – as both a geographical and symbolic space – proves far more resistant to interpretation.

Journeys through Space and Time

As is routinely acknowledged in critical readings of the novel, the journey from London to Dartmoor has a temporal as well as a spatial dimension. It begins on a train – a well-recognised symbol of modernity – and ends in an old-fashioned wagonette, travelling slowly down 'lanes worn by centuries of wheels' (700). For Sir Henry, who has only just arrived from the 'New World' of Canada, the temporal distance covered is even more striking. Describing 'this most God-forsaken corner of the world' in his first report to Holmes, Watson explains:

> When you are once out upon its bosom you have left all traces of modern England behind you, but, on the other hand, you are conscious everywhere of the homes and the work of the prehistoric people . . . As you look at their gray stone huts against the scarred hillsides you leave your own age behind you, and if you were to see a skin-clad, hairy man crawl out from the low door, fitting a flint-tipped arrow on to the string of his bow, you would feel that his presence there was more natural than your own. (712)

Home to creatures 'practically extinct' that live amongst its '[r]ank reeds and lush, slimy water-plants' (708, 759), the moor is reminiscent of a lost primordial world. Thus, it is only appropriate that two of the three characters most closely associated with its primitive and uncivilised land-scape – Selden, the ferocious Notting Hill murderer, Jack Stapleton, the murderous descendent of Sir Hugo Baskerville and, at least for Watson, Holmes himself – are atavistic criminal throwbacks. Read through the lens of criminal anthropology, such characters belong to an earlier, more primitive stage in evolutionary history. Selden is depicted not as a fully evolved man but, rather, as belonging to a lower species. He hides 'in a burrow like a wild beast' (701) and is characterised by 'a terrible animal face' and the agility of a 'mountain goat' (725). In a series of doublings that trouble class and specieal boundaries, Selden is aligned both with Stapleton (they share an intimate knowledge of the moors and are asso-ciated with unusually violent crimes as well as the foreign (Selden plans to escape to South America, the birthplace of Stapleton)) and the titular hound (both are hungry, vicious creatures that haunt the moors by night). Indeed, the description of Selden as 'half animal and half demon' (748) applies equally well to the hound.

In the portrait reading scene that dominates Chapter 13, Stapleton is revealed to be the direct descendent and double of Sir Hugo, the origin and cause of the Baskerville family curse. Having inherited his ancestor's 'wanton and cruel humour' (674) through a father who is, unlike his two brothers, of '"the old masterful Baskerville strain"' (681), he (or Rodger Baskerville to give him his proper name) is '"an interesting instance of a throwback, which appears to be both physical and spiritual"' (750). Although motivated by simple greed – he wishes to eliminate those who stand between him and the family fortune – the strange and ferocious nature of the naturalist's crimes testifies to a primitive and savage nature. Approaching the portrait as might Alphonse Bertillon, the French criminologist and Mortimer's idol, Holmes is able to see past the superficial details of fashion and costume in order to isolate what Bertillon calls the 'the real, actual presence of the person'.[13] This act of circumscription allows the portrait to become legible, even to Watson, who is shocked to see how the 'face of Stapleton had sprung out of the canvas' (750). Significantly, this moment of recognition re-enforces Stapleton's doubling with Selden, who 'sprang to his feet' when confronted by Watson and Sir Henry and, even more telling, the hound itself: 'the dreadful shape which had sprung out upon us from the shadows of the fog' (757). It is, finally, worth noting that the portrait scene, like the map reading episode discussed above, brings together the novel's very different paradigms. If the principle of Bertillonian circumscription produces legibility, it quickly melts into Gothic irrationality as Holmes admits that the hereditary resemblance between the two men is '"enough to convert a man to the doctrine of reincarnation"' (750). Once again, the boundaries between science and superstition blur and fade.

Grimpen Mire

As was recognised by its earliest critics, the Gothic is an affective mode of writing; one that is designed to provoke a physical response in the reader, be that suspense, dread or even terror. And thus Watson has 'tried to make the reader share those dark fears and vague surmises which clouded [their] lives so long' (759). Mortimer's whispered announcement – '"they were the footprints of a gigantic hound"' – for example, is designed to make the reader 'shudder' alongside Watson himself (679). In *The Hound of the Baskervilles*, however, the affective power of the Gothic is complemented by the affective potential of the moor itself; its ability to impact identity already signalled by the proliferation of doubles that inhabit it. Thus, the novel lends itself well to a psychogeographical reading. As suggested by French Marxist critic Guy Debord, psychogeography is the 'study of the specific effects of the geographical environment, consciously organised or not, on the emotions and behaviour of individuals'.[14] As we shall see, the geographical environment of the moors affects not only its inhabitants but, more profoundly, the epistemological framework that they bring to bear upon its mysteries.

From the moment that Watson arrives in Devonshire, he becomes increasingly liable to the influence of his surroundings. On the first night, sat with Sir Henry in a 'little circle of light', he notes that 'one's voice became hushed and one's spirit subdued' (703). As Watson admits the following morning, their circumstances 'tinged my thoughts with sadness' and he confesses to being '"conscious of shadows all around me"' and full of 'vague fears' (712). As if infected by the inchoate nature of his primeval surroundings, the boundaries between subject and environment break down, allowing 'the spirit of the moor [to] sink into one's soul' (712). Under its influence, Watson appears to suffer an existential crisis in which life '"has become like that great Grimpen Mire, with little green patches everywhere into which one may sink and with no guide to point the track"' (711). As inner and outer topographies align, Watson's thoughts become as 'dim and vague' (714) as the outlines of the moor itself.

It is only appropriate that the term 'vague' is employed here and elsewhere to describe Watson's internal and external landscape, for this space is – in stark contrast to the circumscribed and legible topography associated with both London and Holmes's own 'brain-attic' – formless and indefinite. Like 'some fantastic landscape in a dream', it is the repository of '"wonderful secrets"' (700, 707). Its sheer size – Watson describes it as '"vast, and so barren, and so mysterious"' (707) – challenges the 'seeing-is-reading' paradigm described above. Where the circumscribed and legible surface produced by the ordnance map instils false confidence in Holmes – '"I flatter myself that I could find my way about"' (683) – the reality is markedly different. As Stapleton informs Watson, a '"false step yonder means death to man or beast"' and neither will '"know the difference until the mire has them in its clutches"' (707, 708). Believing that he has discovered the reason behind Stapleton's aversion to Sir Henry as a suitor to his sister, Watson claims that it is 'something to have touched bottom anywhere in this bog in which we are floundering' (720). But given that Stapleton's explanation is a lie, designed to hide the true nature of the siblings' relationship, the 'bottom' falls away and, with no firm foundation upon which to interpret events, the 'moor with its mysteries and its strange inhabitants remains as inscrutable as ever' (726).

In a recent exploration of the role of oceanic space in antebellum detective and Gothic fiction, Tyler Roeger argues that the ocean's porousness provided 'a counter imaginary' to the 'geometric stability' of urban space.[15] 'This juxtaposition', he asserts, 'emphasizes the uneasy footing the sea creates for those trying to piece the clues together as they reach for a stable surface that does not seem to exist'.[16] Despite the obvious differences between oceanic space and that of the moor, both 'swallow meaning below the surface' and thus are 'hostile to certainty and conclusion'.[17] It is, therefore, hardly surprising that Watson feels as though a 'dead wall ... [was] built across every path by which I tried to get at the object of my mission' (735). Nowhere, however, is the epistemological threat posed by the moor more obvious than in the thick fog that envelops Grimpen Mire on the night of the hound's attack on Sir Henry. Likened to a 'dense white sea', the fog renders the topography of the moor increasingly illegible. As Holmes admits, it is '"the one thing upon earth which could have disarranged my plans"': '"If [Henry] isn't out in a quarter of an hour the path will be covered. In half an hour we won't be able to see our hands in front of us"' (756). Indeed, it is possible that the paralysis that strikes Holmes, Watson and Lestrade as the hound bursts through the fog is attributable not simply to the affective potency of the creature but, in addition, to the breakdown of the epistemological frameworks by which they read and interpret the world around them.

Although Holmes (just) manages to save Sir Henry as he emerges out of the fog into the 'clear, starlit night' (756), the concept of legibility is not so easily restored. If a 'panoptic view', as Pittard suggests in the passage cited above, renders everything 'visible and immediately comprehensible', the unquantifiable depths of the moor frustrate epistemological certainty. As Mortimer suggests in the early chapters of the novel, there 'is a realm in which the most acute and most experienced of detectives is helpless' (680) and it is significant that once Holmes descends from the heights of the tor onto the moor itself, his power is called into question. Searching for any trace of Stapleton, Watson and Holmes are defeated by the unstable topography of the bog and their sense of agency is dwarfed by the power of the landscape:

> a false step plunged us more than once thigh-deep into the dark, quivering mire, which shook for yards in soft undulations around our feet. Its tenacious grip plucked at our heels as we walked, and when we sank into it it was as if some malignant hand was tugging us down into those obscene depths, so grim and purposeful was the clutch in which it held us ... There was no chance of finding footsteps in the mire, for the rising mud oozed swiftly in upon them.   (760)

Stapleton, along with the possibility of 'certainty and conclusion', is lost forever.

The Man on the Tor

As suggested above, Watson sees Holmes, much like Selden and Stapleton, as closely associated with the moor. The detective appears just as the escaped convict disappears from sight and the metonymic association effectively establishes them as doubles. This perception is reinforced by the fact that both hide amongst the ancient huts scattered across the moor; indeed, Holmes describes Selden as his '"neighbour"' (745). Holmes also shares a number of characteristics with Stapleton. As is often pointed out by critics, both men are characterised by 'hidden fires' (713, 745) while their areas of respective expertise – deduction and entomology – are associated with the nets used to capture their prey (706, 750). The doubling of Holmes and a criminal antagonist is not unusual in the canon – we see it most obviously in his pairing with Moriarty. Here, it is central to the novel's questioning of the various binaries upon which it depends: science/supernatural, rational/irrational, civilised/savage. More generally, such doubling can be read as an acknowledgement that 'the figure of the detective, in the act of social cleansing, could also be dangerously impure, as the mediator between respectable society ... and the criminal'.[18] What is less certain, however, is whether Holmes, like his doubles, has a close association with the moor.

Watson recounts the first sighting of Holmes as follows:

> There, outlined as black as an ebony statue on that shining background, I saw the figure of a man upon the tor ... [T]he figure was that of a tall, thin man. He stood with his legs a little separated, his arms folded, his head bowed, as if he were brooding over that enormous wilderness of peat and granite which lay before him. He might have been the very spirit of that terrible place. (726)

Without doubt, there is something spectral about this scene. It is as if the 'spirit' that Holmes sent to hover over Devonshire in the third chapter has taken on an embodied form. Nor is it insignificant that Watson, waiting within Holmes's hiding place, 'quivered at the vagueness and the terror of [the] interview' (739), thus aligning the detective with the formlessness of the moor. When, however, we separate ourselves from Watson's perspective, it is clear that this 'spirit' is much more closely aligned with the solid and stable topography of London than the shifting surface of the moor.

Portrayed as a 'statue' upon a 'sharp pinnacle of granite' (726), Holmes is associated with fixity rather than flux. Scrutinising his appearance, Watson notes that:

> He was thin and worn, but clear and alert, his keen face bronzed by the sun and roughened by the wind. In his tweed suit and cloth cap he looked like any other tourist upon the moor, and he had contrived, with that catlike love of personal cleanliness which was one of his characteristics, that his chin should be as smooth and his linen as perfect as if he were in Baker Street. (740)

When Holmes's immaculate appearance is put together with his location on the granite and statuesque bearing (which is repeated in the portrait reading scene where he is described as 'a clear-cut classical statue' (749)), they suggest how impervious he is to the affective power of the moor. Unlike Watson and Sir Henry, Holmes remains unaffected by his surroundings. The pointed reference to his status as a tourist, moreover, confirms that he does not belong there. The detective's immunity to the moor is, furthermore, paired with a conscious or unconscious denial of its power to destabilise meaning. How else might one explain, in the face of Stapleton's disappearance, his falsely confident assertion to Watson that, '"I do not know that this place contains any secret which we have not already fathomed"' (760) – an especially inappropriate claim given the moor's resistance to precise measurement – and, back in London, that '"I am not aware that there is anything which has remained a secret to us"' (760–1). Nor is it irrelevant that the final retrospective chapter contains a number of references to repression. As Watson informs the reader, Holmes's 'clear and logical mind would not be drawn from its present work to dwell upon memories of the past' and, as the detective himself admits, '"I cannot guarantee that I carry all the facts in my mind. Intense mental concentration has a curious way of blotting out what has happened"' (761). Only by '"blotting out"' the destabilisation associated with the moor is Holmes able to restore the ideal of legibility established in the early chapters.

Many critics have commented upon the extent to which *The Hound of the Baskervilles* challenges the popular construction of Holmes as the personification of rational positivism. As this chapter has demonstrated, this challenge is clearly linked to the novel's competing topographies, captured most clearly in the flat and legible surface of the ordnance map and the reality of the ever-shifting Grimpen Mire. It is, in conclusion, worth noting the role played by the topography of the narrative itself in exploring this challenge. If, as is largely agreed, the Gothic elements are never adequately contained, structurally or otherwise, surely this is because the linear and connected narrative offered by Holmes in the final retrospective chapter falls flat; like the map itself, it fails to capture the jagged heights and treacherous lows of their adventure on the moors. Here, even more than usual, it is the quality of Watson's writing most despised by Holmes – the '"fatal habit of looking at everything from the point of view of a story instead of as a scientific exercise"' ('The Abbey Grange' 636) – that keeps the reader in its 'tenacious grip'.

A Final Word

As suggested in the opening paragraph of this chapter, the rationale for 'slaying Holmes' stemmed from Doyle's belief that he 'takes my mind from better things'. As he explained in his autobiography: 'All things find their level, but I believe that if I had never touched Holmes, who has tended to obscure my higher work, my position in literature would at the present moment be a more commanding one' (*Memories* 81). This position, Doyle believed, was to be achieved though his carefully researched historical fiction, novels such as *The White Company* (1891) and *Sir Nigel* (1906). Such work, he believed, was on 'a larger and more ambitious scale' than the Holmes stories, which he 'regarded as a lower stratum of literary achievement' (*Memories* 215, 99). Indeed, when asked to write a preface for a new edition of *A Study in Scarlet* he refused, declaring that 'so elementary a form of fiction as the detective story hardly deserves the dignity of a Preface'.[19] Given the lexicon employed to describe his attitude towards different types of literary production, it is easy to read Doyle's career in terms of an evolutionary journey in which he made a conscious effort to progress from a lower and more elementary form of writing to that of a more ambitious, complex and higher nature. Like the moors of Dartmoor, the reading public can be seen to consist of both 'men of education' and 'peasants' (678, 706), those 'who are not content with a mere fiend dog but must needs describe him with hell-fire shooting from his mouth and eyes' (727). It is the latter who clamour for the Holmes stories while the former represent Doyle's ideal audience, those who are able to appreciate his historical writing. Although it is seldom remarked upon, it is significant that the narrative of the Baskerville family curse is interrupted by a parenthetical plea from a father to his sons – from Doyle to his readers – to turn from sensational legend to history proper as Hugo Baskerville 'most earnestly commend[s]' Edward Hyde's *The History of the Rebellion* (1702–4) – the authoritative history of the English Civil War – to the readers' attention (674). Set within this context, *The Hound of the Baskervilles* can be seen as a form of literary regression, an atavistic throwback to an earlier, more primitive period of Doyle's own development. In the penultimate chapter of the novel, Watson describes how the 'tenacious grip' of the mire 'plucked at our heels ... as if some malignant hand was tugging us down into those obscene depths, so firm and purposeful was the clutch in which it held us' (760). Doyle may well have felt the same way about Holmes: the great creation from which he was never able to free himself.

Notes

1. Jon Lellenberg, Daniel Stashower and Charles Foley (eds.), *Arthur Conan Doyle: A Life in Letters* (London: Harper Perennial, 2008), 300.
2. Ibid., 319.
3. Ibid., 477.
4. Maurizio Ascari, *A Counter-History of Crime Fiction: Supernatural, Gothic, Sensational* (Basingstoke: Palgrave Macmillan, 2007), 1.

5. Sigmund Freud, 'The "Uncanny"', in *Art and Literature*, trans. James Strachey. *The Penguin Freud Library*, vol. 14 (London: Penguin, 1990), 335–76 (371, 375).

6. Nicholas Royle, *The Uncanny* (Manchester: Manchester University Press, 2003), 1.

7. Srdjan Smajić, *Ghost-Seers, Detectives and Spiritualists: Theories of Vision in Victorian Literature and Science* (Cambridge: Cambridge University Press, 2010), 71.

8. Ibid., 71–2.

9. Victoria Margree and Bryony Randall, '*Fin-de-Siècle* Gothic', in Andrew Smith and William Hughes (eds), *The Victorian Gothic* (Edinburgh: Edinburgh University Press, 2012), 217–33 (231).

10. Christopher Pittard, *Purity and Contamination in Late Victorian Detective Fiction* (Farnham: Ashgate, 2011), 73.

11. Lynda Nead, *Victorian Babylon: People, Streets and Images in Nineteenth-Century London* (New Haven and London: Yale University Press, 2000), 74–5.

12. Catherine Belsey, *Critical Practice*, 1980, 2nd edn (London and New York: Routledge, 2002), 91–2.

13. Quoted in Ronald R. Thomas, *Detective Fiction and the Rise of Forensic Science* (Cambridge: Cambridge University Press, 1999), 122.

14. Guy Debord, 'Introduction to a Critique of Urban Geography', in Ken Knabb (ed. and trans.), *Situationist International Anthology*, 1955 (Berkeley: Bureau of Public Secrets, 1981), 5–8 (5).

15. Tyler Roeger, 'The Ocean and the Urban: Poe's "The Oblong Box"', *Atlantic Studies* 13:2 (2016), 227–48 (228).

16. Ibid., 235.

17. Ibid., 242, 228.

18. Pittard, *Purity*, 93.

19. Quoted in Daniel Stashower, *Teller of Tales: The Life of Arthur Conan Doyle* (New York: Henry Holt and Company, 1999), 84.

PART III

Holmesian Afterlives

13

BRAN NICOL

Holmes and Literary Theory

On 16 October 2002 British media reported on the rather curious incident of a fictional character being awarded an honorary fellowship by one of the UK's leading professional bodies: the Royal Society of Chemistry.[1] While acknowledging the 100th anniversary of both Doyle's knighthood and the publication of his most celebrated Holmes story, *The Hound of the Baskervilles*, the Society honoured Sherlock Holmes – not his creator, Arthur Conan Doyle – for being 'the first detective to exploit chemical science as a means of detection'.[2] In a ceremony outside Baker Street tube station a gold medal was hung around the neck of the Holmes statue that stands there by a Fellow of the Royal Society, one Dr John Watson.

A fictional detective being awarded a genuine award by a real Dr Watson is typical of the ontological confusion generated by the success of Doyle's creation. In a previous *Sherlock Holmes Companion* to this one, published in 1962, its editors admit in the foreword to being struck by 'the illusion that we were dealing with a figure of real life rather than of fiction'.[3] It is well-known that letters from all over the world addressed to Mr Sherlock Holmes are sent every day to a fictional address, 221B Baker Street, many apparently requesting the detective's help. Despite the persistence of this illusion, the idea of Doyle's creation being credited for its contribution to science rather than literature is a telling one. It suggests that there is something of value in the Holmes canon beyond its literary merit, a quality that opens up questions of knowledge, interpretation and method that are genuinely useful to those involved in scientific investigation. This quality has in fact been there from the outset. One of the French forensic scientists who established the new discipline of modern criminology in the late nineteenth century, Edmund Locard, advised students and colleagues to read Doyle's stories to help them grasp the scientific principles he was advocating.[4]

Holmes's forensic approach to problem-solving is essentially *theoretical* rather than practical in that it relies upon hypotheses rather than action, or, to put it differently, in his investigations, actions are the consequences of hypotheses. His solution to crimes depends upon positing 'as if' scenarios: theorising, in other words. The word theory comes from the Latin word *theoria* meaning contemplation or speculation, thus foregrounding a connection between the literary detective and the literary theorist: both are in the business of explaining something by drawing on general principles and speculating or hypothesising.

More precisely, the theorising in Doyle's stories is the chief mechanism in what Pierre Bayard has called 'the Holmes method', and 'the primary reason', according to Bayard, 'that these texts have become famous.[5] The detective's procedure, as Holmes repeatedly reminds Watson, is to '"see what others overlook"' (192); and, more precisely, as he puts it in 'A Scandal in Bohemia', to '"observe"' instead of simply '"seeing"' (162). The most famous example of this kind of observation is the key event – or, rather, non-event – in 'Silver Blaze': the '"curious incident of the dog in the night-time"' (347). Holmes wonders why it is that a guard dog, normally unfailingly alert, apparently did not bark when something occurred right under its nose on the night of the crime. He notices, in other words, what everyone else had, understandably, overlooked.

In 'A Scandal in Bohemia', as in innumerable examples from the canon, Holmes describes this practice of observation as deduction – '"I see it, I deduce it"' (162). However, the contributors to Umberto Eco and Thomas A. Sebeok's *The Sign of Three* (1983), the most thorough examination of Holmes's method to date – as well as a powerful testament to the value of Doyle's work to literary theory – demonstrate that Holmes does not actually practice deduction in the majority of his cases. Instead, his method is best characterised by what Doyle's contemporary, C. S. Peirce, the American pragmatist philosopher, termed *abduction*. Where deduction is a form of reasoning that proceeds from a general rule to make sense of a particular case (to explain why what happened happened), abduction is at once more complex and less scientific, for it is essentially a matter of forming creative hypotheses, drawing links between things or events, or pointing to how such links embody a rule. In short, abduction involves 'reasoning backwards', supposition and educated guesswork.[6]

Holmes, 'Suspicious Reading' and the 'Mystery to a Solution'

Eco and Sebeok's aim is not to invalidate Holmes's methods, nor to challenge Doyle's status in the history of literature. Their focus, rather, is on what the Holmes method can teach us about how *conjecture* – that is, the act of theorising, hypothesising or inhabiting a world of 'as if' (like the Royal Society of Chemistry awarding Holmes their fellowship, or the people who write letters to the detective at 221B Baker Street) – functions in modern literature and culture.

The pleasure of conjecture is one obvious, though partial, explanation for why Holmes has figured so prominently in literary theory. Theorists, in fact academics more generally, are individuals who like to speculate and contemplate. In his 1971 essay 'Whodunit and Other Questions: Metaphysical Detective Stories in Post-War Fiction', Michael Holquist shows how detective fiction owes its reputation as an intellectual genre, ripe for philosophical speculation and the analysis of literature, to the rise of a particular academic literary culture in the interwar years in America and the United Kingdom. Influential intellectuals who championed the genre (often writing examples of it, too, as in the case of Oxford professors J. I. M. Stewart or C. Day Lewis, writing as Michael Innes and Nicholas Blake respectively) did so because, Holquist argues, detective fiction demonstrates 'the magic of mind in a world that often seems impervious to reason'. There was a particular fascination with Sherlock Holmes, whom Holquist characterises as 'pure mind', the most formidably rational of all detectives and the ultimate intellectual hero, a man devoted, as Franco Moretti later notes, to solving crime for its own sake in the way that dilettantish artists love art for its own sake.[7]

The appreciation of the kind of people who read James Joyce by day and Agatha Christie by night (to paraphrase Holquist)[8] partly explains Holmes's popularity amongst literary theorists. Many of the thinkers familiar to students of literary theory, such as Viktor Shklovsky, Sigmund Freud, Michel Foucault, Roland Barthes, Umberto Eco, Walter Benjamin, Tzvetan Todorov and Fredric Jameson, use detective stories as examples within their work or have written essays on the genre. The French post-structuralists Jacques Lacan and Jacques Derrida (and then Norman Holland and Barbara Johnson) famously debated Poe's 'The Purloined Letter' (1844), Jean Baudrillard entitled one of his books, *The Perfect Crime* (1966) and Julia Kristeva took to writing detective stories herself. The reason for this has to do with more than the fact that those of an academic disposition tend to like conjecture. It is a critical commonplace that detective-work is analogous to critical interpretation. The detective, like the literary critic, is primarily a skilled reader, someone in the business of decoding signs and interpreting narratives. Holmes is therefore a master-reader of texts as much as a detective and his conjectural approach to a puzzle, continually constructing and testing out hypotheses, is mirrored in the reaction of readers to the twists and turns of the stories he or she reads.

More than this, Holmes, in particular, embodies the kind of 'suspicious logic' which literary study in the twentieth and twenty-first centuries, informed by theory, demands. Students are taught not to take what they read or hear at face value, but to look for the 'deeper' meaning beneath the surface. Holmes was in his heyday when the writings of the three thinkers that Paul Ricoeur labels the 'masters of suspicion' – Karl Marx, Friedrich Nietzsche and Sigmund Freud – were becoming influential. Their influence helped institute this 'suspicious' approach to complex literary texts, along with the similarly suspicious or even productively 'paranoid' reading practices required of modernist literature in the first half of the twentieth century, where the reader is required to be hyper-vigilant in analysing patterns or symbols in the text, even interpreting names, colours, etc. in a way which 'in "real life" would clearly be an indication of paranoid behaviour'.[9]

The most influential essay included in Eco and Sebeok's *The Sign of Three*, Carlo Ginzburg's 'Morelli, Freud and Sherlock Holmes: Clues and Scientific Method', originally published in 1980, examines how representative the Holmes method is of a dominant form of suspicious reading that took root in the late nineteenth century. Ginzburg draws a parallel between Holmes's method and the techniques of two of Doyle's contemporaries: the Italian art historian, Giovanni Morelli, and the inventor of psychoanalysis, Sigmund Freud. Between 1874 and 1886, Morelli proposed a new way of determining whether old masters had been forged by insisting that one should concentrate on minor details – such as earlobes, fingernails, or the shape of fingers or toes – rather than the signature elements of a great artist. Freud himself noted the similarity between Morelli's practice and his own method of unlocking a patient's unconscious by focusing on apparently insignificant elements such as dreams, word choice, or slips of the tongue, what Freud called 'the rubbish-heap, as it were, of our observations'.[10]

Ginzburg points out that in the methods of all three figures, Morelli, Freud and Holmes, 'tiny details provide the key to a deeper reality, inaccessible by other methods. These details may be symptoms, for Freud, or clues, for Holmes, or features of paintings, for Morelli'.[11] The value of Ginzburg's analysis is twofold. Firstly, he highlights a striking paradigm shift that establishes a 'suspicious' approach to reading the world as a dominant practice in a range of disparate fields, not just art history, psychoanalysis and detection, but others too, such as medicine and historiography. Secondly, Ginzburg suggests that because the method is so pervasive, it means that modern scientific methods of investigation are dependent upon an older, ancestral form of conjectural logic which can never quite be superseded by modern laboratory techniques. Ginzburg thus both affirms and questions modern scientific rationalism, showing that scientific procedure cannot be detached from an investigative tradition that involves artistry, imagination, and speculation.

This double combination is embodied in the figures of Holmes and Freud and explains why the parallels between them have been frequently explored by literary theorists, writers and thinkers. Steven Marcus has noted that both are prodigious readers of complex narrative texts – the speech, dreams, or symptoms of a patient, in the case of the former, and the story of the crime, in the case of the latter. Nicholas Meyer's novel *The Seven-Per-Cent Solution* (1974) imagines Holmes treated for his cocaine addiction by Freud, and the psychiatrist Michael Shepherd's critique of psychoanalysis, *Sherlock Holmes and the Case of Dr Freud* (1985) argues, along similar lines to the contributors to Eco's and Sebeok's collection, that Holmes's solutions depend more on intuition and illogic than on ratiocination. As well as telling the story of the solution to a mystery, each Holmes case dramatises the complex techniques involved in getting there, or what John Irwin pithily calls, the 'mystery to a solution'.[12]

In a similar vein, in his brilliant contribution to the tradition of reading Holmes through Freud and vice versa, the Lacanian political philosopher Slavoj Žižek has contended that both figures are, in fact, combinations of 'bourgeois scientific rationalism' and a tradition of 'the romantic clairvoyant' without being either, and that this accounts for the special value of the Holmes canon. Žižek points to the fact that both the Freudian case study and Holmes's adventures begin in a similar way, with a mysterious client telling the investigator a seductive but obscure story. There is a wealth of examples from the Holmes canon: the woman paid by her employer to sit with her back to a window in a distinctive blue dress ('The Copper Beeches'), the university professor who is seen crawling on his hands and feet in the dead of night ('The Creeping Man'), the two brothers laughing dementedly at the card-table as their sister sits dead beside them ('The Devil's Foot'). These scenes possess a Gothic power that jars with the outward maintenance of prosaic realism carried by Watson's narration (even though he is actually responsible – as Holmes frequently complains – for sensationalising elements of cases (636)). Žižek argues that such scenes 'exert such a powerful libidinal force that one is almost tempted to hypothesize that the main function of the detective's "rational explanation" is to break the spell they have upon us'.[13] The victory of rational science over irrational Gothic seduction is hard won.

But Žižek goes further and argues that the Holmes method is even more complex in its handling of insignificant details than previously acknowledged because the detective does not simply use the details that others overlook, but takes into account – as the psychoanalyst would – the nature of the deception involved. Holmes's approach is therefore not simply a hermeneutics of suspicion, penetrating through surface to depth, but one that takes account of the complexity of the surface. One of Žižek's examples is from 'The Red-headed League', a story that revolves around a gang who place an advert in a newspaper offering a well-paid job to red-headed men. The explanation behind this, as Holmes realises, is not that the gang have any interest in red-headed men, but that they wish to lure one single man, who happens to have red hair, away from his house beside a bank so they can build a connecting tunnel while he is off the premises: '"it was perfectly obvious from the first that the only possible object of this rather fantastic business of the advertisement of the League, and the copying of the Encyclopaedia, must be to get this not over-bright pawnbroker out of the way for a number of hours every day"' (189). The key to this case is to understand that the advert is not, as it appears, evidence of some insane obsession with red-headed men – a conclusion which would lure the detective in the wrong direction, too – but a ruthlessly practical solution to a problem. Holmes understands that his task is not simply to access the truth covered up by this elaborate lure but to grasp the reason for the peculiar lure itself.

Marxism and the Ideological Fantasy of Detective Fiction

Žižek and Ginzburg approach Holmes's suspicious reading from what might be described as a philosophical angle. Marxist literary theory, another field in which Holmes has figured instrumentally, also considers Doyle's work as representative, but from a materialist point of view. The starting-point for Marxists is the recognition that the Holmesian canon represents a significant moment in literary history for two reasons. First, this was the point when a genre that initially emerged earlier in the nineteenth century with the stories of Edgar Allan Poe (though there are, of course, antecedents) was formalised. Second, the genre developed in a way that crystallised a range of social, intellectual and literary developments at the time, illustrating how literature responds to and helps shape modernity.

From a Marxist point of view the rise and popularity of detective fiction in the nineteenth century is explained by social factors such as a rapidly expanding urban society, which led to fears of anonymous strangers lurking in the crowds of sprawling urban centres like London or Paris. Other such factors would include the series of working-class revolts between 1830 and 1848, which, Ernest Mandel has written, alarmed the bourgeoisie about 'the lower orders … the classes that were ever restive, periodically rebellious, and therefore criminal in bourgeois eyes'.[14] One dimension of the analysis of detective fiction by perhaps its most influential Marxist theorist, Walter Benjamin, is concerned with the detective's special ability to *read* the urban environment and the range of city-dwellers as if both were part of a literary text and, by so doing, create a reassuring fantasy that crime can be understood and prevented. Although Benjamin enjoyed Doyle's fiction, his many discussions of detective fiction do not mention Sherlock Holmes explicitly. However, a range of powerful post-Benjaminian Marxist critiques of Doyle's stories appeared in the late 1970s and early 1980s and build on the idea of the genre's function as a consoling ideological fantasy.

The Marxist exposure of this fantasy concentrates on two things. First, the way that Sherlock Holmes, for all his credentials as a 'superdetective'[15] in fact embodies the individualist ethos central to bourgeois society, and second, the way that classic detective fiction reduces crime, in John Cawelti's words, 'to a puzzle, a game, and a highly formalized set of literary conventions' and therefore transforms an increasingly serious moral and social problem into an entertaining pastime. The result is that 'something potentially dangerous and disturbing [is] transformed into something completely under control'.[16] Marxist critics have noted the class divisions in Holmes's stories, namely the fact that its hero is not a 'plodding' ordinary policeman but 'a brilliant sleuth of upper-class origins'.[17] For Stephen Knight, Doyle's achievement in this respect was to domesticate or naturalise, that is, present as entirely normal, a bourgeois worldview that held that the lower orders must stay as they were while the middle classes could acquire money, property and prestige in order to better themselves. Central to this was the 'subjective individualism' Holmes represents, and his 'bourgeois professionalism', or his combination of a materialistic understanding of the world with egalitarian values.[18] This falsely reassures his readers that crime was, in actuality, petty, unthreatening and solvable, rather than something instrumental to maintaining an inequitable social order.

A similar argument is developed by the Italian theorist Franco Moretti, who argues that there is something evasive about how the Holmes stories narrow everything down to the dastardly schemes of an individual criminal (though it is occasionally a pairing, a small group, or in the case of Moriarty, a complex web) rooted out by a brilliant individual, the detective. This is, for Moretti, a way of evading the possibility that crime might have other and multiple causes, such as the social injustices perpetrated by capitalism.[19]

Narrative Theory and the Question of Literature

A shared feature of both Žižek's psychoanalytic approach and the Marxist perspective of Moretti, Knight and Dennis Porter, is that crime fiction, the most popular of all popular genres, can be considered typical of *all* narrative fiction and, moreover, illuminate how it works. The social and philosophical analysis of these perspectives is founded upon a formalist approach to the genre – i.e. one that never loses sight of how it is structured and narrated – which is not always evident in studies of popular fiction, which, traditionally, have tended to be more sociologically oriented. This formalist basis underpins the analysis of the Holmes stories by narrative theorists. Of all critical analyses, narrative theory puts Doyle's fiction to work most powerfully and suggestively. The best examples insist that detective fiction exposes a tension between the literary and the non-literary which, in turn, raises questions relevant to readers and scholars about what literature is and why we read or interpret it.

The pattern is set by the first formalist analysis of the Holmes stories, one that predates the other theoretical accounts covered so far. The Russian formalist Viktor Shklovsky's essay 'Sherlock Holmes and the Mystery Story' (1929) focuses on the 'prosaic', 'monotonous' and repetitive features of the stories, such as their formulaic beginnings: Watson first enumerates Holmes's adventures and exploits, then a client appears and then Holmes shows off various 'devices of analysis'.[20] Shklovsky explains how Doyle's stories depend upon what he terms a 'slowing' or 'retardation' of the action, effected by analytical digressions, 'false resolutions', enigmatic expressions by the detective, his misconstruing of the meaning of evidence, or Watson's provision of biographical details about Holmes.

Though Shklovsky's purpose is to use what he regards as a less exalted form of narrative, the detective story, to cast light on the handling of mysteries in more complex narratives (such as those by Charles Dickens and Leo Tolstoy), Shklovsky is nonetheless clearly fascinated by what distinguishes detective fiction from other narrative forms. A later theorist in the formalist tradition, Tzvetan Todorov, bases his analysis of the genre in his classic essay 'The Typology of Detective Fiction' (1966) on the way it simultaneously tells two stories in a way that produces a peculiar tension, unique to the genre, between literary and non-literary elements. Todorov's thesis depends upon the Russian formalist division of narrative into two interlocking components: *fabula* (or story), the 'raw material' of a narrative, made up of sequential, causal and chronological elements, and *szujet* (or plot), the ordering of these events into a different, usually non-chronological sequence, to produce suspense, and to withhold or highlight specific elements. In detective fiction, the 'story of the investigation' is the equivalent of this second category, *szujet*, in that it is directly accessible to the reader but is effectively 'non-literary' because nothing much happens (other than the examination of clues, the testing of hypotheses and the gaining of knowledge) and it is narrated in a transparent, imperceptible style. By contrast, the 'story of the crime', equivalent to the *fabula*, exploits an arsenal of literary techniques, such as temporal inversions and multiple subjective points of view, so that the suspense can be maintained and the reader is prevented from guessing the solution too early. Todorov's conclusion is that the 'transparent', non-literary second story naturalises the former, effectively justifying its excessively literary style; in other words reducing it to something that makes sense according to the scientific logic of investigation.[21]

Moretti develops Todorov's insight in his essay 'Clues' (1983) by turning his attention to how, in the Holmes's stories, it is the criminal who produces the underlying story of the crime (*szujet*), one full of gaps and mysteries, a sequence of events that initially confounds the detective's attempts to understand them, while the detective produces the story of the investigation (*fabula*), by filling in the gaps and rendering it all clear, linear and meaningful. By countering the criminal's plot with the story, Holmes's aim is effectively to eliminate the literary elements of the text. According to Moretti, this results in the 'abolition' of narration, as the detective's reconstruction of the story brings the reader back to the beginning. As the only point of the detective story is the end (the solution), it means the journey in getting there is of no importance: reading it is a 'long wait' rather than a 'voyage'.[22] For Moretti, therefore, detective fiction is nothing less than the opposite of the novel, which depends upon development of character and inviting readers to consider their own lives through its themes.

Moretti's and Todorov's analyses of detective fiction show how peculiar a literary form this is: on the one hand eliminating the literary elements of the text but, on the other, knowing it cannot do without the literariness, for a solution without a mystery is uninteresting.[23] A recent complementary theory to the arguments of both these theorists – and, in fact, one that has more far-reaching significance than either – is offered by Pierre Bayard in his forensic dissection and reconstruction of Christie's novel *The Murder of Roger Ackroyd* (1926). The detective story, Bayard argues, is composed of two 'movements'. The 'first movement' (which lasts most of the book) is geared towards opening up meaning, that is 'multipy[ing] leads and solutions' and 'conjuring before the reader's eyes for brief moments a multitude of possible worlds in which different murderers commit different murders'. The 'second movement' (which emerges towards the end of the book) is concerned with 'foreclosing meaning', that is, it 'brutally eliminates different possibilities and privileges a single one, charged … with clarifying all proposed mysteries in retrospect while giving the reader the feeling that it was there in front of him [sic] all the time, protected by his blindness'.[24]

These two movements translate into two contradictory ways of conceiving of the sign. The process of opening meanings up makes the story adhere initially to the critical axiom that signs have multiple meanings: that is, certain events, certain clues, can be interpreted in more than one way. However, the ending effectively asks readers to disavow what they have just learned and accept that, in fact, the sign has all along only meant one thing. There is a definitive explanation of what happened, and other possibilities are revealed to be in fact impossible, or red herrings. But Bayard's point is that the genre cannot have it both ways: either signs can mean many things (as the foundational maxim of post-structuralist literary theory dictates) or they can only mean one thing. And because the detective story must necessarily devote all its energy – all its art, in fact, because it is this element that makes detective fiction a supremely artful genre – carefully to asserting the former, its overall coherence is seriously compromised when it ultimately tries to claim the latter. The 'literary' will always find a way of eluding the clutches of the 'non-literary'.

This theory is the foundation for a series of brilliant forays into what Bayard calls 'detective criticism', in which he pursues some of the possibilities that have been foreclosed in classic detective stories and provides new endings for them. As well as *The Murder of Roger Ackroyd* and Shakespeare's *Hamlet* (which he persuasively reads as detective fiction), Bayard has also turned his attention to *The Hound of the Baskervilles*. *L'Affaire du chien des Baskerville* (2008) (published in English as *Sherlock Holmes Was Wrong*) does more than simply develop a new reading of Doyle's novel, it produces a new writing of it as well, demonstrating remarkably convincingly that Holmes's solution 'simply does not hold up, and that the real murderer escaped justice'.[25] As Bayard's book is partly constructed as a detective story, I shall resist the temptation to spoil the ending. Suffice to say that his solution hinges on the flimsiness of the famous Holmes method. While Holmes makes a number of mistakes in *The Hound of the Baskervilles* (at one point he loses sight of Sir Henry Baskerville, whom he was supposed to protect, and he then unintentionally puts him in a place where he can be attacked by the hound) the main problem is his habit of creating a construction of events before the investigation has properly begun, a construction which he then remains faithful to throughout. Holmes's stubbornness in sticking to this construction means that he 'eliminates other hypotheses, for instance that of accident – defended by the police – or that of a murder committed in some different way'.[26]

Bayard insists that Holmes, for all his and Watson's insistence on the primacy of scientific method, is a creator of fictions. This means that the official rhetoric of the stories, that they are about the conflict between two narratives, one literary and one scientific, is proved misleading. In fact the rational, scientific narrative is a literary conjuring trick sustained by the complicity of Holmes and Watson – and Doyle. Bayard's point is not to convince readers that Holmes is delusional but to show how fiction creates a world and manipulates its readers to believe in it.

Eco's insistence that Holmes indulges in 'creative abduction' rather than deduction is made for the same reason. In his essay, 'Horns, Hooves, and Insteps', Eco considers why the many gratuitous displays of Holmes's brilliant reasoning at the beginning of the stories – such as when, in 'The Cardboard Box', he notices Watson glancing first at a framed portrait of General Gordon on the wall then at an unframed portrait of Henry Ward Beecher and finally at a bare space on the wall, and concludes that his companion was '"thinking that if the portrait were framed it would just cover that bare space and correspond with Gordon's picture there"' (889) – turn out to be correct in the world of the story. His conclusion is that the veracity of Holmes's hypotheses is ensured by the universe of the fiction, which is 'ruled by a sort of complicity between the author [and] his characters' and thus a kind of self-fulfilling logic results: 'If the story's world were the "real" world, Watson's stream of consciousness could have taken so many other directions'. But all fiction is a closed world, and thus Holmes's reasoning happens to be analogous to the truth because the truth has been determined by Doyle. As Eco suggests, Holmes 'has the privilege of living in a world built by Conan Doyle to fit his egocentric need'. Part of this involves the very existence of Watson who, in terms of his narrative function, 'exists just to verify his hypotheses'.[27]

In a similar way to Bayard, whose exercises in 'detective criticism' show how all narrative manipulates the reader, Eco affirms that in the Holmes stories, the author is on the side of the detective, fixing the universe into a single shape, one in which all of Holmes's conjectures are guaranteed to be accurate. Eco's own novel *The Name of the Rose* (1991) – an example of what has been termed 'metaphysical detective fiction', a sub-genre that subverts the conventions of classic detective fiction in order to raise philosophical questions about knowing and being in the mind of the reader[28] – features a medieval detective named Sir William of Baskerville, a Holmes parody who is unable to solve the crime. In Eco's novel, the opposite is true, and the author plays the role of a God who has placed his detective in a universe designed to frustrate his hypotheses rather than support them.

Conclusion: Sherlock Holmes and the Thinking of Literature

In *Reflections on* The Name of the Rose, Eco offers a provocative view of the appeal of detective fiction, one that counters Marxist approaches. Readers turn repeatedly to detective fiction not because the genre permits them a means of confronting the inevitability of death 'safely', nor because it gives them the satisfaction of seeing social order restored by the weeding out of dangerous individuals. Rather, Eco insists, 'the crime novel represents a kind of conjecture, pure and simple ... Every story of investigation and conjecture tells us something that we have always been close to knowing'.[29] The pleasure of reading the Holmes stories is that they enable readers to theorise about the cases they dramatise, about literature and about their own human nature.

Sherlock Holmes himself might best be considered not as a detective or criminologist but as a theorist. His methods are representative of the peculiar combination of scientific technique and a longer-established cultural tradition of conjecture identified by Ginzburg as central to modern forms of investigation. Holmes's ability to read 'suspiciously' is also in tune with the dominant impetus behind literary theory and analysis in the twentieth and twenty-first centuries. It would also not be stretching things too far to describe his creator, Arthur Conan Doyle, as a literary theorist as much as an author of fiction. His Holmes stories are not quite examples of metaphysical detective fiction, like *The Name of the Rose*, but he set out to write fiction that dramatises a method of theoretical thinking and, in so doing, was therefore producing a kind of literary theory.

The programmatic openings to these stories, in which Watson refers to his intention to select 'a few typical cases which illustrate the remarkable mental qualities of my friend, Sherlock Holmes' (888), conceal a literary ambition that is quite radical. Far from dismissing these references to Watson's larger 'project' as simple formulaic exercises in 'anticipation', as Viktor Shklovsky does, we ought to acknowledge that they are part of the elaborate construction of a larger fictional universe that Holmes and Watson inhabit, and in which all their cases have existed (and which perhaps even includes the 'real' 221B Baker Street, or Holmes's recognition by the Royal Chemistry Society). This is the 'as if' world which, as Michael Saler has argued, is typified by the extraordinary capacity of Doyle's stories (along with other examples of fiction from the Victorian period and the first part of the twentieth century) to produce a 'public sphere of the imagination'.[30]

As Todorov recognised, there is a self-reflexive element to the prosaic 'second story' in detective fiction, the story of the investigation. The narrator acknowledges that he is telling not just the story of the crime but the story of how the story about that crime – in other words, the very one he is narrating – came to be told.[31] The central conceit in the expanded universe of Sherlock Holmes, as Watson's opening references to his overall project suggest, is that these stories are not intended to be narratives read for entertainment, so much as case studies designed to exemplify and encourage debate about the Holmes method.

What if, in this spirit, we acknowledge that Doyle was not writing short stories but producing novel exercises in literary theory, the kind that conform to Jean-Michel Rabaté's insistence that literary theory must be understood as a questioning impulse that runs through works of literature and literary criticism as much as it is a canon of theorists and movements that approach the study of literary texts in systematic ways. 'Theory is literature, if you want', Rabaté writes, 'but literature raised to the power of speculation, literature when the term includes the "question of literature" or "the thinking of literature"'.[32] The Holmes stories may be formulaic and repetitive, but they are also thrilling, unnerving, seductive and far from conservative when we consider – as many theorists have encouraged us to do – what they can teach us about literature.

Notes

1. Unsigned, 'Sherlock Holmes honoured for elementary work', *Guardian*, 16 October 2002, [https://www.theguardian.com/education/2002/oct/16/higher education.science, accessed 28 June 2017].
2. 'Sherlock Holmes honorary fellowship', Royal Society of Chemistry, Press Release, 16 October 2002, [www.rsc.org/AboutUs/News/PressReleases/2005/Sherlock-holmes-rsc-fellowship.asp, accessed 28 June 2017].
3. Michael Hardwick and Mollie Hardwick (eds.), *The Sherlock Holmes Companion* (London: Bramhall House, 1962), vii.
4. Ronald R. Thomas, *Detective Fiction and the Rise of Forensic Science* (Cambridge: Cambridge University Press, 1999), 4–5.
5. Pierre Bayard, *Sherlock Holmes was Wrong: Reopening the Case of The Hound of the Baskervilles* (London: Bloomsbury, 2010), 30.
6. Thomas A. Sebeok and Jean Umiker-Sebeok, '"You Know My Method": A Juxtaposition of Charles S. Peirce and Sherlock Holmes', in Umberto Eco and Thomas A. Sebeok (eds.), *The Sign of Three: Holmes, Dupin, Peirce* (Bloomington: Indiana University Press, 1983), 11–54, (18–19).
7. Michael Holquist, 'Whodunit and Other Questions: Metaphysical Detective Stories in Post-War Fiction', *New Literary History* 3:1 (1971), 135–56 (143); Franco Moretti, 'Clues', in *Signs Taken for Wonders: On the Sociology of Literary Forms*, trans. Susan Fischer, David Forgacs, and David Miller (London and New York: Verso, 1983), 130–56 (142).
8. Holquist, 'Whodunit and Other Questions', 147.
9. Paul Ricoeur, *Freud and Philosophy: An Essay on Interpretation* (New Haven: Yale University Press, 1970), 33; Mark Richard Siegel, *Creative Paranoia in Gravity's Rainbow* (Port Washington and London: National University Publications/Kennikat Press, 1978), 15.
10. Sigmund Freud, 'The Moses of Michelangelo', quoted in Carlo Ginzburg, 'Clues: Morelli, Freud and Sherlock Holmes', in Eco and Sebeok, *The Sign of Three*, 81–118 (85).
11. Ibid., 87.

12. John Irwin, *The Mystery to a Solution: Poe, Borges, and the Analytic Detective Story* (Baltimore: Johns Hopkins University Press, 1996), 1.

13. Slavoj Žižek, *Looking Awry: An Introduction to Jacques Lacan through Popular Culture* (Cambridge: The MIT Press, 1992), 49, 60.

14. Ernest Mandel, *Delightful Murder: A Social History of the Crime Story* (London: Pluto Press, 1984), 13.

15. Sita A. Schütt, 'French Crime Fiction', in Martin Priestman (ed.), *The Cambridge Companion to Crime Fiction* (Cambridge: Cambridge University Press, 2003), 59–76 (70).

16. John G. Cawelti, *Adventure, Mystery, and Romance: Formula Stories as Art and Popular Culture* (Chicago: University of Chicago Press, 1977), 105.

17. Mandel, *Delightful Murder*, 15.

18. Stephen Knight, *Form and Ideology in Crime Fiction* (Basingstoke: Macmillan, 1980), 79.

19. Moretti, 'Clues', 143.

20. Viktor Shklovsky, 'Sherlock Holmes and the Mystery Story', in *Theory of Prose*, trans. Benjamin Sher (Normal: Dalkey Archive Press, 1991), 101–16 (105).

21. Tzvetan Todorov, 'The Typology of Detective Fiction', in *The Poetics of Prose*, trans. Richard Howard (Ithaca: Cornell University Press, 1977), 42–52 (44–7).

22. Moretti, 'Clues', 148.

23. Ibid., 148–9.

24. Pierre Bayard, *Who Killed Roger Ackroyd?*, trans. Carol Cosman (London: Fourth Estate, 2000), 67.

25. Bayard, *Sherlock Holmes*, 7.

26. Ibid., 52.

27. Umberto Eco, 'Horns, Hooves, Insteps: Some Hypotheses on Three Types of Abduction', in Eco and Sebeok, *The Sign of Three*, 198–220 (216, 218, 219).

28. Patricia Merivale and Elizabeth Sweeney, 'The Game's Afoot: On the Trail of the Metaphysical Detective Story', in *Detecting Texts: The Metaphysical Detective Story from Poe to Postmodernism* (Philadelphia: University of Pennsylvania Press, 1999), 1–25.

29. Umberto Eco, *Postscript to* The Name of the Rose, rpt. in *The Name of the Rose* (New York: Mariner Books, 2014), 539–76 (564).

30. Michael Saler, *As If: Modern Enchantment and the Literary Prehistory of Virtual Reality* (Oxford: Oxford University Press, 2012), 98.

31. Todorov, 'Typology', 45.

32. Jean-Michel Rabaté, *The Future of Theory* (Oxford: Blackwell, 2002), 8.

14

NEIL MCCAW

Adapting Holmes

On 25 November 1893, the Royal Court Theatre in London staged an evening triple-bill of new short plays. Last on stage at 10pm was a parodical musical skit that *The Times* praised as 'clever enough to make the fortune of any bill'.[1] Titled *Under the Clock*, it was being performed for the very first time, and starred its author, Charles Brookfield, in the lead role. Fast forward more than a century to a crisp spring morning on 27 April 2007 when, outside the British Embassy in Moscow, a commemorative bronze statue of the Russian actors Vasily Livanov and Vitaly Solomin, dressed in the costumes of their most well-known film roles, was being opened to the public. Two cultural events, separated by over a hundred years, thousands of miles and a host of cultural, religious and political differences. Yet, two events linked at their core by their place within the afterlife of the fictional character of Sherlock Holmes – *Under the Clock* as the first ever publicly performed Holmesian adaptation, and the commemoration of Livanov and Solomin owing to their iconic, much-celebrated Russian-language series of films, *The Adventures of Sherlock Holmes and Dr Watson*, produced and broadcast during the last decades of the Soviet Union.

Between these two cultural moments lies more than a century of Holmesian adaptation; re-workings in a multiplicity of cultural forms that have made Sherlock Holmes the most ubiquitous fictional character in the whole of global popular culture. And the origins of this ubiquity can be traced right back to Holmes's creator, Sir Arthur Conan Doyle. For although Doyle was at first resistant when adapters requested licence to create their own versions of the Great Detective – and therein to extend the character's life and adventures beyond the parameters of his original stories – by the end of the nineteenth century he had grasped the commercial potential of a Holmesian adaptation industry and quickly shifted his position. Having initially refused to allow a love interest to be written into the American actor William Gillette's Holmesian stage play, he ended up conceding that Gillette could 'marry or murder or do what you like with him' (*Memories* 102). This willingness to accept a loosening of the ties between his own Sherlock Holmes stories and future adaptive texts was the green light to the growth of the extraordinarily varied range of Holmesian works that have followed since, to the point that now, in the twenty-first century, the setting, adventures and even the very character of the Great Detective have become fundamentally negotiable: 'Holmesland', as Tom Ue labels it, has extended 'well beyond Conan Doyle's stories, genres and media'.[2]

Despite the diversity of Holmes adaptations, it is evident that the question of fidelity/authenticity to Doyle's original works has remained for many adapters a relevant concern. As Stephen Joyce has rightly noted, to a certain extent 'every adaptation of Holmes must deal with the question of authenticity'[3] – the cultural weight of Doyle's canon almost demands this. Even Doyle's more relaxed position about permitting adapters a greater degree of creative freedom in interpreting Holmes was only partial. He did not give up entirely on trying to compel adapters to work to his own strictures, and during his own lifetime a copyright licence was far more likely to be approved if a proposed adaptation (such as the Stoll series discussed below), was perceived to follow either the letter or the spirit of the original Holmes stories, and therein to make evident what Sarah Cardwell calls 'a direct relationship with the culturally established original'.[4]

Thus, it is no surprise that there are many instances in the history of Holmes adaptations where an almost devotional reverence is displayed for Doyle's stories. This is a reverence that accords with one of the key features of Sherlockian scholarship across the twentieth century, first embodied in Ronald Knox's seminal 1911 essay, 'Studies in the Literature of Sherlock Holmes'.[5] Knox and others celebrated a form of scholarship wherein the original Holmes stories became sanctified texts, known as the 'canon' or 'sacred writings' and differentiated from the 'apocrypha' of other writings about Holmes by Doyle and others writers.[6] And it is just such a reverence for the canon that can be seen in a number of twentieth-century adaptations, the first of which perhaps being the series of forty-five short- and two feature-length silent films starring Eille Norwood and produced by Stoll Picture Productions between 1921 and 1923. This series began with a version of *The Dying Detective* (1921) and concluded with *The Sign of Four* (1923), and throughout Norwood strove to bring Doyle's detective to life by transforming himself into what he saw to be the physical embodiment of the character described in the original stories. The actor regularly referred back to these as part of the production process, and even taught himself to play the violin in order to be able to replicate accurately this aspect of Holmes's idiosyncratic behaviour. Norwood also conducted studious research into Sidney Paget's *Strand Magazine* illustrations so as to glean ideas relating to

Holmes's posture and costume – which clearly demonstrates his commitment to Doyle's work, even if, ironically, it also illustrates quite how problematic the notion of fidelity is in relation to Holmesian adaptations, with actors and adapters often drawing as much from previous adaptations as from the original source materials.

The Stoll films were a popular and critical success in the United Kingdom and the United States, with one reviewer noting in particular how 'the stories have been translated to the screen with remarkable fidelity';[7] they may also be credited with ossifying a number of the visual features of the Holmes legend in the public consciousness. Even Doyle praised the films, whilst pausing to point out the limits of their much-celebrated fidelity: '[Norwood] has that rare quality ... which compels you to watch an actor eagerly even when he is doing nothing [as well as] a quite unrivalled power of disguise'. His 'only criticism of the films' was 'that they introduce telephones, motor cars and other luxuries of which the Victorian Holmes never dreamed' (*Memories* 106). Evidently, for him Holmes remained a fundamentally nineteenth-century presence, despite the fact that the Stoll films were themselves speaking to audiences of the 1920s.

The Norwood series embody a fetishisation of the originating stories that has been equally evident at other points in the history of Holmes adaptation. It is tangible again, for example, in the clutch of films starring Arthur Wontner, within which the familiar plots of Doyle's stories are embedded into *The Sleeping Cardinal* (1931), *The Missing Rembrandt* (1932) and *The Triumph of Sherlock Holmes* (1934), or else reproduced wholesale in versions of *The Sign of Four* (1932) and *Silver Blaze* (1936). These films attempted to draw on Doyle's image of the Great Detective, depicting him as angular, physically striking and with a reserved yet intense personality.

After an interlude in which successive film adapters took Holmes further and further away from the parameters of Doyle's stories, most notably with the immensely popular wartime propaganda films starring Basil Rathbone and Nigel Bruce (discussed in more detail below), in the 1960s British televisual versions of the stories went back to the canon and demonstrated concerted attempts to achieve fidelity to this source material. This is especially apparent in the fifty-minute television episodes starring Douglas Wilmer and Nigel Stock (BBC, 1964–5), which even the BBC governors themselves felt should be 'unanimously and unreservedly praised' for their loyalty to the original tales 'on grounds of style, faithfulness and good casting'.[8] Wilmer in particular insisted on working closely from Doyle's writing: 'I felt the shadow of the Sherlock Holmes Society looming over me like a great black bat. I used to say, "They'll tear you apart if you get these details wrong!"'[9] And the overarching ethos of the series was such that even when the actor stepped down from the role and was replaced by Peter Cushing in a series of sixteen more episodes (1968), Cushing himself continued the production convention that saw each member of the cast carrying around copies of the Doyle stories to be consulted during filming, in an ongoing commitment to achieving their much-vaunted, albeit chimeric authenticity.[10]

Perhaps the most pronounced example of an adapter self-consciously trying to faithfully bring to life what they saw as Doyle's own version of Holmes was the Granada television series (1984–94) starring Jeremy Brett. Producer Michael Cox and scriptwriter John Hawkesworth openly shared an explicit commitment to 'set the record straight'[11] and move away from what they viewed as a growing trend towards pastiche and parody that had overtaken Holmesian adaptation during the preceding decade. As Cox noted, 'I started out with the aim of making a series which was as faithful as possible to the original stories'.[12] It was a hallowed fidelity also desired by their lead actor who, in the vein of Wilmer and Cushing, also carried his book of Holmes stories 'around with him on the set and if the directors or the writers departed at all from the story he would want to know why. He was almost puritanical about that'.[13]

The quasi-biblical status of Doyle's writings was made manifest in *The Baker Street File*, a Holmesian reference manual put together by the producers, based on their meticulous reading of the original stories. This manual was identified as the guide text for all of the production crew working on the series, from make-up artists to set designers to actors and film technicians, and each was encouraged to regularly consult this digest of the canon so that it became the foundation for all of their work. The ambition was effectively to 'adhere slavishly'[14] to Doyle's own vision, to ensure that everything that happened on screen had an explicit foundation in the fictional world he had written for his Great Detective.

All of these adaptations that made it their overriding intention to be faithful to Doyle's version of Holmes wrestled with conflicting challenges. On the one hand, they strove to remain true to what they believed to be the essence or spirit of the original work, the world of the 'Holmesian purists'.[15] On the other, commercial realities meant that they were simultaneously attempting to reinvent Holmes 'in a way never before experienced'[16] so as to engage audiences enthusiastically with something more than a simple retreading of familiar ground. And the 'purity' of their quest for fidelity was further complicated (as James Naremore has rightly recognised) by an increasingly 'media-saturated environment ... dense with cross-references and filled with borrowings from movies, books, and every other form of representation'.[17] This goes a long way towards explaining why the lines between Doyle's Sherlock Holmes and the growing body of Holmes adaptation soon began to blur, with even some of the very earliest adapters finding ways of working around copyright restrictions that limited the scope of their creative interpretation whilst still cashing in on the cultural resonance of the Sherlock Holmes name. Thus, in the first decades of the twentieth century we find adaptations depicting Holmes-like characters that are given different names, such as the detective 'Knick Carter' in the silent film *A Black Sherlock Holmes* (1917), a film groundbreaking for featuring an all-black cast, and Douglas Fairbanks's character 'Coke Ennyday' in the farce *The Mystery of the Leaping Fish* (1915). Elsewhere, in the wartime trench literature of World War I, magazines such as *The Wiper's Times* made Holmes a regular feature of their stories, but did so under the disguise of parodic character names such as Herlock Shomes, Barlock Jones, Sherlaw Kombs or Spitlock Phones.

This vibrant market for Holmes pastiche and/or parody was first evidenced by the earliest Holmes film, the thirty-second *Sherlock Holmes Baffled* (1900). This features a generic detective figure with the barest of connections with Doyle and only the famous name and the outline of a crime narrative suggesting it as a Holmes film at all. But it established a precedent for subsequent Holmes films that were 'deliberate, announced revisitation[s]' of the legend,[18] making it the precursor of the rich variety of texts that have taken audiences beyond the Doylean canon. In this category we find overseas productions such as the Danish Nordisk silent films starring Viggo Larsen (1908–09), the German movies made between 1908–14, starring Alwin Neuss, and perhaps most notably William Gillette's four-act play *Sherlock Holmes*, which itself became a film in 1916.

Gillette's play is in itself a fascinating case study of the complex and seemingly never-ending overlap and interrelation of Holmes texts, having been based on a stage adaptation first written by Doyle himself, and then revised by the American actor with a view to taking the lead role. It first opened in New York in October 1899, during the hiatus between the death of Sherlock Holmes at the Reichenbach Falls and his return in *The Hound of the Baskervilles*, and thus a key element of the success of the play as it toured to London, Oslo, Stockholm, Gothenburg, Malmo, Munich and Paris, was how it capitalised on a demand for Holmes that was not at that time being satisfied by Doyle himself. Indeed, the play became so popular that it influenced other Holmes adaptations that followed, including Clive Brook's 1932 film *Conan Doyle's the Master Detective Sherlock Holmes*, which was largely based on the same playscript. And such was the success of Gillette's play that for many audiences he himself became Holmes, resulting in him earning a small fortune as he revived the role well into his eighth decade.

Sherlock Holmes is one of the most prominent examples of a non-Doylean Holmes text/production with a legacy of its own, fundamentally shaping the Holmes legend through its introduction of the Meerschaum pipe and the 'Elementary, My Dear Watson' catchphrase (first coined by P.G. Wodehouse in *Psmith, Journalist* (1915)).[19]

Perhaps most well-known in this Holmes-as-pastiche category of adaptation is the series of films starring Basil Rathbone and Nigel Bruce that premiered in 1939. The series began with a couple of relatively straightforward Holmes films, a retelling of *The Hound of the Baskervilles* and a cut-and-paste story titled *The Adventures of Sherlock Holmes* (also 1939) that sees the detective pitted against his arch-nemesis Moriarty as the latter attempts to steal the English crown jewels. But from this point onwards, after the franchise had passed from Twentieth-Century Fox to Universal Studios, the producers began to take ever more liberties in moving away from Doyle's writings. None of the remaining films take place in the Victorian world synonymous with the Great Detective, or even the earlier twentieth-century world of the later Doyle stories. The next three films in particular see Holmes repackaged for contemporary ideological ends, with *Sherlock Holmes and the Voice of Terror* (1942), *Sherlock Holmes and the Secret Weapon* and *Sherlock Holmes Goes to Washington* (both 1943) forming a triumvirate of anti-Nazi propaganda stories, in which dubious Europeans are demonised and heroic and principled British and Americans are lauded at a time of evident international crisis and indeed panic.

The remainder of the series shifts away from arch-politics but is no less of a diversion from the canon, with a succession of melodramas which include *Sherlock Holmes Faces Death* (1943), *The Spider Woman* (1944), *The Scarlet Claw* (1944), *The Pearl of Death* (1944), *The Woman in Green* (1945) and *Dressed to Kill* (1946). Apart from the ubiquity of Holmes and Watson and the occasional plot resemblance to aspects of the original tales (most explicitly 'The Musgrave Ritual', 'The Six Napoleons' and 'The Five Orange Pips'), these films are almost entirely relocated pastiches. And yet they were still terrifically popular, securing Basil Rathbone in the mind of mid-twentieth-century audiences as their version of Holmes: heroic, ingenious and willing to sacrifice himself in the national cause, fairly and squarely placed within the pantheon of British, and indeed international, greatness.

During the second half of the twentieth century the number of Holmesian pastiches significantly outweighed the number of adaptations more explicitly interested in diligently reproducing the original stories. The first full US TV series, for instance, with thirty-nine instalments starring Sheldon Reynolds (1954–5), offered viewers a range of eccentric non-canonical episode titles which included 'The Case of the Texas Cowgirl' and 'The Case of the

Laughing Mummy'. There were also notable pastiche films, including Billy Wilder's *The Private Life of Sherlock Holmes* (1970), the first major adaptation to explicitly explore Holmes and Watson's sexuality, and a pair of films featuring Christopher Lee in the title role, *Sherlock Holmes and the Leading Lady* and *Sherlock Holmes and the Incident at Victoria Falls* (both 1991), that feature characters created by Doyle, but little else. In addition, there was *Murder by Decree* (1979) – one in a long line of adaptations that brings Holmes face-to-face with Jack the Ripper, as well as parodic romps such as *The Hound of the Baskervilles* (1978) starring Peter Cook and Dudley Moore, and the role-reversal comedy, *Without a Clue* (1988). In the latter, Ben Kingsley and Michael Caine invert the familiar Holmes/Watson relationship with Kingsley's Watson the originator of the Holmes myth, employing out-of-work actor Caine to play the role of the Great Detective in order to perpetuate the charade.

Often these pastiches explore aspects of the Holmes legend that were less developed or else completely overlooked in Doyle's writings, such as Laurie R. King's Mary Russell novels – which feature a fictionalised Holmes student – or Carole Nelson Douglas's extended adventures of Irene Adler, including *Goodnight, Mr Holmes* (1990) and *Good Morning, Irene* (1991). Other adaptations, notably two of the more recent successes, BBC's *Sherlock* and CBS's *Elementary*, explore elements of the canon but do so by resituating the detective in the twenty-first century and, as such, explicitly explore changing social mores and modern technologies. In the former, although the scripts contain a great number of explicit and implicit allusions to the Doyle canon, they also show Holmes at ease within the modern world of smartphones, internet searches and high-level state and personal surveillance. In *Elementary*, on the other hand, what is most contemporary about the series (beyond it resituating events from Victorian London to modern Brooklyn) is the way it implicitly engages with twenty-first century identity politics, featuring as it does amongst other things a female American-Asian Watson, a female Moriarty and an African-American Shinwell Johnson.

At the further extremes of this category of pastiche, Sherlock Holmes is divorced almost entirely from canonical associations, settings and adventures. Across comic books, computer games, ballets, musicals, cartoons, visitor attractions and popular advertising, Holmes is routinely reformulated, with only, in the words of Gérard Genette, 'the most abstract and most implicit [relationship to the author] ... a relationship that is completely silent'.[20] The original character has been refracted through all of Julie Sanders's categories of adaptation: 'version, variation, interpretation, continuation, transformation, imitation, pastiche, parody, forgery, travesty, transposition, revaluation, revision, rewriting, echo'.[21] And within these modes it is just as likely that the starting point for the adapter will be some other aspect of 'the [Sherlockian] franchise as a whole',[22] rather than any specific Doyle material. We can see this in aspects of the animated series *Sherlock Holmes in the 22nd Century*, and within Holmes-themed episodes of other cultural franchises such as *Star Trek: the Next Generation, CSI: Crime Scene Investigation, The Muppets, Teenage Mutant Ninja Turtles, Scooby-Doo* or *Tom & Jerry*. The Holmes figure is removed from Doyle's world and transported into a defamiliarising context, often only playing a marginal, supplementary or incidental role. At times he is little more than a plot device or easily recognisable reference point, such as in Buster Keaton's *Sherlock Holmes Jr.* (1924), where the lead character dreams of becoming a version of Holmes to impress the woman of his dreams, or in *They Might Be Giants* (1971), where George C. Scott's character retreats into a Holmesian psychological fantasy to cope with the death of his wife. In such instances, Holmes is no more than a comforting touchstone, symbolically fulfilling a narrative function rather than serving as a focal character with an agency and importance of his own.

Adaptations such as these reveal the extent to which Sherlock Holmes has become palimpsestuous, continually erased and written over, a name and character resilient and malleable enough to evolve into a nebulous franchise that brings together a range of media and merchandise.[23] Twenty-first-century Sherlock Holmes is as such a multi-dimensional and multi-platform brand, universally recognisable and thus an essentially global popular-cultural figure. And yet, one of the most remarkable aspects of this international Holmesian franchise is that although Sherlock has a cultural currency across the world, the 'cultural globalization'[24] of his name and image has occurred despite the fact that there is no fixed, homogeneous, shared vision of who precisely he is. Instead there are multiple, overlapping, at times competing strands of Holmes-in-adaptation. One minute there might be a cultural vogue for Holmes pastiche, then for the 'formal purism and respectful, heritage' of a Granada TV Sherlock Holmes series which reasserts 'the primacy of Conan Doyle's stories'.[25] This might then give way to a fashion for cartoons (such as in the 1980s with the Japanese-Italian *Sherlock Hound* (1984–5) and Disney's *The Great Mouse Detective* (1986), and more recently with series such as the French-language *Sherlock Yack* (2011–12)). Or the focus could switch to stories of the earlier life of 'Young' Sherlock, as evident in the Spielberg film of that name (1985), and the novel series written by Shane Peacock (2007–) and Andrew Lane (2010–).

What this all means is that twenty-first-century audiences routinely and simultaneously experience Holmes in the most extraordinarily diverse range

of media, on TV, film, in short stories, comic books, graphic novels, computer games and theme parks, as well as in merchandising and advertising.
Which makes any critical focus on the relationship between origin and
adaptation largely a waste of time – at the very least it is insufficient, perhaps
even entirely irrelevant. We do little justice to an adaptation such as BBC's
Sherlock, for instance – written as it is from inside the extended world of
Sherlock Holmes (its writers being Sherlock-literate to the extent that each
episode is littered with subtle and sophisticated allusions to Holmes texts of
all kinds) – if we insist on reading back from this series to Doyle's founding
works. Rather it is more fruitful to view the series as closer to what Benjamin
Poore calls a 'fantasia on the Holmes adventures',[26] a celebration of the rich
tapestry of the Sherlockian franchise past and present, in all its shapes and
colours.

The wisdom of leaving behind the limitations of the adapted vs. adaptive
text binary is demonstrated perhaps most of all by the truly global dimensions of the Sherlock Holmes phenomenon; and *global*, in this sense, means
more than the obvious internationally renowned successes that include not
just *Sherlock*, but also Guy Ritchie's films, *Sherlock Holmes* (2009) and
Sherlock Holmes: A Game of Shadows (2011), starring Robert Downey
Jr. Because for every one of these more universally known Holmesian texts
there are hundreds of others that are much more local, regionally particular
and ethnically specific manifestations of the wider franchise. And each of
these is, if anything, even more poignant as an embodiment of the remarkably seductive power of the Great Detective. For they demonstrate how the
character of Sherlock Holmes has been and continues to be reworked within
the wider process of what Roland Robertson has called *glocalization* –
wherein regional cultures move beyond the homogenising tendencies of
globalisation by reinterpreting and indigenising aspects of wider global
culture in light of their own experiences, values and interests.[27]

In the United States, for instance, where mainstream incarnations of
Holmes such as *Elementary* have been relatively commonplace, the Great
Detective has also been appropriated within subcultural texts. For instance,
as mentioned above, he appears in African-American cultural texts as far
back as the Jim Crow era, when the US state enforced harsh forms of racial
segregation. These include the musical *In Dahomey* (1903), the first full-
length Broadway stage musical written and performed by an all-black cast,
and the 1914 film *The Tale of a Chicken*, also featuring an all-black cast. And
then there is *A Black Sherlock Holmes* – a twelve-minute film produced by
the all-black actors known as the Ebony Players, with the Holmes character
played by Sam Robinson, a cousin of Bill 'Bojangles' Robinson. This film,
despite what might now seem to be its rather outdated racial politics and

ethnic caricatures, as much as any other, shows just how pervasive the character of Sherlock Holmes has been, transcending cultural and ethnic divides and being utilised by people of all ethnic and racial groups.

A Black Sherlock Holmes was the earliest forerunner of other 'Black' reworkings of the Holmes legend, the most recent of which has been the comic-book *Watson and Holmes* (2013–), written by Karl Boller. In this series of adventures both central characters are African-American men who get drawn together as they investigate the criminal underbelly of contemporary Harlem in ways that challenge tabloid stereotypes of black masculinity and sexuality. The reader is privy to the complexities and nuances of their lives as parents, lovers and individuals with careers, and as such the power dynamic of the relationship between Holmes and Watson, as the title implies, is more equitable. Thus, it is a series that connects with the wider Holmesian mythology, but which also fundamentally re-imagines it in terms of the urban social realities of contemporary America.

The glocalisation of Sherlock Holmes is also evident in a number of non-English-speaking countries. Japan, for instance, has its own ethnically specific versions of the Great Detective which have evolved at pace since the first Japanese version of a Holmes story appeared in 1894.[28] Today there is a thriving Holmesian scene, with a particularly developed trend towards animated Holmes adaptations, especially manga, with popular titles including *Sherlock Ninja*, *Dear Sherlock* and *The Black Butler*. Furthermore, the wider world of Japanese Sherlockian animation also features *Sherlock Bones*, *Sherlock Hound*, *Detective Conan* and the esoteric *Puppet Entertainment Sherlock Holmes* – the latter a noteworthy cross-cultural mélange of original Doylean plot outlines and recast narratives and dialogue created by Japanese writers, directors, animators and voice actors. *Puppet Entertainment Sherlock Holmes* (as is the case with many Holmes adaptations produced within this country) turns Holmes into a version of the superhero, with unique powers of a mental and physical nature that he can deploy in order to solve the problems of the world.

The interest in Holmes animation in Russia can be traced back at least as far as the cartoon *Sherlock Holmes and Me* (1985), but the national fascination with Sherlock Holmes is much more long standing; Holmes was first performed by a native actor, Boris Sergeyevich Glagolin, as far back as 1906. That said, Holmes did not begin appearing regularly on Russian/Soviet television until the later 1960s, and the most famous home-grown version of Holmes did not emerge until 1979, with the Lenfilm productions of *The Adventures of Sherlock Holmes and Dr. Watson* starring Livanov and Solomin. These films rework a number of the original stories, and are notable for the detailed care taken by the production team to try to reproduce what they believed to be Doyle's later-nineteenth-century London. There is a meticulous adherence to supposedly authentic plot details and dialogue that makes this whole project one very much in the tradition of the Norwood, Cushing and Brett adaptations, with the producers even deciding to film on location in Latvia on the grounds that there was a street in the old town of Riga that closely matched their imagining of Victorian Baker Street.[29] In addition, a series theme tune was specially composed to resemble a piece of theme music that was, at the time, regularly played on the BBC World Service – as this was seen to represent a traditional, recognisable sense of Englishness. Indeed, throughout the production of the films, as director Igor Maslennikov has pointed out, the overarching aim of the series was to 'play' everything 'in the English style'.[30]

The Livanov series was so popular that it made Sherlock Holmes a firm audience favourite within Soviet/Russian mainstream culture. He was no mere 'imported fad', but rather 'a cultural cornerstone' of the nation.[31] As such, even within a country with a history punctuated by radical political upheaval, Sherlock Holmes came to be seen as a constant, not just popular, but also incrementally etching himself further and further onto the national consciousness. For Livanov himself, this is at least in part because of the core values Holmes embodies, values that speak to the Russian people beyond contemporaneous events or transient political structures. In particular, he has said, it is Holmes's 'readiness to help people' that is key: 'people need help. Now [towards the end of the Soviet period] in our alarming times people are particularly in need of help. People are not reliable, there's no faith that someone in the world will help you out. That's the essence of it'.[32]

The survival, indeed thriving of Sherlock Holmes within restrictive political systems is equally evidenced by the historical relationship the character has with the Chinese people. This long predates the current national obsession with BBC's *Sherlock* – which has more than fifteen million regular viewers who routinely subscribe to the ongoing adventures of characters they have lovingly nicknamed 'Curly Fu' and 'Peanut'. For Doyle's Holmes stories have had a 'far-reaching influence on the overall [shape of] Chinese detective fiction'[33] that can be traced back to 1896 translations of the canon that appeared in the popular *Current Affairs* newspaper. These were followed, in the 1920s, by the 'Huo Sang' novels, written by the author Cheng Xiaoqing (one of the most popular Chinese proponents of detective fiction). These novels feature a lead character that subsequently became known as the 'Shanghai Sherlock Holmes', working alongside his fictional friend and amanuensis to become the 'perfect Holmes-and-Watson pair'.[34]

The modern Chinese appetite for Holmes stories is such that a number of new, ethnically and historically specific versions of the legend have appeared during recent decades. There is the Mandarin film *Sherlock Holmes and the Chinese Heroine* (1994) set against the backdrop of the Boxer Rebellion (1900–1), and the Mandarin-television series *Young Sherlock/Young Detective* (2014), starring Bosco Wong as the fictional investigator Di Renjie. The latter is particularly interesting. First, because the series has its own ethnic and historical particularity owing to its setting in the years of the Tang Dynasty (618–907 CE), which gives the landscape, architecture and costumes a local/regional flavour and infuses the adventures with a nostalgia for an era of self-defined national greatness that chimes with the national adoration of Holmes himself. Second, because the character Di Renjie (the 'Young Sherlock' of the adventures) is an incarnation of an actual Chinese official of the Tang dynasty of the same name thought to be the inspiration for one of the first ever Chinese fictional detectives: 'Judge Dee' of the eighteenth-century *Celebrated Cases of Judge De /Di Gong An*. The name and identity of Sherlock Holmes thus becomes interwoven with that of another detective figure with a particular resonance within Chinese national myth. And the extent of the interrelation is only reinforced by the vast number of more recent adaptations that have featured Di Renjie/Judge Dee, including the screen adaptations of Robert van Gulik's Judge Dee novels (2016–), and the drama serial *Legendary Di Renjie* (2017).[35]

A realisation of the remarkable diversity of the worldwide industry of Holmesian reworkings fundamentally undermines any use of the term *adaptation* that might imply a meaningful degree of coherence among this body of adaptive texts. Any idea of adaptation as a collection of works with 'its own rules, procedures, and textual markers'[36] is woefully inadequate because, within the world of Sherlock Holmes adaptation, everything is up for negotiation, all notions of a hierarchy of source and adaptation are compromised, and 'the authority of all previous versions' has been usurped.[37] If *adaptation* is to have any usefulness as a critical term in considering the remarkable range of the afterlives of the Great Detective then it falls on us to conceive of it in new ways that better come to terms with the rich intertextuality of such 'heteroglot texts'.[38]

One way forward would be to focus not on the way adaptive works link to sources, but instead on their inherent, wonderful fluidity, both as entities in their own right and also as part of the living context of all the other Holmesian works with which they have some kind of relationship. For each adaptation is as much an 'invitation to be rewritten',[39] a creative catalyst for what might follow, as it is a recognisable rewrite of something coherent and measurable that preceded it. The extended Holmes franchise is continually supplemented and reworked, with successive new versions appearing at a global, national and local level with remarkable regularity. And this is what makes Sherlock

Holmes, whoever he (or she) may be, a constantly evolving palimpsest – made and re-made in a shared quest to try to ensure that he always remains fervently *ours*, whomever we are, and where and whenever we may be.

Notes

1. Unsigned, *The Times*, 27 November 1893, 7.
2. Tom Ue, 'Introduction: Holmes at the Matinee', *Journal of Popular Film and Television* 45:2 (2017), 64–7 (66).
3. Stephen Joyce, 'Authentic in Authenticity: The Evolution of Sherlock Holmes on Screen', *Journal of Popular Film and Television* 45:2 (2017), 79–89 (80).
4. Sarah Cardwell, *Adaptation Revisited: Television and the Classic Novel* (Manchester: Manchester University Press, 2002), 12.
5. Ronald Knox, 'Studies in the Literature of Sherlock Holmes', *New Blackfriars* 1:3 (June 1920), 154–72.
6. First collected together in Jack Tracy (ed.), *Sherlock Holmes: the Published Apocrypha* (Boston: Houghton Mifflin, 1980).
7. Lawrence Reid in *Motion Picture News*, quoted in Alan Barnes, *Sherlock Holmes on Screen: The Complete Film and TV History* (London: Titan Books, 2011), 17.
8. BBC Director of Television Kenneth Adam, 21 May1964, quoted in Barnes, *Sherlock Holmes*, 53.
9. Quoted in David Stuart Davies, *Starring Sherlock Holmes* (London: Titan Books, 2007), 86.
10. Tony Earnshaw, *An Actor and a Rare One: Peter Cushing as Sherlock Holmes* (London: Scarecrow Press, 2001), 1.
11. Davies, *Starring Sherlock*, 122.
12. Michael Cox, *Study in Celluloid: A Producer's Account of Jeremy Brett as Sherlock Holmes* (Cambridge: Rupert Books, 1999), 10.
13. David Burke (the first Granada Watson), quoted in *The Perfect TV Detective* (BBC Scotland, 2008).
14. Scott Allen Nollen, *Sir Arthur Conan Doyle at the Cinema: A Critical Study of the Film Adaptations* (Jefferson: McFarland, 2004), 229.
15. Ashley Liening, 'Not Your Grandfather's Sherlock Holmes: Guy Ritchie's 21st Century Reboot of a 19th Century British Icon', *The Oakland Journal* 24 (2013), 35–51 (43).
16. Ibid.
17. James Naremore, 'Introduction: Film and the Reign of Adaptation', in *Film Adaptation* (New Brunswick: Rutgers University Press, 2000), 1–18 (12).
18. Linda Hutcheon, *A Theory of Adaptation* (London: Routledge, 2006), 170.
19. P. G. Wodehouse, *Psmith, Journalist* (London: Everyman, 2008), 132.
20. Gérard Genette, *Palimpsests: Literature in the Second Degree*, trans. Channa Newman and Claude Doubinsky (Lincoln and London: University of Nebraska Press, 1997), 4.
21. Julie Sanders, *Adaptation and Appropriation* (London: Routledge, 2006), 18.
22. Thomas Leitch, *Film Adaptation and Its Discontents: From* Gone with the Wind *to* The Passion of the Christ (Baltimore: Johns Hopkins University Press, 2007), 213.

23. Clare Parody, 'Franchising/Adaptation', *Adaptation* 4:2 (2011), 210–18 (211).
24. Jonathan Friedman, 'Culture and its Politics in the Global System', *Protosociology* 20 (2004), 217–38 (217).
25. Benjamin Poore, 'Sherlock Holmes and the Leap of Faith: the forces of fandom and convergence in adaptations of the Holmes and Watson stories', *Adaptation* 6:2 (2013), 158–71 (163).
26. Ibid., 164.
27. Roland Robertson, 'Globalization or Glocalization?', *The Journal of International Communication* 18:2 (2012), 191–208 (191).
28. See Keith E. Webb, *Sherlock Holmes in Japan* (Bellevue: NextChurch, 1998).
29. 'Curious incidents: the adventures of Sherlock Holmes in Russia', *The Calvert Journal* 10 (2014), [www.calvertjournal.com/comment/show/2817/sherlock-holmes-in-russia, accessed 1 July 2016].
30. Ibid.
31. Ibid.
32. Vasily Livanov, 'BBC Forty Minutes: The Case of Sherlock Holmes'. BBC2, December 1987.
33. Wei Yan, 'Sherlock Holmes Came to China: Detective Fiction, Cultural Meditations, and Chinese Modernity', in Louise Nilsson, David Damrosch and Theo D'haen (eds.), *Crime Fiction as World Literature* (London: Bloomsbury, 2017), 245–56.
34. Jeffrey C. Kinkley, *Chinese Justice, the Fiction: Law and Literature in Modern China* (Redwood City: Stanford University Press, 2000), 188.
35. See Lavinia Benedetti, 'The Metamorphosed Reception of Di Gong An in the West', Paper presented at the annual meeting of the International Communication Association, Boston, MA, 26 November 2014, [http://citation.allacademic.com/meta/p489098_index.html, accessed 21 August 2017].
36. Thomas Leitch, 'Adaptation, the Genre', *Adaptation* 1.2 (2008), 106–20 (106).
37. Leitch, *Film Adaptation*, 234.
38. Leitch, 'Adaptation', 16.
39. Ibid.

15

CATHERINE WYNNE

Neo-Holmesian Fiction

> Our old chambers had been left unchanged ... There were the chemical
> corner and the acid-stained, deal-topped table. There upon the shelf was
> the row of formidable scrap-books and books of reference which many
> of our fellow-citizens would have been so glad to burn. The diagrams, the
> violin-case, and the pipe-rack – even the Persian slipper which contained
> the tobacco – all met my eyes as I glanced round me.   (493)

The disappearance, return and retirement of Arthur Conan Doyle's Sherlock
Holmes has inspired many neo-Holmesian fictions. The above quotation
from 'The Empty House' is Watson's description of the Baker Street apartment following Holmes's resurrection in 1903. It is important to note,
however, that Sherlockian time is different from historical time. As far as
the Victorian and Edwardian reading public was concerned, Holmes's
demise had occurred at the Reichenbach Falls in 'The Final Problem', published in 1893. However, this ten-year absence is condensed to three in
Holmesian chronology (1891–4). The return not only marks Holmes's resurrection but introduces a Holmesian double. Hoping to lure Moriarty's
henchman, Colonel Sebastian Moran, into an assassination attempt, Holmes
places a wax dummy in his image in the window of 221B Baker Street.
Watching events from the titular house directly opposite, Holmes and
Watson capture Moran when he chooses the same location to affect the
assassination. Although the duo then slip back into their Baker Street lifestyle
where nothing seems to have changed, the wax dummy made by
a Frenchman and Moran's German air gun prefigure future alliances and
threats. Significantly, Doyle's tampering with Holmes's mortality fuelled the
appearance of new literary Holmeses which, moulded like the story's waxwork to look somewhat like the original, continue to service the ongoing
fascination with Doyle's detective.

Doyle's further meddling with his character in 'His Last Bow' is also
critical to Holmes's afterlife. Again, historical and Holmesian chronologies
do not match. The story is set in August 1914 as Holmes, who has been
masquerading as a Fenian (an Irish-American revolutionary), thwarts

a German secret agent. The *Strand Magazine* cover of September 1917 depicts the victorious detective smoking a pipe, as well as a note to inform readers that they could send the magazine by free post to the troops. On the cover, an Austin car has replaced the hansom cab of the early Holmes stories; otherwise, three years into the conflict, both Holmes and magazine promise continuity in the midst of chaos. 'His Last Bow' is a war propaganda story published during the Passchendaele offensive on the Western Front. While allied troops were making little progress, Holmes rids the country of the German threat and promises at the story's conclusion that England will be a better place by the war's end: '"a cleaner, better, stronger land will lie in the sunshine when the storm has cleared up"' (980). The title of the story also suggests the end of the previous age as the gentlemanly duel of wits between England's Holmes and Germany's Von Bork is a bloodless conflict that masks the brutal horrors occurring on the Western Front. In Holmesian chronology, 'His Last Bow' is the detective's final story, as he returns to beekeeping in Sussex. Although Doyle continued to write Sherlock Holmes stories until 1929, they are all set prior to August 1914.

Twentieth- and twenty-first-century writers have generated, with varied success, new stories from Holmes's missing years or from the allusions to other cases contained within the canon. Others have invented new scenarios for the character who died but was resurrected, and who retired but lived on as an apiarist. Arguably, the most significant of these recent neo-Holmeses are those created by Anthony Horowitz, Michael Chabon and Mitch Cullin. While Horowitz reenvisions the Victorian world of Doyle's original, Cullin and Chabon force their retired detectives into encounters with worlds torn apart by global conflict: Chabon's elderly Holmes deals with the impact of the Holocaust on a young Jewish boy and Cullin's Holmes visits a Japan devastated by the atomic bomb. By displacing their fictional figures from the stability of Baker Street and presenting them as old men, they question the certainties of Doyle's detective. In addition to providing an overview of Holmesian afterlives from the 1970s to the present, this chapter focuses on the novels of Chabon and Cullin as a particularly revealing case study in neo-Holmesian fiction.

Neo-Holmes

New incarnations of the great detective were already starting to appear within Doyle's lifetime. In his autobiography, *Memories and Adventures*, Doyle reproduces one such example – a short parody by J.M. Barrie. Doyle and Barrie had collaborated on an unsuccessful comic opera and Barrie mocked their theatrical failure by having the two writers visit Holmes for an explanation. As Holmes sees them approach his door he remarks to Watson: '"that big fellow has for years taken the credit for my most remarkable doings, but at last I have him – at last!"' (104). When Doyle, described as '"the brute"', insists that Holmes sits through a performance of the comic opera, threatening that his '"continued existence depends on it"', the detective refuses and proclaims he would rather '"melt into the air"' (105). Barrie's Holmes provides a simple solution to the mystery of their failure by revealing that audiences '"prefer to stay away"' (105). The angry writers draw knives and Holmes starts to melt. The creator of Peter Pan, the boy who never grew up, was thus an early cultivator of the afterlife of Holmes, a character who is constantly resurrected in the Neo-Holmesian novel.

The late twentieth-century revival of Holmes ties into what Cora Kaplan has described as the 'desire to know and to "own" the Victorian past through its remains'.[1] Although Victoriana had its roots in material culture, as the century progressed it 'widened to embrace a complementary miscellany of evocations and recyclings of the nineteenth century' which, by the twenty-first century, included an 'astonishing range of representations and reproductions for which the Victorian . . . is the common referent'.[2] Part of this cult of the Victorian is the cult of Holmes. There is, however, a unique quality to the Holmesian cult: Holmes was extraordinarily popular following the publication of the illustrated stories in the *Strand* from 1891 and the character acquired a life beyond fiction. Letters to and about Holmes, for instance, arrived on Doyle's desk as early as 1890. In 'Some Personalia about Mr Sherlock Holmes' (1917), which was published in the *Strand*, Doyle describes himself as the 'biographer' of the 'notorious' Holmes.[3] 'One of the quaintest proofs of his reality is that I have frequently received autograph books by post asking me to procure his signature'.[4] Doyle remarks that he had not realised what 'an actual living personality Holmes was to many people' until he heard of a group of French schoolboys who, on arrival in London, asked to see Holmes's lodgings on Baker Street.[5]

In his autobiography Doyle relates that he was 'amazed by the concern expressed by the public' over the death of Holmes: 'the general protest against my summary execution of Holmes taught me how many and how numerous were his friends. "You Brute" was the beginning of the letter of remonstrance which one lady sent me, and I expect she spoke for others beside herself. I heard of many who wept' (*Memories* 99). Notably, Barrie's parody describes Doyle as a 'brute', which suggests that Doyle had shared the contents of the enraged fan's letter with him. Young men in the city, according to 'popular but unconfirmed myth', wore black armbands to mourn the death of their hero – a figure who never existed except for the many who believed he was a real person.[6]

Holmes and his world are certainly central to Kaplan's 'astonishing range of representations and reproductions' and, in this way, neo-Holmesian fiction sits alongside the neo-Victorian novel, which may be defined not simply as novels set in the nineteenth century, but texts which engage in a self-conscious *act of (re)interpretation, (re)discovery and (re)vision concerning the Victorians*.[7] Neo-Holmesian fictions vary in their engagement with the nineteenth century: some function as waxwork recreations of Holmes's world, while others more consciously reinterpret a Holmesian world order. The neo-Holmesians further respond to a cultural need for the character's continued existence and the belief, maintained by many fans, that Holmes was real. Like the neo-Victorians, the neo-Holmesians service a literary preoccupation with material and invented pasts and explore what the past may come to mean for readers in the twenty-first century. While the neo-Victorian novel deals in varieties of reinvention, Doyle's Victorian Holmes and his world are already inventions of a writer and, to a certain extent, an artist (Sidney Paget), both of whom endowed the fictional character with aspects of materiality: the Baker Street address and Sidney's use of his brother, Walter, as a model for Holmes.

By establishing the detective's practice in a real place, Baker Street, Doyle provided the character's world with materiality, whilst the fictitious number 221B enabled the cultivation of this imagined and imaginative space. David Bagchi's *The Adventure of Briony Lodge* (2016) is a good example of how neo-Holmesian fictions cleverly play with such notions. In this story, Jerome K. Jerome (a writer friend of Doyle's who published *Three Men in a Boat* in 1889) resides at 221C (the flat above the famous detective). When a troubled young woman is mistakenly deposited at his door rather than Holmes's, Jerome and his friends are drawn into a case. Baker Street also provided a location for fans to send their letters in the twentieth century, and while 221B did not exist, the letters arrived at the headquarters of the Abbey National Bank located at 221. From here staff answered Holmes's letters.[8]

Modern Neo-Holmesian fictions can be dated from Nicholas Meyer's *The Seven-Per-Cent Solution* (1974). Here real and fictional Victorians come together. Set during Holmes's missing years (1891–4), the detective seeks help for his drug addiction from Sigmund Freud. Meyer's *The West End Horror* (1976), set in London's theatre land, introduces a fictionalised Bernard Shaw and Oscar Wilde, with Bram Stoker making a brief appearance as a potential murder suspect. Meyer's postmodern convergence of historical and fictional figures prefigures later re-visionings of literary figures and Victorian social history in the new Holmesian worlds of the twenty-first century. Holmes and Dracula, icons of late Victorian literature, tempted Loren D. Estleman to place them together in *Sherlock Holmes vs. Dracula*

(1978). In the same year Fred Saberhagen produced *The Holmes-Dracula File* using the untold case of the giant rat of Sumatra, which is alluded to in 'The Sussex Vampire', to construct a narrative about a virus, a modern Black Death, which threatens England's stability. Dracula, presented as a more sympathetic figure than his original incarnation, here becomes Holmes's uncle. Michael Dibdin's *The Last Sherlock Holmes Story* (1978) disturbingly casts a deranged Holmes as Jack the Ripper, with Watson watching in horror as he dismembers the final victim. Jamyang Norbu's *The Mandala of Sherlock Holmes* (1999) sees Holmes protect the life of the Tibetan Grand Lama from Chinese imperial ambitions. The Chinese are aided by Moriarty who has escaped the Reichenbach Falls. Both Holmes and Moriarty acquire occult powers, with Holmes infused with the spirit of a deceased Tibetan lama. This is a political text that transforms Holmes to highlight the plight of a contemporary Tibet controlled by the Chinese.

Newer Holmeses are often sympathetic to Doyle's vision of the original character, but frequently act to marginalise or displace him. Laurie R. King's *The Beekeeper's Apprentice* (1994), for example, draws on Holmes's retirement years for her feminist reworking, as Holmes discovers a female apprentice, the orphaned fifteen year old Jewish-American Mary Russell. In this opening novel of King's series, Russell challenges the ageing bee-keeper with her intelligence and is more active than Holmes in solving the novel's crimes. By introducing a female voice, King consciously disrupts the homosocial dynamic of Doyle's stories. The influence of the absent Holmes is also seen in Stuart Fortey's *A Scandal in Scarborough* (2016), which focuses on Sidney and Walter Paget. Walter, the model for Sidney's images of Holmes in the *Strand*, now believes he is the detective, and donning deerstalker and cape investigates a double murder in Scarborough with his reluctant brother. The inept pair becomes involved in British secret service activities and Walter's love interest turns out to be a lesbian British spy. Holmes is also absent from Horowitz's *Moriarty* (2014). Set during Holmes's missing years, Horowitz's protagonist is Athelney Jones, revisioned from Doyle's *The Sign of Four*, who arrives at the Reichenbach Falls and encounters what he believes to be a Pinkerton detective. Jones, who has modelled himself on Holmes, having scrupulously studied his art of detection, fails to realise until the moment of his death that the Pinkerton agent is a disguised Moriarty. The story can be read as a eulogy to the missing Holmes – no one can match the great sleuth.

The Doyle Estate has attempted to control the proliferation of neo-Holmeses by commissioning writers to produce new stories. Commissioned by the Estate, Horowitz's novels and Caleb Carr's *The Italian Secretary* (2005; commissioned by the American representative of the Doyle Estate,

Jon Lellenberg) demonstrate the Doyle family's vision of Holmes in the twenty-first century. Carr creates a Gothic world that draws extensively on *The Hound of the Baskervilles*; the master villain, Lord Francis Hamilton, is modelled on Stapleton, while Carr develops the story of the Baskerville curse in Doyle's novel, in which a servant girl flees over the moor to escape being raped by the degenerate Sir Hugo. Mycroft Holmes asks his brother to investigate the murders at Holyrood House, the former home of Mary, Queen of Scots, fearing that they may be connected with a German threat to Victoria's life. Holmes and Watson discover the pregnant Alison in the wing of the castle where the vicious murder of Mary's secretary, David Rizzio, had been committed centuries before by the Queen's estranged husband and his henchmen. Hamilton and Will Sadler, Alison's seducer, are, in fact, conducting lucrative ghost tours of the castle, believed to be haunted by Rizzio. They murdered the two men, an architect and foreman, whose suspicions were aroused by the activities.

The Gothic atmosphere is enhanced by Sadler's use of a trebuchet (a medieval crane that threw the bodies of plague victims into besieged towns) to fling the murdered men's bodies at the castle walls. Unlike *The Hound* where the supernatural is explained when the Baskerville hound is revealed as a real dog, in Carr's novel Watson sees the ghost of Rizzio as well as the ghost of a murdered girl on Baker Street. The novel's supernatural encounters serve as an acknowledgement of Doyle's championing of Spiritualism; as Holmes comments in *The Italian Secretary*: '"Are ghosts—indeed, are *gods* real? We cannot know, but they are powerful facts of human intercourse"'.[9] The incursion of the supernatural into Carr's novel is, of course, a deviation from the original stories where Holmes refuses to entertain the supernatural. As he famously declares in 'The Sussex Vampire', the '"world is big enough for us. No ghosts need apply"' (1034).

Horowitz's first novel *The House of Silk* (2011) is neo-Victorian in orientation in its revisioning of the past. Here Holmes investigates a transatlantic case of art theft, which consciously emulates but also cleverly deviates from Doyle's 'The Dancing Men' and *The Valley of Fear*. With secret societies, disguised identities and murder in the family, this is the identifiable realm of Doyle's detective. Horowitz, however, moves his Holmes into an entirely new domain of crime. When Holmes investigates the Chorley Grange School for orphaned boys, established by the Society for the Improvement of London's Children (SILC), he uncovers a paedophilia ring involving the school's young boys and upper-class men. The appalling crimes committed on vulnerable boys robs Holmes of the self-assurance and sense of order which generally mark the end of a Doyle story, when the crime has been solved and Holmes and Watson debrief in Baker Street. Horowitz, in contrast, has his Holmes struggle to come to terms with what he encounters. Although Doyle's Holmes solves a spectrum of crimes from murder to blackmail, child sexual abuse does not feature in the canon. Horowitz draws on the work of the late-century social realist novelist George Gissing to cultivate the bleak world of the Victorian underclass and his Holmes explores a crime that Doyle, as a Victorian writer, could not articulate in the pages of a popular family magazine. These new Holmeses of the twenty-first century reappraise the beliefs and injustices of the Victorian world.

Michael Chabon's *The Final Solution*

One of the most significant neo-Holmesian novels of the twenty-first century takes Holmes out of the late Victorian world and situates him in the 1940s, where he confronts societal and global issues. Michael Chabon explains how Doyle was the first writer he 'really fell in love with' and that his first attempt at writing was a Sherlock Holmes story inspired by Meyer's *The Seven-Per-Cent-Solution*.[10] Drawing its inspiration from 'His Last Bow', Chabon's novel introduces us to an aged beekeeper living in the Sussex Downs at the end of World War II. Although Chabon's detective is clearly Holmes, he is never named as such in the novel: 'Years and years ago his name – itself redolent now of the fustian and rectitude of that vanished era – had adorned the newspapers and police gazettes of the Empire, but ... [his] more recent, local celebrity [was] founded almost exclusively on legends of his shyness, irascibility, and hostility to all human commerce'.[11] From his living room chair, he is drawn to the sight of a pale young boy with a handsome African parrot on his shoulder walking along the tracks of the Brighton-Eastbourne line. This, he observes, is a 'promising anomaly' (7).

The world of the retired detective and the boy converge when he prevents the child from urinating on the rail track, thus saving him from potential electrocution. The boy, he discovers, does not or cannot speak while the parrot recites numbers in German in a 'soft, oddly breathy voice, with the slightest hint of a lisp' (11). Holmes later learns that the boy, Linus Steinman, is a traumatised and orphaned Jewish refugee who was smuggled out of wartime Germany. He is placed with the mixed-race family of the local vicar, Reverend Panicker, foregrounding the novel's treatment of the complexities of racial relations. Panicker originates from Kerala, his wife is English and their son Reggie is the 'scourge of the neighbourhood' (17). Here, Chabon draws upon the George Edalji case, a miscarriage of justice that Doyle became involved with in 1906 (and which forms the basis of Julian Barnes's bio-fiction, *Arthur & George* (2004)). Edalji's father was a vicar and a Parsee Indian and his mother was English. Living in Staffordshire, the family became the victims of racist abuse when George, a law student, was accused of maiming cattle. George was exonerated when Doyle, who had trained as an oculist, deployed medical and Holmesian skills to show that George's visual impairment would have made it impossible for him to commit such a crime.

When the corpse of the Panicker's lodger, Richard Shane, is discovered outside the vicarage with a blow to the back of his head and an empty bird cage beside him, Reggie Panicker is arrested. The police believe that Shane was killed when trying to prevent Reggie from stealing the parrot – a business card from a London exotic animal merchant called Black seems to indict Reggie. Holmes, with a flourish drawn from Doyle, dispenses with the police theory by pointing out that Shane, a British intelligence officer masquerading as a salesman, had been assaulted from behind. Holmes's interest in the case centres on the young boy and his desire to recover the parrot. The bird, he discovers, was stolen by Herman Kalb, who works with a Jewish organisation to rescue children from Nazi-occupied Europe. Kalb also murdered Shane who was absconding with the bird. The parrot's constant repetition of numbers excited the curiosity of Shane and Kalb in the mistaken belief that he either had a secret code to a German submarine (of interest to Shane) or the combination of a Swiss bank account (of interest to Kalb). Holmes finds the parrot in a wardrobe in Kalb's London flat and boy and bird are happily reunited.

Chabon's text is deeply embedded in British and European imperial exploitation. Doyle, an upholder of empire, nonetheless set Holmes the task of tackling its abuses, just as he tackled racial abuse with the Edalji case. In 'The Speckled Band', for instance, Holmes rescues a woman from murder by a stepfather who has been conditioned to such violence in India. Indeed, the model for Kalb can be traced to the philanthropist-turned thief Godfrey Abelwhite from Wilkie Collins's earlier narrative of empire, *The Moonstone* (1868). The story of the Moonstone has its origins in an imperial crime, when an Indian temple is raided by British soldiers. The Moonstone ends up in an English house from which Abelwhite steals it. In Chabon's novel, the parrot had endured an unhappy history of abuse with European imperialists before ending up in Nazi Germany where he finds companionship with the boy but also becomes a witness to the crimes of humanity. Indeed, for Stef Craps and Gert Buelens, Chabon's novel, through its mirroring of Nazi Germany and nineteenth-century British and European imperialism, suggests 'continuities and parallels between the Third Reich and the European colonial empires and between the plights of their respective victims'.[12] They read the novel as tracing a line between European imperial exploitation in Africa and the genocide perpetrated on Jews in Nazi Germany. Rather than seeing the Holocaust as an isolated historical event, they argue that Chabon is placing it within the 'realm of colonizing Western modernity'.[13] The false philanthropist Kalb victimises a fellow-Jew by stealing his only companion, and the British officer who reveals Shane's true identity to Holmes wonders how parrot meat would taste (which, given the fact that the parrot relates his own story in the novel, smacks of cannibalism). Evil, the novel suggests, has spread from European colonial violence and is not solely the preserve of the Third Reich.[14] In Doyle's canon evil is generally contained and controlled by Holmes, but Chabon's neo-Holmesian fiction reveals that it is not that simple.

Watson is absent from *The Final Solution* and we assume that he is dead, though glimpses of the relationship with the detective emerge in the story in terms of loss. His absence is marked by the magnifying glass that Holmes uses to examine the scene of Shane's death: 'it was brass and tortoise shell and bore around its bezel an affectionate inscription from the sole great friend of his life' (33). During Holmes's examination of the area the police observe how 'he kept up a steady muttering, nodding his head from time to time, carrying on one half of a conversation, and showing a certain impatience with his invisible interlocutor' (34). Holmes hijacks a drunken Panicker to take him to London to see the exotic animal dealer and the vicar, who is fleeing his failed marriage, functions as a substitute. Watson – '"the one fixed point in a changing age"' (980) – has departed, or remains behind in the Holmesian canon. 'His Last Bow' registers Holmes's departure from a genteel world that never actually existed. Indeed, before writing the story Doyle had witnessed the horrors of the Western Front. In *The British Campaign in France and Flanders* (1920), he recounts a visit to the Hindenburg line, describing 'a tangle of mutilated horses', 'a man with his hand blown off ... holding the arm raised and hanging as a dog holds an injured foot' and 'a shattered man drenched crimson from head to foot'. Such 'ghastly pictures stamped forever upon our memory ... might well haunt one in one's dreams'.[15] Compare such images to the sedate, quasi-theatrical picture of Holmes outwitting Von Bork.

While Doyle's story is designed to provide reassurance in the midst of tumult, Chabon mines the repressed trauma of the canon. *The Final Solution* makes Holmes face the realities of war and the Holocaust. Indeed, Chabon's neo-Holmesian text can be interpreted as trauma fiction in its examination of a young Jewish boy's experience of the Holocaust. Linus is suffering from what psychiatrists would diagnose as post-traumatic stress disorder (PTSD). As a contemporary writer Chabon is working from a definition of PTSD established in 1980, whereby traumatic illness is defined as a 'response to a terrifying and unexpected event', and applying it retrospectively to his story of World War II.[16] Linus is the son of a Berlin psychiatrist who treats the 'bad dreams' of '*Herr Obergruppenfuhrer*' (71) and this high-ranking Nazi protects his psychiatrist from the death chambers for as long as possible. The parrot's repeated listing of numbers is mimicking the boy, who has been counting the numbers on the train carriages that transport Jews to the death camps. During his captivity in Kalb's bedsit the bird sings in the boy's secret voice, 'just as the boy had sung . . . standing in the window at the back of *Herr Obergruppenfuhrer*'s house, overlooking the railroad tracks, watching the endless trains rolling off to the place where the sun came up out of the ground every day, each piece of the train bearing the special claw marks that were the interminable lyrics of the train song' (114). This information is revealed to the reader by the parrot but Holmes remains oblivious to the meaning of the numbers at the narrative's end. This is an inversion of Doyle's Holmes who knows the solution to the crime early on but reveals it only at the close of the story. The fact that the reader has more knowledge than Holmes or the text's adults underlines the fragility of this new Holmesian world, where not everything can be explained.

Holmes, though unaware of the significance of the parrot's repetition of numbers, realises the importance of the parrot to the boy's recovery. Linus suffers from mutism, which was recognised as a 'psychological disorder' of war following the First World War.[17] The parrot ventriloquises the trauma through repeating the act of the boy's counting of trains, vocalising what the boy cannot articulate. Linus's only other communication is to write on a notepad but he reverses the order of the letters or deploys mirror writing, which his guardian, Reverend Panicker, explains to Holmes '"is, according to the doctors . . . related in some way to his inability to speak. Some sort of trauma, no doubt"' (107). Holmes identifies the thief from a clue he obtains from the boy's mirror writing – the boy writes 'blak' (110) on a card and Holmes at first mistakenly believes that he is referring to the seller of rare birds until looking in at Panicker's car window he suddenly realises that the writing is reversed and he thus identifies the villain as Kalb. He returns by train to Sussex with Panicker and the parrot. Waiting at the station are Mrs Panicker and Linus. The parrot resumes his perch on the boy's shoulder and as a goods train travels past, the boy, recovering his voice, starts counting the carriages in German.

Chabon's Holmes, like his Doylean predecessor, is in the business of putting the family, however fractured, back together again. At the end of *The Final Solution*, the Panickers, who are disappointed in themselves and their marriage, achieve reconciliation. Holmes thrusts the bird cage into Reverend Panicker's hands just before alighting from the train back from London, allowing him to assume the role of the hero and surrogate father. Mrs Panicker is now proud of her husband. Reggie has disappeared but Linus, it suggests, will be absorbed into this multi-racial, multi-faith and makeshift family. It is fitting that tentative healing occurs on the railway platform. The German tracks were the site of Linus's initial trauma as he looked out of the window; Holmes looking out of his window at the story's opening sees Linus in danger on the electrified line; and finally, the boy's parrot emerges from a train carriage. All Holmes can do is to help one boy recover his parrot. Ultimately, the fact that there is no final explication of the numbers is important as there can be no final solution. Chabon's neo-Holmesian fiction provides us with a different world order where atrocities like the Holocaust cannot be resolved or even fully understood.

Mitch Cullin's *A Slight Trick of the Mind*

A second prominent twenty-first-century reinvention of Holmes imagines him facing global concerns in the 1940s. Cullin's Sherlock Holmes in *A Slight Trick of the Mind* (2005) is an even more humble figure than Chabon's detective. Here there is no ambiguity about the protagonist's identity when Holmes, a 'slow-walking geriatric', is recognised as the Victorian detective *en route* to a traumatised postwar Japan in 1947.[18] Three interlinked stories make up Cullin's novel: Holmes's Japanese trip, his friendship with his housekeeper's teenage son in Sussex and a previously unrelated case dating from 1904. Each narrative is defined by a sense of loss and longing (death, the impairment of memory and the attempt to recover the dead), incomprehensibility (Holmes's inability to understand his world) and trauma. The dropping of the atomic bomb on Japan makes any solution impossible on a global level. Here Holmes discovers a people exhibiting 'unexpressed desolation' (69).

Cullin's Holmes tries to circumscribe his engagement in the world, focusing his attention on his bees, but the world intrudes. His trip to Japan is prompted by research into royal jelly and prickly ash (a plant native to Japan) which is associated with longevity. Lured there by an individual whom he believes is a fellow bee enthusiast, Holmes discovers that his role for Hensuiro Umezaki is to provide answers to the disappearance of his father decades earlier. When he was a child, Hensuiro's father, then in England, sent a letter to his son and mother informing them that Sherlock Holmes had advised him never to return to Japan. Holmes is at the centre of Hensuiro's unresolved family trauma. However, the problem facing Holmes is that he has no memory of ever having encountered Hensuiro's father and believes that the man lied to his son. Prompted by Hensuiro's longing, Holmes adapts an old case which featured an Asian spy. He uses this as the basis to make up a story about how Hensuiro's father was engaged in British secret service activities and presumed lost on the Cook Islands. The solution, unlike the solutions provided by Doyle's detective, is a lie.

The longing that Holmes sees in Hensuiro is replicated in Holmes's encounters with others. He could 'sense an immense want permeating human existence, the true nature of which he couldn't fully comprehend. And while this ineffable longing had skirted his country life, it still saw fit to visit him on occasion, becoming more and more evident among the strangers who continually trespassed upon his property' (63). While some visitors wanted an autograph or photograph, others wanted a 'laying on of his hands, perhaps a few words, whispered like some healing incantation' (64). While he rebuffs all visitors, he bends his inflexible rule for one woman and her infant. The child cradled at her breast is dead and her soiled hands indicate that she has removed it from its grave. When she thrusts it towards him he 'gently' accepts it, 'holding the baby against his chest' (65). The grieving mother remains mute to his questions but finally declares that '"it's a stupid world"' as she reaches towards him to retrieve her baby (66). Holmes cannot satisfy or alleviate longing.

The loss of babies is at the heart of an old case from 1904, which Holmes is in the process of writing up after his Japanese trip. Mrs Keller has suffered two miscarriages and to alleviate her suffering her husband suggests she take lessons on the armonica (a glass instrument) but then becomes concerned by her obsession, forbidding her to return to the music teacher who has her premises over a bookshop. Keller fails to understand his wife's trauma and instead employs Holmes to investigate her continued absences from home. Holmes discovers that she is not secretly taking lessons but is walking through the bookshop, choosing a book and then sitting in the garden listening to the sound of the armonica emanating from the window before then visiting a botanical garden. A disguised Holmes engages her in conversation in the garden and watches as a worker bee lands on her gloved hand. Woman and bee seem in communion before she gently places it on a flower. Holmes's interest in bees dates to this encounter. The woman has an evanescent quality, which gives the novel its title; as she departs it seems to Holmes that she dissipates like a ghost. Later this gentle creature, with whom Holmes has fallen in love, walks down the tracks towards an oncoming train. Contemplating what made her commit suicide, Holmes concludes that her sensitive nature could not endure her difficulties. The violence of her death is in sharp contrast with her calmness in the garden. Trains, so central to Doyle's stories as they enable Holmes to travel to solve crimes, become in both Chabon's and Cullin's texts associated with horror, trauma and the working out of pain.

Pain defines Holmes's relationship with Roger, the son of his house-keeper, for whom he becomes a father figure after Roger's father, who is a soldier, is killed in conflict. In an attempt to protect the beehives, Roger tries to destroy a wasps' nest whose presence near the hives could prove fatal for the bees. By throwing water over the nest, he infuriates the wasps and they sting him to death. Holmes finds the corpse but is unable to inform Roger's mother of the tragedy. Initially, the bees are blamed for the death until Holmes discovers the wasps' nest and Roger's mistake. When Roger's mother seeks answers from Holmes about the meaning of the tragedy, he is lost: 'he couldn't fabricate an appeasing falsehood to ease her suffering as he'd done for Mr Umezaki; nor could he fill in the blanks and create a satisfactory conclusion, like Dr Watson had often done when writing his stories'. '"Things"', he tells her, '"occur beyond our understanding' and these 'events' are 'exactly what they are . . . and nothing else"' (239). He can offer nothing except the realisation of pain. After his encounter with the woman and her dead baby, he explains why people gravitate towards him: '"I am known for discovering answers when events appear desperate"' (66). Alone in the dead Roger's bedroom, clutching the boy's scrapbook that contains images of 'wildlife and forests, soldiers and war' (230) as well as a desolate image of Hiroshima, Holmes capitulates: 'I haven't a clue' (230). In the world of Cullin's Holmes, the only certainty is that death can come in unexpected forms. His Holmes tries to retain the reticence and restraint of Doyle's detective, but is forced into articulation. While Chabon's Holmes can help bring healing to a traumatised young boy, the world of Cullin's Holmes is without hope. His ninety-three-year old Holmes has no case to solve, other than realising it was wasps and not bees that killed Roger. This provides no consolation. Doyle's Holmes made the world more controllable, Cullin's Holmes lives in a world where there is no control.

For Doyle, Holmes was a 'calculating machine' (*Memories* 108) but for his readers he was and is so much more. Chabon argues that Doyle 'was a real writer. He was in touch with powerful, painful, deep stuff, and it comes through even within this rather tidy framework of the Victorian detective story'.[19] Chabon and Cullin take Holmes out of Baker Street and out of the nineteenth century to provide new neo-Holmesian fictions for contemporary times. Both writers draw impetus from a Doylean Holmes who fought for the causes of the abused and they supply us with new ways of thinking about his significance, challenging the reader to engage with the traumatic legacies of war and empire, with racism and even with the diseases of ageing. The many varieties of neo-Holmesian fictions respond to a global preoccupation with Holmes. They move from playful escapism and reinvention to restaging, reflection, reconsideration and reworking of the Victorian and post-Victorian worlds, while articulating the concerns and issues of their present moments. Neo-Holmesian fictions speak to the neo-Victorian movement, but they anticipate, predate and extend beyond it. A fictional character that has a life beyond fiction, Holmes is both fixed and adaptable. A cultural colossus in his own right, Holmes returns in many forms to service our needs.

Notes

1. Cora Kaplan, *Victoriana: Histories, Fictions, Criticism* (New York: Columbia University Press, 2007), 2.
2. Ibid., 2–3.
3. Arthur Conan Doyle, 'Some Personalia about Mr. Sherlock Holmes', *Strand Magazine* 55 (December 1917), 531–5 (532).
4. Ibid., 533.
5. Ibid.
6. Andrew Lycett, *Conan Doyle: The Man Who Created Sherlock Holmes* (London: Weidenfeld and Nicolson, 2007), 197.
7. Ann Heilman and Mark Llewellyn, *Neo-Victorianism: The Victorians in the Twenty-First Century, 1999–2009* (Basingstoke: Palgrave, 2010), 3. Original emphasis.
8. Richard Lancelyn Green (ed.), *Letters to Sherlock Holmes* (London: Penguin, 1985), 7–8.
9. Caleb Carr, *The Italian Secretary* (New York: Little, Brown, and Company, 2005), 260.
10. See 'A Conversation with Michael Chabon' in *The Final Solution*, by Michael Chabon (London: Harper Perennial, 2005), 5–10.
11. Michael Chabon, *The Final Solution* (London: Harper Perennial, 2005), 7. Further references to this text will be given parenthetically.
12. Stef Craps and Gert Buelens, 'Traumatic Mirrorings: Holocaust and Colonial Trauma in Michael Chabon's *The Final Solution*', *Criticism* 53:4 (2011), 569–86 (569).
13. Ibid., 569.
14. Ibid., 574.
15. Arthur Conan Doyle, *The British Campaign in France and Flanders, 1918* (London: Hodder and Stoughton, 1920), 312.

16. Edgar Jones and Simon Wessely, 'A paradigm shift in the conceptualization of psychological trauma in the 20th century', *Journal of Anxiety Disorders* 21 (2007), 164–75 (164).
17. Ibid., 171.
18. Mitch Cullin, *A Slight Trick of the Mind* (London: Canongate, 2014), 3. Further references to this text will be given parenthetically.
19. 'A Conversation with Michael Chabon', 5.

16

ROBERTA PEARSON

Sherlockian Fandom

Fans, whether of written texts, screen texts or football teams, are emotionally invested in their beloved object, of which they often have great and detailed knowledge. They are also sometimes affiliated with broader communities of like-minded people popularly known as fandoms. The word fan has been in the lexicon since at least the early 1900s, at first associated with supporters of baseball teams. Fans have gathered together in various clubs since at least the 1920s, which saw the rise of science fiction fandom in the United States. Organised Sherlockian fandom began in 1934, with the establishment of the Baker Street Irregulars (BSI), discussed at length below. But the high-profile fandoms of today – from Whovians (*Doctor Who*) to Trekkers or Trekkies (*Star Trek*) to Potterites (Harry Potter) – have their roots in the media fandom of the 1960s, which first arose around the cult television shows *The Man From U.N.C.L.E* (1964–8) and *Star Trek* (1966–9). Fans produced fanzines, in which they commented on their beloved objects and wrote fan fiction, their own extensions of their television heroes' exploits. They also gathered together at conventions, at which they could collectively engage in various activities such as dressing up (or cosplay), quizzes, singalongs and the purchase of paratextual consumables produced by individual fans or commercial industries.

Academics began investigating these and other media fandoms in the 1990s, most notably in Henry Jenkins's seminal work *Textual Poachers: Television Fans and Participatory Culture* (1992). Jenkins and other scholars sought to counter the dominant impression of fans as emotionally immature fantasists over-invested in trivial texts and participating in childish activities. These scholars argued that fans were rational actors resisting dominant media by reworking texts to suit their own, frequently female, desires. Scholarly research into various fandoms established the now thriving academic field of fan studies, complete with monographs, a dedicated journal and conferences. By the twenty-first century, fans and fandom had gone mainstream in both academia and the world at large. The academic research had bestowed a certain degree of legitimacy but, more importantly, media industries had fully embraced their fans, the avid section of the audience, prone to repeat viewings of their favourite films and television programmes as well as the consumption of allied products such as books, games, action figures and transmedia extensions. Industry business models became reliant on the free publicity generated by fan engagement and the revenue streams generated by fan purchases. But some still resist the appellation of fan, preferring terms that connote rational engagement rather than the emotional over-investment and childish practices that were, until recently, the dominant connotations of fandom. For example, BSI members Andrew L. Solberg and Robert S. Katz write that '[s]easoned (i.e., old) Sherlockians must swallow before we admit that what we do for and with our love of Sherlock Holmes fully fits in the fan domain ... We like to think of ourselves as "aficionados" or "devotees"'.[1]

The Baker Street Irregulars (BSI), the world's first and oldest Sherlockian organisation, describes itself on the BSI Trust website as 'part literary society, part social group, and part source of whimsical entertainment'. But not just anyone can partake of this sociality and whimsy. 'One does not join the BSI. One is invited to join ... Membership is generally given after significant accomplishment, and, thus, BSI members are generally accomplished adults, either in the Sherlockian community or in their professions'.[2] The phrases 'literary society', 'significant accomplishment' and 'accomplished adults' indicate that the BSI, or at least its official online presence, seeks to distinguish itself from popular media fandoms such as Whovians, Potterites and the like. The subtext of elitism and exclusivity speaks to current divisions in the Sherlockian community between certain long-standing members, who prefer to call themselves enthusiasts and devotees, and more recent members, who are content to call themselves fans.

Subsequent to the recent proliferation of screen adaptations – *Sherlock* (BBC, 2010–), *Elementary* (CBS, 2012–) and the 2009 and 2011 Warner Bros. films (with a third instalment due for release in late 2020) – the influx of new members into the established community (many of them young, female and accustomed to the practices of media fandom) has led to a dispute over the nature of the BSI. Should it be thought of as an elite literary society or as just another typical fandom? Mystery novelist Lyndsay Faye – author of the well-received Sherlockian pastiche, *Dust and Shadow* (2009), and founding member of the Baker Street Babes – wrote a playful and parodic blog addressing the nomenclature controversy, 'Upon the Clear Distinction Between Fandom and the Baker Street Irregulars':

> It falls to me to discuss certain disturbing tendencies on the part of new devotees to refer to that venerable institution, the Baker Street Irregulars, as

a 'fandom' when it is actually a literary society ... Following the summation of
this article ... fans and traditional Sherlockians alike will have reached a much
clearer understanding, and the unfortunate misnomer of referring to the present Irregulars as a 'fandom' will doubtless cease and be swiftly forgotten.[3]

True to her parodic intention, Faye mounts a very persuasive case for the lack
of distinction between the BSI and fans, enumerating the many strong parallels between the organisation and media fandom customs and mores.

The dislike of being labelled a fan or part of a fandom endures despite the
fact that the appearance of Arthur Conan Doyle's stories in the *Strand
Magazine* in the early 1890s generated a popular Sherlock Holmes fandom
that bears some resemblance to today's media fandoms. The aversion stems
in part from the elite appropriation of the fandom that began in the 1900s, as
academics and journalists laid the foundations for the droll critical commentary known as the Great Game that remains a central element of today's
fandom. This duality between popular and elite appropriations of the character has persisted into the twenty-first century. This chapter focuses upon
the distinctions in class, gender and cultural hierarchy that have shaped
Sherlockian fandom since its inception, tracing its history in the UK and
the US from the late nineteenth century to the present. It employs theoretical
perspectives derived from fan studies, which has often concerned itself with
issues of gender and cultural distinction.

Individual Sherlockian Culture: 1890s to 1930s

Organised Sherlockian fandom began with the founding of the American BSI
and the British Sherlock Holmes Society in 1934, more than four decades
after Holmes's first appearance in *A Study in Scarlet* and four years after the
death of his creator, Arthur Conan Doyle. But between the early 1900s and
1934, Holmes had become a constant feature of popular contemporary
media, appearing on stage and in films, radio, board games, sheet music
and advertising, a cultural pervasiveness noted and enhanced by the popular
press's frequent allusions to the character and his creator. When Doyle
sought to rid himself of his troublesome creation by plunging Holmes to
his death at the Reichenbach Falls in 'The Final Problem', the disappointed
and outraged public barraged him with letters which, according to Jonathan
Cranfield, 'oscillated between emotional bullying and straightforward
abuse'.[4] The press reacted with incredulity, the *Leeds Times*, for example,
mourning the passing of 'the most famous detective probably of any age or
any country'.[5] And when *Strand* publisher George Newnes's financial incen-
tives tempted Doyle into reviving Holmes in 1901, the issues containing the

serialised instalments of *The Hound of the Baskervilles* 'went to seven print-ings, more than any edition before or after'.[6]

The Holmes character also inspired some to take up their pens to add their own contributions to the ever-expanding Sherlockian universe. These wri-ters, both amateurs and professionals, had the same motivations as contem-porary media fans; they sought more knowledge of, and further immersion in, an imaginary world that brought them great enjoyment. In 1894, for example, a reader wrote to the magazine *Tit-Bits* saying that the Holmes stories 'make many a fellow who before felt very little interest in his life and daily surroundings, think that after all there may be much more in life, if he keeps his eyes open, than he has ever dreamed of in his philosophy'.[7] *Tit-Bits* also told its readers about their fellow devotee F. W. B. who 'has been applying the principles of the great detective in various matters connected with actual private life'.[8] As the *Strand*'s sister publication, *Tit-Bits* had a vested interest in cross-promoting Doyle and Holmes in order to boost the readership of both journals. Newnes launched *Tit-Bits* in 1881, aiming the content of 'correspondence, advice columns, contests, new fiction, adver-tisements, and general human interest stories' at 'the often self-taught upper-working and lower-middle classes'.[9] Within a decade the magazine had achieved a weekly circulation of 900,000 copies, second only to the *Daily Mail*'s 1,000,000. The cross-promotional strategies of inquiry columns, competitions and pastiches engendered an early Holmes fandom among its upper-working and lower-middle class readers, as well as among the *Strand*'s more solidly middle-class readers who turned to *Tit-Bits* for further informa-tion concerning the Great Detective.

Those seeking news of Holmes had to write to the *Tit-Bits* inquiry col-umns, since the *Strand* did not publish readers' letters. After the appearance of 'The Final Problem', the editor responded to 'G.' and the 'very many others' who expressed their shock at Holmes's demise saying, 'The news of the death of Sherlock Holmes has been received with most widespread regret, and readers have implored us to use our influence with Mr Conan Doyle to prevent the tragedy being consummated ... Like hundreds of correspondents we feel as if we had lost an old friend whom we could ill spare'.[10] Readers continually inquired about the possibility of Holmes's resurrection. In 1899, the editor replied to 'Three Castles' that '[w]e hope that [Doyle] will continue the series at some time, but when – or if ever – we cannot at present say'.[11] In the meantime, *Tit-Bits* tried to keep the buzz going, an accurate if ana-chronistic term to characterise its strategy. Contests sought to engage readers in Holmes's virtual world. For example, the 'Sherlock Holmes Examination Paper' asked twelve questions about Holmes's methods.[12] As well as quiz-zing readers about the stories, the magazine ran other contests soliciting readers' own Sherlock Holmes stories. The first of these pastiches predated 'The Final Problem', but between 1893 and 1901 (the years of Holmes's absence from the *Strand*), many more appeared as *Tit-Bits* publicised the lucrative character to encourage sales of reprints and perhaps in the hope of the character's eventual return to the pages of its sister magazine.[13]

Tit-Bits' encouragement and engagement of a popular fandom bears some resemblance to the ways in which contemporary media industries construct their fan bases. But at the dawn of the twentieth century, a parallel and independent Sherlockian fandom, bearing less resemblance to contemporary media fandoms, emerged in publications targeted at more upmarket readers. These fans wrote in a spirit of intellectual playfulness that laid the foundation for the Great Game that arguably distinguishes Sherlockians from all other fandoms. The Great Game entails writing commentaries upon the Holmesian canon predicated upon two fundamental precepts: firstly, Holmes and Watson were real people and, secondly, Watson wrote the stories and Doyle was merely his literary agent. Rather than accepting that the canon's many contradictions and gaps result from Doyle's writing hastily to deadline without much concern for continuity, the Great Game's practitioners reason from those fundamental precepts, supplementing their analyses with historical information concerning the Victorian, Edwardian and interwar periods during which Holmes and Watson had their adventures. For example, a Sherlockian might seek to justify Watson's contradictory claims concerning the location of his war wound either in his shoulder or in his leg by considering such factors as the weight, speed and trajectories of the jezail bullets shot by the Afghan fighters during the second Anglo-Afghan War which might have accounted for two wounds being inflicted by the same missile. Sherlockians term these light-hearted conjectures the 'Writings upon the Writings'. By the beginning of the twenty-first century these writings came to constitute a vast torrent of prose from writers of many nationalities, but the speculation upon Watson's authorial shortcomings originated at the beginning of the previous century in the UK and the US.

In 1902 recent Cambridge graduate Frank Sidgwick published 'The Hound of The Baskervilles at Fault (An Open Letter to Dr. Watson)' in the 23 January edition of the *Cambridge Review*. Sedgwick brought 'charges of inconsistency' against the good doctor with regard to the dates on which the related events supposedly occurred.[14] In that same year on the other side of the Atlantic, Arthur Bartlett Maurice also pondered Watson's inconsistencies. Writing in the January issue of *The Bookman*, he notes that in *A Study in Scarlet* Watson had claimed that Holmes knew almost nothing about literature, yet in succeeding adventures the detective cites French aphorisms and quotes Goethe (in the original German) as well as the Latin poet Horace.[15] But it is Monsignor Ronald Knox whom Sherlockians acknowledge (with some dissenting voices) as having produced the most influential of the early Writings upon the Writings and thus as the founder of the Great Game. While a young priest at Oxford in 1911, Knox wrote 'Studies in the Literature of Sherlock Holmes', a parody of German biblical scholarship presented to the University's Gryphon Club and subsequently published in the *Blue Book Magazine* in 1912 and then again in *Blackfriars* in 1920.[16] Once again, the author points to Watsonian inconsistencies, but at much greater length than his predecessors. Why does Watson's wife call her husband James in 'The Man with the Twisted Lip' (1891) when the stories are written by John H. Watson? Did Professor James Moriarty have a brother also called James? Did Holmes attend Oxford or Cambridge? On what dates did the stories take place? The fact Sherlockians continue to debate these and other matters of similarly pressing import more than a hundred years after Knox delivered his talk attests to his foundational status in the fandom.

In the late 1920s and throughout the 1930s, culturally elite British and American Holmes enthusiasts contributed to an outpouring of Writings on the Writings. The 1930s alone saw the publication of one or more Sherlockian articles in the following magazines: *The Bookman, Cambridge Review, The Colophon, Real Detective, Cornhill Magazine, New Statesman, The Times Literary Supplement, Oxford Magazine, Guy's Hospital Gazette, The Lancet, The American Journal of Surgery* and *The Saturday Review of Literature*.[17] More important in terms of their influence upon future generations of Sherlockian scholars, a number of book-length studies also appeared during this period. In 1928, Knox reprinted his seminal contribution in *Essays in Satire* (Sheed and Ward). Sydney Roberts, Cambridge professor (and later vice-chancellor), responded to Knox's arguments in a booklet titled *A Note on the Watson Problem* (Cambridge University Press, 1929) and then expanded his arguments in *Doctor Watson: Prolegomena to the Study of a Biographical Problem* (Faber & Faber, 1931). Three other foundational monographs followed in quick succession: T. S. Blakeney's *Sherlock Holmes: Fact or Fiction* (John Murray, 1931); archaeologist H. W. Bell's *Sherlock Holmes and Doctor Watson: A Chronology of Their Adventures* (Constable and Company, 1932) and literary critic and columnist Vincent Starrett's *The Private Life of Sherlock Holmes* (MacMillan, 1933). In 1934, Bell published the first edited volume of scholarly Sherlockian essays, *Baker-Street Studies* (Constable and Company); the book contains chapters by members of the early Sherlock Holmes Society of London, such as Roberts and the well-known mystery novelist Dorothy L. Sayers, but also includes one by the American Starrett.

Baker-Street Studies testifies to the development of a trans-Atlantic interpretive community and network of elite Sherlockian enthusiasts. Whereas Knox had fabricated fictitious critics to rail against, these writers knew each other, or at least each other's Writings on the Writings, and engaged in playful debates on the Watsonian inconsistencies. They were of the same class and overwhelmingly of the same gender, Sayers being one of the few female players of the Great Game in that period. Their writing acquired cultural legitimacy through being published in the period's most reputable journals and issued by its leading publishers. A fandom that began as a popular entertainment in *Tit-Bits* had transformed into an elite pastime in upmarket books and periodicals. In 1946, Sayers commented that '[t]he game ... was begun, many years ago, by Monsignor Ronald Knox. Since then, the thing has become a hobby among a select set of jesters here and in America'.[18] By that time, a hobby practiced by individuals had morphed into a collective activity, with the simultaneous formations of the BSI and the Sherlock Holmes Society in 1934. What follows focuses upon the former, which has been almost constantly active in one form or another since that date, whilst the latter rather quickly disbanded, only re-emerging several years later in 1951. Hence the Baker Street Irregulars have legitimate claim to being the oldest continuous organised fandom in the Sherlockian world and, indeed, one of the most long-established organisations in all of fandom.

Collective (But Male-Only) Sherlockian Culture: 1934–1991

Christopher Morley, American journalist, novelist, essayist and poet, was prominent amongst Sayer's select set of 'jesters', particularly in his role as columnist for the weekly magazine *The Saturday Review of Literature*. A Sherlock Holmes enthusiast since early adolescence, Morley, from the 1920s onward, used the magazine as a platform for Sherlockian news and speculation, with his fellow contributors occasionally joining in the fun from their own columns. After a cocktail party on 6 January 1934 to honour Holmes's birth date as determined by textual evidence, Morley regularly mentioned the Irregulars in his column, but this was a proto-BSI constituted only by Morley's friends. Later that year Morley wrote the column that led directly to the BSI's official launching; it includes a letter supposedly from Tobias Gregson (the detective who features in *A Study in Scarlet*) claiming to have been given a crossword puzzle found in the favourite chair of Mycroft Holmes, brother of Sherlock, at the Diogenes Club. Morley reprinted the puzzle, all the clues and answers based on the canon, saying that 'All those who send me correct solutions ... will automatically become members of the Baker Street Irregulars'.[19] A third of the successful entrants were women, but

Morley decided not to invite them to the founding dinner on 7 December 1934.[20]

As George Mills argues in his history of the early BSI, the organisation was 'born from a distinctive group of journalists and men of letters in a growing New York literary scene'.[21] When Morley's crossword puzzle and subsequent dinner expanded the membership beyond his own social circle, doctors, lawyers and successful industrialists augmented the men of letters' ranks. Although the BSI was founded at roughly the same time as science fiction fan clubs in New York, Los Angeles and Boston, Michael Saler argues that the former's high social status protected them from the 'dismissive scorn commonly endured by fantasy fans ... [They] were eminent professionals who couldn't be dismissed as maladroit teenagers, dreamy escapists, or hopeless cranks'.[22] A memo sent to BSI members by Edgar W. Smith, first editor of *The Baker Street Journal*, indicates their awareness of – and desire to preserve – their culturally respectable status. 'Every effort will be made to maintain a level of scholarship for the quarterly which will hold its circulation to modest figures by assuring the complete indifference of *hoi polloi*'.[23]

Newspapers of the 1940s validated this self-perception; the *New York World-Telegram*, for example, describes the BSI as a 'super-duper Holmes fan club with a highbrow membership', while the *New York Sun* observes that 'There are no professional detectives in the [Baker Street Irregulars] although there are writers, doctors, lawyers and other professional men – including a psychiatrist'.[24] Despite the *Sun*'s insinuation that members might benefit from a psychiatrist's care, legitimate cultural institutions continued to confirm the BSI's self-proclaimed cultural legitimacy. A search for the term 'Baker Street Irregulars' in the archives of *The New York Times*, the US' paper of record, results in more than 200 articles dating back to the 1940s; these include coverage of the annual dinner and reviews of Sherlockian books authored by BSI members. Fordham University Press has for several decades published *The Baker Street Journal* while Harvard's Houghton Library hosts the BSI archives.

But after more than three decades of male camaraderie and cultural confirmation, the revolutionary tides of the 1960s surged even onto the staid shores of the Sherlockian world. A small band of students at Connecticut's all-female Albertus Magnus College, brought together by their shared fannish enthusiasms, including love of the Great Detective, began corresponding with eminent Baker Street Irregulars. But they realised that '[h]owever good we got at the game, we would never be good enough to dine with them'. In the spirit of the age, they decided to picket the 1968 annual dinner, brandishing poster board signs declaring, 'We Want In!', 'BSI Unfair to Women!', 'Let Us In Out of the Cold!'.[25] The BSI kept them out in the metaphorical cold, but the six protesters became the 'Founding Mothers' of the Adventuresses of Sherlock Holmes (ASH), initially a female-only society, which for many years hosted an annual dinner scheduled opposite the BSI's, as well as autumn and spring gatherings of the female faithful.

Then in 1991, the BSI's new leader, Thomas Stix, made the unilateral decision to invest six prominent female Sherlockians including, in an act of belated justice, Katherine McMahon, one of the original solvers of Morley's crossword puzzle, Evelyn Herzog, by now ASH's leader under the title of 'Principal Unprincipled Adventuress', and Julia C. Rosenblatt, co-author of *Dining with Sherlock Holmes* (1976) and BSI spouse. Rosenblatt, drawing on husband Albert's insider knowledge, writes of the divisions amongst the BSI concerning Stix's decision. Those who opposed admitting women 'said it was a matter of numbers, that it was simpler to keep the BSI to a manageable size if it were men only. Others wanted the BSI to be a gathering where it was always 1935'. Those who favoured admitting women 'saw it as a matter of social justice. It was not fair to exclude women from the self-styled pre-eminent group of Sherlockian scholars'.[26] Despite the dissenters, in the following years the Irregulars admitted more women to their ranks. But in the twenty-first century an influx of young females into the Sherlockian community proved even more threatening to a small number of old-guard BSI who harked back to the Sherlockian Golden Age of the 1930s when the group revelled in its exclusiveness and cultural legitimacy.

Collective Sherlockian Culture: The Twenty-First Century

Established in 2011, The Baker Street Babes describe themselves as 'an all-female group of Sherlock Holmes fans dedicated to approaching the fandom from a female point of view'.[27] The Babes' outright declaration of their fannish and female perspectives distinguishes them from both the BSI and ASH. Their affirmation of fandom contrasts with the BSI's insistence on being a literary society and not a fandom. Whilst the Babes stress their female perspective, ASH, despite its roots in the 1968 protest, was assimilationist, its members desiring nothing more than full admittance into Sherlockian fellow-ship and the Great Game on an equal footing with the men. But those original ASH members, like today's Babes, were also popular culture fans – the Founding Mothers bonded not only over Sherlock Holmes but over *Star Trek*. As Herzog suggests in recounting the history of the organization to an ASH gathering, '[w]e came to share many, many enthusiasms ... It needn't have been the Canon that took first place among us – had things been only slightly different this might be a *Star Trek* convention [that I'm addressing]'.[28] The original ASH had almost as strong an engagement with the emerging media fandom as they did with established Sherlockian fandom.

But male traditionalists took affront even from fans and fan-like behaviour associated with Holmes adaptations. In 1988, *Baker Street Journal* editor Philip Shreffler wrote an editorial bemoaning the attitudes and behaviours of new members attracted to the Sherlockian community by the critically well-received television series starring Jeremy Brett (Granada, 1984–94). According to an introduction to a 2013 reprint of the editorial, '[a]t that time, Jeremy Brett fandom threatened to overwhelm more traditional forms of Sherlockian sensibility, and Shreffler's acute observations offered a way to think about the vast gulf between the Holmes fan and the Holmes devotee'.[29] Legitimate Sherlockians, opined Shreffler, should be 'devoted to the world where it is always 1895 and always 1934', aspiring to 'the Old World gentlemanly and ladylike milieu in which Sherlock Holmes lived and, later, from which the Baker Street Irregulars were born' rather than adopting the 'casual ... ambiance associated with life in the mid-to-late twentieth century'. Most importantly, believed Shreffler, '[t]he devotee is a person of language, of words; the fan is more commonly a person of half-ideas, half-expressed. The devotee is comfortable in genteel, dignified Sherlockian surroundings; the fan ... is at home at a science-fiction convention'.[30]

Shreffler's editorial embodies the scorn Saler identifies as endured by fantasy fans, and from which the BSI had for years been exempt. Fans endured this scorn for decades, but, as noted above, the late twentieth- and early twenty-first centuries witnessed the mainstreaming of fandom. Despite this mainstreaming, the denigration of young, female fans has not only persisted but, in some cases, grown louder, as seen in the 2014 'Gamergate' controversy in which male videogame players vigorously contested the right of females to participate in the fandom, as well as in the cultural stereotype of the clueless fangirl. The Babes arose both from fandom's mainstreaming and from the lingering denigration of the females who dare to enter those male preserves.

The Babes' founder Kristina Manente initiated the group's podcast in response to the male-hosted podcast *I Hear of Sherlock Everywhere*. Manente stated that she 'wanted to give a voice to young female fans. We're poked fun at constantly by the media and those who don't necessarily understand fan culture, but while we may have quirks and in-jokes, there's an amazing level of scholarship and discussion happening'.[31] Each podcast draws between 5,000 and 10,000 listeners, but episodes focusing on the BBC's *Sherlock* have proven most popular, sometimes doubling the size of the audience. In a testament to fandom's current perceived value, both *Sherlock*'s producer, Sue Vertue, and PBS, the public service television network that broadcasts the programme in North America, have involved the Babes in their publicity strategies.[32] Members of the Babes have also appeared in the mainstream media, including NBC, The Today Show, CBS, USA Today and FOX.[33] In addition to their prominent media profile, The Babes have become an integral part of the Sherlockian community, invited to the annual BSI dinner and hosting an annual ball open to all during the January weekend in New York City celebrating Holmes's birthday. Betsy Rosenblatt, Baker Street Irregular and professor at Whittier Law School, acknowledges that the first of these balls 'felt revolutionary', attracting as it did a broad spectrum of attendees including 'traditional Sherlockians, fans of just the adaptations, young people, old people, pretty darn old people'.[34]

As *The New York Times* reported, the Babes' conspicuous divergence from the old elitist mode elicited a reaction from a breakaway group of old guard Irregulars already disgruntled by the erosion of distinctions between their once-cherished literary society and typical fandom. Declining to attend any of the January weekend's official activities, they instead hold meetings for a small group of the like-minded, with Jon Lellenberg, American agent for the Conan Doyle Estate and formerly the BSI's official historian, acting as unofficial leader. The *Times* reporter writes that many Sherlockians think that Lellenberg has 'led a rear-guard action aimed at marginalizing ... new admirers', particularly the Babes. Lellenberg and friends edited a pamphlet for distribution at their 2013 meeting that lamented the BSI's 'embrace of the Babes'. Amongst the pamphlet's authors was the aforementioned Philip Shreffler, who contributed an update of his 1988 editorial, 'The Elite Devotee Redux' that the Babes obtained, scanned and made publicly available on their Tumblr site.[35]

According to the editorial introduction, 'a new fan movement', emerging in 'circumstances all too similar to those that prompted his 1988 editorial', impelled Shreffler to pen his update – that new fan movement, of course, is the one centering around the BBC's globally popular *Sherlock* (2010–). Shreffler bewails 'the conflation of Sherlockians as established in the twentieth century with its present practice by those whose primary adherence to Holmes is through the BBC's *Sherlock*'. He bemoans the fact that the *Baker Street Journal* 'has embraced' the term 'Sherlockian fandom' and characterises as 'somewhat chilling' a *Journal* editorial offering an 'egalitarian ... "Welcome to your new home!"' to fans. (This welcome is, of course, in sharp contrast to original editor Smith's desire to exclude hoi polloi.) Shreffler focuses his ire on Babes' founder Manente, noting that 'she was somewhat fawningly fêted, to our surprise and discomfort' at a BSI gathering. He particularly derogates Manente's colloquial and contemporary pod-cast speaking style, comparing it to a 'potting shed on which is scrawled derogatory graffiti'.[36]

Shreffler's 1988 editorial did not elicit much push-back, but twenty-five years later circumstances had changed. Factors such as the admission of women into the BSI, the media's wholehearted embrace of the Babes, and the cultural mainstreaming of fandom now rendered Shreffler's opinions offensive to many. Christopher Roden, founder of the Arthur Conan Doyle Society and long-standing BSI, dismissed Shreffler's views as 'bigoted and pigheaded'.[37] Posted on the Babes' Tumblr site, the essay 'drew hundreds of links and sarcastic comments'.[38] Babe Lyndsay Faye responded by pointing out that Holmes originated, and remains, in popular culture. 'Sherlock Holmes is a *detective,* and therefore a *genre fiction hero,* who was printed in *disposable paperback magazines*, and as such belongs heart and soul to what Mr Shreffler mockingly calls the "lightest-weight popular culture" … He was the great shame of his author's life, the darling of *popular stage plays* and *popular films'.*[39]

After the 'Shreffgate' incident, as the Babes term it, Manente nonetheless expressed optimism about a future fandom forged by traditionalists and new members together. 'The vast majority of traditional Sherlockians are incredibly welcoming and very excited about the surge of new, young people entering into their world. There's no right or wrong way to enjoy your love of something, and that's something that we really want to hammer home and promote, as do, I think, most of those in the traditional world'.[40] But, despite Manente's declaration that there is no 'right or wrong way' to love Holmes, the Babes still wanted to demonstrate their Sherlockian chops by playing the Great Game in the traditional manner established in the 1930s. In 2015 they published a collection of Sherlockian scholarship entitled *The One Fixed Point in a Changing Age: A New Generation on Sherlock Holmes* and edited by Babes Manente, Maria Fleischhack, Sarah Roy and Taylor Blumenberg. In calling for contributions, the Babes said that it 'would be really good to prove that we are more than just "silly fans", and that we can be just as scholarly as the big boys'.[41]

The publication of the collection may signal the conclusive integration of the female and of the self-proclaimed fan into Sherlockian culture. But such integration should not overwrite the contested history that preceded it, a history that reveals the interplay of class, gender and cultural legitimacy. In Sherlockian circles, scholarship has been primarily associated with the 'boys', the founding fathers of the Great Game and their BSI descendants whose cultural elitism and gender bestowed legitimacy upon their activities. The integration of the assimilationist ASH, who self-consciously chose Sherlockian fandom over media fandom, did not constitute a threat either to the BSI's established customs and mores or to their cultural legitimacy. But self-avowed fan girls, in the form of the Baker Street Babes, were perceived by some as threatening the BSI's cultural legitimacy through their importation of the language and practices of contemporary media fandom. Ironically, however, the Babes themselves, like their ASH predecessors, sought full integration into the Sherlockian world by demonstrating that they too could play the Great Game, thus privileging the BSI's established customs and mores over media fandoms' language and practices.

Notes

1. Andrew L. Solberg and Robert S. Katz, 'Fandom, publishing and playing the Grand Game', *Journal of Transformative Works and Cultures* 23 (2017), [http://dx.doi.org/10.3983/twc.2017.0825, accessed 12 May 2017].
2. Baker Street Irregulars Trust, 'BSI History – An Introduction', [www.bsitrust.org/2015/01/bsi-history.html, accessed 10 May 2017].
3. Lyndsay Faye, 'Upon the Clear Distinction Between Fandom and the Baker Street Irregulars', *Criminal Element*, 30 November 2012, [www.criminalelement.com/blogs/2012/11/upon-the-clear-distinction-between-fandom-and-the-baker-street-irregulars-lyndsay-faye-sherlock-holmes-arthur-conan-doyle-elementary, accessed 13 May 2017].
4. Jonathan Cranfield, 'Sherlock Holmes, Fan Cultures and Fan Letters', in Tom Ue and Jonathan Cranfield (eds.), *Fan Phenomena: Sherlock Holmes* (Bristol: Intellect, 2014), 66–79 (74).
5. Quoted in Zach Dundas, *The Great Detective: The Amazing Rise and Immortal Life of Sherlock Holmes* (Boston: Houghton Mifflin Harcourt, 2015), 118.
6. Cranfield, 'Sherlock', 75.
7. *Tit-Bits*, n.d., quoted in Michael Saler, *As If: Modern Enchantment and the Literary Prehistory of Virtual Reality* (Oxford: Oxford University Press, 2012), 118.
8. *Tit-Bits*, 8 June 1895, quoted in ibid.
9. Ann McClellan, '*Tit-Bits*, New Journalism, and early Sherlock Holmes fandom', *Journal of Transformative Works and Cultures* (2017), [http://dx.doi.org/10.3983/twc.2017.0816, accessed 13 May 2017].
10. *Tit-Bits*, 6 January 1894, quoted in ibid.
11. *Tit-Bits*, 1 April 1899, quoted in ibid.
12. McClellan, '*Tit-Bits*'.
13. *Tit-Bits*, 3 December 1892, quoted in ibid.
14. 'Frank Sidgwick's 1902 Essay', BSI Archival History, [http://www.bsiarchivalhistory.org/BSI_Archival_History/Sidgwick_essay.html, accessed 14 May 2017].
15. 'Some Inconsistencies of Sherlock Holmes', *The Bookman* (January 1902), 446–7, (US version), *The Arthur Conan Doyle Encyclopaedia*, [https://www.arthur-conan-doyle.com/index.php?title=Some_Inconsistencies_of_Sherlock_Holmes, accessed 14 May 2017].

16. R. A. Knox, 'Studies in the Literature of Sherlock Holmes', *Blackfriars* 1:3 (1920), 154–72.
17. Kate M. Donley, 'Early Sherlockian Scholarship: Non/fiction at play', *Journal of Transformative Works and Cultures* 23 (2017), [http://dx.doi.org/10.3983/twc .2017.0837, accessed 15 May 2017].
18. Dorothy L. Sayers, *Unpopular Opinions* (London: Victor Gollancz, 1946), 7.
19. Christopher Morley, 'The Bowling Green: Sherlock Holmes Crossword', *The Saturday Review of Literature* (19 May 1934), 703.
20. Julia C. Rosenblatt, 'From outside to inside', *Journal of Transformative Works and Cultures* 23 (2017), [http://dx.doi.org/10.3983/twc.2017.0920, accessed 15 May 2017].
21. George Mills, 'The scholarly rebellion of the Early Baker Street Irregulars', *Journal of Transformative Works and Cultures* 23 (2017), [http://dx.doi.org/10 .3983/twc.2017.0864, accessed 15 May 2017].
22. Saler, *As If*, 123.
23. Edgar Smith, 'Memo to the Baker Street Irregulars' (11 October 1945), quoted in Mills, 'The scholarly rebellion'.
24. Jon L. Lellenberg, *Irregular Crises of the Late 'Forties* (New York: BSI, 1999), 48; Jon L. Lellenberg, *Irregular Proceedings of the Mid 'Forties* (New York: BSI, 1995), 298, both quoted in Saler, *As If*, 124.
25. Evelyn Herzog and Peter Blau, 'A duet: With an occasional chorus', *Journal of Transformative Works and Cultures* 23 (2017), [http://dx.doi.org/10.3983/twc .2017.0932, accessed 17 May 2017].
26. Rosenblatt, 'From outside to inside'.
27. Baker Street Babes, 'About the Baker Street Babes', [http://bakerstreetbabes.com/, accessed 20 May 2017].
28. Evelyn Herzog, 'Boys and Girls Together', *The Serpentine Muse* 26:4 (2009), 22–3.
29. 'The Elite Devotee or How The Sherlock Fandom Is A Horrible Embarrassment To The Sherlockian World by Philip Shreffler', [http://bakerstreetbabes .tumblr.com/post/41481263409/the-elite-devotee-or-how-the-sherlock-fan dom-is-a, accessed 20 May 2017].
30. Ibid.
31. Lisa Granshaw, 'Meet the Baker Street Babes, the first all-female Sherlock Holmes podcast', *The Daily Dot* 4 (December 2013), [https://www.dailydot.com/parsec/ fandom/sherlock-holmes-baker-street-babes-fans-podcast/, accessed 20 May 2017].
32. Ibid.
33. 'Elite Devotee'.
34. Quoted in Jennifer Schuessler, 'Suit Says Sherlock Belongs to the Ages', *The New York Times* (6 March, 2013), [http://www.nytimes.com/2013/03/07/books/suit- says-sherlock-belongs-to-the-ages.html?_r=0, accessed 12 August 2014].
35. Ibid.
36. Reprinted in Lyndsay Faye, 'When the Shreff Hits the Fangirl: A Public Apology', [http://bakerstreetbabes.tumblr.com/post/41884893346/when-the-shreff-hits- the-fangirl-a-public-apology, accessed 15 May 2016].
37. Quoted in Schuessler, 'Suit Says Sherlock'.
38. Ibid.

39. Faye, 'When the Shreff Hits the Fangirl'.
40. Quoted in Granshaw, 'Meet the Baker Street'.
41. Baker Street Babes, 'Call For Entries! The One Fixed Point In A Changing Age: Essays on Sherlockiana By Online Fandom', 28 October 2012, [http://bakerstreet babes.com/call-for-entries-the-one-fixed-point-in-a-changing-age-essays-on-sherlockiana-by-online-fandom/, accessed 12 December 2016].

Biographies, Primary and Reference Materials

Dirda, Michael, *On Conan Doyle: or The Whole Art of Storytelling*. Princeton: Princeton University Press, 2012.

Doyle, Arthur Conan, *Memories and Adventures*. Cambridge: Cambridge University Press, 2012.

The Narrative of John Smith, ed. Jon Lellenberg, Daniel Stashower and Rachel Foss. London: British Library Publishing, 2011.

'Some Personalia about Mr. Sherlock Holmes', *Strand Magazine* 55 (December 1917), 531–5.

Dundas, Zach, *The Great Detective: The Amazing Rise and Immortal Life of Sherlock Holmes*. Boston: Houghton Mifflin Harcourt, 2015.

Gibson, John Michael and Richard Lancelyn Green (eds.), *The Unknown Conan Doyle: Letters to the Press*. London: Secker and Warburg, 1986.

Hall, John and Sidney Paget, *'I remember the date very well': A Chronology of the Sherlock Holmes Stories of Arthur Conan Doyle*. Romford: Ian Henry, 1993.

Hodgson, John A., 'Arthur Conan Doyle', in Charles J. Rzepka and Lee Horsley (eds.), *A Companion to Crime Fiction*. Oxford: Wiley-Blackwell, 2010. 390–402.

Lancelyn Green, Richard and John Michael Gibson, *A Bibliography of A. Conan Doyle*. Oxford: Clarendon, 1983.

Lellenberg, Jon, Daniel Stashower and Charles Foley (eds.), *Arthur Conan Doyle: A Life in Letters*. London: Harper Perennial, 2008.

Lycett, Andrew, *Conan Doyle: The Man Who Created Sherlock Holmes*. London: Weidenfeld and Nicolson, 2007.

Miller, Russell, *The Adventures of Arthur Conan Doyle: A Biography*. London: Harvill Secker, 2008.

Orel, Harold (ed.), *Sir Arthur Conan Doyle: Interviews and Recollections*. Basingstoke: Macmillan, 1991.

Sims, Michael, *Arthur and Sherlock: Conan Doyle and the Creation of Holmes*. London: Bloomsbury, 2017.

Stashower, Daniel, *Teller of Tales: The Life of Arthur Conan Doyle*. New York: Henry Holt and Company, 1999.

General Sources on Sherlock Holmes and Victorian Detective Fiction

Ascari, Maurizio, *A Counter-History of Crime Fiction: Supernatural, Gothic, Sensational*. Basingstoke: Palgrave Macmillan, 2007.

Auden, W. H., 'The Guilty Vicarage', *Harper's Monthly* 196:1176 (1948), 406–12.

Baggett, David and Philip Tallon (eds.), *The Philosophy of Sherlock Holmes*. Lexington: University Press of Kentucky, 2012.

Binyon, T. J., *'Murder Will Out': The Detective in Fiction*. Oxford: Oxford University Press, 1990.

Boltanski, Luc, *Mysteries and Conspiracies: Detective Stories, Spy Novels, and the Making of Modern Societies*, trans. Catherine Porter. Cambridge: Polity, 2014.

Boström, Mattias, *The Life and Death of Sherlock Holmes: Master Detective, Myth, and Media Star*. London: Head of Zeus, 2017.

Cawelti, John G., *Adventure, Mystery, and Romance: Formula Stories as Art and Popular Culture*. Chicago: University of Chicago Press, 1977.

Clark, John D., 'Some Notes Relating to a Preliminary Investigation into the Paternity of Nero Wolfe', *Baker Street Journal* 6:1 (1956), 5–11.

Clarke, Clare, *Late Victorian Crime Fiction in the Shadows of Sherlock*. Basingstoke: Palgrave Macmillan, 2014.

Clausen, Christopher, 'Sherlock Holmes, Order, and the Late-Victorian Mind', *Georgia Review* 38:1 (1984), 104–23.

Clausson, Nils, 'Degeneration, *Fin-de-Siècle* Gothic, and the Science of Detection: Arthur Conan Doyle's *The Hound of the Baskervilles* and the Emergence of the Modern Detective Story', *Journal of Narrative Theory* 35:1 (2005), 60–87.

Cohen, Michael, *Murder Most Fair: The Appeal of Mystery Fiction*. Madison: Fairleigh Dickinson University Press, 2000.

Cook, Michael, *Detective Fiction and the Ghost Story: The Haunted Text*. Basingstoke: Palgrave Macmillan, 2014.

Eliot, T. S., '*The Complete Sherlock Holmes Short Stories*: A Review', in Philip A. Shreffler (ed.), *The Baker Street Reader: Cornerstone Writings About Sherlock Holmes*. Westport: Greenwood, 1984. 17–19.

Glazzard, Andrew, *The Case of Sherlock Holmes: Secrets and Lies in Conan Doyle's Detective Fiction*. Edinburgh: Edinburgh University Press, 2018.

Hardwick, Michael, and Mollie Hardwick (eds.), *The Sherlock Holmes Companion*. London: Bramhall House, 1962.

Haycraft, Howard, *Murder for Pleasure: The Life and Times of the Detective Story*. New York: Biblio and Tannen, 1976.

Haynsworth, Leslie, 'Sensational Adventures: Sherlock Holmes and His Generic Past', *English Literature in Transition, 1880–1920* 44:4 (2001), 459–85.

Jann, Rosemary, *The Adventures of Sherlock Holmes: Detecting Social Order*. New York: Twayne Press, 1995.

Kayman, Martin A., *From Bow Street to Baker Street: Mystery, Detection, and Narrative*. New York: St Martin's Press, 1992.

Kerr, Douglas, *Conan Doyle: Writing, Profession, and Practice*. Oxford: Oxford University Press, 2013.

Kestner, Joseph A., *Sherlock's Sisters: The British Female Detective, 1864–1913*. Farnham: Ashgate, 1997.

Knight, Stephen *Crime Fiction Since 1800: Detection, Death, Diversity*, 2nd edn. Basingstoke: Palgrave Macmillan, 2010.

Form and Ideology in Crime Fiction. Basingstoke: Macmillan, 1980.

Towards Sherlock Holmes: A Thematic History of Crime Fiction in the 19th Century World. Jefferson: McFarland, 2016.

Knox, Ronald A., 'Studies in the Literature of Sherlock Holmes', *Blackfriars* 1:3 (1920), 154–72.

Lehman, David, *The Perfect Murder: A Study in Detection*. Ann Arbor: University of Michigan Press, 2000.

Mandel, Ernest, *Delightful Murder: A Social History of the Crime Story*. London: Pluto Press, 1984.

Merivale, Patricia and Elizabeth Sweeney (eds.), *Detecting Texts: The Metaphysical Detective Story from Poe to Postmodernism*. Philadelphia: University of Pennsylvania Press, 1999.

Messent, Peter, *The Crime Fiction Handbook*. Oxford: Wiley-Blackwell, 2013.

Naidu, Sam (ed.), *Sherlock Holmes in Context*. Basingstoke: Palgrave Macmillan, 2017.

Nilsson, Louise, David Damrosch and Theo D'haen (eds.), *Crime Fiction as World Literature*. London: Bloomsbury, 2017.

Ousby, Ian, *Bloodhounds of Heaven: The Detective in English Fiction from Godwin to Doyle*. Cambridge: Harvard University Press, 1976.

Panek, LeRoy Lad, *After Sherlock Holmes: The Evolution of British and American Detective Stories, 1891–1914*. Jefferson: McFarland, 2014.

Parker, Ben, 'The Method Effect: Empiricism and Form in Sherlock Holmes', *Novel* 49:3 (2016), 449–66.

Pittard, Christopher, 'From Sensation to the *Strand*', in Charles J. Rzepka and Lee Horsley (eds.), *A Companion to Crime Fiction*. Oxford: Wiley-Blackwell, 2010. 105–116.

Purity and Contamination in Late Victorian Detective Fiction. Farnham: Ashgate, 2011.

Porter, Dennis, *The Pursuit of Crime: Art and Ideology in Detective Fiction*. New Haven: Yale University Press, 1981.

Priestman, Martin, *The Cambridge Companion to Crime Fiction*. Cambridge: Cambridge University Press, 2003.

Crime Fiction: From Poe to the Present, 2nd edn. Tavistock: Northcote House, 2012.

Detective Fiction and Literature: The Figure on the Carpet. New York: St Martin's Press, 1991.

Putney, Charles R., Joseph A. Cutshall King and Sally Sugerman (eds.), *Sherlock Holmes: Victorian Sleuth to Modern Hero*. Lanham: The Scarecrow Press, 1996.

Redmond, Christopher, *Lives Beyond Baker Street: A Biographical Dictionary of Sherlock Holmes's Contemporaries*. London: MX Publishing, 2016.

Roth, Marty, *Foul & Fair Play: Reading Genre in Classic Detective Fiction*. Athens: University of Georgia Press, 1995.

Saler, Michael, '"Clap if You Believe in Sherlock Holmes": Mass Culture and the Re-Enchantment of Modernity, c.1890-c.1940', *The Historical Journal* 46:3 (2003), 599–622.

As If: Modern Enchantment and the Literary Prehistory of Virtual Reality. Oxford: Oxford University Press, 2012.

Shreffler, Philip A., *Sherlock Holmes by Gas-lamp: Highlights from the First Four Decades of the* Baker Street Journal. New York: Fordham University Press, 1989.

Smajić, Srdjan, *Ghost-Seers, Detectives and Spiritualists: Theories of Vision in Victorian Literature and Science*. Cambridge: Cambridge University Press, 2010.

Steiff, Josef, *Sherlock Holmes and Philosophy: The Footprints of a Gigantic Mind*. Chicago: Open Court, 2011.

Sussex, Lucy, *Women Writers and Detectives in Nineteenth-Century Crime Fiction*. Basingstoke: Palgrave Macmillan, 2010.

Symons, Julian, *Bloody Murder: From the Detective Story to the Crime Novel*, rev. edn. London: Pan, 1994.

Watson, Kate, *Women Writing Crime Fiction, 1860–1880*. Jefferson: McFarland, 2012.

Werner, Alex (ed.), *Sherlock Holmes: The Man Who Never Lived and Will Never Die*. London: Ebury Press, 2014.

Worthington, Heather, *Key Concepts in Crime Fiction*. Basingstoke: Palgrave Macmillan, 2011.

The Rise of the Detective in Early Nineteenth-Century Popular Fiction. Basingstoke: Palgrave Macmillan, 2005.

The Publishing Context and Illustrations

Ashley, Mike, *Adventures in the Strand: Arthur Conan Doyle and the* Strand Magazine. London: British Library Board, 2016.

The Age of Storytellers: British Popular Fiction Magazines 1880–1950. London: British Library Press, 2006.

Cairney, Maria, 'The Healing Art of Detection: Sherlock Holmes and the Disease of Crime in the *Strand Magazine*', *Clues* 26:1 (2008), 62–74.

Cox, Howard and Simon Mowatt, *Revolutions from Grub Street: A History of Magazine Publishing in Britain*. Oxford: Oxford University Press, 2014.

Cranfield, Jonathan, 'Sherlock's Slums: The Periodical as an Environmental Form', *Textual Practice* 28:2 (2014), 215–41.

Twentieth-Century Victorian: Arthur Conan Doyle and the Strand Magazine, *1891–1930*. Edinburgh: Edinburgh University Press, 2016.

Daly, Nicholas, *Modernism, Romance and the* Fin de Siècle: *Popular Fiction and British Culture, 1880–1914*. Cambridge: Cambridge University Press, 1999.

Dawson, Janis, 'Rivaling Conan Doyle: L.T. Meade's Medical Mysteries, New Woman Criminals, and Literary Celebrity at the Victorian *Fin de Siècle*', *English Literature in Transition 1880–1920* 58:1 (2015), 54–72.

Greenfield, John, 'Arthur Morrison's Sherlock Clone: Martin Hewitt, Victorian Values, and London Magazine Culture, 1894–1903', *Victorian Periodicals Review* 35:1 (2002), 18–36.

Hammond, Mary, *Reading, Publishing and the Formation of Literary Taste in England, 1880–1914*. Farnham: Ashgate, 2006.

Hewitt, Martin, *The Dawn of the Cheap Press in Victorian Britain*. London: Bloomsbury, 2014.

Hoberman, Ruth, 'Constructing the Turn-of-the-Century Shopper: Narratives about Purchased Objects in the *Strand Magazine*', *Victorian Periodicals Review* 37:1 (2004), 1–17.

Hollyer, Cameron, 'Author to Editor: Arthur Conan Doyle's Correspondence with H. Greenhough Smith', *ACD: The Journal of the Arthur Conan Doyle Society* 3 (1992), 11–34.

'"My Dear Smith": Some Letters of Arthur Conan Doyle to his *Strand* Editor', *Baker Street Miscellanea* 44 (1985), 1–24.

Jackson, Kate, 'George Newnes and the "Loyal Tit-Bitites": Editorial Identity and Textual Interaction in *Tit-Bits*', in Laurel Brake, Bill Bell and David Finkelstein (eds.), *Nineteenth-Century Media and the Construction of Identities*. Basingstoke: Palgrave, 2003. 11–26.

George Newnes and the New Journalism in Britain 1880–1910: Culture and Profit. Farnham: Ashgate, 2001.

Klinefelter, Walter, *Sherlock Holmes in Portrait and Profile*. New York: Syracuse University Press, 1963.

Kooistra, Lorraine J., *The Artist as Critic: Bitextuality in* Fin de Siècle *Illustrated Books*. London: Scolar, 1995.

Leech, George W., *Magazine Illustration: The Art Editor's Point of View*. London: Pitman, 1939.

McDonald, Peter D., 'The Adventures of the Literary Agent: Conan Doyle, A.P. Watt, Holmes, and *The Strand* in 1891', *Victorian Periodicals Review* 30:1 (1997), 17–26.

British Literary Culture and Publishing Practice, 1880–1914. Cambridge: Cambridge University Press, 2002.

Mussell, James, *Science, Time and Space in the Late Nineteenth-Century Periodical Press*. Farnham: Ashgate, 2007.

Newnes, George, 'Introduction', *Strand Magazine* 1 (1891), 3.

Pittard, Christopher, 'The Victorian Context: Serialization, Circulation, Genres', in Christine Berberich (ed.), *The Bloomsbury Introduction to Popular Fiction*. London: Bloomsbury, 2015. 11–29.

Pound, Reginald, *Mirror of the Century: The* Strand Magazine *1891–1950*. London: Heinemann, 1966.

Redmond, Donald A., *Sherlock Holmes Among the Pirates: Copyright and Conan Doyle in America, 1890–1930*. New York: Greenwood Press, 1990.

Stock, Randall, 'Sidney Paget: Paintings by the Numbers', *Baker Street Journal* 59:1 (2009), 6–10.

Werner, Alex, 'Sherlock Holmes, Sidney Paget, and the *Strand Magazine*', in Alex Werner (ed.), *Sherlock Holmes: The Man Who Never Lived and Will Never Die*. London: Ebury Press, 2014. 101–25.

Zieger, Susan, 'Tobacco Papers, Holmes's Pipe, Cigarette Cards, and Information Addiction', in *The Mediated Mind: Affect, Ephemera, and Consumerism in the Nineteenth Century*. New York: Fordham University, 2018. 54–86.

Englishness and Imperialism

Arata, Stephen, *Fictions of Loss in the Victorian* Fin de Siècle: *Identity and Empire*. Cambridge: Cambridge University Press, 1996.

Berberich, Christine, '"Isn't this worth fighting for?": World War I and the (Ab)Uses of the Pastoral Tradition', in Petra Rau (ed.), *Bodies-at-War: Conflict, Nationhood and Corporeality in Modern Literature*. Basingstoke: Palgrave Macmillan, 2010. 26–45.

Brantlinger, Patrick, *Rule of Darkness: British Literature and Imperialism, 1830–1914*. Ithaca: Cornell University Press, 1990.

Burrow, Merrick, 'Conan Doyle's Gothic Materialism', *Nineteenth-Century Contexts: An Interdisciplinary Journal* 35:3 (2013), 309–23.

Doyle, Arthur Conan, *Dangerous Work: Diary of an Arctic Adventure*, ed. Jon Lellenberg and Daniel Stashower. Chicago: University of Chicago Press, 2012.

Featherstone, Simon, *Englishness: Twentieth-Century Popular Culture and the Forming of English Identity*. Edinburgh: Edinburgh University Press, 2009.

Gillespie, Michael Allen and John Samuel Harpham, 'Sherlock Holmes, Crime, and the Anxieties of Globalization', *Critical Review* 23:4 (2012), 449–74.

Harrington, Ellen Burton, 'Nation, Identity and the Fascination with Forensic Science in Sherlock Holmes and CSI', *International Journal of Cultural Studies* 10:3 (2007), 365–82.

Harris, Susan Cannon, 'Pathological Possibilities: Contagion and Empire in Doyle's Sherlock Holmes Stories', *Victorian Literature and Culture* 31:2 (2003), 447–66.

Hendershot, Cyndy, 'The Animal Without: Masculinity and Imperialism in *The Island of Doctor Moreau* and "The Adventure of the Speckled Band"', *Nineteenth Century Studies* 10 (1996), 1–32.

Huh, Jinny, 'Whispers of Norbury: Sir Arthur Conan Doyle and the Modernist Crisis of Racial (Un)Detection', *MFS: Modern Fiction Studies* 49:3 (2003), 550–80.

Kumar, Krishan, '"Englishness" and National Identity', in David Morley and Kevin Robins (eds.), *British Cultural Studies: Geography, Nationality and Identity*. Oxford: Oxford University Press, 2001. 41–55.

Matzke, Christine and Susanne Muhleisen (eds.), *Postcolonial Postmortems: Crime Fiction from a Transcultural Perspective*. Amsterdam: Rodopi, 2006.

McCrea, Barry, *In the Company of Strangers: Family and Narrative in Dickens, Conan Doyle, Joyce, and Proust*. New York: Columbia University Press, 2011.

McLaughlin, Joseph, *Writing the Urban Jungle: Reading Empire in London from Doyle to Eliot*. Charlottesville: University of Virginia Press, 2000.

Mukherjee, Upamanyu Pablo, *Crime and Empire: The Colony in Nineteenth-Century Fictions of Crime*. Oxford: Oxford University Press, 2003.

O'Dell, Benjamin D., 'Performing the Imperial Abject: The Ethics of Cocaine in Arthur Conan Doyle's *The Sign of Four*', *The Journal of Popular Culture* 45:5 (2012), 979–99.

Oak Taylor-Ide, Jesse, 'Ritual and the Liminality of Sherlock Holmes in *The Sign of Four* and *The Hound of the Baskervilles*', *English Literature in Transition, 1880–1920* 48:1 (2005), 55–70.

Reitz, Caroline, *Detecting the Nation: Fictions of Detection and the Imperial Venture*. Columbus: Ohio State University Press, 2004.

Said, Edward, *Orientalism*. New York: Vintage, 1979.

Siddiqi, Yumna, *Anxieties of Empire and the Fiction of Intrigue*. Cambridge: Cambridge University Press, 2008.

Thomas, Ronald R., 'The Fingerprint of the Foreigner: Colonizing the Criminal Body in 1890s Detective Fiction and Criminal Anthropology', *ELH* 61:3 (1994), 655–80.

Thompson, Jon, *Fiction, Crime, and Empire: Clues to Modernity and Postmodernism*. Urbana and Chicago: University of Illinois Press, 1993.

Trower, Shelly, 'On the Cliff Edge of England: Tourism and the Imperial Gothic in Cornwall', *Victorian Literature and Culture* 40 (2012), 199–214.

Ue, Tom, 'Holmes and Raffles in Arms: Death, Endings, and Narration', *Victoriographies* 5:3 (2015), 219–33.

Wiltse, Ed, '"So Constant an Expectation": Sherlock Holmes and Seriality', *Narrative* 6:2 May (1998), 105–22.

Wynne, Catherine, *The Colonial Conan Doyle: British Imperialism, Irish Nationalism, and the Gothic*. Westport: Greenwood Press, 2002.

Holmes and London

Beckson, Karl, *London in the 1890s: A Cultural History*. New York: W.W. Norton, 1992.

Briggs, Asa, *Victorian Cities*. London: Penguin, 1980.

Dyos, H. J. and Michael Wolff (eds.), *The Victorian City: Images and Realities*, 2 vols. London: Routledge & Kegan Paul, 1973.

Freeman, Nicholas, *Conceiving the City: London, Literature, and Art 1870–1914*. Oxford: Oxford University Press, 2007.

Harper, Lila Marz, 'Clues in the Street: Sherlock Holmes, Martin Hewitt, and Mean Streets', *Journal of Popular Culture* 42:1 (2009), 67–89.

Harrison, Michael F., *In the Footsteps of Sherlock Holmes*, rev. edn. Newton Abbot: David and Charles, 1971.

Jaffe, Audrey, 'Detecting the Beggar: Arthur Conan Doyle, Henry Mayhew, and "The Man with the Twisted Lip"', *Representations* 31 (1990), 96–117.

Joyce, Simon, *Capital Offenses: The Geography of Class and Crime in Victorian London*. Charlottesville: University of Virginia Press, 2003.

Langbauer, Laurie, *Novels of Everyday Life: The Series in English Fiction 1850–1930*. Ithaca: Cornell University Press, 1999.

Metcalf, Priscilla, *Victorian London*. London: Cassell, 1972.

Moretti, Franco, *Atlas of the European Novel 1800–1900*. London: Verso, 1998.

Nead, Lynda, *Victorian Babylon: People, Streets and Images in Nineteenth-Century London*. New Haven: Yale University Press, 2000.

Sennett, Richard, *The Fall of Public Man: On the Social Psychology of Capitalism*. Cambridge: Cambridge University Press, 1977.

Smith, Philip Thurmond, *Policing Victorian London: Political Policing, Public Order, and the London Metropolitan Police*. Westport: Greenwood Press, 1985.

White, Jerry, *London in the Nineteenth Century*. London: Vintage, 2008.

Wolfreys, Julian, *Writing London (Volume 2): Materiality, Memory, Spectrality*. Basingstoke: Palgrave, 2004.

Power and Surveillance

Belsey, Catherine, *Critical Practice*, 2nd edn. London: Routledge, 2002.

Derrida, Jacques, 'Before the Law', in Derek Attridge (ed.), *Acts of Literature*. London: Routledge, 1992. 181–220.

'Force of Law: The "Mystical Foundation of Authority"', in Gild Anidjar (ed.), *Acts of Religion*. London: Routledge, 2002. 228–98.

Fillingham, Lydia Alix, '"The Colorless Skein of Life": Threats to the Private Sphere in Conan Doyle's *A Study in Scarlet*', *ELH* 56:3 (1989), 667–88.

Foucault, Michel, *The Birth of the Clinic*, trans. A. M. Sheridan. London: Routledge, 2003.

Discipline and Punish: The Birth of the Prison, trans. Alan Sheridan. London: Penguin, 1984.

'The Order of Discourse', in Robert Young (ed.), *Untying the Text: A Post-Structuralist Reader*. London: Routledge, 1981. 48–78.

Ginzburg, Carlo, 'Morelli, Freud, and Sherlock Holmes', in Umberto Eco and Thomas Sebeok (eds.), *The Sign of Three: Dupin, Holmes, Peirce*. Bloomington: Indiana University Press, 1983. 89–118.

Miller, D.A., *The Novel and the Police*. Berkeley: University of California Press, 1988.

Nietzsche, Friedrich, 'On Redemption', in *Thus Spoke Zarathustra*, trans. Graham Parkes. Oxford: Oxford University Press, 2005. 119–23.

Stone, Marjorie, 'Dickens, Bentham, and the Fictions of the Law: A Victorian Controversy and Its Consequences', *Victorian Studies* 29 (1985), 125–54.

Takanashi, Kyoto, 'Sherlock's "Brain-Attic": Information Culture and the Liberal Professional Dilemma', *PMLA* 132:2 (2017), 250–65.

Tambling, Jeremy, *Literature and Psychoanalysis*. Manchester: Manchester University Press, 2012.

Welsh, Alexander, *George Eliot and Blackmail*. Cambridge: Harvard University Press, 1985.

Gender and Sexuality

Barsham, Diana, *Arthur Conan Doyle and the Meaning of Masculinity*. London: Routledge, 2000.

Clark, John D., 'Some Notes Relating to a Preliminary Investigation into the Paternity of Nero Wolfe', *Baker Street Journal* 6:1 (1956), 5–11.

Crompton, Constance, 'Dissimulation and The Detecting Eye: Female Masculinity In "A Scandal in Bohemia"', *Nineteenth-Century Gender Studies* 7:3 (2011): http://www.ncgsjournal.com/issue73/crompton.htm

Godfrey, Emelyne, *Masculinity, Crime and Self-Defence in Victorian Literature: Duelling with Danger*. Basingstoke: Palgrave Macmillan, 2011.

Kestner, Joseph, *Sherlock's Men: Masculinity, Conan Doyle, and Cultural History*. Farnham: Ashgate, 1997.

Light, Alison, *Forever England: Femininity, Literature and Conservatism Between the Wars*. London: Routledge, 1991.

Longhurst, Derek, 'Sherlock Holmes: Adventures of an English Gentleman 1887–1894', in *Gender, Genre and Narrative Pleasure*. London: Unwin-Hyman, 1989. 51–66.

Macdonald, Kate (ed.), *The Masculine Middlebrow, 1880–1950: What Mr. Miniver Read*. Basingstoke: Palgrave Macmillan, 2011.

Miller, Elizabeth Carolyn, *Framed: The New Woman Criminal in British Culture at the* Fin de Siècle. Ann Arbor: University of Michigan Press, 2008.

Pamboukian, Sylvia, 'Old Holmes: Sherlock, Testosterone, and "The Creeping Man"', *Clues* 35:1 (2017), 19–28.

Plain, Gill, *Twentieth-Century Crime Fiction: Gender, Sexuality and the Body*. Edinburgh: Edinburgh University Press, 2001.

Queen, Ellery, *In the Queens' Parlor and Other Leaves from the Editors' Notebook*. New York: Simon & Schuster, 1957.

Redmond, Christopher, *In Bed with Sherlock Holmes: Sexual Elements in Arthur Conan Doyle's Stories of the Great Detective*. Toronto: Simon & Pierre, 1984.

Schaub, Melissa, *Middlebrow Feminism in Classic British Detective Fiction: The Female Gentleman*. Basingstoke: Palgrave Macmillan, 2013.

Skovmand, Michael, 'The Mystique of the Bachelor Gentleman in Late Victorian Masculine Romance', in Michael Green (ed.), *English and Cultural Studies: Broadening the Context*. London: John Murray, 1987. 45–59.

Small, Douglas, 'Sherlock Holmes and Cocaine: A 7% Solution for Modern Professionalism', *English Literature in Transition 1880–1920* 58:3 (2015), 341–60.

Smith, Andrew, *Victorian Demons: Medicine, Masculinity and the Gothic at the* Fin-de-Siècle. Manchester: Manchester University Press, 2004.

Stout, Rex, 'Watson Was a Woman', *The Saturday Review of Literature* 23:19 (1 March 1941), 3–4, 16.

Surridge, Lisa, '"Are Women Protected?" Sherlock Holmes and the Violent Home', in *Bleak Houses: Marital Violence in Victorian Fiction*. Athens: Ohio University Press, 2005. 216–46.

Walkowitz, Judith R., *City of Dreadful Delight: Narratives of Sexual Danger in Late-Victorian London*. Chicago: University of Chicago Press, 1992.

Adaptation, Fandom and Neo-Holmesian Fiction

Barnes, Alan, *Sherlock Holmes on Screen: The Complete Film and TV History*, updated edn. London: Titan, 2011.

Boström, Mattias and Matt Laffey, *Sherlock Holmes and Conan Doyle in the Newspapers*, 3 vols. Wantage: Wessex Press, 2016.

Cardwell, Sarah, *Adaptation Revisited: Television and the Classic Novel*. Manchester: Manchester University Press, 2002.

Cox, Michael, *The Baker Street File: A Guide to the Appearance and Habits of Sherlock Holmes and Dr Watson, specially prepared for the Granada Television Series*. Chester: Calabash Press, 1997.

A Study in Celluloid: A Producer's Account of Jeremy Brett as Sherlock Holmes. Cambridge: Rupert Books, 1999.

Craps, Stef and Gert Buelens, 'Traumatic Mirrorings: Holocaust and Colonial Trauma in Michael Chabon's *The Final Solution*', *Criticism* 53:4 (2011), 569–86.

Davies, David Stuart, *Starring Sherlock Holmes*, rev. edn. London: Titan, 2007.

Earnshaw, Tony, *An Actor and a Rare One: Peter Cushing as Sherlock Holmes*. London: Scarecrow Press, 2001.

Farghaly, Nadine (ed.), *Gender and the Modern Sherlock Holmes: Essays on Film and Television.* Jefferson: McFarland, 2015.

Gillis, Stacy and Philippa Gates (eds.), *The Devil Himself: Villainy in Detective Fiction and Film.* Westport: Greenwood Press, 2002.

Haining, Peter, *The Television Sherlock Holmes.* London: Virgin, 1994.

Heilman, Ann and Mark Llewellyn, *Neo-Victorianism: The Victorians in the Twenty-First Century, 1999–2009.* Basingstoke: Palgrave, 2010.

Hoel, Camilla Ulleland, 'The Final Problem: Constructing Coherence in the Holmesian Canon', *Authorship* 6:1 (2017): https://www.authorship.ugent.be/article/view/4836

Kaplan, Cora, *Victoriana: Histories, Fictions, Criticism.* New York: Columbia University Press, 2007.

Kaye, Marvin (ed.), *The Game is Afoot: Parodies, Pastiches and Ponderings of Sherlock Holmes.* New York: St Martin's Press, 1994.

Kelley, Gordon E., *Sherlock Holmes: Screen and Sound Guide.* London: Scarecrow Press, 1994.

Lancelyn Green, Richard (ed.), *The Further Adventures of Sherlock Holmes.* London: Penguin, 1985.

(ed.), *Letters to Sherlock Holmes.* London: Penguin, 1985.

Leitch, Thomas, *Film Adaptation and Its Discontents: From* Gone with the Wind *to* The Passion of the Christ. Baltimore: Johns Hopkins University Press, 2007.

Liening, Ashley, 'Not Your Grandfather's Sherlock Holmes: Guy Ritchie's 21st Century Reboot of a 19th Century British Icon', *The Oakland Journal* 24 (2013), 35–51.

McCaw, Neil, *Adapting Detective Fiction: Crime, Englishness and the TV Detectives.* London, Continuum, 2011.

McClellan, Ann K., *Sherlock's World: Fan Fiction and the Reimagining of BBC's Sherlock.* Iowa City: University of Iowa Press, 2018.

Nollen, Scott Allen, *Sir Arthur Conan Doyle at the Cinema: A Critical Study of the Film Adaptations.* Jefferson: McFarland, 2004.

Pearson, Roberta, 'It's Always 1895: Sherlock Holmes in Cyberspace', in Karen Hellekson and Kristina Busse (eds.), *The Fan Fiction Studies Reader.* Iowa City: University of Iowa Press, 2014. 44–60.

'Sherlock Holmes, the *De Facto* Franchise', in Lincoln Geraghty (ed.), *Popular Media Cultures: Fans, Audiences, and Paratexts.* Basingstoke: Palgrave, 2015. 186–205.

Peschel, Bill (ed.), *The Early* Punch *Parodies of Sherlock Holmes.* Hershey: Peschel Press, 2014.

Sherlock Holmes Great War Pastiches and Parodies I: 1905–1909. Hershey: Peschel Press, 2016.

Sherlock Holmes Great War Pastiches and Parodies II: 1915–19. Hershey: Peschel Press, 2016.

Ping, Zhang, 'Sherlock Holmes in China', *Perspectives* 13:2 (2009), 106–14.

Poore, Benjamin, *Sherlock Holmes from Stage to Screen: Post-Millennial Adaptations in British Theatre.* Basingstoke: Palgrave Macmillan, 2017.

'Sherlock Holmes and the Leap of Faith: the forces of fandom and convergence in adaptations of the Holmes and Watson stories', *Adaptation* 6:2 (2013), 158–71.

Porter, Lynette (ed.), *Sherlock Holmes for the 21st Century: Essays on New Adaptations*. Jefferson: McFarland, 2012.

Who is Sherlock? Essays on Identity in Modern Holmes Adaptations. Jefferson: McFarland, 2016.

Reynolds, William and Elizabeth A. Trembley (eds.), *It's a Print! Detective Fiction from Page to Screen*. Bowling Green: Bowling Green University Popular Press, 1994.

Ridgway Watt, Peter and Joseph Green, *The Alternative Sherlock Holmes: Pastiches, Parodies and Copies*. London: Routledge, 2003.

Rosenblatt, Betsy and Roberta Pearson (eds.), 'Sherlock Holmes Fandom, Sherlockiana, and the Great Game', Special Issue of *Transformative Works and Cultures* 23 (2017): https://journal.transformativeworks.org/index.php/twc/issue/view/27

Sanders, Julie, *Adaptation and Appropriation*. London: Routledge, 2006.

Smith, Daniel, *The Sherlock Holmes Companion: An Elementary Guide*. London: Aurum, 2016.

Stein, Louisa Ellen and Kristina Busse (eds.), *Sherlock and Transmedia Fandom: Essays on the BBC Series*. Jefferson: McFarland, 2012.

Steinbrunner, Chris and Norman Michaels, *The Films of Sherlock Holmes*. London: Citadel, 1991.

Ue, Tom, 'Imagining Sherlock Holmes', Special Issue of *Journal of Popular Film and Television* 45.2 (2017).

Ue, Tom and Jonathan Cranfield (eds.), *Fan Phenomena: Sherlock Holmes*. Bristol: Intellect Press, 2014.

Vanacker, Sabine and Catherine Wynne (eds.), *Sherlock Holmes and Conan Doyle: Multi-Media Afterlives*. Basingstoke: Palgrave Macmillan, 2013.

Wei Yan, 'Sherlock Holmes Came to China: Detective Fiction, Cultural Meditations, and Chinese Modernity', in Louise Nilsson, David Damrosch and Theo D'haen (eds.), *Crime Fiction as World Literature*. London: Bloomsbury, 2017. 245–56.

Webb, Keith E., *Sherlock Holmes in Japan*. Bellevue: NextChurch, 1998.

Reading Sherlock Holmes Through Theory

Bayard, Pierre, *Sherlock Holmes was Wrong: Reopening the Case of* The Hound of the Baskervilles, trans. Charlotte Mandell. London: Bloomsbury, 2010.

Who Killed Roger Ackroyd?, trans. Carol Cosman. London: Fourth Estate, 2000.

Benjamin, Walter. *Charles Baudelaire: A Lyric Poet in the Era of High Capitalism*, trans. Harry Zohn. London and New York: Verso, 1983.

Bennett, Tony (ed.), *Popular Fiction: Technology, Ideology, Production, Reading*. London: Routledge, 1990.

Delamater, Jerome H. and Ruth Prigozy (eds.), *Theory and Practice of Classic Detective Fiction*. Westport: Greenwood Press, 1997.

Doyle, Arthur Conan, *Sherlock Holmes: The Major Stories with Contemporary Critical Essays*, ed. John Hodgson. London: Bedford Press, 1994.

Eco, Umberto, 'Horns, Hooves, Insteps: Some Hypotheses on Three Types of Abduction', in Umberto Eco and Thomas A. Sebeok (eds.), *The Sign of Three: Holmes, Dupin, Peirce*. Bloomington: Indiana University Press, 1983, 198–220.

Eco, Umberto and Thomas A. Sebeok (eds.), *The Sign of Three: Holmes, Dupin, Peirce*. Bloomington: Indiana University Press, 1983.

Freud, Sigmund, 'Criminals from a Sense of Guilt', in *On the History of the Psycho-Analytic Movement, Papers on Metapsychology and Other Works*, trans. and ed. James Strachey. *Standard Edition of the Complete Psychological Works of Sigmund Freud*, vol. 14. London: Hogarth Press, 1957. 332–3.

'Totem and Taboo', in *Totem and Taboo and Other Works*, trans. and ed. James Strachey. *Standard Edition of the Complete Psychological Works of Sigmund Freud*, vol. 13. London: Hogarth Press, 1955. 1–161.

'The "Uncanny"', in *Art and Literature*, trans. and ed. James Strachey. *The Penguin Freud Library*, vol. 14. London: Penguin, 1990. 335–76.

Haycraft, Howard (ed.), *The Art of the Mystery Story: A Collection of Critical Essays*. New York: Simon and Schuster, 1946.

Holquist, Michael, 'Whodunit and Other Questions: Metaphysical Detective Stories in Post-War Fiction', *New Literary History* 3:1 (1971), 135–56.

Irwin, John, *The Mystery to a Solution: Poe, Borges, and the Analytic Detective Story*. Baltimore: The Johns Hopkins University Press, 1996.

Marcus, Laura, 'Detection and Literary Fiction', in Martin Priestman (ed.), *The Cambridge Companion to Crime Fiction*. Cambridge: Cambridge University Press, 2003. 245–68.

McHale, Brian, *Constructing Postmodernism*. London: Routledge, 1992.

Moretti, Franco, *Signs Taken for Wonders: On the Sociology of Literary Forms*, trans. Susan Fischer, David Forgacs and David Miller. London and New York: Verso, 1983.

'The Slaughterhouse of Literature', *Modern Language Quarterly* 61:1 (2000), 207–27.

Most, Glenn W. and William W. Stowe (eds.), *The Poetics of Murder: Detective Fiction and Literary Theory*. San Diego: Harcourt, Brace, Jovanovich, 1983.

Pyrhönen, Heta, 'Criticism and Theory', in Charles J. Rzepka and Lee Horsley (eds.), *A Companion to Crime Fiction*. Oxford: Wiley-Blackwell, 2010. 43–56.

Rushing, Robert, *Resisting Arrest: Detective Fiction and Popular Culture*. London: The Other Press, 2007.

Sebeok, Thomas, 'Give Me Another Horse', in Rocco Capozzi (ed.), *Reading Eco: An Anthology*. Bloomington: Indiana University Press, 1997. 276–82.

Sebeok, Thomas A., and Jean Umiker-Sebeok, '"You Know My Method": A Juxtaposition of Charles S. Pierce and Sherlock Holmes', in Umberto Eco and Thomas A. Sebeok (eds.), *The Sign of Three: Holmes, Dupin, Peirce*. Bloomington: Indiana University Press, 1983. 11–54.

Shklovsky, Viktor, 'Sherlock Holmes and the Mystery Story', in *Theory of Prose*, trans. Benjamin Sher. Normal: Dalkey Archive Press, 1991. 101–16.

Todorov, Tzvetan, 'The Typology of Detective Fiction', in *The Poetics of Prose*, trans. Richard Howard. Ithaca: Cornell University Press, 1977. 42–52.

Žižek, Slavoj, *Looking Awry: An Introduction to Jacques Lacan through Popular Culture*. Cambridge: The MIT Press, 1992.

Crime and Science

Accardo, Pasquale J., *Diagnosis and Detection: The Medical Iconography of Sherlock Holmes*. Rutherford: Farleigh Dickinson University Press, 1987.

Beer, Gillian, *Darwin's Plots: Evolutionary Narrative in Darwin*, George *Eliot and Nineteenth-Century Fiction*, 3rd edn. Cambridge: Cambridge University Press, 2009.

Clausson, Nils, 'Degeneration, *Fin-de-Siècle* Gothic, and the Science of Detection: Arthur Conan Doyle's *The Hound of the Baskervilles* and the Emergence of the Modern Detective Story', *Journal of Narrative Theory* 35:1 (2005), 60–87.

Darwin, Charles, *The Descent of Man and Selection in Relation to Sex*, ed. James Moore and Adrian Desmond. London: Penguin, 2004.

On the Origin of Species by Means of Natural Selection, ed. William Bynum. London: Penguin, 2009.

Davie, Neil, *Tracing the Criminal: The Rise of Scientific Criminology in Britain, 1860–1918*. Oxford: Bardwell Press, 2005.

Ellis, Havelock, *The Criminal*. London: Walter Scott, 1901.

Frank, Lawrence, *Victorian Detective Fiction and the Nature of Evidence: The Scientific Investigations of Poe, Dickens, and Doyle*. Basingstoke: Palgrave Macmillan, 2003.

Galton, Francis, *Finger Prints*. London: Macmillan, 1892.

Gibson, Mary, *Born to Crime: Cesare Lombroso and the Origins of Biological Criminology*. Westport, CT: Praeger, 2002.

Goldsmith, Hilary A., 'Darwin and the Detective: Aspects of the Darwinian Worldview and the Sherlock Holmes Stories of Arthur Conan Doyle', *Clues* 28:2 (2010), 19–28.

Goring, Charles, *The English Convict: A Statistical Study*. London: His Majesty's Stationery Office, 1913.

Gould, Stephen Jay, *The Mismeasure of Man*. New York: Norton, 1981.

Greenslade, William, *Degeneration, Culture and the Novel: 1880–1940*. Cambridge: Cambridge University Press, 1994.

Horn, David G., *The Criminal Body: Lombroso and the Anatomy of Deviance*. New York: Routledge, 2003.

Hurley, Kelly, *The Gothic Body: Sexuality, Materialism, and Degeneration at the* Fin de Siècle. Cambridge: Cambridge University Press, 2004.

Jann, Rosemary, 'Sherlock Holmes Codes the Social Body', *ELH* 57:3 (1990), 685–708.

Karschay, Stephan, *Degeneration, Normativity and the Gothic at the* Fin de Siècle. Basingstoke: Palgrave Macmillan, 2015.

Lankester, Edwin Ray, *Degeneration: A Chapter in Darwinism*. London: MacMillan, 1880.

Leps, Marie-Christine, *Apprehending the Criminal: The Production of Deviance in Nineteenth-Century Discourse*. Durham and London : Duke University Press, 1992.

Levine, George, *Darwin and the Novelists: Patterns of Science in Victorian Fiction*. Chicago: University of Chicago Press, 1988.

Lombroso, Cesare, *Criminal Man*, ed. and trans. Mary Gibson and Nicole Hahn Rafter. Durham: Duke University Press, 2006.

Lombroso, Cesare and Gina Lombroso Ferrero, *Criminal Man According to the Classification of Cesare Lombroso*. London: G. P. Putnam's Sons, 1911.

Lyell, Charles, *Principles of Geology*, ed. James Secord, abridged edn. London: Penguin, 1997.

Mighall, Robert, *A Geography of Victorian Gothic Fiction: Mapping History's Nightmares*. Oxford: Oxford University Press, 2003.

Neill, Anna, 'The Savage Genius of Sherlock Holmes', *Victorian Literature and Culture* 37 (2009), 611–26.

Nordau, Max, *Degeneration*. New York: D. Appleton and Company, 1895.

Numbers, Ronald L. and John Stenhouse, *Disseminating Darwinism: The Role of Place, Race, Religion, and Gender*. Cambridge: Cambridge University Press, 2001.

O'Brien, James, *The Scientific Sherlock Holmes: Cracking the Case with Science and Forensics*. Oxford: Oxford University Press, 2013.

Pick, Daniel, *Faces of Degeneration: A European Disorder, c.1848-c.1918*. Cambridge: Cambridge University Press, 1989.

Richter, Virginia, *Literature After Darwin: Human Beasts in Western Fiction, 1859–1939*. Basingstoke: Palgrave Macmillan, 2011.

Rudwick, Martin J., *Georges Cuvier, Fossil Bones, and Geological Catastrophes*. Chicago: University of Chicago Press, 1997.

Sekula, Allan, 'The Body and the Archive', in Richard Bolton (ed.), *The Contest of Meaning: Critical Histories of Photography*. Cambridge: The MIT Press, 1992. 342–88.

Shermer, Michael, *In Darwin's Shadow: The Life and Science of Alfred Russel Wallace*. Oxford: Oxford University Press, 2002.

Thomas, Ronald R., *Detective Fiction and the Rise of Forensic Science*. Cambridge: Cambridge University Press, 1999.

Willis, Martin, *Literature and Science*. Basingstoke: Palgrave Macmillan, 2014.

Vision, Science, and Literature 1870–1920: Ocular Horizons. London: Routledge, 2011.

Wynne, Catherine, 'Sherlock Holmes and the Problems of War: Traumatic Detections', *English Literature in Transition* 53:1 (2010), 29–53.

Journals

Baker Street Journal: An Irregular Quarterly of Sherlockiana
The Sherlock Holmes Journal
ACD: The Journal of the Arthur Conan Doyle Society

Websites:

The Adventuresses of Sherlock Holmes:
https://ash-nyc.com/
The Arthur Conan Doyle Encyclopaedia:
https://www.arthur-conan-doyle.com/index.php/Sherlock_Holmes
The Baker Street Babes:
http://bakerstreetbabes.com/
The Official Site of the Sir Arthur Conan Doyle Literary Estate:
http://www.arthurconandoyle.com/
Sherlockian.Net:
https://www.sherlockian.net/

The Strand Magazine: An Illustrated Monthly on The Internet Archive:
https://archive.org/details/TheStrandMagazineAnIllustratedMonthly
The Universal Sherlock Holmes by George Vanderburgh (University of
Minnesota):
https://www.lib.umn.edu/scrbm/ush/intro

INDEX

Cambridge Companions To ...

AUTHORS

Oscar Wilde edited by Peter Raby

Tennessee Williams edited by Matthew C. Roudané

August Wilson edited by Christopher Bigsby

Mary Wollstonecraft edited by Claudia L. Johnson

Virginia Woolf edited by Susan Sellers (second edition)

Wordsworth edited by Stephen Gill

W. B. Yeats edited by Marjorie Howes and John Kelly

Xenophon edited by Michael A. Flower

Zola edited by Brian Nelson

TOPICS

The Actress edited by Maggie B. Gale and John Stokes

The African American Novel edited by Maryemma Graham

The African American Slave Narrative edited by Audrey A. Fisch

Theatre History by David Wiles and Christine Dymkowski

African American Theatre by Harvey Young

Allegory edited by Rita Copeland and Peter Struck

American Crime Fiction edited by Catherine Ross Nickerson

American Gothic edited by Jeffrey Andrew Weinstock

American Literature of the 1930s edited by William Solomon

American Modernism edited by Walter Kalaidjian

American Poetry Since 1945 edited by Jennifer Ashton

American Realism and Naturalism edited by Donald Pizer

American Travel Writing edited by Alfred Bendixen and Judith Hamera

American Women Playwrights edited by Brenda Murphy

Ancient Rhetoric edited by Erik Gunderson

Arthurian Legend edited by Elizabeth Archibald and Ad Putter

Australian Literature edited by Elizabeth Webby

The Beats edited by Stephen Belletto

British Black and Asian Literature (1945–2010) edited by Deirdre Osborne

British Literature of the French Revolution edited by Pamela Clemit

British Romanticism edited by Stuart Curran (second edition)

British Romantic Poetry edited by James Chandler and Maureen N. McLane

British Theatre, 1730–1830, edited by Jane Moody and Daniel O'Quinn

Canadian Literature edited by Eva-Marie Kröller (second edition)

Children's Literature edited by M. O. Grenby and Andrea Immel

The Classic Russian Novel edited by Malcolm V. Jones and Robin Feuer Miller

Contemporary Irish Poetry edited by Matthew Campbell

Creative Writing edited by David Morley and Philip Neilsen

Crime Fiction edited by Martin Priestman

Dracula edited by Roger Luckhurst

Early Modern Women's Writing edited by Laura Lunger Knoppers

The Eighteenth-Century Novel edited by John Richetti

Eighteenth-Century Poetry edited by John Sitter

Emma edited by Peter Sabor

English Literature, 1500–1600 edited by Arthur F. Kinney

English Literature, 1650–1740 edited by Steven N. Zwicker

English Literature, 1740–1830 edited by Thomas Keymer and Jon Mee

English Literature, 1830–1914 edited by Joanne Shattock

English Melodrama edited by Carolyn Williams

English Novelists edited by Adrian Poole

English Poetry, Donne to Marvell edited by Thomas N. Corns

English Poets edited by Claude Rawson

English Renaissance Drama edited by A. R. Braunmuller and Michael Hattaway (second edition)

English Renaissance Tragedy edited by Emma Smith and Garrett A. Sullivan Jr.

English Restoration Theatre edited by Deborah C. Payne Fisk